973 H894 1988
Hughes, Richard T. (Richard
Thomas
Illusio

D0687051

Date Due

DISCARDED

COLUMBIA BIBLE COLLEGE

1444 00029 0213

ILLUSIONS
of
INNOCENCE

Protestant Primitivism in
America, 1630–1875

•

Richard T. Hughes
and C. Leonard Allen

Foreword by Robert N. Bellah

The University of Chicago Press
Chicago and London

RICHARD T. HUGHES is professor in the Religion Division, Pepperdine University.
C. LEONARD ALLEN is associate professor in the College of Biblical Studies, Abilene
Christian University.

The University of Chicago Press, Chicago 60637
The University of Chicago Press, Ltd., London
© 1988 by the University of Chicago
All rights reserved. Published 1988
Printed in the United States of America

97 96 95 94 93 92 91 90 89 88   5 4 3 2 1

Library of Congress Cataloging-in-Publication Data

Hughes, Richard T. (Richard Thomas), 1943–
    Illusions of innocence: Protestant primitivism in America,
1630–1875 / Richard T. Hughes and C. Leonard Allen; foreword by
Robert N. Bellah.
        p.   cm.
    Bibliography.
    Includes index.
    ISBN 0-226-35917-4
    1. Protestant churches—United States—History.   2. Primitivism—
History.   3. United States—Church history.   I. Allen, Crawford
Leonard.   II. Title.
BR517.H84 1988
973—dc19   88–837
                                                            CIP

To our teachers
at the University of Iowa
T. Dwight Bozeman
Sidney E. Mead
James C. Spalding

Contents

•

Foreword

•

The comparative study of religion has discovered the widespread presence of conceptions of *Urzeit* and *Endzeit* (origin time and end time) in religions of the most diverse sort over a very great historical span. It is therefore not surprising that these conceptions should turn up in America. Nevertheless, though many have written about American conceptions of the *Endzeit*, usually some form or other of Christian millennialism, Hughes and Allen have done us the great service of highlighting the importance of the *Urzeit*, in this case mainly, though not exclusively, in the form of Protestant primitivism, a topic much less adequately explored in the literature. Of course, the themes of origin and end are deeply interrelated: last things often involve a return to first things; primordium becomes millennium when the end of times is heralded by "the restoration of all things." Yet in our most future-entranced of cultures it is instructive to see how often we have hankered for an earlier time when all was well, when we had not fallen into the guilt of history, when we experienced the innocence that is our birthright as Americans. Hughes and Allen reveal to us both the vitality of this idea and its dangerous proclivity to self-deception.

No civilization was more preoccupied with the origin time than classical China. It was the ancient kings who laid down the proper pattern of human existence. Even Confucius, who played so crucial a role in the original formulation of the classical tradition, was already looking far into the past for his exemplars, seeing his own time as one of confusion and degeneration. Most intellectuals in the more than 2,000-year history of imperial China kept their eyes glued to the primordial mists of the earliest period of Chinese history when things were as they ought to have been. In China, too, the dialectic of origin time and end time was operative so that there were recurrent periods when the project of restoring the primordium took on millennial overtones, not the least important of which came toward the very end of imperial history in the late nineteenth century. But China is a good contrast to the West because there the fascination with the origin usually overpowered expectations about the future whereas with us expectations about the end have usually overshadowed concern for origins.

Within the West a concern with the primordium, though never as central as concern with the millennium, is not unique to America—Hughes and Allen trace a considerable interest in that subject to certain strands of Reformation thought on the Continent and in England—but, relatively speaking, it is in America that the theme has particularly flourished. It is not hard to see why. Although the Western Hemisphere was early on called "the new world," its newness was thought of as the newness of pristine beginnings. As John Locke put it, "In the beginning all the world was America." The pristine newness of America (to Europeans) was the result not only of the fact that it was newly discovered; America's newness fit readily into categories of the European mind that were salient in the first centuries after the discovery. Hughes and Allen discuss interestingly two of the sources of these categories. One was the Reformation, or that part of Reformed thought which saw the major task to be the weeding out of centuries of distorted tradition and a return to the condition of the earliest Christian church. To Protestants with this idea an "errand into the wilderness" made sense, for it would be the uncontaminated wilderness of the New World where the original institutions would have the best chance of being recovered. The other source was the Enlightenment, of which Locke, raised as a Protestant, was so important a precursor. The Enlightenment wished to submit all existing traditions and structures of power to the judgment of reason, and reason itself rested on nature. Where but in America would nature be most likely to speak with the voice of reason? The enormous popularity of Benjamin Franklin among educated Parisians at the time of Louis XVI derived in part from the fact that he was viewed as the living embodiment of American natural wisdom.

The authors of this book have done us the further service of showing how the preoccupation with the innocence of origins affected our understanding of American nationhood from the very beginning. At the birth of the Republic American consciousness drew heavily on Protestant and Enlightenment currents of thought, so that it was all too easy to think of our country as an expression of primordial reason, direct, as it were, from the hand of God. Our mission to the world was to represent an idea of freedom that we took to be perfectly natural because we did not recognize the cultural particularity of the Protestantism and Enlightenment from which we had derived it. The frightening consequences of this lack of self-consciousness are amply spelled out in the following pages.

This book deals with the problem of American primitivism from 1630 to 1875, but fortunately our authors have allowed themselves to speculate about the continued vitality of their theme right up to the present. In the Epilogue they argue stunningly that Allan Bloom's enormously popular book *The Closing of the American Mind* owes some of its popularity to its primitivist theme: it describes a period of pristine academic excellence in the past from which we have regrettably fallen away. Others have commented on the heavy overtone of nostalgia in Bloom's book and I wrote a review of it entitled "Academic Fundamentalism?" in which I pondered whether Bloom might be considered "an urbane, highly educated Jerry Fallwell" (*New Oxford Review*, July–August, 1987). But neither I nor anyone else, so far as I know, has shown so conclusively the classic American pattern of Bloom's book which puts him in the company of such unlikely bedfellows as the Primitive Baptists and the Latter-day Saints. In a footnote to the epilogue the authors kindly exempt *Habits of the Heart* from the charge of primitivism, pointing out that my co-authors and I attempted to place the traditions we discussed in the context of America's historic particularities and therefore avoided absolutizing them. Yet it would be hard to say that the popular success of our book is not due in part to a primitivist reading of it as exalting the simplicity of the early nineteenth-century small town from which we have now sadly fallen away, however much we tried to insist that that was not our message. Such is the persistence of powerful cultural archetypes.

We need history that helps us understand who we are and what we should become while also telling us as honestly as possible what we have been. Richard Hughes and Leonard Allen have given us a book which is exemplary in these regards.

Robert N. Bellah

Preface

•

American history is fraught with ironies and illusions—a fact that every student of America's past is prepared to admit. Less understood are the sources for those illusions. While the sources may be many, one in particular is little understood because, according to its own inner logic, it stands outside of history and is therefore no fit subject for historical analysis. This is the myth of restoring first times which has informed so much of American life for 350 years.

The restoration perspective has worked in American life in two important ways. Some Americans have enshrined first times as an ideal to be approximated and even as a kind of transcendent norm that stands in judgment on the ambiguities of the present age. In this case, the myth of first times has been a beacon summoning Americans to perfection. On the other hand, some Americans have fully identified their religious denomination or even their nation itself with the purity of first times. The illusion thereby fostered in the minds of these Americans is that they are an innocent and fundamentally natural people who, in effect, have stepped outside of history, thereby escaping the powerful influences of history, culture, and tradition. These Americans therefore have often confused the historic particularities of their limited experience with universal norms that should be embraced, they have thought, by all people in all cultures and all times.

The threat to freedom implicit in this latter conviction is obvious. The irony, however, lies in the fact that a powerful appeal to freedom often has supplied the central content of the myth of first times in American life. From time to time, therefore, throughout American history, both in the specific religious traditions and in the nation at large, a persistent and tenacious paradox has emerged: the spectacle of a people, convinced of its own pure beginnings, compelling others to be free. This book, therefore, explores not only the phenomenon of restoring first times but also the relation of the restoration ideal to the illusion of innocence in America. Our story begins with the settlement of the Massachusetts Bay Colony and continues through most of the nineteenth century.

The myth of first times was no quirk or aberration from the theological norms of Anglo-American culture. On the contrary, it was central, even pivotal, in many instances. That it was seldom argued and defended in a programmatic way may suggest to some that it was a theme of no serious consequence. It appears to us, however, that the myth of first times was a fundamental assumption, a given that required no definitions and elaborations since everyone already understood its logic and importance. This certainly was true of the New England Puritans as Dwight Bozeman has argued in his recent book, *To Live Ancient Lives*. And in later American history, this assumption, so central to the Puritan mind, seemed an obvious way of making sense of what everyone knew experientially, namely, that America was a wholly new order of the ages, now set free from the constraining web of history and conforming instead to the pattern of first times.

The casual reader, scanning the table of contents or even briefly perusing the text itself, might conclude that this book is chiefly about Puritans, Baptists, "Christians," and Mormons. To an extent this is true. But this book goes far beyond a mere analysis of these religious traditions. Rather, it employs these traditions as windows on the larger American experience in an attempt to understand the peculiar logic of the restoration theme in the American context.

The importance of these groups is apparent when one considers the two periods that most clearly defined the identity of the American people—the Puritan epoch and the revolutionary epoch. In the first instance, the Puritans virtually defined colonial identity through their frequent articulation of the special tasks to which God, they believed, had called them. And in the second, the popular religions of the early nineteenth century reflected in powerful ways a revolutionary identity already in place. Mormons, Baptists, and "Christians" were no mere cults, destined to strut upon the American stage and then to die. In fact, one of the principal reasons for their immense, collective appeal to so many thousands of Americans at the time was their uncanny accuracy in reflecting the myth of first times that was so central to the American ethos. One might even argue that Mormons and "Christians" were, in fundamental ways, creations of that ethos. At any rate, the strong ideological ties that bound these traditions to the larger culture suggest that understanding the restoration impulse in these three traditions—Mormons, Baptists, and "Christians"—will take us far in understanding the dynamics of American identity.

While examining Puritans, Baptists, Mormons, and "Christians" in some detail, we also have sought, expecially in chapters 1, 8, 9, 10, and the epilogue to examine some of the ways by which Americans have employed the myth of first times in the service of the nation itself. What we have done in this regard is more suggestive than comprehensive or definitive, and we hope that other scholars will go beyond our preliminary work to explore the full range and meaning of the myth of first times in American life, culture, and politics. At the same time, it is striking that so few scholars have examined this dimension of American identity.

There seem to be at least two reasons for this oversight. One is the power of the myth itself, a power to which all Americans, including historians, are susceptible. The other is the persistent inclination of historians to regard the restoration impulse, when they find it in various sectarian traditions, as exceptional—an aberration from American norms. The argument typically employed implicitly suggests that no Americans could be victimized by so naïve a perspective unless they were also victims of economic deprivation, social disorder, or some sort of chaotic disruption. In this view, the restoration impulse is essentially compensatory and flourishes among the displaced, the disoriented, or the dispossessed. Thus, for example, Rhys Isaac entirely missed the power of the restoration ideal—as ideal—among the Separate Baptists of Virginia and finally concluded that this form of "evangelicalism can be seen as a popular response to a mounting sense of social disorder." Similarly, Gordon Wood has argued that the appeal of popular religion in the early nineteenth century—embracing, among others, the restoration–oriented Baptists, "Christians," and Mormons—was due to "a social disintegration unequalled in American history." And Nathan Hatch, who acknowledged a variety of social and intellectual sources for the "Christian" movement of the early nineteenth century, nonetheless finally explained the "Christians" as a response to "a pervasive collapse of certainty within popular culture"—an example of "what became of American religion in these years . . . when traditional values were being turned upside down."[1]

We do not quarrel with the interpretation that social disintegration can intensify mythic perspectives, especially a perspective that symbolically removes one from the chaotic present and places one instead in an idealized time of pure beginnings. But to explain the restoration impulse—or restoration-oriented traditions—almost exclusively in terms of chaos or social disintegration implicitly suggests that the impulse is aberrant and will subside when order is restored. Such an understanding obscures the power and persistence of the myth of first times in Anglo-American history and essentially removes any reason to examine this perspective in the larger American context.

Our objective, therefore, is not only to call attention to the dynamics of the restoration ideal in the American context but also to suggest that this impulse has been a far more significant part of American life and culture than typically has been supposed. Indeed, the myth of first times has appeared with such frequency and power in American life that it may well be one of the "habits of the heart"—a phrase first turned by Alexis de Tocqueville and recently popularized by Robert Bellah and four colleagues in a book bearing that title. It is striking how near Tocqueville came to putting his finger squarely on the myth of first times. While failing to recognize all its sources, he clearly described the profound alienation from history that characterized Americans in his age.

> The woof of time is every instant broken and the track of generations effaced. Those who went before are soon forgotten; of those who come after, no one has any idea. . . . Thus not only does democracy make every man forget his ancestors, but it hides his descendants and separates his contemporaries from him; it throws him back forever upon himself alone and threatens in the end to confine him entirely within the solitude of his own heart.[2]

Here was the root and core of the "individualism" that Tocqueville described and that Bellah and his associates lament. Thus, these more recent authors warn that

> we are parts of a larger whole that we can neither forget nor imagine in our own image without paying a high price. If we are not to have a self that hangs in the void, slowly twisting in the wind, these are issues we cannot ignore.[3]

Our concern, like that of Bellah and his colleagues, is that Americans learn fully to admit and appreciate the finite historic context in which they inevitably live and move and have their being. And we are convinced that American admission of finitude will occur much more readily when Americans stare squarely in the face their persistent myth of first times. America's failure to take history seriously may yet determine that this nation will one day simply "hang in the void, slowly twisting in the wind." This, indeed, is an issue we dare not ignore.

Acknowledgments

•

It is a pleasure for us to acknowledge the many debts we have accumulated over the twelve years in which this book has taken shape. Catherine L. Albanese, Henry Bowden, James Burrow, Richard Bushman, Mike Casey, W. Royce Clark, Robert Flanders, Samuel S. Hill, Hiram Lester, Sidney E. Mead, Ronald Numbers, R. L. Roberts, John Robinson, Winton Solberg, and James C. Spalding kindly read and criticized portions of the manuscript. Their assistance has proved invaluable.

The Graves Award, administered through the American Council of Learned Societies, facilitated work on primitivism in American culture in the summer of 1976. Two chapters began as projects in National Endowment for the Humanities summer seminars. Chapter 8 had its inception in an NEH seminar in 1975 under the direction of Robert N. Bellah at the University of California, Berkeley, and chapter 9 grew out of an NEH seminar in 1981 under the direction of George B. Tindall at the University of North Carolina, Chapel Hill. We are especially grateful to the NEH for its support and to Bellah and Tindall for their encouragement and criticism. We offer special thanks to the Cullen Research Foundation of Abilene Christian University for several summer stipends making possible travel to archives and extended periods of writing. We also are grateful to Brigham Young University and expecially to Tom Alexander, James Allen, and Milton Backman, Jr., of BYU who facilitated research for chapter 6. Don Haymes provided stimulation and encouragement at a crucial stage in our work, and Martin Marty assisted us significantly near the end. The dedication expresses the great debt we owe our teachers at the University of Iowa.

We also thank the libraries and their staffs that generously served us in many way: Bill Sumner and the staff of the Southern Baptist Historical Commission; David McWhirter, James Seale, and the staff of the Disciples of Christ Historical Society; the American Baptist Historical Society; the Southern Historical Collection at the University of North Carolina; the

Harold B. Lee Library of Brigham Young University; the University Library of the University of California, Berkeley; the Library of Congress; the Huntington Library; W. J. Berry, Sr., of the Primitive Baptist Library; and the staff of the Brown Library of Abilene Christian University, and especially R. L.Roberts, former archivist of the ACU Center for Restoration Studies.

For their dedicated work in preparing the manuscript we thank Roberta Brown, Carla Anderson, and Marisue Meyer and her staff at the ACU Word Processing Center: Angie Allen, Carla Claybrook, Karol Kyles, and Rhonda Royal. And to Mark Wentz, our graduate assistant, we extend our gratitude for efficient, prompt, and always good-natured attention to the seemingly endless details of proofreading and correction. We wish to thank the staff at the University of Chicago Press for their encouragement and assistance.

We also express our thanks to several publishers and journals for granting permission to reprint, with revisions, the following articles and chapters: Richard T. Hughes, "Soaring with the Gods: Early Mormons and the Eclipse of Religious Pluralism," in Jerald C. Brauer, ed., *The Lively Experiment Continued* (Macon, Ga.: Mercer University Press, 1987) (chapter 6); C. Leonard Allen, "Baconianism and the Bible in the Disciples of Christ: James S. Lamar and *The Organon of Scripture*," *Church History* 55 (March 1986): 65–80 (chapter 7); Richard T. Hughes, "From Primitive Church to Civil Religion: The Millennial Odyssey of Alexander Campbell," *Journal of the American Academy of Religion* 44 (March 1976): 87–103 (chapter 8); idem, "A Civic Theology for the South: The Case of Benjamin M. Palmer," *Journal of Church and State* 25 (Autumn 1983): 447–67 (chapter 9).

We also are grateful for permission to adapt substantial portions of the following two articles: Richard T. Hughes, "From Civil Dissent to Civil Religion—and Beyond," *Religion in Life* 49 (Autumn 1980): 268–288 © 1980 by Abingdon Press (chapter 1); idem, "Recovering First Times: The Logic of Primitivism in American Life," in Rowland A. Sherrill, ed., *American Recoveries: Religion and the Life of the Nation* (Urbana: University of Illinois Press, forthcoming) (chapter 1 and epilogue).

We also thank Mr. and Mrs. J. McDonald Williams for their unselfish support of our work on a variety of projects and especially for their assistance in facilitating the color work for the dust jacket of this volume.

Finally, we thank our wives—Jan and Holly—for their support for this project over a very long period of time, and our children for fresh and stimulating glimpses into the meaning of life and growth in the American setting.

ONE

Restoring First Times in the Anglo-American Experience

When J. Hector St. John de Crevecoeur observed that "the American is a new man, who acts upon new principles; he must therefore entertain new ideas, and form new opinions," he was only offering a realistic assessment of American life, labor, and social structures as he perceived them.[1] There were others, however, in Crevecoeur's generation and the next who infused the image of American newness with a mythic dimension. For these interpreters, Americans were new in that they had been cut loose from the constraints of history and time and stood on the threshold of a radically new age which was wholly discontinuous with all previous epochs. Thus, Charles Pinckney argued in 1787 that the American situation was simply "unexampled" in the past, and Gulian Verplanck told students at Union College in 1836 that America was "without a parallel in past history."[2] Three years later, a writer in the *Democratic Review* contended that America had little connection with the histories of modern nations "and still less with all antiquity, its glories, or its crimes. On the contrary, our national birth was the beginning of a new history, . . . which separates us from the past and connects us with the future only."[3] Poetically, Walt Whitman captured the essence of this sentiment in *Pioneers! O Pioneers!*:

All the past we leave behind,
We debouch upon a newer, mightier world, varied world.

And graphically, the great seal of the United States captured the sentiment of radical American newness when it pictured all human history prior to America as a barren and arid wilderness from which emerged the American *novus ordo seclorum* (new order of the ages) in 1776.

That millennial visions are implicit in this understanding is obvious, and anyone even casually acquainted with American religion in this period knows that millennialism of various kinds flourished in America between the Revolution and the Civil War. Intrigued by the various

visions of millennial newness and the way those visions related to American purpose and identity during this period, scholars have explored the
meaning of nineteenth-century American millennialism in painstaking
and minute detail.[4] Most scholars writing on this subject, however, have
failed to recognize that generally implicit in the rhetoric of American
newness and millennialism was the fundamental theme of recovery—
recovery of something primal, ancient, and old. To be sure, most Americans were not concerned to recover their recent past, or even an ancient
past which was merely history, fully as corrupt and degenerate as the
recent past from which they had sprung. But they were concerned to
recover the primordial past that stood behind the historical past. The
objective of their recovery was, to use the language of Mircea Eliade,
sacred time, not profane time—the time of the gods, not the time of
humankind.

Implicit in this conception is the notion of a fall from primal purity
and rightness, and it was history—the long duration of human time—
that embodied the disastrous aftermath of that fall. Understood in this
way, millennialism was itself a kind of recovery of sacred time. Far from
depicting a vacuous, contentless vision of the last age, most millennial
visions elaborated a very specific content drawn from a first age whose
perfections had been lost or obscured in a fall but that might be recovered or restored in the millennial dawn.

A few scholars have sensed the importance of the notion of recovery
in the American experience and have written cogently and suggestively
regarding this theme. Fred Somkin, in his book *Unquiet Eagle,* finds it
notable that delegates to the constitutional convention looked to the
classic world for instruction rather than to the England of the commonwealth. This meant, Somkin argues, that the delegates sought to identify
"with a universalism that transcended the mere homeland." Then
Somkin makes the crucial point:

> In the classic, archetypal forms of political life were to be found
> the rights of man, as distinguished from the rights of En-
> glishmen. Such a point of view argued an American alienation
> from the grasp of an organic, efficacious past, as though America
> were itself a kind of rebuke to time. An appeal to the nature of
> man, rather than to his history, evidenced a faith in something
> that had emerged unscathed from the gauntlet of historical
> time.[5]

Further, Somkin clearly recognizes that America's newness was
predicated precisely on her oldness, that is, on her identification with
primordial norms. Thus while writing of America's "unprecedented-

ness" and of her "utterly new beginning," Somkin also can write that "America . . . , by cleaving to the primitively old, to that which had not grown old through the agency of time, gained the possibility of continuing to be always new."[6] This description comes close to suggesting the image of America straddling the stream of history, with one foot planted squarely in the primordium and the other in the millennial dawn. In this way America became "a providential conspiracy against time, . . . an attempt to outwit time by an evasion of the exigencies of temporal causality." None of this means, of course, that Americans were ahistorical or unhistorical or failed either to know or to appreciate the past. Quite to the contrary. "As record, as deposit, the past undoubtedly existed," Somkin observes, "but Americans contested the extent of its jurisdiction."[7]

Contesting the extent of the jurisdiction of the past is precisely what Sidney Mead had in mind when he wrote of the sense of "historylessness" that American denominations in the nineteenth century so often manifested. Contending with one another in the new free market of souls, created and sustained by religious freedom and pluralism in the new nation, both right-wing denominations and left-wing sects sought legitimacy by claiming to duplicate primitive Christianity more closely than the others. In so doing, Mead observes, sects and denominations in America became both radically new and radically old at one and the same time so that all, to one degree or another, embraced "the idea of building anew in the American wilderness on the true and ancient foundations."[8]

I

One of the chief contentions of this volume is that recovery of primal norms has been a fundamental preoccupation of the American people. In the quest for identity, both the nation and the nation's religious traditions have employed this perspective with striking regularity.

The concern to identify with pure beginnings is a legacy of the Protestant Reformation, though this legacy survives in the twentieth century in a myriad of forms, some of which are explicitly Protestant and denominational and some of which are broadly cultural and political. One might argue, for example, that American foreign policy, often dominated by redemptive themes, rests ultimately on the conviction that America has restored pure, natural, and primal norms while other nations remain snared in the web of history, tradition, and artificial contrivance. America's task, therefore, is redemptive precisely because America, at the level of fundamental identity, transcends the vicissitudes of history and the constraints of finitude. Put another way, American institutions—especially democracy and free enterprise—are simply natural and reflect the way the Creator intended things to be from the beginning.

In the mid-1980s, a spate of pro-American, anti-Soviet films reflected these themes at the popular level. *Rocky IV* was a notable case. When Rocky Balboa trained for his great fight with the Russian giant, Drago, he trained in the Siberian wilderness as a fundamentally natural man. Instead of lifting manufactured weights, Rocky lifted timber and stones. He pulled crude sleds across the Siberian terrain and jogged on mountain tops. He was the American—the natural man. In stark contrast, Drago was contrived and artificial. He trained on the latest scientific equipment and jogged in a modern, scientific gymnasium. If Rocky was the natural man, Drago was preeminently a product of modern science and technology. And when Rocky finally defeated the Russian giant, the Soviet crowd, responding enthusiastically to the compelling attraction of the natural man, began to chant, "Rocky, Rocky, Rocky." The symbolism was clear: America, the natural, primal, and pure nation, once again had defeated the hosts of history, time, and artificial contrivance.

To describe this perspective, we employ in this book the terms *primitivism* and *restorationism* interchangeably, for the heart of this perspective is the concern to "restore" what seems to be "primitive" or prior to the mere traditions of history. This American perspective descends ultimately from a sixteenth-century tradition that viewed antiquity, and especially the primitive Christian church, as the standard for all subsequent Christian faith and practice. In England this viewpoint emerged with extraordinary power when Christian Humanism and Reformed theology made common cause under the catalytic influence of William Tyndale's covenant theology. The uniqueness of this perspective, at least in Christian history, appears when contrasted with the other dominant tradition of the Reformation, the theology of Martin Luther. Luther had virtually no interest in resurrecting the primitive Christian church as a norm for his own age, and severely chastised Andreas Bodenstein von Karlstadt, who attempted to model the church in Wittenberg after a supposed apostolic pattern. The particular content of Karlstadt's theology Luther viewed as beside the point. It was the theological method itself that Luther viewed as demonic, for it "destroys faith, profanes the blood of Christ, blasphemes the gospel, and sets all that Christ has won for us at nought."[9] Luther was not so much concerned with returning to an earlier time as he was with finding a place to stand, a ground of being (*ontos*), in his own time.

Noting the radical difference between Luther's theological method and that of Christian Humanism and much of the Reformed tradition,

Gordon Rupp and George Yule prefer to speak of "patterns of Reformation" rather than Reformation per se. Both distinguish between the overriding *sola gratia* theology of Luther and the other major way of doing theology in the Reformation period, a method Rupp describes as "plans of salvation" and Yule describes as "reformation by biblical precedent."[10] In our view, a workable and suggestive way of distinguishing between Luther's theological method and the theological method of much of Reformed Christianity is to distinguish between *ontological reform,* where the primary question is How can I find a merciful God, or a place to stand? and *primordial reform,* where the primary question is What was the ancient tradition? It was this latter question that dominated both the worldview and the theological method of Christian Humanism, the Reformed tradition, and the Puritans. When Rationalism finally revolted against Puritan dominance and intransigence in England, it was able to extricate itself from Puritan preoccupation with the primitive church and apostolic practices, but it did not extricate itself from the basic question of primordial reform, namely, the question concerning some kind of ancient or primitive norm.

II

Before sketching briefly the historic development of primordial reform, and its manifestations in both Puritanism and the Enlightenment, we need to view primordial reform from a phenomenological perspective. Here the works of Mircea Eliade regarding sacred and profane time in primitive religions prove helpful. Eliade argues that for the primitive person the only real time, and therefore "sacred time," was primordial time; that "profane time" was "the 'unreal' *par excellence,* the uncreated, the nonexistent: the void"; and that primitive man sought, through periodic rituals and festivals, to repeat the paradigmatic activities of the gods, thus making primordial time or real time contemporary. Through the restoration of sacred, primordial time, primitives transformed profane chaos into sacred cosmos—a world possessing reality and wholeness.[11] This epitome of Eliade's argument makes clear what we mean by primordial reform: *chronos* is reversed until profane history is transcended and the believer stands squarely in the first age.

In applying such a construction to the Christian tradition, the critical question is, of course, How is it possible to apply essentially non-historical categories to a historical religion? The answer lies in recognizing that any human history, if that history has more than a formal and factual significance, bears mythical and symbolic power. To the degree that the factual history outweighs the power of the myth, and a certain distance is maintained between the particular history that is normative and the believer's own time, then we may speak of a particular religious tradition as being historical. In such cases a certain objectivity remains. But when the normative history is swallowed up in myth to such an extent that the believer loses the clear distinction between his own time and the primal time, then that historic tradition has lost its historicity. At that point, the particular time that was merely normative now has become the eternally repeatable primordium within which the believer lives and moves and has his being and apart from which life itself has no meaning or significance.

A classic illustration, drawn squarely from the American situation, is the Church of Jesus Christ of Latter-day Saints, which contends that the church established during the apostolic primordium but subsequently lost from the face of the earth was restored once and for all by the prophet Joseph Smith. All efforts by Mormons to verify the facts of this historical norm (the primordium) or the facts of its recovery (the restoration) are beside the point, because efforts to verify are not for the sake of the believer but rather for the sake of the outsider. The power of the myth emanating from the particular history has already grasped the believer, and no amount of verification or lack of verification can possibly make any difference. Put another way, whether the history has any objective reality is beside the point; the myth carries existential reality and that alone is sufficient. Only as the power of the myth diminishes does the history require repeating, and this repetition occurs only for the sake of reinforcing the myth. In this case history enlarges the myth, rather than the myth being constrained and refined by the facts of history. Moreover, Mormons, while fond of repeating their own particular history, typically do not repeat the larger history that lies behind their own. They typically either ignore or dismiss as an aberration from the primordial norm the eighteen centuries of Christian history that precede. Mormons are utterly ahistorical in taking this approach, and yet they are part of a historic tradition—the Judeo-Christian faith. In their case, however, the power of the myth outweighs and even obscures the facts of the history that produced them.

The student of Christian history, therefore, should be aware that a historical religion quickly may become ahistorical when its adherents either deny or attempt to transcend the particular history that produced them. Once one perceives this possibility, it becomes difficult to dismiss the insights of Eliade for a study of certain aspects of Christian history. Indeed, the concept of the primordium may be far more applicable to certain dimensions of Christian history than is immediately apparent.

For, as Eliade describes it, the primordial event was precisely whatever the believer understood to be primordial. Eliade's treatment of Walt Whitman's *Homer* helps us understand this conception of the relativity of primordial time: "Whitman expressed with force and glamour the obsession with the primordial, the absolute beginning. He enjoyed 'reciting *Homer* while walking beside the Ocean' because *Homer* belonged to the *primordium;* he was not a product of history—he had founded European poetry."[12] Similarly, for many strands of the Reformed and English Protestant traditions, the examples of Israel, Jesus, the apostles, and the primitive church belonged to the primordium; they were not products of history—they had founded the only real history there was, Christian history now understood as the primitive church and the Protestant era. All intervening history was profane.

Eliade himself makes it clear that the notion of a primordial norm is not universally applicable to Christianity and that it would be faulty to apply it to theologies like that of Luther. Utilizing the rubric "Christianity" but describing a Christianity dominated by a radical conception of *sola fides* and *sola gratia,* Eliade contends that

> in Christianity . . . the *basileia tou theou* [kingdom of God] is already present "among" those who believe, and . . . hence the *illud tempus* [former or first time] is eternally of the present and accessible to anyone, at any moment, through *metanoia* [repentance]. Since what is involved is a religious experience wholly different from the traditional experience, since what is involved is faith, Christianity translates the periodic regeneration of the world into a regeneration of the human individual.[13]

Primordial reform, however, differs significantly from what Eliade describes here. We turn now to a brief history of this tradition.

III

The primordial dimension of the English Reformation and Puritanism drew essentially from three sources: Christian Humanism, the Reformed tradition of the Continent, and the covenant theology of William Tyndale. Christian Humanism, through its concern to restore both the source documents of primitive Christianity and the morals of Christian antiquity, provided the springboard for primordial thinking in the Reformation period. The writings of Desiderius Erasmus, for example, reflect a deep reverence for the ancient Christian writings over against the scholastic theology of his own age, and a concern that people learn to live according to the *philosophia Christi.* The following passage from the *Paraclesis* typifies the Erasmian emphasis:

> Why devote the greater part of life to Averroes rather than to the gospels? Why spend nearly all of life on the ordinances of men and on opinions in contradiction with themselves? . . . Let us all, therefore, with our whole heart covet this literature [the Scriptures], let us embrace it, let us fondly kiss it, at length let us die in its embrace, let us be transformed in it, since indeed studies are transmuted into morals.[14]

Erasmus, to be sure, never suggested that the apostolic church provided a model for the church of the sixteenth century. As Abraham Friesen has pointed out, Erasmus was prohibited from taking that step, on the one hand, by his commitment to the traditions of Christendom and, on the other hand, by his Neoplatonic conception of Christ by which Christ's perfection could only be reflected, not duplicated.[15] But at the same time the basic structural presuppositions of chronological reform were present in his thought—the supremacy of Christian antiquity and the preeminence of the *philosophia Christi.*

It is critical at this point to note that Christian Humanism influenced practically every sixteenth-century reformer who embraced primordial reform. The early English Catholic reformer John Colet, whose humanism was beyond question, provides a notable case in point. William Clebsch has demonstrated that Colet's conception of reform, while predicated on the Pauline corpus, nevertheless differed radically from the posture of Luther. As Clebsch puts it, "that which is particularly Coletian . . . is the fastening . . . upon the Pauline writings as descriptive of the pure primitive Church, for a model of individual and corporate Christianity."[16] Nowhere in the sixteenth century is Eliade's conception of the transformation of chaos into cosmos through the repristination of the primordial norm more thoroughly typified than in the thought of Colet. According to Colet, the Edenic state of nature had been reestablished in primitive Christianity and thus restoring apostolic life and teachings also meant restoring the primordial norm in the most objective sense possible.

> It was the purpose of Christ, himself the author of nature, to express nature herself among men, and to bring back to the order and beauty of nature what had diverged from order, and to reform the human race, all deformed as it was, and disfigured and abominable. . . . This could not be done without some mighty living force, which, being in all its fulness in one, might be poured out from that one upon the many; which might go

forth, and recall, restore, win back and re-establish for mankind their pristine state.[17]

Colet's theology epitomized the recovery of the primordial norm. The sources of that norm were twofold: nature and revelation—the same two traditions that would converge, now in this way and now in that, to shape the contours of the Anglo-American primordium for generations to come.

The notion of primordial reform, however, was not popularized by Colet and had to await the Marian Exiles for its full-blown development. But when at last the Exiles developed this theme, they did so with a profound sense of urgency rooted in the covenant theology of William Tyndale. For Tyndale, England was a "new Israel," and just as God had smitten ancient Israel for covenant-breaking, so God would smite England with "hunger, death, murrain, pestilence, war, oppression, with strange and wonderful diseases, and new kinds of misfortune and evil luck" if England failed in her covenant duties.[18] But, Tyndale wrote in the preface to his 1534 New Testament, "If we meke oure selves to god, to kepe all his lawes, after the ensample of Christ: then God hath bounde his selfe vnto vs to kepe and make good all the mercies promysed in Christ throwout all the scripture."[19]

The implications of Tyndale's covenant theology for primordial reform were obvious, especially given the milieu of Christian Humanism present in England during the early and mid-sixteenth century. But what was merely an implication became clear during the first year of Edward's reign when injunctions were issued ordering every pastor to obtain Erasmus's *Paraphrases* on the New Testament as a study guide to the New Testament. Significantly, a strong dose of Tyndale's covenant theology was appended to Erasmus's *Paraphrase* in the prefaces written by Nicholas Udall and Thomas Key. This joining of Erasmus and Tyndale in the same volume clearly implied that England could fulfill the covenant through a return to the sources and morals of Christian antiquity. This volume circulated so widely that, by the time the primitivist impulse from the Continent began shaping English theology later in the reign of Edward VI, a unique blend of Tyndalic deuteronomism and Erasmian Humanism had already prepared the ground.

The continental influences on England during Edward's reign came from a host of sources, to be sure, but principally from the Reformed theologians of Zurich and Strassburg. While the Zurich theologians Huldreich Zwingli and Heinrich Bullinger both upheld a profound doctrine of justification by faith, both also were Christian Humanists who strongly advocated primordial reform. Bullinger, for example, was quite explicit that "the church should hold tightly to no other form than that transferred and established by the Lord and the Apostles and should remain unchanged," and he even sought to approximate the primitive traditions in his rejection of musical instruments in the Great Minster: "The organs in the churches are not a particularly old institution, especially in these parts. Since they do not agree with the apostolic teaching (I Cor. 14) the organs in the Great Minster were broken up on the 9th of December in the year 1527. For from this time forth neither singing nor organs in the Church was wanted."[20] Zwingli and Bullinger profoundly influenced the English theological scene through letters, commentaries, Bullinger's *Decades of Sermons,* and through the proto-Puritan John Hooper. Further, their influence was sufficiently extensive to prompt King Edward himself to write the senate of Zurich on October 20, 1549, regarding the "mutual agreement between us concerning the Christian religion and true godliness."[21]

The Strassburg influence on England came primarily from Peter Martyr Vermigli and Martin Bucer, though it is Bucer who demands our attention in this context. Bucer, in his *De Regno Christi* presented to Edward VI in 1550, clearly called for primordial reform, but his chief contribution lies in the fact that he placed his call for primordial reform squarely within the context of the national covenant. Thus, for the first time in England, the presuppositions of Tyndalic deuteronomism and Erasmian Humanism had been combined to create an explicit and urgent demand that England—the entire *corpus christianum*—become the primordial kingdom of Christ, lest England be afflicted with the wrath of God.[22] Bucer, in other words, called for a Christian civil religion. Consistent with this appeal, Bucer's model was not the apostolic church of the first century but rather the Constantinian church and society, which was for him the Christian primordium that should be replicated in his own time.

The appeal to a Christian priordium within the context of a national covenant—a phenomenon that would become common in America— became commonplace within the early Puritan movement as it grew up among the Marian Exiles. But more to the point, this primordial appeal became the basis for a powerful dissenting tradition that emerged at this time. The Geneva Bible, produced by the Exiles, provides an important case in point. The preoccupation of the translators with the national covenant is well known. Within that context the advancing of true religion meant to the Exiles the faithful reproduction of the primitive church revealed in the Word of God. Thus, in the dedicatory to Queen Elizabeth, the translators charged her to build up the church "according to the word of God. . . . For if it was not lawful for Moses to build the material Tabernacle after any other sort than God showed him by a pattern . . . , how can it be lawful to proceed in this spiritual building any other way, than Jesus Christ the Son of God, who is both the foundation, head and chief corner stone thereof, hath commanded by his word?" Dan G. Danner, who has analyzed carefully the theology of the Geneva Bible, has summarized this theme: "No man has the authority to exceed the bounds of scripture, either to add to, or take from. . . . Whatever is not commanded by God's Word 'touching his service, is against the word.' Only the Bible is God's authority which contains norms for worship and piety."[23] The recovery of the biblical pattern was at one and the same time the recovery of a primordium that had been lost in the previous years of darkness and ignorance. The Exiles believed, therefore, that "it hath pleased [God] to call us into this marvelous light of his Gospel, & mercifully to regard us after so horrible backsliding and falling away from Christ to Antichrist, from light to darkness, from the living God to dumb and dead idols, & that . . . we are . . . received again to grace with most evident signes and tokens of Gods especial love and favor."[24] These Exiles had a keen awareness of stepping, as Eliade would put it, from profane time into sacred time, from the present as present into the present as primordium, and it was this awareness that propelled their dissent.

It is within this context that John Knox's controversy with Richard Cox in Frankfurt makes sense. Knox developed his well-known covenant theology in response to Mary Tudor's accession to the throne in 1553, an event that the proto-Puritans among the Exiles typically interpreted as God's scourge on England for failing sufficiently to reform the church. In *An Admonition or Warning,* completed in 1554, Knox summarized the covenant: "This is the league betwixt God and us, that He alone shall be oure God, and we shall be his people: He shall communicate with us of his graces and goodness; We shall serve him in bodie and spirit: He shall be oure safeguard from death and damnation; We shall seek to him, and shall flee from all strange Gods."[25] Thinking in covenantal terms, Knox argued with Richard Cox in Frankfurt that the Anglicans failed to exercise godly discipline. The real issue, which Knox failed to articulate but which Richard Vander Molen perceptively observes, was *what kind* of discipline should be imposed. For Anglicans, any principle of discipline was of necessity historically conditioned. They were willing therefore to accept national church traditions. Knox and his followers, on the other hand, sought to return to a first-century norm for a method of discipline uncontaminated by subsequent historical and cultural influences. Cox strongly suggested to Knox that such an ideal was illusory and that even his concern to approximate a first-century norm was historically and culturally conditioned.[26]

Following the Exile, the compulsion to duplicate the Christian primordium in the present time became a central feature of Puritan dissent. Sixteen years after Knox's *Admonition,* Thomas Cartwright argued, in his Cambridge lectures on Acts (1570), that the government of the first Christian church in Jerusalem was presbyterian and that therefore, ipso facto, presbyterian church government should be employed in the present age. Indeed, so insistent was Cartwright that the church of his own day replicate the primitive church that, taking his cue from Tertullian, he found the very silence of scripture prohibitive. As Cartwright put it, "The scripture denieth that, whiche yt noteth not." Moreover, Cartwright was convinced that the further one moved in time from the first apostolic communities, the more corrupt the church became, so that by the end of the first five hundred years of Christian history the true church hardly existed at all.[27] Indeed, Donald McGinn has argued that the heart of the entire controversy surrounding Cartwright's famous *Admonition to Parliament* was the question of the primitive church. Two years after the *Admonition* was published, Walter Travers published what B. R. White calls "the most systematic exposition of presbyterian churchmanship during this period for English Puritans," *De Disciplina Ecclesiastica,* translated that same year by Cartwright into English and entitled *A full and plaine declaration of ecclesiasticall discipline.* Travers there argued the same point, namely, that the Bible provided a perfect pattern for ecclesiastical discipline "which is common and general to all the church and perpetual for all times."[28]

Other and later Puritans repeated this basic argument almost ad nauseum. Although agreed on the fact of a perfect ancient pattern, they disagreed continually on its features. The Separatist Henry Barrow, for example, judged the Marian Exiles, for all their primordialist sentiments, to have missed the mark. But, generously, he excused them.

> It can be no wonder that those godly men so unexpert and unexercised in this heavenly work, never having lived in, seen, or heard of any orderly communion of saints, any true established church upon earth of so many hundred years, ever since the general defection under Antichrist so much foretold of in the Scriptures, no marvel, I say, if they erred in setting up the frame. But what then? Should we therefore justify or persist in their errors? Especially should we reject the true pattern of Christ's Testament which reproveth our works, and showeth us a better course?[29]

12

And the Separatist turned Congregationalist John Robinson put his case in a classic form that illustrates well the phenomenological perspective of Eliade. "We do believe, by the word of God," he wrote, "that the things we teach are not new, but old truths renewed; so are we not less persuaded, that the church constitution in which we are set, is cast in the apostolical and primitive mould, and not one day nor hour younger, in the nature and form of it, than the first church of the New Testament."[30]

In New England the primordial theme was equally as pronounced. The great tutor of the New England Puritans, William Ames, had affirmed that scripture was "not a partial, but a perfect rule of Faith and manners," and within that context the New England Puritans perpetuated the venerable primordialist tradition.[31] The *Cambridge Platform* of 1648 argued, for example, that church government is "exactly described in the word of God . . . so that it is not left in the power of men, officers, Churches, or any state in the world, to add, diminish or alter any thing in the least measure therein." This, clearly, was a way of urging conformity to the once-for-allness of the primordial norm and rejecting merely historical traditions as of any value whatsoever. Likewise William Bradford, in *Of Plymouth Plantation,* recalled how Satan had opposed the truth in England, reluctant that "his kingdom should go downe, the trueth prevaile; and the churches of God reverte to their anciente puritie; and recover their primitive order, libertie, and bewtie."[32] Bradford here was recalling the time when primordial theology was a tool for dissent.

But in New England what once was the basis for dissent became the basis for an established church. Nowhere is this shift more apparent than in John Cotton's affirmation that the New England Way was as close as could be to what "the Lord Jesus [would erect] were he here himselfe in person." The shift appears in Cotton Mather's smug proclamation that "the Churches of New England are [not] the most *regular* that can be; yet I do say, and am sure, that they are very like unto those that were in the first ages of Christianity." Not surprisingly, Edward Winslow wrote in 1646 that the Bay churches had not borrowed from the Plymouth churches or vice versa. Rather, the Bay churches "advised with us," and we "accordingly shewed them the Primitive practice for our warrant. . . . So that here also thow maist see they set not the Church at Plimouth before them for example, but the Primitive Churches were and are their and our mutuall patterns and examples."[33]

Later in the seventeenth century a major shift took place in English religious thought, a shift from Puritanism to the Enlightenment. Puritanism was credited with causing bitter societal divisions, war, bloodshed, the fragmentation of English society, and finally, regicide. The Puritans' efforts to construct a new established order in England by returning to the ancient Christian primordium now seemed a failure, and sober and reasonable men and women sought diligently for a new theological glue that might once again bind their world together. Lord Herbert of Cherbury first adumbrated this new theology that sought to reduce religion to a set of essentials on which all reasonable persons could agree. The source for this new theology was not something highly particular, knowable only to a few, but rather highly universal, knowable to all: the source was nature.

IV

For all the theological changes involved in the shift from orthodoxy to the Enlightenment, however, one thing did not change, and that was the theological method. The quest for the primordium persisted; the rationalists simply substituted one book—the book of Nature—for another and exchanged the primordium of the early church for the primordium of Eden. The basic theological question continued to be What is truth? And the old assumption that truth resided in antiquity continued to prevail. The basic difference was that the rationalists carried their quest for truth to an antiquity far older than the Christian antiquity they were rejecting. As one Enlightenment thinker put it, the antiquity they sought was as old as creation.

The appeal to antiquity was especially strong among the Jeffersonians in the American Enlightenment. No one made the point more clearly than Thomas Paine in *Rights of Man,* where he argued that human rights are rooted in the original creation and can be justified by appealing only to the original creation.

> The error of those who reason by precedents from antiquity, respecting the rights of man, is that they do not go far enough into antiquity. They do not go the whole way. They stop in some of the intermediate stages of an hundred or a thousand years, and produce what was then done, as a rule of the present day. This is no authority at all, . . . but if we proceed on, we shall at last come out right; we shall come to the time when man came from the hand of his Maker. . . . We have now arrived at the origin of man, and at the origin of his rights.[34]

The Jeffersonians could argue that all men were created equal because the created order of things, they supposed, had remained virtually unchanged since the creation itself. Thus to study the creature was to study the creation, and to attend to nature was to attend to Eden. Again, Paine made the point well.

> All men are born equal, and with equal natural rights, in the
> same manner as if posterity had been continued by *creation*
> instead of by *generation*. . . . Consequently every child born
> into the world must be considered as deriving its existence from
> God. The world is as new to him as it was to the first man that
> existed, and his natural right in it is of the same kind.[35]

From an Eliadian perspective it might well be said that, for Paine, the
birth of a human being was a sort of sacred festival making contemporary
the primordial, creative activity of the gods.

But if this were true, then why had so many human governments
denied the God-given rights of man? Here Paine sketched a theory of the
fall:

> because there have been upstart governments, thrusting them-
> selves between, and presumptuously working to *un-make*
> man. . . . It is not among the least of the evils of the present
> existing governments in all parts of Europe that man, consid-
> ered as man, is thrown back to a vast distance from his Maker,
> and the artificial chasm filled up with a succession of barriers, or
> sort of turnpike gates, through which he has to pass.[36]

Paine described these barriers erected between human beings and the
original creation as kings, parliaments, magistrates, priests, nobility, and
Peter. But lo, in these latter days, Paine argued, the barriers had been
destroyed and a restoration had occurred. The creative activity of the
gods had been made contemporary in the eighteenth century with the
founding of the American republic and the recovery of the primordial
rights of man.

> In viewing this subject, the case and circumstances of America
> present themselves as in the beginning of a world; and our
> inquiry into the origin of government is shortened by referring
> to the facts that have arisen in our own day. We have no occasion
> to roam for information into the obscure field of antiquity, nor
> hazard ourselves upon conjecture. We are brought at once to
> the point of seeing government begin, as if we had lived in the
> beginning of time. The real volume, not of history, but of facts, is
> directly before us, unmutilated by contrivance, or the errors of
> tradition.[37]

It is significant that Paine did not regard history as the real volume of
facts. History, for Paine, had been transcended, and the facts of the matter
were to be found in nature. Given these peculiarly primordialist presuppositions, it is hardly surprising that Daniel Boorstin should write that

"the Jeffersonians reasoned that man . . . had no significant past. . . . By merging man into the whole natural universe, the Jeffersonians had in fact alienated themselves from the humanistic past."[38] Methodologically, though not theologically, the Jeffersonians were at one with the Puritans.

Thus when Jefferson, like Herbert of Cherbury, sought to transcend real or potential religious combustions, he did so by appealing to a faith common to all humankind since it could be learned from nature. Deploring the fruits of Christian orthodoxy, which he described as "castes of inextinguishable hatred to one another," Jefferson sought to transcend both theological particularities and the social repression that insistence on those particularities created. Indeed, he sought, as he put it, to unite people "in those principles only in which God has united us all," namely, the principles that "there is only one God, . . . that there is a future state of rewards and punishments, [and] that to love God with all thy heart and thy neighbor as thyself is the sum of religion," formulations all derived from the primordium of nature.[39] The primordial qualities of these doctrinal statements are made explicit in the Declaration of Independence, which specifically identifies God as "Nature's God" and describes the moral order as an endowment from this God and thus "unalienable." But this theme became even more explicit in Jefferson's earlier draft of the Declaration, which read, "We hold these truths to be sacred & undeniable; that all men are created equal & independent, that from that equal creation they derive rights inherent & inalienable."[40] The rights to life, liberty, and the pursuit of happiness were therefore, to borrow a phrase from the Puritan John Robinson, "not new, but old truths renewed . . . and not one day nor hour younger, in the nature and form of it" than the original creation.

To be sure, this effort to push behind primitive Christianity to the original creation was the difference that made all the difference, theologically, between Puritanism and the Enlightenment. For in spite of the primordial qualities of Enlightenment thought, this new theology was not concerned with restoring finite forms and structures, as had been the case with Puritanism. It rather was an effort to go behind the finite forms and structures to the one universal reality that all people could confess— the sovereignty and providence of God.

Even the early Mormons, who sometimes despaired of their treatment at the hands of the United States government, readily proclaimed their faith in the primal and therefore universal dimensions of the U.S. Constitution. Parley P. Pratt, one of the original Twelve Apostles of the Latter-day Saints who suffered brutal imprisonment in Missouri for his faith, unequivocally affirmed:

In the principles of the Constitution formed by our fathers . . . there is no difficulty, that is, in the laws and
instruments themselves. They embrace eternal truths, principles of eternal liberty, not the principles of one peculiar
country, or the sectional interest of any particular people, but
the great, fundamental, eternal principles of liberty to rational
beings.[41]

In one sense, the theology of the Enlightenment was similar to the
theology of Luther, for it stripped away human intermediaries between
human beings, affirming the sovereignty of the Creator and the finitude
of the creation. And, like Luther, the Enlightenment thinkers taught that
God could be depicted and known through a variety of theological
formulations, and that those formulations should never be taken as absolute or mistaken for God himself. This is what Sidney Mead meant when
he wrote that the Enlightenment thinkers "plumbed for the universal
which is dressed and disguised in the particularities of doctrine and
practice that distinguish one sect from another."[42]

This kind of theology held profound implications, for the effort to
transcend finite forms and symbols resulted in the simultaneous tran-
scendence of both civil dissent and civil religion. Civil dissent was
transcended because, at least in theory, all particular finite forms would
be permitted. And civil religion was transcended because no particular
finite form would be regarded as absolute. Henceforth the glue that
would bind this commonwealth together would not be common agreement on a particular set of theological assertions, as with the Puritans, but
rather common agreement on the one assertion that all theological assertions are equally finite but also equally viable ways of plumbing for the
universal.

V

Once again, the radical differences between Puritan and Enlightenment
theological content should not obscure the fact that Puritans and Enlightenment thinkers shared a common theological method—the quest
for the primordium. And it was at least partly due to this common method, and partly due to the pervasiveness of the Puritan heritage to which
virtually all Americans of the time more or less had fallen heir, that the
primordium of the primitive church and the primordium of nature could
become so thoroughly amalgamated in the thinking of so many in this
period. One of the earliest to amalgamate these two categories was John
Wise. In *Vindication of the Government of the New England Churches*
(1717), Wise argued first that "the Churches in New-England; and the

Primitive Churches are Eminently parallel in their Government." But if the Congregational government preserved the original Christian primordium, it also preserved the "Original State and Liberty of Mankind . . . found peculiarly in the Light of Nature."[43] Or again, Jefferson provides a case in point. Like the humanist Colet 250 years earlier, Jefferson was convinced that the first age of the Christian faith had re-pristinated successfully the virtues of the primordium of nature. Thus he said, "I adhere to the principles of the first age; and consider all subsequent innovations as corruptions of his religion, having no foundation in what came from him [Jesus]." Or again, in 1821, Jefferson wrote to Timothy Pickering that "when . . . we shall have unlearned everything which has been taught since his day, and got back to the pure and simple doctrines he inculcated, we shall then be truly and worthily his disciples; and my opinion is that if nothing had ever been added to what flowed purely from his lips, the whole world would at this day have been Christian." But Jefferson was not without hope. Quite to the contrary, he was "happy in the prospect of a restoration of primitive Christianity," though he admitted that he "must leave to younger Athletes to encounter and lop off the false branches which have been engrafted into it by the mythologists of the middle and modern ages."[44] And significantly, this restoration of primitive Christianity would take place in nature's nation, under the auspices of nature's God, and its theology would be nature's as well. Boorstin was right in observing that Jefferson "came close to making Jesus a Son of Liberty, and a member of the American Philosophical Society."[45]

Similarly, on the Puritan side of things, an Abraham Keteltas could link the primordium of nature, which heralded civic liberties for all people, with the primordium of the Christian church, which heralded the universal, magisterial rule of Jesus Christ. The Revolution, he told his flock in a sermon of 1777, was not only "the cause of the oppressed against the oppressor [and] . . . the cause of liberty against arbitrary power," but was also "the cause of pure and undefiled religion against bigotry, superstition, and human invention . . . [and] the cause of reformation against popery." In an interesting theological paradox, he admonished his parishioners to pray for the time when "universal love and liberty . . . shall prevail" and when "the kingdoms of this world are become the kingdoms of our Lord and his Christ (Rev. 11:15)."[46]

This amalgamation of Jesus and Eden had taken place within the relatively short span of fifty years. The millennial fervor that had characterized the Great Awakening had possessed a single focus: "the new and most glorious state of God's church on earth," that is, "a new world in a spiritual respect," as Jonathan Edwards aptly put it.[47] But during the next fifty years, while the colonists fought the Battle of Armageddon on three successive fronts—the Great Awakening, the French and Indian War, and the American Revolution[48]—the God of Nature stole stealthily into their hitherto undefiled and sacrosanct Christian temples, put on Christian garb, and in that disguise began to receive the homage that previously had been reserved for Jesus Christ alone. Many Americans now celebrated the primordium of nature, with its liberties for all people, as a uniquely Christian phenomenon, and Timothy Dwight could proclaim that "this continent will be the principal seat of that new, that peculiar kingdom, which shall be given to the saints of the Most High."[49] Though Dwight never would have admitted it, a significant shift in outlook had taken place: the Most High had become the God of Nature, though dressed in Christian garb, and his saints were U.S. citizens who more and more assumed that they constituted a Christian nation. What was emerging was a new American faith, one that was neither the religious establishment of the Puritans nor the religionless "theology of the Republic" adumbrated during the Revolution. Rather, the new faith was a unique blend of Christ and nature, of the primordium of the early church and the primordium of the creation. It was, in fact, the beginnings of the civil religion Robert Bellah described several years ago.[50] But more to the point, all the elements of this new civil religion were rooted in the common conviction that America had transcended history and had made the ancient primordium contemporary in the new Republic.

As Americans progressively collapsed Christ and nature into a single, common primordium, they increasingly, though not always consciously, infused the open-ended dimensions of Enlightenment thought with implied particularities. In this way, the primordium as judgment on all particular assertions became instead a primordium marked by highly particularized assertions. This clearly was the case as the new civil religion blossomed into full flower in the mid-nineteenth century in the doctrine of Manifest Destiny. John L. O'Sullivan, who helped popularize the notion in the 1840s with reference to the Oregon Territory, virtually relegated to oblivion any historical tradition that might have cautioned restraint: "We have a still better title than any that can ever be contructed out of all these antiquated materials of old black-letter international law. Away, away with all these cobweb tissues of rights of discovery, exploration, settlement, continuity, &c."[51] Instead of looking to the legal traditions of a profane history to adjudicate the claim, O'Sullivan identified the interests of the Republic with a sacred dimension that stood completely outside the bounds of profane history.

> Our Claim is by the right of our manifest destiny to overspread
> and to possess the whole of the continent which Providence has
> given for the development of the great experiment of liberty and
> federative self-government entrusted to us. It is a right such as
> that of the tree in the space of air and earth suitable for the full
> expansion of its principle and destiny of growth—such as that of
> the stream to the channel required for the still accumulating
> volume of its flow.[52]

Clearly, America's destiny was "manifest" because it was rooted in the
primordium rather than in the "cobweb tissues" of finite human history.

VI

It is hardly surprising that the Puritan legacy and the Enlightenment
perspective could amalgamate so thoroughly in the revolutionary and
early national periods. For while these two traditions differed profoundly at the level of theological *content,* at the level of theological
method they both were committed to restoring pure beginnings. The
Christian Humanists had heralded the reality of the restoration many
years before, but that reality still had not been realized in the affairs of
humankind. Countless thousands of Western Christians had longed to
view, in their lifetimes, a restoration of that pure and primal age but to no
avail.

But all those countless thousands of Christians had not lived to view
the American Revolution. From the perspective of many who lived during and following the Revolution, that event was the infinitely grand,
cosmic battle that, now at last in these latter days, had begun the process
of making the primordium contemporary. "Behold, all things have become new" was the common sentiment. And so they had. Americans of
that time had simply never known freedom to this extent. But what was
new also was what was old, for the open-ended quality of life that characterized the new nation appeared to be the same open-ended quality of
life that had characterized the first man and the first woman in the
Garden.

Because the experience was both new and old at one and the same
time, it could be conceptualized in either primordial or millennial terms.
The quest for the millennium during the revolutionary period and thereafter, so well understood by historians, was often a quest for the
primordium. Advocates of the millennial age frequently derived their
vision from the rich panoply of images that filled the mythic accounts of
the golden age (or golden ages) that existed when the gods created the
cosmos (or its functional equivalent). In other words, the millennium
typically constituted a restoration of the primordium, and all profane

history that had intervened between these two end times was obscured, ignored, and transcended. As Crevecoeur said, this American was a new man. But he also was a very old man. And it is this old man who, by and large, has failed to receive the attention from historians that he deserves.

Within this early nineteenth-century context, a host of new movements, all given to the celebration of the ancient primordium, rapidly gained popularity in the young Republic. Among these new movements were Shakers, Baptists, Disciples of Christ, Mormons, and utopian communes such as Oneida and Hopedale. Significantly, all these movements prospered during the years following the Revolution when the primordial/millennial fervor was at its height. It is certainly worth considering whether William Warren Sweet's thesis—that those churches that prospered on the frontier were those churches that creatively followed the frontier—might profitably stand some emendation to the effect that those churches that prospered in the westward-moving, primordial nation were those churches that depicted most vividly the ancient primordium to a primordial people.

Precisely here lies the significance of the traditions and denominations considered in this book: most were fundamentally American in that they drank deeply of the wellsprings of restoration thought at those times when the primordial waters washed over the emerging American soul and shaped the American character. The Puritans, of course, indelibly stamped the American character during the early colonial period and etched there a deep and abiding concern for pure beginnings. Reinhold Niebuhr in fact observed that "the New England conception of our American virtue began as the belief that the church which had been established on our soil was purer than any church of Christendom."[53] And then, when the nation was born, the Jeffersonian Enlightenment, first, and then the Scottish Common Sense tradition deposited fresh and lasting layers of primitivist thought on the already powerful Puritan concern for first times. When one adds to all of this the radical newness of the American political experiment and the millennial fervor that characterized so many Americans at that time, one has the key ingredients that contributed to a profound sense of historylessness in the early national period.

The point is simply this: Mormons and "Christians" came to birth and Baptists experienced significant growth and popularity precisely when numerous factors converged to make the appeal to pure beginnings a powerful dimension of American popular culture. In this context, and in the face of a bewildering array of Christian denominations, sectarians found that the appeal to pure beginnings was the surest way to cut through the confusion of religious pluralism. To proclaim one's own sect a reproduction of the ancient, apostolic order was to annoint one's sect the one, true church while all others were merely historic, tradition laden, and therefore false. Further, while we can adduce various reasons for the popularity of each of these movements, one point we surely must consider is that each reflected primordial concerns to a primordial people and even offered the hope of hastening the realization of America's promise in a microcosmic community of faith. In this sense, these three groups were fundamentally unlike the old, established churches of Europe that had been imported to America's shores. Those older denominations were America's adopted children who, by living in the parent's house for many years, gradually took on the parent's traits. But Mormons and "Christians" were genetic children, nurtured in the parent's womb, born in the parent's house, and inheriting the spiritual and mental characteristics of the one who gave them birth. Baptists, while adopted, were adopted in early childhood and, further, were the natural children of close relatives. Thus they absorbed the spiritual characteristics of their foster parent with little difficulty. For these reasons, Baptists, Mormons, and "Christians" are significant, in a way that many other denominations are not, for what they can tell us about the shape and texture of American life and culture in the early national period. We have focused primarily on these three groups precisely because they offer such telling clues to the character of the American people.

VII

Beyond the question of parent-child relations, however, lies the more fundamental issue of the interaction between restoration and liberty in the American experience—and this is the second major consideration of this book. The primitivism embraced by the founders of this Republic was broad and open-ended, avoiding the particular in the interest of what seemed to them the universal. In this conceptual milieu, liberty would flourish. But time and again, zealots of one faith or another would particularize and even absolutize the primordium, elevating one conception of the primordium to standard and authoritative status. On these terms, liberty was possible only for those who conformed themselves to the particularized and absolutized norm.

At times American patriots, totally identifying the primal state of things with America itself, Americanized the primordium. Here, for example, was Thomas Paine, who supposed that by viewing the birth of the nation he also was gazing on the creation, or John L. O'Sullivan who so Americanized the primordium that neither history nor law had any bearing on territorial claims. As a result of such thinking, the British lost

Oregon, but far more disastrous were the losses in life and property sustained by both Mexicans and native Americans. While virtually identifying the new American nation with the primordium, primitivists in this nation consigned both Mexicans and Indians to the finite sphere of human history and proceeded to extinguish not only their liberties but, in many instances, their lives.

Undeniably the issue here was cultural pluralism, and it was ironic that a nation committed to pluralism within its own boundaries, at least for people of light skin, would resist so strenuously the ways and traditions of people of color and in nearby regions. Even more ironic was the fact that primordial theology, employed by the founders to secure liberty, could be particularized so that those not sharing in the "primal particularities" were simply excluded from the blessings of freedom.

In this tendency, however, the nation was not unique, for these patterns were repeated over again by numerous religious groups in America, themselves struggling with the issue of pluralism. For some, such as Puritans and Mormons, identifying themselves with the ancient order of things was the most effective way of blunting the religious legitimacy of others. For others, such as Roger Williams, the early Baptists, and the early "Christians," the appeal to pure beginnings was the very basis for their claim to religious liberty, both for themselves and for others. But once again, irony intruded, and both Baptists and "Christians" finally particularized and absolutized the primordium on their own terms and came to use the primitive church ideal not so much to promote freedom as to define the bounds of the true church.

Not only have sectarians employed the restoration theme to legitimate their traditions, but patriots have employed the theme to legitimate the nation and/or its ideals. Thus, when Alexander Campbell's followers absolutized their version of the primordium, Campbell began looking more to Protestant America and less to his primitive church as the last, best hope for unity in freedom and diversity. So well rooted was the restoration perspective in the American experience that with the advent of the Civil War, even southern clerics such as Benjamin M. Palmer employed primitivism to deny freedom to blacks and to defend both slavery and the Confederacy. Even in twentieth-century U.S. politics, the restoration theme has persisted with extraordinary vitality. Several presidents constructed foreign policies around its presuppositions, most notably Woodrow Wilson and Ronald Reagan, and two noted scholars implicitly have described the genius of American ideals in terms of the restoration sentiment. Here, on the one hand, Sidney E. Mead appeals to first times to describe the "theology of the Republic" which, he contends, always stands in judgment on the particular contents of American culture.[54] In this, Mead's vision recalls the prophetic sort of primitivism employed by Roger Williams and Thomas Jefferson. On the other hand, Allan Bloom, in his attempt to re-open the American mind, draws unsparingly on the restoration sentiment but in a way radically different from Mead's use of the theme.[55] Like John Cotton, John L. O'Sullivan, and Benjamin Palmer, Bloom absolutizes particular manifestations of the primordium and, in the interest of opening the mind, ironically provides for its closing. In this, Bloom strikingly illustrates the illusions that the restoration sentiment often generates.

Clearly, the restoration ideal has not been the exclusive property of a few eccentric Christian sects. It has informed the fundamental outlook of preachers and presidents, of soldiers and scholars. Indeed, the restoration perspective has been a central feature of American life and thought from the earliest Puritan settlements, and now continues to exercise a profound influence on the thinking and behavior of the American people. Nowhere can the effect of this perspective be discerned more clearly than in the bounds it sets—and continues to set—on human freedom.

This book, then, explores the long and often illusory quest to restore first times—a quest that has led American primitivists, from early Puritans to the present, either to restrict or to enlarge the sphere of human liberty. The intersection of primitivism and freedom in the American experience is richly nuanced and textured. We have sought to capture these rich nuances not only by exploring restoration traditions from Puritans to Mormons but also by focusing our attention in several instances on representative but relatively little-known spokespersons of these traditions. Thus the reader will meet not only John Cotton, Roger Williams, and Alexander Cambell, but also Parley Pratt, Walter Scott, James R. Graves, James S. Lamar, and Benjamin M. Palmer. Each of these persons was an articulate defender not only of the ancient order of things, as he understood that order, but also of what he viewed as the rightful place of freedom in American life. Further, in addressing these two themes together, and in struggling with their balance and relationship, these leaders were but crossing and recrossing an intersection of long-standing in American life—one that continues to bear, sometimes in ominous ways, on the American present and future.

TWO

The Constraints of "True Antiquity": John Cotton and the New England Way

In 1630 the celebrated Puritan preacher John Cotton stood at dockside in Southampton, England, to deliver the farewell sermon to John Winthrop and four hundred others preparing to sail for Massachusetts aboard the *Arbella*. Several of his friends and colleagues were among the group, and three years later Cotton himself would join them. For this momentous occasion he had chosen as his text 2 Samuel 7:10: "Morever I will appoint a place for my people Israel, and I will plant them, that they may dwell in a place of their own, and move no more." Building on the conviction that God's people always must live in the land God had appointed them, Cotton proceeded to justify the people's plans "to transplant themselves, and set up a new Commonwealth." He held up New England as a place, providentially provided, for religious refugees to seek the "liberty and purity of [Christian] Ordinances," and he insisted that the colony they raised up there must be in harmony with "the first Plantation of the Primitive Church."[1]

This last phrase of Cotton's was not a stray thought, a mere rhetorical adornment. It was rather a reflection of the primitivist orientation that had become a major component of Puritan thought and a central feature of Cotton's own thinking. The New England enterprise, in this outlook, was to consist of a massive restoration of the "first and best times" set forth in the biblical primordium, not of an experimental reaching for the new and untried. Indeed, the chief problem that long had unsettled Cotton, Winthrop, and many other English Puritans was the "human invention" still enshrined in the Church of England. In Massachusetts, therefore, they hoped to cast out all that was "new" and "invented" and return both church and the civil order to the sacred standards of "True Antiquity."

This current of primitivist thinking ran deep in the Puritan movement, though Puritan scholars have paid it only scant attention. As Dwight Bozeman notes in his ground-breaking book *To Live Ancient Lives,* the bulk of scholarly work in American Puritanism has been done in almost total disregard of its primitivist strain.[2] This chapter explores that primitivist strain, first by sketching its background and broad contours, then by focusing on a case study of John Cotton. Cotton was the most prominent minister of Massachusetts' founding generation and a chief architect of the New England Way, and in his New England career we see clearly the role of primitivist ideas. Visible too is the ironic interplay of primitivism, liberty, and illusion.

I

The primitivist or restoration strain, as we saw briefly in chapter 1, had a long history in the development of Reformed Protestantism. The Reformed emphasis on "biblical precedent" and the "law of Christ" left a deep mark on English religion during the reign of Edward VI. Together with the deuteronomic biblicism of William Tyndale, this emphasis gave primitive events recorded in scripture—and especially the primitive church—enormous prestige and made this vision a potent tool in the hands of a spectrum of English polemicists in the sixteenth century. From Thomas Cranmer, to John Jewel, to John Foxe, to Thomas Cartwright and Walter Travers, early English Protestants regarded the first age of the church as a time of purity, freshness, vigor, and of unadulterated conformity to the will of God. Archbishop Cranmer, for example, viewed the age of the early Fathers as the "golden time" of the church and sought to rehabilitate that tradition. Bishop Jewel wrote: "We have searched out of the Holy Bible, which we are sure cannot deceive, one sure form of religion, and have returned again unto the primitive church of the ancient fathers and apostles."[3] As Leonard Trinterud noted of this age, the terms *pure, purity,* and the like suggested a return to the unadulterated, "to the true, original primitive church—away from the pollutions of the papacy, the monks, and the 'accretions of the pure gospel.' " "Nothing in early Elizabethan religion," he added, "was quite so sacred as the primitive church. Upon it hung the entire case of English religion against Rome, whether that case was argued by the Queen, by Bishop Jewel, by John Foxe, or by any other spokesman."[4] There was widespread agreement that the primitive church was in some sense normative for the contemporary church and that the purity of the period of beginnings should be recovered.

By the 1560s, however, early Puritans turned against the defenders of the Elizabethan Settlement the very argument concerning the primitive church that those defenders had used so forcefully against the Roman Catholics. The English Church, Puritans such as Cartwright argued, did not yet conform to the primitive pattern; "human invention" still was rife and must be brought more rigorously under the control of biblical precedent. One of the early Puritan agendas for achieving this further restoration can be seen in the "first open manifesto of the Puritan party," a tract of 1572 entitled *An Admonition to Parliament.* Its overriding concern was for "a church rightly reformed according to the prescript of God's word." Such a church would display three basic marks: the preaching of the word, proper observation of the sacraments, and faithful administration of discipline. Further, in structure and in practice it would be bound by biblical precedent: nothing was to be done "but that which you have the expresse warrant of God's word for." Holding up the best Reformed churches of the Continent as examples, the authors urged Parliament "altogether [to] remove the whole Antichrist, both head, body, and branch, and perfectly plant that puritie of word, that simplicitie of the sacraments, and severitie of discipline, which Christ hath commanded to his church." If God's plagues on the nation were to be averted, then right religion must be established; this meant that "nothing in this mortal life is more diligently to be sought for and carefully to be looked into than the restitution of true religion and reformation of God's church."[5]

This concern for "restitution of true religion"—and the persistent appeal to the sole authority of scripture on which it rested—became a central feature of the Puritan movement. Though scholars often have observed this feature of Puritan dissent, the larger pattern of ideas and terms undergirding it—the primitivist orientation—has gone largely unexplored. Dwight Bozeman goes so far as to contend that primitivism comprises a "major coherence" in English dissenting thought and that neglect of this dimension has led to a host of misconceptions on the part of scholars in the field. Scholars eager to highlight the forward-thrusting, modernizing elements of the Puritan movement and thus to explain the rise of modern notions of progress, Bozeman argues, generally have pushed into the background those elements that resist alignment with this futurist orientation, and in so doing have missed a major key to understanding the Puritan mind.[6]

Confronting the definitional confusion on the part of recent interpreters of Puritanism, Bozeman proposes that "the distinctive and conscious concerns of Puritan dissent tended to revolve around three interacting centers": *moralism, pietism,* and biblicist *primitivism.* The moralistic emphasis, adumbrated through the channels of Reformed covenant theology, involved "a stress upon the moral transformation, performance and purity of individuals and their communities."[7] The pietistic dimension, which emerged in its developed form only in the

1580s, was marked by "a preoccupation with the self and its subjective states"; the central themes included preparation for conversion, warfare with the flesh, quest for assurance of salvation, and the practice of prayer and meditation.[8] Biblicist "primitivism," the third and least familiar of the defining features, involved "a reversion, undercutting both Catholic and Anglican appeals to a continuity of tradition, to the first, or primitive, order of things narrated in the Protestant Scriptures." Such an orientation pervades the Puritan literary remains and forms "an entire substructure of meanings" that, though seldom reflected on by the Puritans in any systematic way, nevertheless shaped and controlled the theological agenda of the movement at several different levels. The primitivist outlook, in short, "was integral in numberless ways to the very meaning of the 'Puritan' vision both within the English church and in the early New England Colonies."[9] Recognizing and reconstructing this major pattern of ideas, Bozeman asserts, will have a number of important consequences. Among other things, it will force a sharp qualification of the many recent assertions of the movement's modernizing impact; more important, it will contribute significantly to clarifying the definitional muddle that has marked recent Puritan studies.

The pattern of Puritan primitivism is characterized chiefly by an elemental belief in the power and exemplary authority of an ancient "first time," a time when supernatural power and presence had transformed ordinary history into an extraordinary time full of precedential authority. This ancient primordium—dramatically reported in the Old and New Testament scriptures—was the "great time" when God intervened at will, transporting his chosen actors far beyond the realm of the commonplace and giving their lives unparalleled force and significance. It was the time when truth was fullest and clearest, when humankind could be seen at its highest and best. The primordium, in short, was the time of unmatched purity and simplicity. Postprimordial time, in sharp contrast, had brought nothing but an ever-increasing decline from the original standards and a mounting loss of supernatural power.

As we shall see in subsequent chapters, later American primitivists shared this vision but essentially split it in two. Alexander Campbell, for example, chiefly bemoaned the decline from original standards that characterized postprimordial time, while his contemporaries, the Mormons, lamented the loss of supernatural power.

For Puritans, however, original standards and supernatural power formed an inseparable unity. The dictum of Thomas Cartwright, therefore, became a central theological instrument of Puritanism: "That is true whatsoever is first; that is false whatsoever is later." Centered in this intense devotion to the *first,* the primitivist pattern gave rise to an array of terms that recur throughout the vast range of Puritan writings, terms such as *primitive, ancient, pattern, model, imitation, purity, simplicity, invention, addition, novelty,* and *innovation.* Such terms form a major part of the standard Puritan vocabulary and serve as signposts to the primitivist or restorationist assumptions underlying much Puritan belief and action.[10]

Puritan primitivism was rooted in a long tradition of primitivist dissent going back to monastic reform movements, Lollardy, Waldensianism, and Christian humanism; it made up an intellectual heritage which the Puritans accepted as a master of course. Furthermore, the Puritans inherited from the Protestant Reformation what Bozeman calls the "Protestant Epistemology," a distinctive set of ideas produced when "antirationalist influences from nominalist, humanist and other sources were joined with a conviction of the radically fallen character of the human faculties, the central authority of the Bible, and the primitive church." Central to the Protestant Epistemology was the rigorous restraint of all rational and imaginative activity. Because all religious truth was fixed and complete, not subject to change or embellishment, the mind's role was simply to recover what had been given in full, not to discover or create anything new. Primitivist ideas served only to heighten the demand for intellectual restraint, especially in Reformed Protestantism; because of the inventive and fanciful propensities of the human mind, it must be brought ever more rigorously under the jurisdiction of the "great time," the time when every precept for ordering both human life and the church had been given. Without such restraint, "human invention" led to wild and disastrous extension of divine prescription: the "elaborate discursive, logical, speculative, and fanciful capacities of the mind were prone to unfurl out of all proportion to the simple cognitive tasks that lead to Redemption." The shocking results of unchecked "invention" appeared, Reformed Protestants believed, in the career of Roman Catholicism which over the centuries had produced "a vast sprawl of ecclesiastical paraphernalia," all of it a gross addition to simple, primordial doctrine and worship.[11]

To a lesser degree such convoluted "invention" still marked the Anglican church and formed the basis of much Puritan protest. Bozeman argues in fact that Puritan "commitment to the preservation and intensification of the . . . [Protestant Epistemology] over against a persistent Anglican advocacy of invention" became a major defining theme of the Puritan movement. The widespread Anglican concern to give human "reason" a broader province in religious matters and the corresponding defense of *adiaphora* or "things indifferent" stood in sharp contrast to the growing Puritan concern for restraint of reason's inventive capacity.

With his *Laws of Ecclesiastical Polity* published in the 1590s, the Anglican apologist Richard Hooker brought the distinctly Anglican view into clear focus, and in so doing set upon a major departure from the Reformed heritage. Whereas the original Reformed theologians had been concerned to limit the reach of reason, Hooker wished to expand it. By minimizing the impact of the Fall on the faculties of reason and severely limiting the precedential nature of the scriptural record, Hooker argued that many areas of church affairs were open to and indeed required rational and practical "invention." In matters "necessary to Salvation," scripture was fixed and unchanging, but in many other areas scripture's jurisdiction was not absolute. Many biblical precepts and patterns, Hooker insisted, were historically relative, suitable to the particular circumstances of the time. Hooker judged the very quality of early Christian "simplicity," so vaunted by the Puritans, to be a temporary accommodation to a simple uncultured age; by contrast, official English Christianity, with all its regal vastness and traditional institutions, required ecclesiastical "laws" far different from those of more "primitive" ages. Scorning the primitivist drive "to draw all things under the determination of bare and naked scripture," Hooker in short sought to retrieve "human capacity, judgment and wit" from the narrow strictures of the Protestant Epistemology.[12]

In the decades following Hooker's work, Anglican apologists continued to press and consolidate their claim on ecclesiastical "invention," the departure from strict Reformed biblicism. In turn, the Puritans' campaign against "men's devices" and their "unyielding devotion to the biblical primordium in all its sacred finality" continued unabated. In this growing divergence, Bozeman argues convincingly, one finds the deepest distinction between Puritan and Anglican theological method. The distinctively Puritan element was an exaltation of the virtues of "first" times and patterns and a recognition of "the encompassing claim of the Great Time to order the actions of men."[13]

II

From the early vestarian movement of the 1560s down to the Great Migration of the 1630s, the English Puritan movement took shape largely under the impact of such primitivist aspirations. In the 1620s the rise of the Laudian "high church" party with its stricter enforcement of the official liturgy and introduction of new "inventions" into the worship brought increasing pressure on Puritan nonconformists and set in motion plans for colonization of America. The Puritan hopes for restoration of primordial ordinances in England seemed to ebb away, and the prospects for divine retribution on a covenanted people seemed imminent. As the Great Migration got under way, Puritans defined its basic agenda with the same primitivist categories that had fired their concerns since the 1560s. The religious concerns of the Bay Colony, in short, took the form of a restorationist crusade.

This conclusion, however, flies in the face of most recent assumptions about the conscious intent of the colony's founders. Most often cited are the words of John Winthrop in the "Modell of Christian Charity": "Men shall say of succeeding plantations: the Lord make it like that of New England; for we shall be as a City upon a Hill, the eyes of all people are upon us." The conventional reading of this passage, following Perry Miller's brilliant argument for an "errand into the wilderness," has stressed the founders' intent to create an exemplary, world-redeeming Bible commonwealth, an organized task force dedicated to setting up a beacon to guide the nations of the world to their final redemption.[14] In this form, the idea of the "errand" has entered the textbooks as the standard explanation of the reason for emigration. Recently, however, dissenters from the "errand" have tended to see New England primarily as a haven for persecuted dissidents rather than as a light to the nations and have tended to stress the variety of motives for leaving the homeland.[15] To these voices Bozeman adds his own in what is to date the most searching and pointed critique of the conventional view of Winthrop's famous words. Bozeman argues flatly that, with the exception of the brief reference in the "Modell," the Bay project "nowhere in the entire corpus [of first-generation writings] is pictured as a redemptive city upon a hill, a light to the nations or a decisive pattern for English, European or worldwide reform." The conventional reading, furthermore, ignores the overall thrust of Winthrop's sermon. The point was to urge "Christian charity" in the face of the challenges and perils of fashioning a "due form of Government both civil and ecclesiastical." If read in this light, "the famed text is nothing more than a momentary embellishment of the argument, a touch of rhetorical hyperbole rephrasing a popular biblical text (Matthew 5:14)." The famous text itself, Bozeman concludes, sees the great impact upon "all people" as based not on the success of the New England colony, but rather on its failure; thus, Winthrop warned, "if we shall deal falsely with our God in this work . . . we shall be made a story and a byword throughout the world."[16]

If no overarching world-redeeming "errand" propelled the Puritan colonists, what were the "reasons moving [them] to transplant themselves"? From his assessment of the large body of materials addressing this issue left by first-generation New Englanders, Bozeman finds two major categories of reasons: (1) the desire to find a refuge from the constricting and foreboding conditions in England, and (2) the long-standing Puritan desire to escape "man's devices" and win "liberty of the ordinances."[17] A large percentage of the material falls into the first category, stressing exilic themes and the need to find a "place of refuge." The problem was twofold: the likely prospect of catastrophic divine judgment on England due to her failure to maintain covenant standards, and the more immediate matter of continual persecution for nonconformity. Underlying these concerns was the deep current of primitivist grievances: "human inventions," "ceremonies," and Anglican "innovation." Recalling why they had chosen "to fly into the Wilderness from the face of the Dragon," Thomas Shepard and John Allin, for example, looked back to the "time when humane Worship and inventions were growne to such an intolerable height, that the consciences of God's saints and servants inlightened in the truth could no longer bear them." And John Eliot, some years later, wrote that "the cause of our coming into New England . . . [was] that we might be freed from the ceremonies and have liberty to enjoy all the pure ordinances of Christ . . . without . . . human additions and novelties."[18]

If flight from "ceremonies" and "inventions" was the negative motivation, the positive was desire for "liberty of the Ordinances," the freedom to administer the primitively certified forms of ecclesiastical polity and worship that had been stifled in the homeland. John Cotton wrote in the early 1640s that "it was the principal end of their coming, to enjoy the presence of the Lord in the liberty and purity of His ordinances." John Norton, arriving in 1636, wrote that "the sole cause of our transplanting ourselves over the Atlantic ocean . . . was liberty, to walk peaceably in the Faith of the Gospel." This constantly repeated theme was expressed perhaps most clearly in *New Englands First Fruits*: "our endeavor is to have all his own Institutions, and no more than his own and all those in their native simplicity without any human dressings; having a liberty to enjoy all that God commands, and yet urged to nothing more than he commands."[19] Instead of the exemplary mission on behalf of the world usually put forth, the four-thousand-mile voyage to the New England wilderness was moved, in short, primarily by the intense desire to have "Christ and his ordinances in their primitive purity." /

This brief survey of the primitivist strain of Puritan thought suggests that, to a degree considerably beyond what scholars have recognized, the New England Puritan enterprise took the form of a restorationist crusade. Shaped by the Protestant Epistemology and given intensity by six decades of frustrated crusading against profane "ceremonies," the early Bay colonists hoped, in the free air of a new land, to serve their God in the enthralling simplicity of the ancient Great Time, stripping away once and for all the ruinous corruptions of profane time. They sought new liberties—to live, as it were, in the absorbing drama of the primordium. But irony intruded, as we shall see. Having established their vision, absolutized it, and convinced themselves that all their practices were primitively certified, they would restrict sharply the liberty of those whose primordium took on a different shape or whose piety sought broader bounds. To explore this irony, we turn now to a more focused case study—the New England career of John Cotton.

III

When John Cotton (1584–1652) arrived in the New World in September 1633 at the age of forty-eight he was one of the most highly educated and highly respected Puritan preachers in England. He had placed himself squarely in the Puritan camp as early as 1602 when he became a fellow of Emmanuel College in Cambridge University. With the influential Lawrence Chaderton steering a precariously strict Puritan course, Cotton and the other Emmanuel students worshiped regularly without the officially prescribed Prayer Book and even partook of the Lord's Supper sitting around a table in imitation of apostolic precedent. Cotton was to spend ten years at Emmanuel College, taking his master of arts in 1606, receiving ordination in 1610, and earning his bachelor of divinity in 1613. During those years he served as tutor, dean, lecturer, preacher, and catechist. His mastery of languages was phenomenal, but he achieved his greatest fame as a preacher. In 1612 he received a call from St. Botolph's Church in Boston, Lincolnshire, and soon, while many other churches endured poor preachers or restricted preaching, that congregation was enjoying a "feast of preaching." Over the next twenty years Cotton's preaching brought him an ever-growing reputation and a devoted following. He became one of the most respected and influential Puritans of his time.[20]

Despite his steady rise in eminence, Cotton wrestled throughout his English career with the perennial Puritan concern over "ceremonies," a concern that arose, as we have seen, out of the intense primitivist regard for pure originals. Faced with the Canons of 1604, which required strict adherence to the official liturgy and polity, Cotton and some of the other ministers with Puritan leanings attempted to walk the narrow path between conformity and separation. Early in his ministry Cotton wrote that "in matters of ceremonies . . . pertaining to the worship of God: an argument doth hold from the negative, to disallow what is not found in the Scriptures expressly or by good consequence." Believing that conformity to such ceremonies was sinful, he drew together a group of his

parishioners which covenanted together to eschew the offensive ceremonies and "to follow after the Lord in the purity of his Worship."[21] But
troubles and doubts ensued. He was suspended for nonconformity, then
reinstated. In the early 1620s he confessed that his views were still in flux;
in a letter to his bishop he expressed the need for more time for "better
consideration of such doubts as yet remain behind." But with the stricter
enforcement of ceremonies under William Laud in the late 1620s, which
soon pushed Puritan leaders into separation and emigration, Cotton
began to stiffen in his convictions. Finally in April 1632, summoned
before Laud and the High Court and fearing suspension or perhaps
imprisonment, he fled into the Puritan underground where he soon
decided to follow his friends to the New World. When in 1634 he reflected on his "Reasons for . . . removal to New-England," he spoke of
the danger he faced for his "witness against the Levitical ceremonies"
and of New England as God's providential refuge from high-church
"inventions." In this he resembled most early emigrants. Cotton later
could remind his Massachusetts congregation that "you have left your
Trades, friends, country, and have put your self upon a changeable and
hazardous Journey because your consciences could not submit to
Ceremonies."[22]

On arrival in Boston, Cotton was chosen teacher of First Church, a
position in which he was charged with doctrinal oversight and preaching. During the first three years he entertained reservations about some
of the practices of the New England churches, especially the requirement
of making an explicit church covenant an "essential cause of the church
without which it can not bee," but by 1636 he was able to endorse such a
practice, even traveling to Salem to apologize for his earlier criticism of
it.[23] Cotton himself was to become the leading defender of the ideal of a
gathered or covenanted church and the very one who attached to it the
name "Congregationalism." Meanwhile, he focused his energies chiefly
on preaching and met with immense success. After only a few months of
Cotton's ministrations, Winthrop wrote that "more and more were converted and added to that church, than to all the other churches in the
bay."[24] Such results were in keeping with what, to Cotton, was the central
task of the preacher: opening the doctrine of salvation to sinners and
articulating, as an instrument of the Holy Spirit, the experience of grace
so that the elect might be settled and joyous in their estate. In his preaching, Cotton worked within the bounds of Reformed soteriology, tracing
the process of salvation from election, to justification, sanctification, and
finally glorification. Like most other New England divines he stressed the
sovereignty of grace throughout the process and upheld the primacy of
justification over sanctification, but his stress on the utter passivity of the

sinner and his complete reliance on the inner work of the Holy Spirit aroused suspicion and eventually trouble.[25]

The controversy that erupted focused on Anne Hutchinson, one of Cotton's former parishioners in old Boston, and her group of sympathizers. Accusing the other Massachusetts ministers of being legalists preaching a "covenant of works," Hutchinson claimed faithfully to follow Cotton's preaching of a covenant of "free grace." The magistrates and ministers increasingly grew alarmed, engaging in protracted and heated debate over the issues. Confusion and disorder mounted, confirming to the ministers the insidiousness of the errors and the urgent need to remove the contagion. "By advancing free-grace," Thomas Shepard wrote, the antinomians

> deny, and destroy all being and evidence of inherent grace in us; by crying up Christ, they destroy the use of faith to apply him; by advancing the Spirit, and revelation of the Spirit, they destroy or weaken the revelation of the Scriptures; by depending on Christ's righteousnesse and justification, without the works of the Law, they destroy the use of the Law and make it no rule of life unto a Christian.[26]

The fear, in short, was that, in a commonwealth where the citizens' adherence to God's law so directly affected the adherence to civil law, the exalting of the Spirit's work and scorning of divine laws would undermine the very foundations of moral and civil order. As the controversy rose to its climax, Cotton was bombarded with questions from his fellow ministers but was slow in distancing himself from the Hutchinsonians. Finally, when he concluded that the antinomians apparently sought nothing less than a social revolution, and when he saw them being brought to trial for heresy and sedition, Cotton satisfied the other ministers with his orthodoxy and joined with them in the synod attempting to gather up and root out all the "loose opinions." When Anne Hutchinson herself was brought to trial she was found guilty and banished. In the judgment of the officials, both her anticlerical agitation and her blatant reliance on personal "revelations" posed a serious threat to the social order of the colony.[27]

Because of Cotton's prominent role in the heated controversy, his reputation reached a low point, but he rebounded in the years that followed to become a principal architect of the New England Way.[28] In the 1640s, most of his published writings dealt with ecclesiology, particularly with his concern that the order and form of the New England churches reflect that of the primitive apostolic churches. Though Cotton never completely concurred with the more "legal" doctrine of such ministers as Shepard and Bulkeley, he did stress increasingly the importance of laws, outward forms, and correct observances to the well-being of a godly commonwealth. In 1638, for example, Cotton wrote to one of the exiled antinomians at Aquidneck: "I know not how you can build up either church or commonwealth on the Holy Spirit alone, for it would then be 'an house without a foundation.' "[29] The necessary foundation, Cotton believed, was provided by pure ordinances and discipline drawn strictly out of biblical archetype.

In his intensified concern for ecclesiastical form in the years immediately following the Antinomian Controversy, Cotton stood squarely in the stream of restorationist thought that earlier had heightened his agitation over "ceremonies" and had driven him to seek "liberty of the ordinances." This quest for pure forms and ordinances was a central part of the larger quest for duplication of the authentic church of primordial times. Recovery of the pure church, in Puritan emphasis, involved a passion for both a regenerate membership and those visible forms that "Christ did institute or the Apostles frame"; it involved, more simply, moral sanctification and biblical restoration. The two emphases were closely related: strict allegiance to biblical form and precedent, Puritans believed, would enable the Covenant of Grace to become visible in the lives of the converted. The central distinctives of New England Congregationalism—individual church covenants, visible sainthood, strict discipline, closed communion, and restriction of baptism to children of covenanted members—all arose out of this dual concern. The primitively given ordinances, Puritan ministers believed, provided the very channels through which vital piety was built up and safeguarded. Seen in this light, Cotton's turn toward matters of ecclesiastical form and practice can be tied closely to his concern for personal conversion and godliness, for both concerns were rooted in the conviction that one found divine purity in the "ancient" and "first."

IV

We stress here that this devotion to "firstness" was absolutely fundamental to Cotton's whole outlook, and especially to his development of congregational theory in New England. It was a mind-set, as we have seen, long nurtured and intensified in the Puritan ranks, and its importance to the shaping of New England Puritanism would be difficult to exaggerate. Bozeman has assembled several of Cotton's most striking and explicit expressions of this mind-set from the 1620s, the time when he was still wrestling with Anglican ceremonies:

> no new traditions must be thrust upon us . . . [but] that which
> [we] have had from the beginning. . . . True Antiquity . . . is that

which fetches its original from the beginning. . . . True Antiquity is twofold. 1. From the first institution . . . of a thing, . . . 2. That which fetches its beginning from God, though it were of later times, . . . and as he is the ancient of days, so is that good; as Baptism and the Lord's Supper, though they were not in the world before Christ's coming in the flesh, yet being from God they have true Antiquity. . . . [If a religious form] have no higher rise than the [patristic] Fathers, it is too young a device, no other writings besides the Scripture can plead true Antiquity. . . . All errors are aberrations from the first. [In sum], live ancient lives; your obedience must be swayed by an old rule, walk in the old ways.[30]

From Old England to New, "True Antiquity" became, in theory at least, the final test of ecclesiastical form and practice. With all the theological skills at his command, John Cotton attempted to demonstrate, to all who had eyes to see, that the New England churches were in fact nothing more than the "first" churches restored, advancing no innovations but walking resolutely in the "old ways."

In developing his congregational theory, Cotton drew heavily on the ecclesiastical theory worked out by a small group of dissenters that had attempted to chart a middle course between Presbyterianism and radical Separatism in the first quarter of the seventeenth century. Most prominent among the group were Paul Baynes, Robert Parker, Henry Jacob, and William Ames. As the originators of nonseparating congregationalism, these men deeply influenced Cotton and the other leading ministers of the founding generation. Particularly important were the works of Ames, especially *The Marrow of Sacred Divinity* and *A Fresh Suite against Human Ceremonies* (1633); many of Cotton's ideas on church polity, in fact, can be found here. Throughout the writings of these men run, significantly, the primitivist themes of withdrawal from ceremonies and recovery of original simplicity.[31]

Between 1634 and 1643 Cotton wrote six works addressing issues in congregational theory and practice; the longest and fullest was written about 1642 and entitled *The Way of the Churches of Christ in New-England*.[32] Focusing more on actual New England practice than on theoretical matters, this work discussed the formation of a church, the admission of members, the proper officers of a church, the proper observance of the ordinances, and other matters of form and polity. Like Ames, Cotton believed that a church could be no larger than a single congregation and that it must originate in an explicit church covenant. He gave a lengthy, detailed description of how a church was gathered: the group of prospective church members, made up of at least seven men, first examined one another's doctrinal soundness and experience of saving grace; then, with ministers of nearby churches and some of the civil magistrates present giving their approval, the prospective members entered into a covenant, pledging to uphold the laws of God and the purity of the congregation. Once gathered in this way, the congregation then selected its officers: a pastor or teacher, ruling elders, and deacons. When persons presented themselves for membership thereafter, they were examined by the elders, presented to the congregation for examination, and finally, having attested satisfactorily to the genuineness of their experience of grace, they were asked to profess their faith and subscribe to the church covenant. Such a means of forming churches, Cotton believed, was the old way, rooted firmly in God's covenantal dealing with Israel and continued in his dealings with Christians in all ages. It troubled him somewhat that the New Testament gave no clear example of the practice, but he had a ready answer. "In the days of the New Testament," he wrote, "the magistrates and princes of the earth being aliens and enemies to the church, the apostles thought it meet to speak of this covenant not plainly but as it were in parables and similitudes."[33] Such a procedure, he was confident, always had been required of the churches in the "purest times" and was now essential in keeping out the unregenerate who crowded the English parish churches.

Whether arguing for church covenants or against human "ceremonies," Cotton's concern was fashioning every practice "according to the primitive pattern." No aspect of the church's worship or government are men to administer "of their own heads"; rather, they are "to dispense all according to the will of Christ revealed in his Word." All set forms of worship "devised and ordained by men" must be rejected, for "if such set formes had been an ordinance of the Lord . . . the Lord himselfe, or at least some of the Apostles, or Prophets, would not have held back that part of Gods Counsell, from the Church."[34] The divine instructions given in the primitive time were full and complete, needing and allowing no supplementation or adornment. "The primitive apostolic church," Cotton exulted, "was . . . the most completely and abundantly fair, of all that have ever been before it, or shall be after, upon the face of the earth." Consequently, he concluded, "there is no false way, but is an aberration from the first institution."[35]

The length to which restorationist ardor for the "first institution" could be carried appears in two issues spanning Cotton's ministerial career, one from 1611, the year after his ordination, the other from the 1640s. In 1611, while still a fellow of Emmanuel College, Cotton wrote a treatise arguing that the Lord's Day should be observed from evening to evening, not from morning to morning as was common practice in

England. He urged an evening-to-evening observance because it had been set forth in "the first institution of time" and thus was "the old and good way." Furthermore, it had been "the practice and judgment of the primitive Church." "I see no footstep of Christ or his disciples . . . that goe before us in this path," he concluded, "to call us to begin the Christian Sabbath from the morninge." Cotton's practice, though it never gained a wide following in England, did prevail in New England's Sabbath observance.[36]

The other issue, surfacing late in Cotton's career, concerned the corporate singing of the church. In the late 1630s, Cotton and several other leading ministers were assigned the task of making a more strict and literal rendering of selected psalms which, when set in meter, could be used in congregational singing. The work was completed and published in 1640, and usually is known as the Bay Psalm Book. In a preface to the volume, Cotton noted that in the worship of ancient times songs had been "sung by a joynt consent and harmony of all the Church in heart and voyce," not by an "order of singing Choristers." The standard had been the Davidic Psalter; therefore, all other hymns, even those "invented by the gifts of godly men in every age of the church," were prohibited, for they were contrived and illicit additions to the primitive standard. With the new metrical Psalter to guide congregational singing, Cotton expressed his confidence that "as we doe injoye other ordinances, soe . . . wee might injoye this ordinance also in its native purity."[37]

A few years later Cotton enlarged on his preface, arguing at great length against the church's right to "invent . . . spiritual songs." Though Christians may "compose a spirituall Song fit for their private solace," such humanly devised songs are "not fit to be sung in the solemn Assemblies of the Church," for they lack the spirit and life of those psalms divinely sanctioned in the Great Time. Cotton saw a crucial difference between "set formes" of prayer and "set formes" of songs for worship: the former were "devised and prescribed by men" while the latter were "appointed by God" in both the Old and New Testaments. God strictly forbade human "inventions for worship" but "never forbid himselfe to divise and appoint what forme of worship he pleased"; however, God did give human beings the "liberty of inventing Tunes" since God had not chosen to reveal the original Hebrew tunes. Further, Cotton believed that the use of musical instruments in worship, even though permitted in ancient Israel, was inappropriate. "Singing with Instruments in Old Testament times," he wrote, "was typicall, and so a ceremoniall worship, and therefore is ceased. . . . No voyce now [is] to be heard in the Church of Christ, but such as is significant and edifying . . . which the voyce of instruments is not." In the matter of congregational singing, as in all others, Cotton concluded, the great imperative was recovery of "the purest times," for in the centuries after Christ worship had been cluttered with "inventions" that "savoured rather of superstition that of pure Primitive Devotion."[38]

The congregationalism coming into full view in Massachusetts, Cotton little doubted, conformed almost exactly to the exemplary "first institution." Though some charged that the congregational way "is but of yesterday, newly sprung up, unknown and unheard of in the former ages of the church," it is in fact, Cotton countered, "the old way, . . . yea so old, as fetcheth [its] antiquity from the ancient of days, and from the Lord Jesus." Though the presbyterian pattern may be ancient, it is not "so ancient, as the way of our Congregational government of each church within itself, by the space of three hundred years." Further, the congregational discipline—the attempt to limit the church to a regenerate membership—"is the same . . . wherein the primitive church walked for the first three hundred years." Cotton rejoiced in such strict biblical conformity, for in it lay great spiritual power: as churches "come nearer to the primitive pattern," he wrote, "so they may expect a freer passage of the presence and blessing of the Holy Ghost with them." The Massachusetts churches evidently were flowing with such spiritual power for, in Cotton's judgment, they were the very churches that "the Lord Jesus [would erect] were he here himselfe in person."[39]

V

If Cotton and the other Massachusetts leaders sought to bring the churches under the strict control of biblical precedent, they sought with almost equal ardor to do the same for the political and social life of the colony. Standing firmly in the Reformed tradition of investing the civic order with redemptive significance, the Bay Colony ministers and magistrates all saw their task as claiming the social realm for the kingdom of God and structuring it to serve redemptive purposes. The divine will for the civic order, like that for the church, found its fullest and most complete expression in the Great Time of ancient Israel and the apostolic church. Civic matters, like the religious, therefore, required shaping so far as possible according to biblical rule and pattern. This assumption was self-evident and virtually unquestioned among the early New Englanders as they sought to raise up a holy commonwealth in the wilderness. Thomas Shepard, for example, wrote in the late 1630s that "the whole Scriptures contain the perfect rule of all moral activities"; John Cotton cited with approval William Perkins's view that "the word, and scriptures of God doe conteyne a . . . platforme, not onely of theology, but also of . . . ethicks, economicks, politiks, church-government, prophecy, [and] academy."[40] Whether fashioning a body of laws for the new colony, restricting the franchise to church members, deciding the qualifications and power of magistrates, expelling dissidents and heretics, or fighting the native Americans, Bay Colony Puritans turned their most careful attention to biblical example and precept, under whose goverance they sought to bring all significant social and civic structures.

The intensity of this drive in early New England must be explained in part by the idea of the national covenant, which, especially since the time of William Tyndale in the 1530s, had served as a powerful impetus for continuing reformation. As we saw in the previous chapter, Tyndale's belief that God had entered into a conditional covenant with England was reinforced in the 1550s by Martin Bucer's *De Regno Christi,* the annotations of the Geneva Bible, and John Foxe's *Acts and Monuments.* The idea took firm root in the Puritan movement and, from the 1560s down to the Civil War and Interregnum, provided preachers and polemicists with a powerful weapon against all who resisted further reformation. Puritans drew the basic elements of the doctrine from biblical Israel: England, like Israel, had entered into a covenant with God; the terms of the covenant required that national life conform strictly to biblical law; if the divine standards were maintained the nation would prosper, but negligence or rebellion would provoke God's disfavor and eventually bring national calamity, just as in Israel of old; godly sorrow and repentance, however, could divert divine wrath and restore the nation to its blessed and favored position.[41]

When set in this framework the Puritan striving to restore the church of "first and purest times" takes on immense significance. Thomas Cartwright expressed the significance in typical Puritan form: the church and the state, he argued, are "lyke unto Hippocrates twinnes whych were sicke togither and well togither. . . . Neyther is it to be hoped [that] the commonwealth shall flourish untill the church be reformed." He concluded that the weight of the church "(if it fall) will eyther quite pull down the commonwealth or leave it as none whych feare God will take any pleasure in it."[42] Stirred by such convictions, English Puritan leaders pressed relentlessly for recovery of the primitive order, for only in this way could covenental safety be assured. When, after decades of agitation, their efforts appeared to have failed and the prospects for divine judgment on the nation seemed imminent, many Puritans fled to a place of refuge where they could find liberty to institute all of "God's appointments." In their hard-won place of refuge, the immigrants, intensely set on achieving what they had been unable to achieve when faced with the intransigent English monarchs and their bishops, quickly adapted the national covenant to the colonial enterprise.

The close tie between the demands of the national covenant and recovery of ancient "first" institutions was everywhere assumed in early New England. To achieve in society the level of moral order that would avert God's judgment and call down blessings, the Puritan theorists believed that there must be steady effort to return both church and government to the biblical fountainheads. In the civic order this meant that such magistrates as Hezekiah, Josiah, and other godly kings of ancient Israel faced the solemn duty of establishing and protecting true religion and exercising rigorous, moral vigilance throughout society. The godly magistrate, like the faithful minister, was to press for recovery of pure and divinely instituted originals and see that his constituency maintained them; indeed, the very office itself was to be patterned after primitive biblical models. In the early "Modell of Church and Civil Power," prepared in 1636 to warn the Salem church of Roger Williams's heresies, a committee of ministers summarized the prevailing concept of magistracy:

> we willingly grant that Magistrates upon due and diligent search what is the counsell and will of God in his Word concerning the right ordering of the church, may and ought to publish and declare, establish and ratifie such Lawes and Ordinances as Christ hath appointed in his Word for the well ordering of church affaires, both for the gathering of the Church, and the right administration of all the Ordinances of God amongst them in such a manner as the Lord hath appointed [at first].[43]

As a warrant for such magisterial duties, the authors of the "Modell" needed only to recite the refrain, "Thus did Josiah."

With such biblical models before them, the Massachusetts magistrates took their role as guardian of the churches with utmost seriousness. In 1630 they levied a tax for the support of ministers and in 1638 passed a law compelling every inhabitant to contribute for this purpose; in 1631 they restricted the right of voting and of holding political office to church members; and in 1637 the general court passed a law excluding any from the colony who did not meet the test of orthodoxy.[44] In general the magistrates permitted no church to be gathered without their permission and punished or expelled those persons guilty of moral or scriptural offenses. Slackness in their duty, they believed, endangered seriously the peace and order of the colony; failure in suppressing heresy and promoting the bibilical form of religion invited God's displeasure and punishment. But through diligence in the work of conforming church and society to ancient and unalterable divine law, they would help bring into being, as Cotton put it, a "visible state of a new *Hierusalem,* which shall flourish many yeares upon Earth, before the end of the World."[45]

Because of his stature in the young colony, John Cotton assumed a prominent role in the development and defense of New England's civic order. Though John Norton, Cotton's successor at First Church in Boston, later could note with some amazement that Cotton was "above other men [in] declining irregular and unnecessary interesting of himself in the actions of the Magistrate," still he quickly was drawn into the deliberations and soon emerged as perhaps the leading clerical spokesman for the New England Way. In Perry Miller's terse characterization, Cotton became "the mouthpiece of the ruling oligarchy."[46]

Two early, closely related works by Cotton reflect his views and, to a large degree, those of most others in the early years of Massachusetts. The first, written in 1636 for a committee of magistrates and ministers charged with formulating a code of law, Cotton entitled *An Abstract, or The Lawes of New England* (often referred to as "Moses His Judicials"). The second work, written to a fellow minister in 1637, he entitled *A Discourse about Civil Government in a New Plantation Whose Design Is Religion.* In the *Discourse* Cotton argued that the ideal form of government was not democracy but theocracy; in such a government leaders were not elected by all the citizens but rather by the saints or those in full fellowship with a properly ordered Church of Christ. With the saints electing saints as magistrates, the laws of God could be upheld securely and thus divine rule extended over all of society. But Cotton was careful to distinguish church from state. In the theocracy he envisioned there would be separate but closely parallel civil and ecclesiastical governments, both patterned faithfully after biblical models. The church was a spiritual institution designed for the salvation of souls; the state was a temporal institution charged with upholding order, justice, and piety.

The one lent full and sympathetic support to the other, though neither must cross a carefully demarcated line. Ministers, for example, could not serve as magistrates, nor could magistrates infringe on the rights of ministers to deal with moral and doctrinal offenses in a "church-way." But magistrates most certainly were to serve as "nursing fathers" to the church, and ministers most certainly were to be called on, as the need arose, to advise the magistrates. In the *Discourse* and other writings, one of Cotton's central concerns was to fashion a delicate balance between the two realms, giving each its proper liberties and each its proper bounds. "It is most wholesome," Cotton later wrote in a sermon, "for Magistrates and Officers in church and Common-wealth, never to affect more liberty and authority than will do . . . the People good." It is their duty, Cotton continued, "to be studious of the bounds which the Lord hath set: and for the People, in whom fundamentally all power lyes, to give [only] as much power as God in his word gives to men." For all stations in society, he concluded, whether magistrates, ministers, family members, or servants, "let there be due bounds set. . . . Let them be duely observed, and give men no more liberty than God doth."[47]

The concern of Cotton and his Massachusetts colleagues for the "bounds" of liberty prompted an effort, begun in May 1636, to formulate a body of laws for the colony. The moving force behind the effort, it appears, was a group of freemen seeking to limit the discretionary power of magistrates and thus provide safeguards against arbitrary government. Cotton and two other ministers, Hugh Peter and Thomas Shepard, were appointed to "make a draft of laws agreeable to the word of God." By October of that year Cotton, apparently having done most of the work himself, presented to the general court "a model of Moses his judicials, compiled in an exact method." Drawing heavily, though not exclusively, on Old Testament legal codes, Cotton sought to bring all aspects of public life— "bodies, goods, lands [and] liberties of the people"—under the sacred jurisdiction of the "first" and most perfect legal code, that of Moses.[48]

To understand Cotton's draft of "Moses His Judicials" and the debate that surrounded it for several years, we first must see more clearly the Reformed rationale for Christian use of the Old Testament. As we have seen, the Puritan leaders, in defining the office of magistrate and in laying out the contours of a godly commonwealth, drew heavily on Old Testament archetypes and precedents. Such appeals reflect a "proportional" reading of the two testaments rooted in Reformed covenant theology. Scripture contained two covenants, the Puritans believed, a covenant of grace and a covenant of law. These two covenants, however, did not correspond to the two parts of the Bible called Old and Nest Testaments. The covenant of grace began with Adam after the fall and was focused in God's selection of Abraham; the covenant of law began when God covenanted with the Israelites at Sinai. The two covenants existed side by side in the scriptural record until Christ's coming opened the covenant of grace more fully and extended it to the Gentiles. Christ, rather than beginning a new covenant, broadened and deepened the original covenant of grace and elevated the covenant of law to a more spiritual, less ceremonial plane.[49]

With such a reading of scripture, the Puritans bound the two testaments firmly together in the economy of redemption, with the result that the Old Testament occupied a large place in their studied devotion to primordial rule and exemplar. Cotton could write, for example, that "a great part of the New Testament, or covenant is expressly delivered in the books of the Old Testament. . . . [They] hold forth the Doctrine, Worship, Order and Government of the New Testament to such who have not a vaile laid over their hearts"; any change in the New, he added, was not "by way of abrogation or diminution, but by way of accomplishment and enlargement."[50] Without such a "proportional" reading of the Old and New testaments, Cotton and his fellow divines insisted, there was a dangerous tendency to break redemptive history in half at Christ's appearing, thus denying the church's link to Israel and obscuring the fact that God worked the divine will not only internally in the souls of believers but also externally through a people in outward covenant with him. This was precisely the problem, Cotton charged, with Roger Williams. To insist, as Williams did, that after Christ's coming God had no literal covenanted nation but only a spiritual nation called out from among many nations was nothing less than seditious, for it exploded the divinely appointed civic order and invited divine judgment.

Cotton's enthusiasm for "Moses His Judicials" also must be viewed against the backdrop of Puritan support for the Mosaic judicial laws, which intensified in the 1570s. Protestant theologians long had distinguished between "ceremonial," "judicial," and "moral" law in the Old Testament. In the view of earlier Reformed theologians such as John Calvin, Christ's coming had superseded both the ceremonial laws detailing religious ritual and the judicial laws regulating everyday life, leaving in force only the moral law (summarized in the Ten Commandments). But the rise of Puritanism, with its primitivist concern for expanding biblical rule in the life of the nation, brought increasing support for the Mosaic judicials. Thomas Cartwright, William Perkins, and William Ames became the leading theorists. They argued that the judicials were binding not in every case or in every detail, for a considerable number of the laws were historically relative, but rather when they were interpreted "according to equity" and carefully "proportioned" to the contemporary setting. It was this tradition of high regard for the judicials that shaped the view of Cotton, Winthrop, and most early New Englanders. Through continual recourse to the "Archetype or first draught of Magistracie"— an archetype found in Moses, "the greatest Law-giver that ever was,"— they hoped, as Samuel Ward put it, "to repair the ruines of the dying world [by] renew[ing] government to the primative beauty of it."[51]

Such a renewal was the goal of Cotton's draft. In ten chapters, most of them laced heavily with scriptural citations, Cotton treated the role of magistrates, the franchise, protection of the colony, control of commerce, collection of taxes, rights of inheritance, penalties for criminal trespasses, and international relations. Of all the chapters the fullest and most important was the one treating capital offenses. With particularly full documentation from the Mosaic codes, Cotton cited sixteen crimes deserving death: blasphemy, idolatry, witchcraft, consultation with witches, obstinate and aggressive heresy, worshiping God with a graven image, Sabbath breaking, sedition and insurrection, rebelliousness in children, murder, adultery, incest, sodomy, intercourse with a woman during her menstrual period, "whordome of a maiden in her fathers house," man-stealing, and bearing false witness. Three additional capital crimes were recommended but were not drawn from biblical prescription—willful perjury, treason, and reviling the magistrates. Though the list appears shockingly severe by modern standards, it was considerably more moderate than English law of the time; Cotton, for example, drew on biblical guidelines to propose that thieves not be hanged but rather sentenced to make restitution as part of their punishment. For lesser crimes such as profanity, drunkenness, fornication, or slander, the penalties included whipping, fines, or branding. Cotton's draft represents, in general, a comprehensive and systematic application of Moses's judicials to the civic order of the Bay Colony. It was based squarely on the primitivist belief that, as Thomas Shepard put it, "Moses' judicials bind all nations, so far . . . as they contain moral equity." Cotton himself put it more sharply: "The more any law smells of man, the more unprofitable."[52]

Cotton's draft of "Moses His Judicials" received careful and prolonged consideration by the Massachusetts leaders. It was the focus of a formal discussion by a group of ministers and was studied and debated for several years by members of the general court. In 1639 it finally was rejected. The rejection appears to have hinged not on the proposals' strong biblicism and employment of primordial archetypes—for that was standard procedure—but on its failure to satisfy the group determined to limit magisterial power. In any case, Cotton's work exercised significant influence on the judicial codes that eventually were adopted—the famous *Body of Liberties* (1642) and the *Laws and Liberties of Massachusetts* (1648).[53] All these codes partook of the almost unquestioned belief that, whatever the civic issue, the answer lay in sacred archetype—if not in exact imitation of the archetypes then at least in continual return to them and careful extrapolation from them.

VI

The progress toward the adoption of a judicial code reflects a period of steady institutionalization and consolidation of power in the Bay Colony. Faced with challenges from more radical ideas, which were fairly widespread and had been from near the beginning, Cotton and the other leaders adjusted and extended their religious and civic policies to meet the challenges. The Antinomian Controversy, for example, provoked strong repressive measures, as we have seen; the court feared that Hutchinson and her followers might, "upon some revelation, make some sudden eruption upon those that differ from them in judgment."[54] The antinomian emphasis on the priority of the Holy Spirit over the demands of the law led, many feared, to a radically egalitarian view of society, seriously undermining the Puritan ideal of order, discipline, and social calling. To curb such threats, the general court passed laws screening immigrants for orthodoxy, repressing dissent, and in general ensuring the colony's fidelity to the terms of the national covenant.

In the 1640s concern over the spread of radical ideas grew, bringing a push for greater control and harsher measures. According to Cotton, it was a time in New England when the "Spirit of Error" ran rampant and the hearts of the people had become like "Tinder, ready to catch and kindle at every sparke of false light." And Peter Bulkeley of Concord expressed his alarm over a "generation in the Land, that are altogether looking after new light and new truths" with "itching ears, itching minds, and itching tongues also, itching to be fed with, and to be inventing novelties."[55] One person who helped cause such alarm was Samuel Gorton, a radical spiritist or "enthusiast" who had been banished from Plymouth Colony in 1639. Outraged by Gorton's letters, in which he had paraded his many blasphemous and heretical ideas, and long disturbed by his garrulous nature, the Massachusetts magistrates brought Gorton and his followers to Boston in 1643 to stand trial as heretics and enemies of the civic order. They forced Gorton, under penalty of death, to answer a set of doctrinal questions. He complied and his answers proved satisfactory, but he adamantly refused the magistrates' demand that he retract his earlier insults and heretical statements. Narrowly voting down the death penalty, the court sentenced Gorton and his followers to wear irons and to do hard labor. Gorton later claimed that Cotton was among those ministers who, in their sermons, "encouraged the people in their lawfulness of dealing [severely] with us."[56]

The Gorton episode proved damaging to the Bay Colony's reputation in the homeland, for shortly after his release, Gorton traveled to England where he publicized the intolerance of the New England Puritans and particularly the abridgment of his rights as an Englishman. He won his case before the Commission for Foreign Plantations and in 1646 published a lengthy narrative of his trials in Massachusetts. The book caused serious embarrassment, so much so that Edward Winslow, the colony's agent in London, published a full-scale rebuttal.[57] There followed a rising tide of criticism aimed at New England's treatment of dissenters and a growing belief in England, even among the colony's supporters, that the Bay Colony was no longer fit to serve as a model for reformation. The prominent English Independent Hugh Peter, for example, wrote in a letter to John Winthrop, Jr., in 1646: "None will come to you because you persecute[;] cannot you mend it?" Another English critic charged that the repressive tactics of the Bay colonists made them "stinke every where." Still another wrote to Winthrop: "As for my good opinion of persons of New England, I do acknowledge some have lost it and I thinke deservedly." During these years there was strong pressure on Massachusetts to bring its policies toward dissenters into line with the more lax policies developing in England.[58] But rather than bow to the pressures and adjust their policy, New England instead heightened its repression of dissent, stiffening in its resolve to maintain what it took to be the standards and strictures of "True Antiquity."

John Cotton emerged as an ardent defender of New England's firm stance against the rising arguments for toleration and religious liberty. Following Roger Williams's banishment, for example, one John Hall, a member of the Roxbury church, had acquired a portion of the tract entitled *A Most Humble Supplication,* written by an anonymous member of a General Baptist church in London, and had sent it to Cotton asking for his comments. The tract posited the complete separation of church and state as a foundation for the practice of liberty of conscience, arguing that magisterial coercion was entirely inappropriate for the maintenance of a true Christian church. Cotton's answer represents well the views of New England's leaders in the 1640s.[59] He began by distinguishing between "Points of Doctrine" that are "fundamental" and others that are "circumstantiall or lesse principall." Any tolerance of wrong belief in the fundamental doctrines was dangerous, and even the less central points— where some latitude was allowable—could be held with such "Arrogance and !mpetuousnesse" that the civil peace was disrupted. Such basic errors and such a spirit of rebelliousness could not be tolerated without putting souls in jeopardy, hindering the course of reformation, threatening civil peace, and eventually calling down divine judgment. They must be stopped.

The proper course of action, Cotton believed, was admonition by the ministers, as directed by apostolic precedent (Titus 3:10). Scripture clearly taught that the "erronious and blind Conscience . . . cannot but be convinced . . . of the dangerous Errour of his way, after once or twice Admonition." If, after such admonitions have been "wisely and faithfully dispensed," the person persists in his error, he no longer can be said to possess a blind conscience; rather, he must be viewed as a sinner against his conscience and to have forfeited his right to toleration. At this point the godly magistrate properly may step in and use appropriate force to silence the offender, thus protecting the spiritual and temporal welfare of the state.[60]

Through the 1640s and the 1650s, Cotton's theory for control of heresy and dissent guided New England practice. That practice took a more severe turn in the encounter with Baptists in the early 1650s. Though the Massachusetts courts had disciplined numerous Baptists in the 1640s, it was not with the severity unleashed in the summer of 1651. John Clarke, Obadiah Holmes, and John Crandall, all Baptists from Rhode Island, had come to the Bay Colony to edify a small group of fellow Baptists. They were arrested, imprisoned, found guilty of holding private worship services on the Sabbath and rejecting infant baptism, and sentenced to pay a large fine or be whipped. Holmes refused to pay and, after a two-month imprisonment, received a public whipping. Cotton agreed with the severe measure imposed by Governor Endicott and the court and preached against any toleration of such "soul-murderers."[61]

Later that year John Clarke traveled to England with Roger Williams and there published *Ill Newes from New-England,* an account of his and his companions' treatment at the hands of the Bay Colony magistrates.[62] Stung by the publicity, the Massachusetts leaders asked Thomas Cobbett, minister at Lynn, to prepare a rebuttal. In it Cobbett began with a lengthy defense of the magistrates as "Christs Vice-Regents" and thus as the "nursing Fathers and Mothers of his church." Cobbett's central arguments, not surprisingly, were primitivist: the sanction for Massachusetts' action was to be found in biblical archetype and instruction. Thus godly magistrates who took coercive action against Baptists imitated King David and other "good kings" of the Old Testament; they also emulated Christ as he drove the money changers from the temple in "one of his most glorious Acts." The idea of toleration that Clark had defended in his "scandalous pamphlet," Cobbett concluded, was nothing less than "that Great Antichrists masterpiece."[63]

News of the persecution of Baptists provoked further dismay in England and quickly prompted strong letters charging New England with self-righteousness. For example, Sir Richard Saltonstall, himself a former Massachusetts magistrate, wrote Cotton and John Wilson a letter of protest in 1652. "It doth not a little grieve my spirit," he wrote,

> to hear what sadd things are reported dayly of your tyrany and persecutions in New-England as that you fyne, whip and imprison men for their consciences. First you compel such to come into your assemblies as you know will not joyne with you in worship, and when they show their dislike thereof . . . , then

you styrre up your magistrates to punish them for such (as you conceyve) their publick affronts.

"These rigid ways," he added, "have layed you very low in the hearts of the saynts." Saltonstall closed by stating his hope that "you do not assume to yourselves infallibility of judgment, when the most learned of the Apostles confessed he knew but in part and saw darkly as through a glass."[64] Attempting to justify their treatment of the Baptists, Cotton replied with more heat and sarcasm than usual. "If our wayes (rigid wayes as you call them) have layd us low in the hearts of Gods people, yea, and of the saints (as you stil them)," he snapped, "wee do not believe it is any part of their saintship." Faced with the sharp question as to how the New Englanders could coerce others when they themselves once had fled coercion, Cotton asserted that "there is a vast difference between mens inventions and Gods institutions. Wee fled from mens inventions, to which wee else should have been compelled. Wee compell none to mens inventions."[65] Cotton expressed supreme confidence that the New England ministers and magistrates, unlike the Anglican authorities they had opposed, had indeed discerned the will of God on all central matters and thus had judged the Baptists' errors correctly. The conclusion was clear: because the Bay Colony's religious and civic institutions were nothing more or less than the primitive institutions divinely established in the Great Time, the leaders could claim divine sanction for all their coercive measures.

VII

In the years that followed, the coercive measures grew still more harsh, particularly in the persecution—and in a few cases, execution—of Quakers. John Norton's work *The Heart of New-England Rent* (1660), written after New England had enacted its harshest laws against dissenters, reflects the heightened severity and the theological shift that accompanied those laws. "All experience proveth," Norton wrote, "that the bitter root of Heresie, hath never prevailed where Doctrine, Catechism, and Discipline have been upheld in their purity and vigor." He added that "Religion admits of no eccentric notions." The great irony here is, as Philip Gura has pointed out, that the Puritan movement from its very beginning had been propelled by just such "eccentric notions." It had been a movement of intense and persistent dissent against traditional norms and had insisted, throughout much of its history, on a "further light" from God. But now, ironically, with the institutionalization of dissent, the codification of Congregationalism, and the defensive attempts to preverse their primitively pure and settled way from corruption, the Puritan leaders could allow little room for the very religious experimentation that first had stirred such upheaval in England and that eventually had brought the Puritans to the New World. Now Norton could assert baldly that "the rule of Doctrine, Discipline, and Order is the *Center of Christianity,*" not the working of God through the Spirit which for earlier Puritan divines, and especially for John Cotton, had provided the center.[66] Indeed, as we have seen, Cotton himself placed more and more emphasis on "Doctrine, Discipline, and Order"; his eighteen-year career in New England had convinced him that continual questing for "further light" brought only social disruption and divine displeasure.

The irony of this development is heightened when we see that the call for "further light" had served not only as a convenient tool of dissent throughout the decades of Puritan agitation in England but in fact as a key restorationist slogan. It was an appeal based squarely on the Protestant Epistemology, invested with all the features of primitivist constraint. When Cotton, for example, had issued the call for continuing reformation, envisioning a "far greater light than yet shines," he had had no thought whatsoever of continuing revelation, for the body of divine truth had been revealed fully in primitive times and underwent not the least bit of change in succeeding centuries. He envisioned, therefore, not a progression in truth itself but rather a progression in understanding of that truth; "further light" was found by a deeper and more diligent opening of the ancient and fixed body of truth contained in scripture, a process that, due to the strong human propensity for "invention," conceit, and spiritual dullness, must be ongoing. Thus Cotton warned that, though New England's churches evidence "a greater face of reformation than in any [other] churches," they cannot "rest in Reformation and formes of it."[67] Richard Mather in like manner objected to a certified doctrinal platform for the Massachusetts churches because it would make them unreceptive to "further light." Others insisted, on the same basis, that New England must resist the "conceit of having already attained a perfect reformation."[68]

New England Puritans, however, did not resist. They were God's New Israel and finally saw virtually no gulf between their vision for church and society and God's. They had stripped away all illicit "human inventions," all the encrustations of profane time, and had restored all of God's original ordinances and laws to their pristine form. Their performance of covenant duties admittedly was lacking, but their perception of those duties surely was not. Through the doorway of myth and imagination, they had reentered, as it were, the sacred primordium.

Out of such heady confidence arose both the Puritans' greatest achievement and their greatest failures. By identifying themselves so closely with ancient Israel and attempting to transfer the principles of nationhood in theocratic Israel directly to their own colony, the Puritans sought order, stability, and social cohesion, and indeed they achieved that goal to a remarkable degree, fashioning a profoundly conservative social order unmatched in its time.[69] But such identification with Israel and the primordium ultimately proved pretentious, for in the process they claimed the same divine prerogatives for treatment of "canaanites" (Indians), heretics, and dissenters. They claimed a divine right to Indian lands and in fact sought the disintegration of Indian culture and its replacement by "civilized" English mores and religion.[70] But such is the power and such the temptation of the restoration impulse—to so identify with the sacred and unparalleled "first" age that, though one gains a powerfully unifying sense of divine purpose, at the same time one's own sense of finitude grows clouded. Divine justification for denying legitimacy to others lies therefore close at hand. Even the moderate and restrained John Cotton found the lure of this temptation difficult to resist.

THREE

The Quest for "Soul Liberty": Roger Williams and Puritan Dissent

If the primitivist impulse helped draw John Cotton and other defenders of the New England Way into a rigidity that easily denied the legitimacy of dissent, it performed just the opposite function in the thought of Roger Williams (1603?–1683). In place of religious conformity, Williams sought "soul liberty." In his view, only toleration of dissent could liberate divine truth from the polluted bins of history and prepare the ground for a reemergence of the original divine order. To the extent that his Puritan brethren forced consciences and restricted liberty, he charged, they had joined themselves to the corrupt and decaying order of things and fell tragically short of the full restoration they sought.

A series of polemical exchanges between Cotton and Williams in the years following Williams's banishment from Massachusetts throws into sharp refleif the issues that separated the two men. Beginning with a published letter by Cotton (attempting to convince Williams of his errors) and a published reply by Williams, the exchange escalated with Williams's classic work, *The Bloudy Tenent of Persecution, for Cause of Conscience* (1644), and Cotton's sharp reply, *The Bloudy Tenent of Persecution, Washed and Made White in the Bloud of the Lambe* (1647). Williams had the last word in his rambling, convoluted, sometimes eloquent rejoinder, *The Bloody Tenent Yet More Bloody(1652).*[1] The famous debate has been the subject of frequent, intense, and sometimes enlightening scrutiny, but missing throughout most of the literature is the crucial recognition of the primitivist issues underlying the debate.[2] Missing is the key insight that, however great the differences between Cotton and Williams, they were united upon the assumptions of the Protestant Epistemology and the additional primitivist constraints produced by aggressive and prolonged Puritan dissent. This biblicist primitivism led both men, for example, ultimately to resist the more radical spiritism that characterized many dissenters in early New England; though both men had strong leanings in that direction, both finally recoiled against those who sought the Spirit's guidance into ever new truth.[3] Both alike came to share a disdain for the radicals' boundless revelations, for the social upheavals they caused, and for other products of "human invention"; both maintained a profound passion for the fixed forms and final truths revealed in the biblical primordium. By seeing this profound similarity more clearly, perhaps we can see the well-known differences more clearly as well.

This chapter focuses on Roger Williams's primitivist vision and how that vision stirred his unceasing calls for liberty of conscience and religious toleration, calls that John Cotton found heretical, seditious, and not surprisingly, a product of "human invention."

1

On February 5, 1631, Roger Williams, age twenty-seven, and his wife arrived in Boston.[4] Fresh from theological studies at Cambridge and a brief stint as a household chaplain for a wealthy Essex Puritan, Williams was received warmly and invited to join the Boston church. He also was honored with an invitation to fill the prestigious post of teacher temporarily left vacant by John Wilson (and later held by John Cotton). But after consulting with members of the church, he declined the offer. "I durst not officiate," he explained, "to an unseparated people, as, upon examination and conference, I found them to be." John Winthrop wrote that Williams refused the offer "because they would not make a public declaration of their repentance for having communion with the churches of England, while they lived there."[5] Though the Boston church was based on a covenant and was thus congregational in form, and though it accepted only regenerate members and exercised rigorous discipline, Williams felt it needed to repent publicly of its impure former association. A geographical separation was not enough. With this insistence Williams revealed the strict Separatist views toward which he had moved between 1627 and 1631.[6]

After his refusal at Boston, Williams ministered briefly with the Separatist congregation at Plymouth, then moved to Salem where he assisted Samuel Skelton in the teaching ministry. The magistrates' concern over Williams deepened when in late 1633 they read a treatise in which Williams argued that the Bay Colony had no right to the land they occupied except to the extent that they "compounded with the natives," and that as a result of this illicit possession the royal patent should be returned to England. According to a later comment by Williams, the "great sin" of the New England patent lay in the fact that "Christian kings (so called) are invested with Right by virtue of their Christianitie, to take and give away the Lands and Countries of other men."[7] Though Williams appeared "penitently" before the general court and satisfactorily affirmed his allegiance to the king, his relentless pursuit of Separatist principles led to further troubles in the months that followed.

In July 1635 Williams again was called before the court, this time for arguing, as he had done on his arrival in Boston, that magistrates had no authority to punish those who violated the first table of the Ten Commandments, except when they also disturbed "the civil peace." As in his objection to the patent, Williams here was protesting the illicit mingling of church and world, of the things of God and the things of man; just as it was blasphemous to call Europe "Christendom," so it was a profanation of the church to establish and uphold it by civil power. His opposition struck hard at the ideal of a holy commonwealth that the magistrates and ministers struggled to define and maintain. The leaders were aroused and determined to remove or silence the persistent threats. In the presence of the assistants and a number of leading ministers invited for the hearing before the court, Williams heard the charges and was given until the next court meeting (eight weeks) to consider them. At that time he was either to "give satisfaction to the court, or else to expect the sentence." Throughout this time the ministers continued their attempt to deal with him in a "church way"; Cotton, for example, says that he "spent a great part of the Summer in seeking by word and writings to satisfie his scruples."[8]

At the October meeting of the court, to which all the ministers had been summoned, charges were brought against Williams for two letters he had written—one to the Boston church, the other to Salem. The court offered him a month's respite and further consultation but he refused. They chose Thomas Hooker to debate him, but Hooker "could not reduce him from any of his errors." The following morning, therefore, they officially banished Williams from the Bay Colony.[9] Due to illness, he was given a six-week respite; it was later extended until the following spring under the condition that he not "go about to draw others to his opinions." But by January 1636 someone reported to the authorities that Williams "did use to entertain company in his house, and to preach to them, even on such points as he had been censured for"; furthermore, "he had drawn about twenty persons to his opinion," according to Winthrop, "and they were intended to erect a plantation about the Narragansett Bay, from whence the infection would easily spread into these churches, (the people being, many of them, much taken with the apprehension of his godliness)."[10] On these grounds, the magistrates decided on immediate deportation, but Williams was warned of the plan and escaped into the wilderness.

Williams's winter flight took him, after considerable time at an Indian settlement, into Narragansett territory, where he established the
settlement of Providence Plantations. There, amid the hardships and
trials of fashioning a permanent settlement with an effective government,
Williams continued his quest for the "due order of the Lord," for a
church duplicating the primitive apostolic church in purity and in practice. In the unrestricted atmosphere of Providence, he entered a period
of intense intellectual ferment and theological reorientation spanning
roughly the years 1636 to 1644. He engaged in vigorous, often polemical,
correspondence with such men as John Winthrop, Peter Bulkeley, John
Cotton, and Hugh Peter, setting forth his views on the nature of the
church, scriptural grounds for separation from the Church of England,
the demands of ecclesiastical purity, the evangelization of the Indians,
and other topics.

A central theme of his polemics in the period just after his banishment was the charge that reformation was incomplete among the
Massachusetts churches, that they had failed to separate the church from
the world and thus restore the purity of the first age. In letters to
Winthrop and Cotton he bemoaned the fact that in matters of Christian
worship and polity they were still "asleepe"; he implored God to wake
up "my honoured Contreymen, to see how . . . they sleep, insensible of
much concerning the purity of the Lord's worship." He warned that
"though you have come farr yet you never came out of the Wilderness to
this Day." Restitution of the primitive pattern meant a complete separation or walling off of the church from the world; when this was not done
thoroughly the church was corrupted. While the Bay Colony church
members might be exemplary in their personal morality, their churches
were impure. He advised them to "abstract your selfe with a holy violence from the Dung heape of this Earth." Winthrop, Cotton, and the
other Bay Colony leaders, he urged, should make every effort to "cleanse
*themselves from all filthiness both of flesh and spirit, and to finish holiness
in the feare of God.*" Williams promised that he would "mourne dayly,
heavily uncessantly till the Lord looke down from Heaven, and bring all
his precious living stones into one New Jerusalem." Williams himself
took this advice so seriously that, according to Winthrop, he refused for a
time to engage in worship with anyone except his wife.[11]

Williams's preoccupation with ecclesiastical purity and the theological ferment it stirred in him during the years immediately following
his departure from Massachusetts propelled him along a course often
taken by sectarians of the time who claimed a "further light." This course
followed the classic pattern of "falling off," a term used in reference to
those who passed from one church to another in their religious quest.

Williams's own theological "falling off" was compared by his contemporaries to that of John Smyth, the Separatist turned Baptist. Smyth professed that "wee are inconstant in erroer: that wee wou'd have the truth, though in many particulars wee are ignorant of it: We will never be satisfied in indevoring to reduce the worship and ministery of the Church, to the primitive Apostolic institution from which as yet it is so farr distant."[12] Like Smyth, Williams's search for the "primitive Apostolic institution" led him to question and reject his baptism in the Church of England and to embrace the believers' baptism practiced by the Baptists. Judging from Winthrop's reports, Williams reached this position regarding baptism at least by 1638. Winthrop reported that in March 1639 Williams was "emboldened" to embrace the principles of "Anabaptistry" by one Katherine Scott, a sister of Anne Hutchinson. He and Ezekiel Holyman, a former resident of Salem, rebaptized each other along with about ten other people. "Mr. Williams and many of his company, a few months since, were in all haste rebaptized," Winthrop added later, "and denied communion with all others."[13]

Only a few months after his rebaptism, however, Williams once again "fell off" to a more radical theological position, this one shaping the course of his remaining life and forming the base for his public career as a controversialist. He left the Baptist congregation at Providence, renounced his baptism, and evidently never associated himself with a church again.[14] His long quest for "the first pattern" of God's church, his restless preoccupation with ecclesiastical purity, his efforts to "finish holiness in the feare of God," all prompted in him now a profound theological shift. The implications of this shift he found disturbing and his contemporaries found utterly shocking. Not only had there been a "falling away . . . from the first primitive *Christian* state or *worship*," as all Puritans accepted in some fashion, but the church in fact had been extinguished; there had been a "desolation of Zion," a "total routing of the *Church* and *Ministry* of *Christ Jesus*."[15] The New Testament pattern, he now believed, showed churches formed only by apostles or apostolic messengers who were given authority by Christ. The medieval apostasy had broken the succession of those who possessed this authority; no ground remained therefore for establishing churches "after the first pattern." The task now, Williams believed, was not founding churches but denouncing the errors in Christianity, and waiting—waiting for the impending restitution of the church and its ordinances by God or God's duly authorized messengers.

Thus his search for the true church continued. Finding the pattern of the apostolic church ever before him, he looked for and longed for its reappearance. To John Winthrop's query, in a letter written to Williams six months after his banishment, "From what spirit, and to what end do you drive?" Williams replied: Like you, I "seek Jesus who was nailed to the gallows, I ask the way to lost Zion, I witness what I believe I see patiently . . . in sackcloth."[16]

II

Though Roger Williams came to believe that the authentic church had not existed for over a thousand years—since shortly after Constantine's time—and that it could not be restored by mere human activity, he nonetheless held strong convictions about what that pure church looked like and how it should stand in relation to society. With the theorists of the New England Way he shared a large core of primitivist assumptions and terminology; with them he looked intently to "the practice of the Primitive Church of Jerusalem."[17] He disagreed most basically with them not over the primacy of biblical archetypes or the firm rejection of all "human invention" but rather over the nature and structure of the archetype. The New Testament pattern alone provided the "pattern" for the church, Williams believed, whereas most churchmen since Constantine had set up the "best patterns of the kings of Judah" as their model.[18] The trouble with the Massachusetts leaders, he charged, was a fateful misunderstanding of the proper Christian archetype and a lack of courage to live in full conformity with archetypal norms.

An important factor in this disagreement over primitive models was the typological exegesis of the Bible. Christian exegetes valued the typological method because it allowed them to affirm the historicity of the Old Testament events while at the same time investing those events with specifically Christian meaning. The Protestant Reformers had used the method extensively, and the Puritans stood within this rich theological heritage. In the famous debate between John Cotton and Williams, therefore, the issue was not the use of typology itself but rather the extent to which Christ's coming abolished the historical "types" and replaced them with spiritual "anti-types."[19] Both Cotton and Williams agreed that "*Canaan* was *Typical* [while] Christ's kingdom is spiritual"; they agreed that "the Body being come, Types and shadows vanish."[20] But they disagreed over the relation of literal to spiritual, of shadow to reality.

Williams believed that the events, laws, and institutions of Israel had found completion in the New Testament with Christ's incarnation and thus were "dead." He argued that the meaning of "the whole *Church* of *Israel, Roote,* and *Branch,* from first to last . . . [is now] *figurative* and *Allegorical.*" Failure to make the correct distinction between type and antitype—the one physical and "shadowish," the other spiritual and substantive—was the key hermeneutical mistake, Williams charged, that caused John Cotton and those of like mind to become mired in "a Babylonish mixture of the Old and New Testament." Cotton, he insisted, acted as if "the *letter* . . . is yet in force."[21] In contrast, Cotton believed that, though Christ had fulfilled the "ceremonial duties" of Israel, he "never abolished a National Civil State nor the judicial laws of Moses." For him, some Old Testament types were simultaneously literal and spiritual. For example, Israel provided, at the literal level, a permanent divine pattern for civil government and, at the spiritual level, a prefigurement of Christ and the church. He claimed that Williams, by rejecting the literal continuity, "transforms all the Scripture into an Allegory."[22] Thus Cotton upheld a literal-spiritual continuity between the Old and New Testaments and between the Old Testament and the Bay Colony. Two typological approaches are at work here: Cotton employed typology conjunctively to bind the testaments together, while Williams employed it disjunctively to set the New Testament apart from the Old as a religious authority.

The typological method, Williams recognized, was fraught with dangers if used improperly. "The applying of the *times* and *persons* each to the other," he observed, "requires a more than ordinary *guidance* of the finger or holy *Spirit* of *God*."[23] Williams believed he had received such guidance when God had called him directly to serve as a "witness" decrying the religious error of the times. By the "applying of the times and persons each to the other" he believed he had set the proper bounds for the biblical model of the pure church. Because of the gulf between the testaments opened up by Christ's incarnation, the New Testament, and it alone, now served as the archetype for the form and function of the church.

With the baseline of scripture drawn tightly around the New Testament, Roger Williams found there an exact, perfect pattern for the ordering of the church and in fact for most of the affairs of the Christian's life. The New Testament is "the *golden Rule* [which], if well attended to, will discover all crooked *swervings* and *abberations*." The first churches of Christ pictured there are "the *lights, patternes,* and *presidents* to all succeeding Ages." Every practice must be done "either by way of *command, Promise,* or example."[24] Williams believed, with many others who adopted a program for the restitution of primitive Christianity, that everything not authorized explicitly by Christ and the apostolic writings must be rejected.

Williams's Puritan brethren held a similar conviction about the strict jurisdiction of apostolic norms. But Williams believed that his brethren, having affirmed such norms in theory, were not willing to apply them consistently. When it came to using the civil sword for enforcing true religion and rooting out heresy and idolatry, they could display no apostolic command or example supporting such a practice. The New Testament apostles never addressed, either in word or writing, the civil states in which they lived. A state church, Williams never tired of reminding people, "is not the *Institution* of the *Lord Jesus Christ.*" Where, he asked, can you "now find one footstep, Print or Pattern in this Doctrine of the son of God, for . . . a Nationall Church?"[25] Under the covenant with Abraham and Moses there *was* a state church, there *was* authority to put the recalcitrant to death, but now, under the rule of Christ, what authority is there to "follow that pattern of Israel" and punish those failing to follow the "rules of the *Gospel?*" Where is the "least footing" in the New Testament for such a practice? Cotton admitted that Christ gave none; magistrates therefore must turn for their guidance to Moses and the prophets, "who hath expounded him [Christ] in the Old Testament." Williams objected. The Old Testament, he said, prophesied Christ or typed Christ, not expounded him; it was Christ rather who was the "fulfilling, opening, and *expounding*" of the Old Testament.[26] With his death and resurrection he "typed out" the Old Testament, making any appeal to it for the ordering of church and society illegitimate.

Insistent on confining every appeal for scriptural authority or precedent to the New Testament, Williams set out a view of church and society that, despite similar doctrines and a similar appeal to the apostolic church, differed greatly from that of the Massachusetts Puritan fathers. His own deep sense of isolation from his brethren, and alienation from the dominant cultural-ecclesiastical model of his time, helped him identify not with the deuteronomic theology of Israel's national "church," but with the despised and persecuted Christians of the first-century church who in their sufferings were made one with their despised and crucified Lord. He saw in the New Testament not a church triumphant in earthly power and glory, sustaining itself by force, but a church weak in earthly might, lacking in outward splendor and sustained only by its reliance on God. The difference, to Williams, was like the difference between night and day. One depended on earthly power, the other solely on divine power. The one persecuted dissenters and heretics; the other *was* persecuted as dissenter and heretic. The one refused, partly out of fear of losing its power and sway over people, to exclude the unregenerate from its assemblies; the other refused, out of fear of standing impure before God, to include them. The one did not expect to be perfect; the other could accept nothing else. The two views of church and society were based on two very different biblical archetypes.

This sharp divergence from the dominant ecclesiastical model brought with it, or perhaps was in part caused by, a view of Christ's spiritual lordship over the believer and the church, a lordship manifested not in temporal might and glory but in humiliation and suffering. For Williams, the dominant image of the New Testament church was the image of a suffering church, a church under the cross, despised by the world, persecuted by the strong and mighty, and honored to imitate Jesus in his sufferings as an outcast. Christ exercised his lordship not with the physical sword but with the sword of the Spirit, not in material prosperity but in spiritual well-being, not in the wilderness of the world but only in the garden of his church. Those living under this lordship in no way depended on temporal lords for their strength and well-being.

Williams's typological distinction between Old and New Testaments is crucial here. In Williams's view, failure to recognize the uniqueness of Old Testament Israel, the abrogation of the Mosaic ceremonial and judicial regulations, and the replacement of an earthly, geographic kingdom with a spiritual one detracted seriously from the significance of Christ's appearance on the earth, for in his appearance Christ radically changed the nature of God's kingdom. Whereas with Israel under Moses the spiritual and civil were united in one nation, after Christ the civil and spiritual were two entirely different spheres. The temporal features of God's kingdom under Israel now applied in a spiritual way to the church, the new Israel of God. Mixing the two realms disparaged the work of Christ and misconstrued the nature of his lordship.

Williams's affirmation of Christ's spiritual lordship deeply affected his understanding of both Christian discipleship and church-state relations. The implications for discipleship appear in Williams's insistence that those following Christ most closely are those "content with a poor and lowly condition in worldly things." In this they were like Christ. He was a glorious king, mighty and full of splendor, only in his spiritual kingdom, though in the world's eyes he had "the esteeme of a mad man, a Deceiver, a Conjurer, a Traytor against Caesar, and destitute of an house wherein to rest his head."[27] Christ's lowliness and suffering in his worldly estate served as a model for his faithful followers: they should not expect any better treatment at the hands of the world than was given Jesus himself. Thus for Williams one prime mark of the true church was that it was always a suffering church.

In this conviction, Williams stood within the tradition created by John Foxe and others in the sixteenth century. In Foxe's myth of the English martyrs, the true church is never the "most multitude" but always the "little flock," marked by affliction, persecution, and suffering. This view became a central theme in the apocalyptic tradition of sixteenth-century English Protestantism, though in the later years of the century there arose the tendency to identify the persecuted "little flock" not with the faithful, but with the English nation itself.[28] It also became a prominent theme in sectarian protests against the established church of England in the seventeenth century. Sectarian writers often claimed that an experience of persecution on behalf of cherished beliefs had conferred on them a deep sense of God's approbation. Williams shared this sectarian experience and outlook. His own banishment from Massachusetts and isolation amid the savagery and hardships of the wilderness strengthened his identification with the huddled bands of believers in the early church and throughout history who had faced expulsion, hardships, and death. Furthermore, it bound him to a Christ whom he saw as despised and rejected yet reigning over a spiritual kingdom that could not be shaken.

Williams's deep conviction that the true church was always a suffering and persecuted church pervades his controversial writings and illustrates further how his views contrasted with Cotton's. Cotton looked to the deuteronomic theology of ancient Israel and saw that God assured earthly peace and prosperity to his people when they "flourish in *holiness,*" but Williams argued to the contrary that those who are most holy and faithful are most persecuted, as "is the most evident in all the New *Testament,* and all mens new and fresh experience."[29] For Cotton, the reforming magistrate was necessary in upholding true religion and thus ensuring civil peace and prosperity. Williams retorted that while scripture promises that godliness brings a better life and that those who seek first the kingdom will prosper in some sense, these promises by no stretch of the imagination prove that Christ's followers will have outward prosperity in the present evil world. If one makes the proper typological distinction between national and spiritual Israel, thus taking the New Testament as the sole model, he then will see that, far from a national prosperity being promised for the establishment of true religion, scripture promises only persecution for God's people, a persecution that appears heavier for the most zealous and faithful.

Expectations of prosperity, peace, honor, and riches, Williams insisted, are worldly expectations. Christian expectations, in contrast, are only "paine and *sorrow,* yea *poverty* and *persecution,* untill the great day of *refreshing,* near approaching"; until then, Christians can expect only to be "like a woman in travel" (*sic*). Cotton's demand for civil maintenance of religious uniformity to ensure peace and well-being, therefore, fits under "the portion of this *world.*"[30] Williams felt that Cotton in fact probably was deceiving himself in an attempt to "escape the bitter sweeting of *Christ's* cross" and the "*portion* of *sorrow* and *suffering*" that has been the usual lot of Christians in the world. Indeed, Williams charged that schemes for a godly commonwealth were promoted as subtle devices to keep the church from "the *Cross* or *Gallows*" of Christ; they salve the consciences of those unwilling to separate themselves from the world and cloak the minister's carnal desire to protect and enhance his worldly portion. Since the apostasy, Williams believed, the clergy had disdained a humiliated, crucified Christ and had fashioned for themselves "*Pompous* and *Princely, temporall* and *Worldly Christians*" with the goal of attaining authority, wealth, and power. And the nearer they got to worldly wealth and ease through these means, the "further and further have they departed from *God,* from his *Truth,* from the *Simplicitie, Power* and *Puritie* of *Christ Jesus* and true *Christianitie.*"[31]

The life of the Christian, for Williams, was always a life lived under the cross of suffering, persecution, and humiliation. This pattern of suffering found its biblical precedent, he believed, in Acts 17:6, where the apostles were seen as people who "turned the world upside down," as people who stirred up the sinful consciences of worldly people with the preaching of a crucified Christ. They incurred the wrath of evildoers, the scorn and rage of the crowds, the vicious opposition of the religious elite, and the persecution of rulers eager to protect their own power and position. Christ's true disciples will always find it so, to some degree. They must be prepared, he warned, to stand virtually alone against a whole city or a whole society, for the argument of numbers is always against God. Christ's spiritual lordship, with its implications for Christian discipleship, was summed up vividly by Williams in *Mr. Cotton's Letter Lately Printed, Examined and Answered:*

> If him thou seekest in these searching times, mak'st him alone
> thy white and soules beloved, willing to follow and be like him
> in doing, in suffring; although thou find'st him not in the restau-
> ration of his Ordinances, according to his first Patterne. Yet shall
> thou see him, raigne with him, eternally admire him, and enjoy
> him, when he shortly comes in flaming fire to burne up millions
> of ignorant and disobedient.[32]

III

Williams's understanding of Christ's spiritual lordship undergirded his view of church-state relationships. If for the individual Christian Christ's spiritual rule meant a lowly worldly estate and a despised minority status, then for the church as a whole it meant that spiritual and temporal comprised two entirely separate realms.

In Old Testament Israel, Williams observed, God had used only one government for both the civil and spiritual realms, but after Christ, God had chosen in the divine wisdom to administer the two realms through two distinct governments, one religious and one civil. Christ's lordship now was exercised not with physical weapons and coercion, which were part of the civil realm, but only with the "two-edged sword" of the Spirit. Now "the *Civil Magistrate* hath his charge of the *bodies* and *goods* of the *subject*" while "the *spiritual Officers, Governors* and *overseers* of *Christs City* or *Kindgome,* [hath] charge of their *souls,* and *soule safety.*"[33] The duties of the state, under the new dispensation inaugurated by Christ, were entirely secular; the duties of the church were entirely spiritual. By mingling these two realms, as Williams thought Puritans in both England and New England were doing, one fell into *"Babylonish* and *confused mixtures"*; one preferred Moses over Christ; one confused the garden of the church with the wilderness of the world.

By making such a radical separation between the spiritual and the temporal kingdoms, between the church and the state, Williams set forth a view that was nearly inconceivable to all but a tiny minority in the early seventeenth century. The General Baptists had published a series of tracts arguing for such a separation, most notably *A Short Declaration of the Mistery of Iniquity* (1612) by Thomas Helwys, *Religions Peace* (1614) by Leonard Busher, *Objections: Answered by Way of Dialogue* (1615), and *A Most Humble Supplication* (1620); Williams repeated virtually the same arguments, but they were still as unpopular and unacceptable in the 1640s as they had been in the 1620s.[34]

The heart of Williams's argument was an appeal to the actual practice of the primitive apostolic churches. According to Williams, when one looks at the primitive churches pictured in the New Testament, one does not find the mixing of civil and spiritual as in the Old Testament. The churches at Philippi and Rome, for example, stood apart from the cities of Philippi and Rome, as far apart as the heavens from the earth. Williams pointed out further that the apostle Paul never charged civil authorities with spiritual duties and never placed on their shoulders the defense of divine truth. Since the rulers themselves usually were carnal or dead in sin and thus possessed no ability to discern spiritual truth, Paul would "have put out the eye of *Faith* and *Reason* and *Sense* at once" by giving them such responsibility. Cotton essentially agreed with Williams, stating that an appeal to Herod, Pilate, or Caesar would be like "a poor *sheep* [complaining] to the *Wolves* of the *Wolves heresies.*" Rather than appealing to such corrupt magistrates, Cotton argued, Christians must profess the gospel, then as the gospel has some effect, urge the magistrates to do their spiritual duty. The fact that no godly magistrates existed in the first century, Cotton believed, did not invalidate their legitimacy in a properly ordered society.[35] In sharp contrast, Williams viewed magistrates as essentially unqualified to judge in spiritual matters, for "Scripture and all *History*" clearly shows that kings and rulers seldom have judged properly those who should be punished and those who should not.

Williams pushed the argument further. He argued that, since the church suffered fiery trials during the first three hundred years of its existence and clearly had no weapons but the spiritual, Cotton (by his doctrine) must view the church of that period—God's "heavenly *Garden*"—as "over-growne" with idolaters and hypocrites for lack of civil coercion to support and purge it. In truth, however, the church was not overgrown with falsehood during those three hundred years; in fact the "*Garden of Christ* was never fairer since."[36] The primitive church, he believed, was the purest God's church had ever been, yet possessed no civil sword to maintain it.

Reduced to its simplest form, Williams's argument against civil interference in spiritual affairs and against religious persecution in matters of conscience was this: "Christ Jesus never directed his Disciples to the civill Magistrate for help in his cause."[37] Those who set up Constantine, Theodosius, Henry VIII, and other kings and queens of England as antitypes of Israel's kings greatly misconstrued the instructions of Christ "in the very first *institution*"; for Christ himself was the antitype, "the *Spirituall King* of the Church," the new king of Israel. Furthermore, the New Testament nowhere provided a "*patterne* and *president*" for magistrates as "*Keepers* of both *Tables.*" Instead, God now charged the spiritual well-being of the church to the apostles, whom Christ called the "foundation of the Church," and to the "ordinary Officers . . . appointed to be the shepherds or Keepers of the flock of *Christ.*"[38] For Williams, civil oversight of religion could not be justified except by mutilating the New Testament pattern, either by going backward to the Old Testament pattern or forward to the Constantinian pattern. By moving either direction one usurped and denied the authority of Christ.

All of this flew in the face of the conventional wisdom of the day—that "Civill peace cannot stand intire, where religion is corrupted."[39] But the conventional wisdom, Williams believed, was based on a misreading of both the Bible and history. In reading the Bible, its proponents failed to take into account the uniqueness of Old Testament Israel and thus to see that God's literal blessings and cursings on national Israel are now, since Christ, spiritual blessings and curses on spiritual Israel, the church. And thus, because of this distinction, Williams said that he dare not assent to the view that "every sin, even originall sinne hurts the Civill State." Some sins do, he agreed, but "*blindnes* of *minds, hardnes* of *heart, inclination* to choose or worship this or that *God,* this or that *Christ,* beside the true, these hurt not remotely the *Civill* state."[40] Further, the conventional wisdom was based on a misreading of history. Many governments, Williams asserted, have enjoyed long periods of peace and prosperity "notwithstanding their *Religion* is so corrupt, as that there is not the very Name of *Jesus Christ* among them." While God in his "deep *councels* and *times*" does indeed bring both temporal and eternal judgment upon antichristian states, the common maxim that "the *church* and *Commonweale* are like *Hipocrates twins,* weep and laugh, flourish and fade, live and die together" is clearly proven false by "diverse *ages* of temporal prosperity to the *Antichristian Kingdom.*"[41] For Williams a commonwealth was no more or less a commonwealth with or without Christianity in its borders.

What does hurt the state, Williams believed, is the violent suppression of those judged as false teachers and heretics. Persecution for the sake of conscience, not false religion, is the chief cause of civil upheaval and divine judgment. God, Williams believed, could tolerate false worship or no worship in a commonwealth far more than enforced conformity and persecution for conscience. Far from prospering nations that root out false religion by the sword, God actually prospers them, if at all, when they show mercy to oppressed consciences. Williams, in fact, ventured the theory that God destroyed nations for idolatry or false worship only when that was joined with the "bloody *doctrine* of *persecution*" and after God had sent "witnesses" who were rejected and persecuted.[42]

If the state is not endangered by toleration of religious error within its borders, it was equally true for Williams that God's elect people are not endangered by toleration of error in false churches. Christians do not have to worry about magisterial protection or an "arm of flesh" to purge out corruption, for God mightily supplies his spiritual army with every weapon and spiritual shield necessary for accomplishing its mission. Christ's true witnesses certainly possess weapons, but they are weapons more in keeping with the witnesses' lowly and humble condition, weapons that the world laughs at and despises. They have "1. *Christs bloud.* 2. The *Word* of their *testimonie.* 3. Their *owne bloud.*" They are equipped with a "*two edged sword* out of his *mouth*" able to cut out heresy and punish the heretic far beyond any physical punishment or coercion.[43]

The wall of separation that Williams erected between the church and the world, between carnal and spiritual governance, was a direct outgrowth of the profound archetypal shift that marked his theological development. His stress on a New Testament precedent for every church practice, his typological exegesis of scripture that helped elevate the New Testament as the sole pattern, and his conception of Christ's spiritual lordship all combined to create an archetype of the pure church that his contemporaries found heretical. For Williams, God's kingdom was a spiritual kingdom ruled by a spiritual king, with spiritual defenses and weapons, and promised spiritual or heavenly rewards. No matter that the worldly estate of the subjects was poor and despised—so was that of their king; one could not be a true subject, in fact, and seek earthly power, glory, or wealth. The holy commonwealth of the Puritans, Williams felt, provided just such a guise for seeking earthly power, a cloak for human pretensions; the true New Testament church, in contrast, was a sweet refuge for the powerless and downtrodden, a hiding place for the humble and contrite.

IV

By 1643, when he embarked on his first return trip to England, Williams was firmly established in the primitivist vision outlined above. For the rest of his life, both in New England and in Old, this vision stood behind and controlled his numerous engagements with the swirling debates of his time—debates over liberty of conscience, ministerial authority and regulation, and church-state relations.

His stay in England during 1643 and 1644 provides a particularly important example. With the beginning of civil war in 1642, the attention of New Englanders had been trained on the homeland, for they saw in these events the initial stages of the national reformation for which they had sought unsuccessfully and for which they finally had left England to seek for themselves. In 1642 a day of thanksgiving had been declared in Massachusetts for the success of Parliament against the king, and by 1644 twelve special fast days had been observed in Massachusetts. A small but steady stream of New Englanders began returning to support the parliamentary or Puritan cause.[44] Throughout New England excitement grew over the prospects of a Puritan victory in England. Only in Rhode Island, according to the Baptist immigrant Gregory Dexter, did the colonists "stay quiet and drie from the streams of blood spilt by the warr in our native country"; only there did they resist being "consumed with the overzealous fire of the Godly and Christian magistrates."[45] With all eyes fixed on the homeland, Roger Williams found himself, as on a great stage, in a propitious position to hold up his unique primitivist vision before his fellow colonists with new clarity and force.

Williams arrived in England in June 1643 to obtain from Parliament a charter for Rhode Island. Since the preceding October, Parliament had been engaged in open warfare against the forces of Charles I, and by May of 1643 Parliament, due to a military stalemate, was seeking reinforcements from Scotland. Aid from Scotland, however, hinged on

Parliament's active commitment to further ecclesiastical reform, a commitment the Scots thought would move England toward a presbyterian system like their own. Under pressure to acquire military aid from the Scots, Parliament ratified in 1643 a bill for gathering an assembly of clergymen to guide their efforts at reform. As a result the Westminster Assembly of Divines, made up largely of Puritan clergymen, began its work on July 1, 1643.[46]

After some preliminary business Parliament directed the Assembly of Divines, in mid-October, to the business of formulating "such a discipline and government as may be most agreeable to God's holy word and most apt to procure and preserve the peace of the church." Immediately the differences within the assembly emerged and fostered intense debate. The debates gave rise to distinct groups or lobbies that in press and pulpit vociferously advocated the plan of church government they thought most suitable. One of these groups advocated presbyterianism patterned after the Scottish model. Another group, the Independents, advocated a congregational polity. That group was made up primarily of five so-called Dissenting Brethren; they were supported in London by a small group of ministers, including John Archer, John Goodwin, and the New England ministers Hugh Peter and Thomas Weld who were in London at the time. They all were committed to the vision of a gathered church and the communion of saints, while at the same time seeing the need for a national church to preserve the social order.[47] These developments Roger Williams no doubt followed closely, though much of his time was consumed in lobbying to gain his charter, in earning his own living, and for a time, in helping supply wood to London's poor after royalist forces had cut off the supply of coal from Newcastle.[48]

In the midst of intensifying debates in the Westminster Assembly, the five Dissenting Brethren published their *Apologeticall Narration* in January 1644. The authors recounted how they had perceived, before most of their brethren, the "sinful evil of those corruptions in the publique worship and government of the Church" and how that, deprived of the "publique exercise" of their ministries, they had fled to the Netherlands. At first they had seen no further than the "*dark part*" of the Anglican ecclesiology: the "superstitions adjoyned to the worship of God, which have been the common stumbling block and offence of many thousand tender consciences . . . ever since the first Reformation of Religion." But in exile they had had the liberty to search the Bible for the true pattern of church government, to inquire into the "*light part*" or "positive part of *Church-worship* and Government." They had begun "to search out what were the first Apostolique directions, pattern and examples of those Primitive Churches recorded in the New Testament." They had done this objectively, they insisted, because they "had no new Common-wealths to rear, to frame Church-government unto, . . . to cause the least variation . . . from the Primitive pattern." Only the Bible had guided their efforts. They had examined, to be sure, the various Reformed churches and the polity of the New England churches but nonetheless had stood as "unengaged spectators" evaluating these churches and drawing out their practice "nakedly according to the word."[49]

In this objective search for the New Testament pattern, they claimed to have found "cleare and certaine" principles "not onely *fundamentall* and essential to the being of a Church, but *superstructory* also for the well-being of it." Indeed, they were confident that scripture contained "rules and ruled cases for all occasions whatsoever" if they were but able to discern them. Such "rules," they believed, provided for autonomous congregations, "ruled by their own Elders," retaining the right and duty of discipline "within themselves," and subject to no presbyteries or assemblies except in an advisory capacity. Scripture was clear in these "rules," they felt. At the same time, however, they were aware of their own frailty in the task of discernment, and thus added that in all points where they "saw not a cleare resolution from scripture, example, or direction," judgment should be held back "untill God should give . . . further light." In setting forth this pattern, they rejected both Separatism and Presbyterianism: "We believe the truth to lye and consist in a *middle way* betwixt that which is falsely charged on us, *Brownisme;* and that which is the contention of these times, the *authoritative Presbyteriall Government* in all the subordinations and proceedings of it."[50]

Though each congregation was to be autonomous and administer its own discipline, each was accountable to the state in the case of gross error. Heresy and schism, they envisioned, would be kept down in most cases, not by the acts of an ecclesiastical board, but by censure and withdrawal of communion on the part of other churches. The role of the magistrates, then, would be to "assist and back the sentence" of the churches. In this way, the Dissenting Brethren believed, they would give as much or more power to the magistrates than "the principles of the Presbiteriall government will suffer them to yeeld."[51] This stress on the key role of magisterial power in reforming and maintaining the church was a central theme in the *Apologeticall Narration.* "The crucial significance of this tract in the debate," according to David Walker, "is to be found in the fact that what it offers to parliament as an alternative to theocratic Presbyterianism is an at least equally theocratic Congregationalism."[52]

The response sparked by publication of the *Apologeticall Narration* was immediate and intense. The first counterattack came in the same month from the Scottish commissioners to the assembly. In their *Reformation of Church-Government in Scotland, Cleered from Some Prejudices,* they argued, in a manner similar to that of the Dissenting Brethren, that the Church of Scotland had been reformed using only the New Testament churches as pattern and guide. In their churches, as a result, "there was to be seen a representation of the Primitive and Apostolike times and a new resurrection from the dead."[53] Parliament's duty, they believed, was to further the cause of reform by setting up presbyteries throughout England according to the divine pattern.

It was in the midst of this debate between Independents and Presbyterians concerning the type of church government that Parliament should impose that Roger Williams published his *Queries of Highest Consideration,* challenging the reform programs of both groups. Appearing in early February, the tract addressed a number of the concerns commonly treated in sectarian pamphlet literature: it rejected imposition of the Solemn League and Covenant, appealed for complete religious toleration, and argued for the Separatist view of an autonomous, gathered church. But beyond these particular issues, Williams's primitivist ecclesiology led him to focus on a more foundational issue: the legitimacy of any program for ecclesiastical renewal that gave civil magistrates authority over Christ's church. As he had done earlier in the Bay Colony, Williams challenged the very assumption underlying the agendas of both the Dissenting Brethren and the Presbyterians—the assumption that true religion must be established and upheld by the state. Parliament, he reminded them, was simply the representative of the populace; establishing religion and carrying out reform by the "representative Common-weale" of the nation simply subjected the church to the vagaries of political fortune and, in the process, imposed the will of the unregenerate masses on the holy spouse of Christ. How can one subject the high and holy things of God, he asked, to "the vain uncertain and changeable Mutations of this present evil world?" Magisterial reform, he concluded, had made England a religious weathercock, whirling about rapidly with the changing political currents. It had been responsible for spiritual rape "in forcing the consciences of all men to one Worship, which a stronger arm and Sword may soon (as formerly) arise to alter."[54]

Simple historical observation, Williams believed, provided overwhelming evidence that all "[human] Reformations are fallible." The Independents, who were arguing for a limited and carefully defined toleration, had perceived this fallibility to some degree. They believed that, with the "further light" God was revealing, many had seen the error of their previous convictions and that, as they received more light, they might be forced to change their views again. Their own congregational polity, they believed, was part of this light; many were agreeing that it "was the Primitive Way, and is the purest, and [that] the Presbyterian Way is but a step thereto, and will rest here as its center, and end in this as its perfection."[55] Because human perception of religious truth was often dim, clouded by human traditions and inherent limitations, some toleration should be exercised toward those who received new, clearer insights into the scriptural pattern. In 1645 the anonymous Independent author of *The Ancient Bounds* queried the Presbyterians:

> Why may you not in a while see cause to exchange your present judgment for a better? Why may there not be more truth yet behind? Is that which is perfect come, or are we come yet to that measure of the stature of the fulnesse of Christ? . . . May not errors for a time, have the credit of Truths? As many Episcopall Doctrines now rejected, might be instanced in; hath not every truth its set time, the *fulness of time* to be born into the world.[56]

Despite such an insistence on the fallibility of present human judgments, the Independents still envisioned a fairly uniform religious establishment, with toleration granted for their congregational "light" but not for the "light" of the Separatists, Baptists, or other radicals.

Williams's sense of the finitude of human judgment ran deeper. Addressing the Dissenting Brethren and Scottish commissioners, and noting their many godly characteristics, he asked:

> Have there not been as excellent and heavenly Reformers as your selves . . . whose professed Reformation you now dislike? Who shall outshine many of the Waldensian Reformers for Holynesse, Zeale, patience? Where is, or hath that pretious man been found, who hath (for personall excellencies) outshined *Luther?* and who shall o'retop those glorious Cedars *Bishops, Doctors,* &c burnt for Christ Jesus in Queen *Maries* days?[57]

They were all godly people and "excellent reformers, full of zeal for the true sevice of God," but their work "now seems to be beside the first Pattern." What makes present-day reformers, he asked, so certain that they are exempt from such errors and limitations in judgment? The fact is, he asserted, that even God's most beloved people often have been slow in perceiving and obeying God's will.

Throughout his writings, Williams reiterated this theme as he argued for complete liberty of conscience. For example, against Cotton's position that doctrinal fundamentals are so clear that a person who did not accept them after one or two admonitions would be sinning against his conscience, Williams asserted that "Fundamentals of Christian worship

[are] not so easie and sure." Godly, regenerate people, despite their "inward and secret *fellowship* with God," may live and die in "false *Ministries* of *Word* and *Prayer*" even though they are admonished repeatedly and have turned on them the bright light of God's word. Williams noted that Cotton and the New England ministers, though they now had renounced the English practice of "common" prayer, earlier had practiced it in England in the face of many arguments against it, arguments that had seemed weak and unconvincing at the time. How can they presumptuously assume, therefore, that truth can be found so easily and, further, that religious uniformity can be imposed and persecution proceed on such grounds? Williams concluded that all of God's "own dear People" are often "sad, drowsie and unkinde" in their "*answer* to the *knocks* and *calls*" of Christ and that "in all their awakening acknowledge how sleightly they have listened to the checks of their own *consciences.*"[58] As a result, both magistrates and clergymen must be extremely cautious in dividing the sound from the unsound, the obedient from the disobedient, the orthodox from the heretic, for all have a certain spiritual sluggishness about them and blind spots that may be the object of "further light."

All of these considerations led Williams to reject the Puritan vision of ecclesiastical reform conducted by magisterial pronouncement. The strongest factor was lack of any scriptural precedent. "What Precept or Pattern," he asked, "hath the Lord Jesus left you in his last Will and Testament for your *Synod* or Assembly of Divines?" The usual proof text cited for such a practice, he noted, is Acts 15–16, which records the proceedings of the Jerusalem Council; but it refers only to the collaboration of individual congregations and is most certainly not "a Pattern for a Nation or Kingdome . . . to reforme or forme a Religion." He further questioned use of the name itself: "in what part of Christs Testament is found that title, *The Assembly of Divines?*" The title, if used at all, should refer to all the children of God as they assembled together in particular congregations.[59]

The reform agenda of the Independents and Presbyterians, in Williams's view, mutilated the scriptural pattern in numerous ways. The most serious distortion was the conclusion that they were justified in waging a holy war to further reformation. Many Presbyterians and Independents believed not only that the national welfare depended on establishment of pure religion but that, through such efforts, the millennial age or "latter-day glory" of the church would dawn. Thus when conflict arose with Charles I, they quickly interpreted the parliamentary cause as a holy crusade against forces of evil threatening both church and nation. Many interpreted the war as an advanced phase of God's great campaign against the forces of Antichrist.

Williams decried such views. He saw them as the inevitable results of mixing the temporal and spiritual kingdoms. The fortunes of Christ's kingdom, he believed, depended not at all on the fortunes of a particular nation. Against the advocates of holy war, he wrote: "since the Lamb of God and Prince of Peace hath not in his Testament given us a pattern, Precept or Promise, for the undertaking of a civill War for his sake: we Querie how with comfort to your Souls you may incourage the English Treasure to be Exhausted, and the English Blood to be spilt for the Cause of Christ?"[60] To those saying that Christ's "Kingdome then was not of this world, but now it is or shall be," Williams pointed to the scriptures promising only suffering and persecution for all who *live godly in Christ Jesus.*" Christ's saints did not reign in this corrupt world but only in the heavenly kingdom. The apocalyptic battles of Daniel and Revelation— often identified with contemporary military activity by Puritan ex- egetes—symbolized for Williams only spiritual battles waged with purely spiritual weapons. In Williams's view, John the Apostle spoke of no "other ammunition and artillerie, used by the Saints, but what we find in *Pauls* Christian Magazine, *Ephes.* 6."[61]

Williams strongly opposed, in most of its major features, the method propounded by the official Puritan clergy for restoration of the primitive order of the church. Purification and regulation of the church, he be- lieved, were not properly the task of Parliament, the Westminster Assembly of Divines, the New England general court, or any other institu- tion outside the particular congregations of saints. Allowing such bodies to lead reform violated the scriptural pattern, underestimated the finitude of human judgment, forced consciences, and promoted violent "holy" wars. In contrast, Williams saw the task of restoration as God's alone; ultimately only God could repristinate the church according to its original pattern.

V

Though the positive work of restoration was God's alone, God had used, throughout the centuries of the church's dissolution, an elite group of "witnesses" to carry out the negative part of restoration. Drawing on the distinction between the "darke" and "light" parts of reformation made by the Dissenting Brethren, Williams restricted all efforts in the present age to the "darke" part. "The Sufferings of Gods Witnesses since the Apostacie," he wrote, "have . . . been only right against the darke part, the Inventions, Abominations and Usurpations of Anti-christ." The "light part" or actual restoration was not a present possibility, for each succeeding reformation was still discovering and decrying more corruption, still reforming the previous reformations, and in this uncertainty and instability all positive efforts at reformation were incomplete and misguided. The witnesses could do no more than attack error, denounce corrupt practices, and await the time when the "*light* part would . . . arise in its brightnesse."[62]

In using the term "witness" Williams drew on the apocalyptic imagery of Revelation interpreted by the English martyrological tradition. He referred specifically to Revelation 11:3–12 which speaks of two witnesses who testify on Christ's behalf for 1,260 days after the destruction of the holy city. Using historicist exegesis, Williams interpreted the two witnesses as actual persons who had earned the title of Christ's martyrs or witnesses by their sufferings or deaths. He specifically identified these witnesses with the many leaders of religious dissent since the fall of the church—Wyclif, Hus, Luther, John Foxe, and the Separatists, for example.[63]

The "witnesses" were called to their vocation by God's "immediate" or direct inspiration. Throughout the many centuries of the church's wilderness exile they had testified courageously against antichristian error and often had been driven into hiding or slain for their testimony. At the same time, however, many of the witnesses had "more or less submitted to Anti-christ" by not separating themselves completely from false churches and corrupt worship; many of them had been "ignorant of . . . that holy way of worship, which Christ himselfe at first appointed." But despite the many errors of the witnesses, God in his mercy had hidden their failures and accomplished much good through them.

> All the *wisedome, mercy, goodnesse,* and *piety* that is in us, is but a *drop* to the *Ocean* of that which is in the *Father* of *mercies,* who with infinite *pity* and *patience,* passeth by the *ignorances* and *weaknesses* of his Children. Hence *Luther* and other *Monks, Cranmer* and other *Bishops, Calvin* and other *Presbyterians,* God hath graciously covered their *Failings,* and accepted his owne *Grace* of good *Desires,* good *Affections* and *Endeavors,* though many wayes defiled with sin.[64]

Though Williams believed that Luther, Calvin, and other "precious Witnesses" had not erected churches "after the first pattern (as they conceived they did)," he did believe that they had been mighty witnesses against the enemies of truth.

In contrast to Antichrist's kingdom with its power, might, and temporal glory, the witnesses of Christ always appeared heretical, schismatic, and ineffective. In keeping with the spiritual nature of his kingdom, God always had "chosen the *poore* of the *World:* and the *Witnesses* of Truth . . . are cloathed in *sackcloth,* not in *Silke* and *Sattin.*" In all periods of history they had received the same charge: "You are *Hereticks, Schismaticks, factious, seditious, rebellious.*" As a result they seldom enjoyed visible success in their work; all temporal success, in fact, was irrelevant to their cause, for only faithfulness and spiritual success was important. While all those who had wandered off after the Beast reveled in their dependence on the temporal sword, in persecution of dissenters, and in magisterial might, the witnesses depended solely on the "two-edged *sword*" of God's Word. All their victories contrasted sharply with those of this world, "for when they were slaine and slaughtered, yet then they conquer."[65] They proclaimed no temporal judgments on nations and rulers as the Old Testament prophets did, and they did not stir up rulers to persecute antichristians as the leaders of "Christendom" had done since the time of Constantine. Instead, they played only a small role in the restoration of the church, a role carried out in patient suffering, courageous testimony, and humble reliance on Christ who set the supreme example of perseverance in suffering.

Roger Williams's own experience of suffering and persecution convinced him that he had been chosen as one of God's witnesses. In the opening pages of *Mr. Cottons Letter Lately Printed, Examined and Answered,* published in early February 1644 as a companion piece to *Queries of Highest Consideration,* Williams gave an extended account of his banishment from the Bay Colony. In preaching against the patent, against the tendering of civil oaths to the unregenerate, and against the laxity of unseparated churches, Williams said that he had served as "a faithful Watchman on the walls to sound the Trumpet and give the Alarum." When the people did not heed the call, he then had withdrawn voluntarily from all the churches "resolved to continue in those evils," hoping that "the act of the Lord Jesus sounding forth in me (a poore despised Rams horn) . . . shall in his owne holy season cast down the strength and confidence of those inventions of men in the worshipping of the true and living God." After his withdrawal from the churches, however, he was banished from the colony and "exposed to the miseries, poverties, necessities, wants, debts, hardships of Sea and Land." And, like most faithful witnesses throughout history, he was charged with bringing such suffering upon himself by clinging stubbornly to heretical and inflammatory views.[66] But through it all he gained a deep sense of being chosen for the honored task of testifying on behalf of the gospel. "It pleased God," he wrote, "to lay a *Command* on my *Conscience* to come in as his poor Witnesse in this great Cause." Shortly after his banishment, when Winthrop asked him, "What have you gained by your new-found practices?" he replied: "I have gained the honor of one of his poor witnesses, though in sack-cloth." In this role he hoped to "be ready not only to be banished, but to die in New England for the name of the Lord Jesus."[67]

Williams understood his work as writer and controversialist to be an essential part of his function as a witness. He wrote and debated, it seems, not so much to win people to his viewpoint, for he was not naïvely optimistic about the chances of that, but to support and strengthen the resolve of fellow witnesses. Williams hoped that by boldly controverting the generally accepted ideas of the godly commonwealth—magisterial reform, religious uniformity, and a millennial rule of the saints—he would inspire conviction and courage in other witnesses and stir up boldness in their testimony.

In stressing the witnesses' part in the "*darke* part" of restoration, Williams differed sharply from the Presbyterians and Independents in the Westminster Assembly and from defenders of the New England Way. Looking to the holy commonwealth as the overarching model for reform, Puritan divines believed that toleration of religious error in the nation would cause civil disorder and, more important, hinder the progress of restoration and invite God's judgment. The Independents *did* argue for a limited toleration but still thought within a national framework. Williams, in contrast, argued that complete liberty, not uniformity, furthered the cause of restoration. The illicit mixing of church and state had corrupted the church in the first place, and, he thought, such a mixture presently impeded restoration. Liberty of conscience would give the witnesses— Christ's true reformers—freedom to attack corruption and to expose all the religious error shielded under the persecuting sword of popes, magistrates, and parliaments. Liberty would speed the work of restoration by giving the witnesses freer course in dividing truth from error and lifting up the scriptural pattern of the church from amid the jumbled mixtures of church and state. Liberty, in short, would enable the witnesses to complete their testimony in preparation for "the bright Appearance of the Lord Jesus" and the final restoration of the church. By "bright Appearance" Williams referred not to a personal appearance of Christ on the earth, but rather to a mighty flash of his "brightness," bringing mass conversions and a prolonged golden age of the church.[68]

VI

Throughout his life, Williams continued to ponder the great issues of the day, always confounding error when he saw it and steadfastly bearing witness to the truth as he knew it. A sharp and ironic sense of the past enhanced his vision. He saw clearly that human beings possessed an extraordinary capacity for naïve and inflexible certitude in religious matters and that, most often, this smug certitude became a cloak for self-serving ends and a justification for mistreating others. Divine truth, he believed, was not easily discovered. Across the centuries it had become intricately entangled in a morass of "human invention," diluted by the vested interests of popes and potentates, and covered over by the glitter of worldly preferment. Only in the rough and tumble of free expression and debate could recovery of the "old" and "pure" way proceed. But even under such free conditions, Williams was convinced, recovery always would be stifled, for the corruption and loss had been too great and the human capacity for conceit and blindness was too pervasive. God alone could perform the great and final act of recovery.

Meanwhile, until that time came, Williams thought it not too much to hope that John Cotton and his brethren in New England, who already had received great beams of "further light," might receive still another one—this one enabling them to bear with each other in their differences and breathe the common air together in peace.

Finally, looking ahead, we see that Williams and Cotton provide paradigms for subsequent uses of the restoration theme in American history. For Williams, the radical finitude of human existence, entailing inevitable failures in understanding and action, makes restoration of necessity an open-ended concept. The absolute, universal ideal existed for Williams without question. But the gap between the universal and the particular, between the absolute and the finite, was so great that it precluded any one-on-one identification of the particular with the universal. Closing the gap would come only at God's behest and initiative. In the meantime, the best one could do was *approximate* the universal, an approximation that occurred only through a diligent search for truth. For this reason, freedom was absolutely essential. In taking this position, Williams prefigured a whole host of American restorationists, including Isaac Backus, Barton W. Stone, and Thomas Jefferson, among others. The affinity of Williams with Jefferson is particularly notable. Though coming at the question of toleration with strikingly different interests and motives, both were restorationists who sought to approximate the universal embedded in first times, through free and open debate. Williams surely would have agreed with Jefferson, when he proclaimed in "A Bill for Establishing Religious Freedom" in Virginia, "that truth is great and will prevail if left to herself; that she is the proper and sufficient antagonist to error, and has nothing to fear from the conflict unless by human interposition disarmed of her natural weapons, free argument and debate; errors ceasing to be dangerous when it is permitted freely to contradict them."[69]

On the other hand, the gap between the particular and the universal, in Cotton's view, essentially had been closed. New England Congregationalists, Cotton thought, had retrieved the perfections of first times and had embodied those perfections in their churches. The restoration ideal for Cotton, therefore, was fundamentally a closed construct which precluded dissent and debate and produced instead coercion and repression. In this, Cotton prefigured a tradition of American restorationists radically different from the Williams-Backus-Stone-Jefferson variety.

Ironically, however, many in this absolutist, coercive tradition began their restoration careers employing the restoration ideal as a tool of dissent and a means to freedom. This is true of both individuals and denominations that finally absolutized their dissent and the grounds of their freedom. Thus, for example, in the Baptist trajectory, one moves from an Isaac Backus to a James R. Graves in little more than a century. In the Churches of Christ, one moves from the freedom-loving Barton W. Stone to an Arthur Crihfield with his *Heretic Detector* in a matter of years. And Roger Williams, who despaired of a complete restoration apart from a decisive act of God, finally and ironically had his vision fulfilled in the Mormon prophet, Joseph Smith, who took a similar position but claimed that God had acted decisively in him and that, through him, the restoration was now complete. Even Thomas Jefferson's vision, which denied a one-on-one identification of the universal with the particular, was fully capable of ironic transformation. Thus, Benjamin Palmer could defend the Confederacy on the grounds that it was a virtual repristination of ancient, universal ideals, including the political ideals of the American founding fathers. And other Americans such as Andrew Jackson, James K. Polk, John L. O'Sullivan, and William McKinley viewed as a universal maxim the judgment that no particular could fully express the universal: then, ironically, they identified this universal with a particular state.

The remainder of this book is an explication of these two versions of the restoration vision originally propounded on these shores by John Cotton and Roger Williams. Subsequent chapters also inquire how the vision represented by Williams evolved in time into a closed, coercive system. To begin this inquiry, we turn first to the Baptist tradition.

FOUR

The Ancient Landmarks: Baptist Primitivism from the Separates to James R. Graves

The primitivist impulse, as we have seen, is the longing to return to an idealized, primordial past, to a time when things were pure, unworn, and unobscured by willful human embellishments. The irony, however, is that the effort to restore primitive or first-time ideals may result in either a call for untrammeled liberty or a demand for narrow conformity. As we have seen, the Puritan standing order in New England, with its deep primitivist undergirdings, restricted religious liberty and expelled dissenters, while Roger Williams, an equally ardent primitivist, insisted on complete liberty as the most healthy environment for pure religion.

The Christian primitivism that in various forms has coursed through American culture in the subsequent three centuries exhibits this dual tendency. On the one hand, incessant appeal to primitive liberties has been a powerful force against arbitrary and tyrannical power, whether in governments or in churches; on the other hand, the sense of innocence and self-righteousness that almost inevitably results from identification with the primordium has led in turn to coercion and curtailment of freedom.

I

The Baptist tradition, the subject of this chapter, provides an illuminating case study of these dynamics. From the inception of the Baptist tradition in early seventeenth-century Holland and England, Baptists were an illegal and persecuted minority, and from their ranks arose, not surprisingly, some of the earliest and most forceful arguments for complete liberty of conscience in matters of religion. Roger Williams, a Baptist for only four months, borrowed and developed these arguments in early New England, and they became mainstays of the Baptist dissenting tradition in America. From John Clarke of Rhode Island, whose *Ill News from New England* (1651) publicized the persecution of Baptists in the early Bay Colony, to the Separate Baptist Isaac Backus, who campaigned tirelessly for religious liberty in the revolutionary epoch, Baptists in colonial America played an important role in the complex and astonishing shift from religious establishment to disestablishment, or to use Sidney Mead's phrase, from "coercion to persuasion."[1]

Particularly under the impact of the Great Awakening which marked the beginning of their meteoric growth, Baptists more and more demanded freedom from the restraints of traditional civil and ecclesiastical laws. The free stream of God's grace, the revivalists felt, must not be dammed up by human laws and institutions. "The command of heaven is, *Let them run down,*" Isaac Backus asserted, "put no obstruction in their way. No, rather be in earnest to remove everything that hinders their free course." The dominant theme among Baptists was that "truth certainly could do well enough if she were once left to shift for herself,"[2] a contention they surely shared with America's founding fathers. Though the Baptists held deep convictions about the bounds of God's truth and the shape of the true church, they were concerned—at least in their rhetoric—more with lifting old human bounds than with establishing new ones.

The triumph of religious liberty and disestablishment in the early national period, coupled with the emergence of the Baptists as one of the largest denominations in America, brought about inevitable shifts in the Baptist outlook, however. In their intense competition with Methodists, Presbyterians, and "Christians," especially in the southern frontier regions, Baptists solidified doctrinal differences, staked out and defended boundaries with passionate invective, and upheld familial pride with all the zeal of one still insecure in her newfound status. On a preaching tour in Virginia and North Carolina, Isaac Backus wrote, for example, that the "Methodists have followed the Baptists thro' the country with much zeal, but they earnestly strike against the most essential doctrines of the gospel. . . . To hold up light against their errors, and others, is of great importance in this time when many have an ear to hear."[3] Though Backus still had confidence that unfettered truth needed nothing more than the spirited preaching of Baptists in order to prevail, the tactics of Baptists grew more harsh and authoritarian. In the decades that followed, many Baptists, to be sure, were a part of the fragile and ever-shifting pattern of denominational cooperation that developed, but, as Mead noted, "finally each sect stood by itself against all others, a law unto itself in defense of its peculiar tenets which it implicitly held as absolute."[4] In such an atmosphere, Baptists often transformed the reality of religious freedom into a mythology of freedom: the rhetoric of freedom continued, but it often meant in actual fact that non-Baptists were free only to join the true church or to remain in error.

Nowhere in the Baptist tradition is this transformation seen more starkly than in James R. Graves and the Landmark Baptist movement he inspired. By the mid-1850s Graves had become the most powerful person among Baptists in the Southwest and for over three decades remained a vituperative and unyielding champion of the Baptist cause against all non-Baptist denominations. The central thrust of his extensive writings was "to establish the fact in the minds of all, who will give me an impartial hearing, that Baptist churches are the churches of Christ, and that they *alone* hold, and have alone ever held, and preserved the doctrine of the gospel in all ages since the ascension of Christ."[5] Graves supported his sharp exclusivism at almost every point by powerful primitivist appeals. In his view, Christ founded his church and left in the New Testament a precise, finely detailed blueprint for its organization, worship, ordinances, and practice; since he was its only king and lawgiver, human beings had no business changing or adding anything. Any religious society, therefore, "not organized according to the pattern of the Jerusalem church" could not sustain any claim to be a church of Christ. On this basis Graves attacked pedo-baptists and Campbellites as heretical innovators, rejecting their "societies" as true churches and their ministers, ordinances, and practices as invalid. All such churches had been organized since the primitive or first age of the church. In contrast, Christ had founded the true church—the Baptist church—in the apostolic period and had preserved it without interruption through all the antichristian darkness of the ages.[6] Graves appealed therefore for Baptists of his day to close ranks and cease the dangerous practices of accepting "alien immersions," permitting "pulpit affiliation," and encouraging union meetings.

In his constricted ecclesiology, Graves never lost the traditional Baptist rhetoric of freedom. Instead, he put it to work as a polemical tool against non-Baptist denominations. Not only were Methodist, Anglican, Presbyterian, "Christian," and Roman Catholic "societies" not true churches, but in fact they were un-American and inimical to the progress of civil liberty. "Pure religion,—not *priestism,*" Graves said, "is the only guarantee and conservator of civil and religious liberty."[7] Though such "anti-republican" groups had a right to exist, they could further the cause of liberty and defeat tyranny only by embracing the Baptists' "biblical" model. Thus, in the primitivist Landmark system, Graves replaced the ideal of freedom with conformity and the unfettered search for religious truth with the duty to embrace his own version of that truth. Though legal

81

coercion was no longer a ready possibility and indeed repugnant to Baptists, one could not escape the conclusion that being a true American meant being a Baptist.

II

James Graves and the Landmark Baptists promulgated their virulent sectarianism within a pervasive primitivist or restorationist framework. The primitivist outlook was not an isolated phenomenon in the nineteenth-century South or in the Baptist tradition itself. The virgin land of America spread out in vast array before the westward-moving settlers, giving them a sense of the new, the fresh, and the innocent. And the denominations that migrated with the settlers found their most appealing message in the simple teachings of Jesus and the practice of the primitive church. They found no better way of outdistancing their competitors for the souls of people than arguing that their own church conformed most closely to the pure biblical pattern. As John Nevin wrote in irritation in 1849, every sect sought to appear "aboriginal, self sprung from the Bible, or through the Bible from the skies."[8]

This atmosphere certainly provided a hothouse for the caustic primitivism of the Landmark Baptists in middle Tennessee, but the seeds actually had been planted over two centuries earlier at the beginning of the Baptist tradition. As an outgrowth of English Puritanism in the early seventeenth century, the Baptists shared the intense concern for the "restitution of true religion" that lay at the heart of Puritan dissent. They shared with English congregationalists the desire to "search out what were the first Apostolique directions, pattern and examples of those Primitive Churches recorded in the New Testament, as that sacred pillar of fire to guide us."[9] They shared with John Cotton and his New England colleagues the disdain for all religious practices "devised and ordained by men." For example, John Smyth, the Puritan Separatist turned Baptist, wrote that he could never rest until he had reduced "the worship and ministery of the Church, to the primitive Apostolic institution from which as yet it is so far distant." And Thomas Helwys, leader of the General Baptist group that broke with Smyth in 1610, wrote that only the Baptist position fully duplicated the apostolic practice of adult immersion upon a profession of faith.[10] Though the early Baptists were divided between General Baptists (holding a "general" atonement) and Particular Baptists (holding a "particular" or "limited" atonement), both groups shared such primitivist assumptions.

In America, the Particular Baptists became the dominant group by the early eighteenth century, with their center of activity in the middle colonies. In 1707 five of these churches united to form the Philadelphia Baptist Association, and this association set the pattern for the mainstream of Baptist life for a century. The primitivism of its English Puritan ancestors continued, though mitigated somewhat by the strong creedalism that developed. The Philadelphia Confession of Faith, a modified version of the Westminster Confession, along with *A Short Treatise of Church Discipline,* exercised great influence over the Particular or Regular Baptist churches in the eighteenth century. At the same time, however, Particular Baptists held up the Bible as the "only rule of faith and obedience" and, in theory at least, gave it precedence over any human creed. All assumed that confessional standards served no other purpose than upholding the doctrine and polity of the primitive church.[11] On this basis, Particular Baptists in America advanced significantly beyond their English forerunners by developing a strong system of association among churches. Though the Philadelphia Confession specified that the association exercised no "church-power" and should not infringe on the autonomy of each congregation, the associations were attacked frequently by churches fearing a usurpation of their freedom. Particular Baptists sometimes supported the associational pattern with appeals to scriptural precedent, but they most often defended that pattern as an expedient means of fostering the spiritual unity of small churches facing a hostile culture.[12]

With the strong creedalism and growing pattern of association, the early primitivism was softened but certainly not lost. A striking example appears in Morgan Edwards, prominent preacher in Philadelphia in the 1760s and early Baptist historian. Edwards combined an irenic spirit uncharacteristic of most Baptists of the time with an ardent primitivism. On the one hand, he minimized the differences between Baptist groups such as the Regulars and Separates, stressing that believers' baptism was the only essential common denominator; on the other hand, he found in the New Testament a detailed blueprint for church order and practice that must be followed exactly in order to have a "church complete."

In what was probably the first book written in America on the polity and practice of Baptist churches, Edwards outlined in careful detail and with copious scriptural references "the customs of primitive churches."[13] Every aspect of church life, Edwards insisted, must take its rise from "the Bible, and the Bible only." Regarding church officers, scripture authorized "*teachers; elders; deacons; deaconesses;* and *clerks.*" The number of each could vary, but the New Testament example dictated that a church should "have more than one of each sort."[14] Regarding church ordinances or rites, Edwards listed thirteen that were "of divine original and perpetual continuance in the church": baptism, the Lord's Supper, laying on of hands, the right hand of fellowship, the love feast, foot washing, the kiss of charity, anointing the sick, collecting for the saints, fasting, feasts, funerals, and marriage. And where specific instructions were given for observing the rites, they were to be followed. The Lord's Supper, for example, should be observed "every Lord's day evening" just like the "Primitive Christians": the New Testament precedent prescribed the evening, and even the very name "supper" required it, for "any other time makes it the Lord's breakfast or the Lord's dinner."[15] The collection for the saints should be taken on the first day of the week because scripture issued a "command and example" to do so. Women should not speak in the church because "it is unprecedented in scripture." Church members in general were "tied to rules" and bound to scriptural "orders" regarding all behavior toward fellow Christians, toward the world, and toward sister churches. Even associations, of which Edwards was a strong supporter, were authorized by the gospel for the well-being of the churches.[16]

The fact that Edwards's book was not adopted officially by the Philadelphia Association, as he hoped it would be, suggests that not everyone shared its primitivist rigor; at the same time, however, the book provides telling insight into the restorationist impulse that coursed through the "Philadelphia tradition."[17]

III

The ecclesiastical pattern set by the Philadelphia Association exercised wide influence in the eighteenth century, but it was not the primary stream that fed the primitivism of the Landmark Baptists in the nineteenth century. The primary influence came through the Separate Baptist movement that emerged out of the Great Awakening in New England and spread rapidly throughout the South after 1755.[18] What was interpreted as outpourings of God's grace in the preaching of such men as Jonathan Edwards and George Whitefield brought about the dramatic conversion of thousands of people and caused great furor in the Congregational churches of New England's standing order. Three parties emerged: (1) an "Old Light" faction opposing the revivalists' extreme emotionalism, the insistence on a dramatic conversion experience, and the practice of lay preaching and itineracy; (2) a *conservative* "New Light" faction recognizing the work of God in the revival but seeking to curb the pietistic excesses; and (3) a *radical* "New Light" faction that withdrew and formed separate churches rather than remain in ones tolerating an unregenerate membership and squelching the free work of the Spirit.

The *radical* New Lights or Separates wanted overthrow, not reform, of the old system. They sought to restore the golden age of the early Puritan era, the time when churches required a testimony of saving faith from everyone seeking membership. The effect of this pietistic awakening was to make the individual believer, not the educated clergy of the established church, the new source of authority. Isaac Backus, an early Separate leader, put it bluntly: "The common people claim as good right to judge and act for themselves in matters of religion as civil rulers or the learned clergy."[19] They could take upon themselves such a right because they now saw that one learned divine truth in the conversion experience and by the power of the Spirit, not through the accumulated wisdom of human tradition or learning.

From the ranks of these Separate Congregationalists emerged the Separate Baptists, led chiefly by Backus. Many Separates became Baptists because the practice of infant baptism worked against the ideal of a pure church composed only of the regenerate. Separate congregations therefore earned the label "nurseries of baptists." Further, Separates were troubled by not finding in the New Testament any express command for baptizing infants. To embrace believers' baptism thus seemed to many a logical stopping place in their quest, so much so that for a time, according to Backus, it appeared that all Separates would become Baptists.[20] Backus himself accepted believers' baptism by immersion in 1751 and in 1756 formed a Separate Baptist church in Middleborough, Massachusetts.

At the heart of the Separate Baptist faith, like that of the Separate Congregationalists, was the unmediated experience of salvation through the work of the Spirit. Such experience left little room for human conventions, clerical rule, or civil regulation. The result was patent disregard for denominational conformity and a passion for conforming their Christianity to the original practice of Jesus and the apostles. The "New Light" experience thus threw open the doors for overturning and restoring. They therefore elevated the Bible as the "perfect rule" for the church and viewed with suspicion creeds and confessions of faith as detriments to individual liberty. The Separate Baptist John Leland, for example, though a moderate Calvinist, denied following any guide but "the wind of heaven"; creeds, he added, were nothing but a "Virgin Mary between the souls of men and the scriptures": they "check any further pursuit after truth, confine the mind into a particular way of reasoning, and give rise to frequent separations."[21] Separate Baptists above all sought freedom in the Spirit. Though the Bible provided the only rule for proper church order and was to be followed carefully, many of these Baptists extended a spirit of mutual forbearance regarding the precise details of biblical form lest rigid patterns lead back to the conformity they had sought so ardently to escape.[22] In this, the Separates prefigured the "Christian" movement of Barton W. Stone which, by the early nineteenth century, they would influence profoundly.

Despite this forbearance, however, concern for the form of the visible church stayed near the forefront in Separate Baptist thinking. Backus focused the issue when he stated that "there are things not essential to salvation which are necessary in the visible building [of the church]."[23] This primitivist concern for the ancient forms emerges clearly as a motivation for Backus's extensive history of the early Baptists in America. In the preface to volume 2, he claimed that the New Testament reveals only one form of church order: in the apostolic age churches were constituted through baptism by immersion after a profession of faith; each congregation was entirely autonomous; and each was overseen by bishops acting more as servants than as rulers. But with the rise of infant baptism, the use of "heathen philosophy" to interpret scripture, and secular rulers to enforce church teaching, a dark period of "antichristian apostasy" ensued. During this long night of departure from the New Testament, however, God was not without witness to divine truth. Instead, such groups as the "Waldenses, Petrobuscians, Wicklifites, and Hussites" bore witness to God's church as "an assembly of true and real saints" opposed to using secular power for its advancement. And in the present day, Backus concluded, despite the continuing "inventions of men," the strife, the "endless confusion," and "contests for preeminence," a restoration was occurring: a "great and effectual door is now opened for terminating these disputes, and for a return to the primitive purity and liberty of the Christian church. To trace out the evil effects of apostasy, and to promote . . . such a return, is the great design of this and the former volume."[24] The primitivist outlook stated so clearly here by Backus remained a central feature of the Separate Baptist movement.

The most spectacular phase of the Separate Baptist awakening occurred not in New England but in the South. The amazing growth of this movement throughout the South derived largely from the work of two powerful and tireless evangelists, Shubal Stearns (1706–1771) and his brother-in-law Daniel Marshall (1706–1784).[25] They moved from Connecticut to northwestern Virginia in 1754. Then a year later, with a group of fifteen other Separate Baptists, they settled at Sandy Creek, North Carolina, near the Virginia border. The settlers immediately formed a church. By the time the Sandy Creek Association was organized three years later, it included three churches with over nine hundred members. Morgan Edwards, who visited the area in 1772, wrote that the Sandy Creek church "in 17 years, is become mother, grandmother, and great grandmother to 42 Churches, from which sprang 125 ministers, many of which are ordained and support the sacred character as well as any set of clergy in America." He added that "all the separate baptists sprang hence: not only eastward towards the sea, but westward towards the great river Mississippi, northward to Virginia and southward to South Carolina and Georgia." The Sandy Creek church was the fountainhead, and "her converts were as drops of morning dew."[26]

This remarkable growth resulted in large part from the fervency and drive of the uncultured evangelists and their ability to identify closely with the uprooted and often disinherited settlers who poured into the backwoods of the Piedmont region. The Baptist message was "well adapted to the conditions of us in these parts," said one of the preachers, "being chiefly on vital and experimental subjects."[27] With evangelistic fervor and great displays of emotion, the Separate Baptist preachers in the South perpetuated the revivalistic patterns begun in the Great Awakening. The mushrooming growth came despite severe persecution by the Anglican church and civil magistrates. Mobs attacked preachers, destroyed property, made threats, and even shot people on occasion. The Baptists were lambasted for their ignorance, crudity, and sedition and became the objects of gross rumors. The Baptist David Thomas reported that no "atrocious villany . . . has not been laid to our charge." In all the upheavals, powerful social forces were at work making the Separate Baptists at once a threat to the traditional order and an attractive haven for the lowly.[28]

In this atmosphere the primitivist outlook intensified. An experimental faith, to be sure, remained at the center of Separate Baptist ecclesiology. Each member was expected to know the time and place of her conversion and be able to narrate that experience to the satisfaction of the congregation. But combined with this intense pietism was a heightened concern to duplicate the New Testament church by practicing all its forms and ordinances. The two emphases—pietism and biblicism—were linked together: every person who has had "Christ formed in his soul," James Ireland asserted, "would be found conforming to every gospel precept and falling in with every known duty."[29] In the attempt to isolate all scriptural forms and duties, thus duplicating the primitive church, most southern Separates observed what Morgan Edwards termed the "nine Christian rites." The rites included baptism, the Lord's Supper, foot washing, the love feast, the kiss of charity, laying on of hands, anointing the sick, the dedication of children, and the right hand of fellowship.[30] Separates also appointed elders, deacons, and deaconesses in the churches because they found these offices precedented in scripture. In the extreme concern for apostolic duplication, some of the churches even experimented with ordaining "apostles" and instituting other rites thought to be of apostolic origin.[31] Appeals to the "Apostles and primitive Christians" and to scriptural "precedent" pervade Separatist Baptist writings, reaching something of a climax in David Thomas's claim that the Baptist church will be found "exactly corresponding with the rule and line of the Gospel in every part of it." He added that the Baptist church, above all others, possessed a "primeval rectitude."[32]

A natural part of this heightened primitivism was a strong rejection of creeds and confessions of faith. Since the Bible alone was the measuring rod for all doctrine and practice, confessions were unnecessary; even more, they could be harmful, especially when used—as they often had been—to restrict the freedom of individual churches.[33] Some of the churches did include a doctrinal summary in their church covenants, but they adamantly refused to adopt a confession that would be imposed on the churches as a whole. Such antipathy for many years exacerbated the conflict with the Regular Baptists and helped stall the Regulars' repeated attempts at union with the Separates. When fragile unions did begin to occur in the 1770s, the Regulars' insistence that Separates subscribe to the Philadelphia Confession was met with compromise. In Virginia, for example, Separates and Regulars united in 1787 on a compromise confession proposed by John Leland. Separates accepted the London Confession but, "to prevent it from usurping a tyrannical power over the consciences of any," added the provision that "[not] every person is bound to the strict observance of everything therein contained."[34] By thus giving superficial allegiance to the confession, the Separates maintained allegiance to the Bible alone as the only binding confession. Such resistance to enforced doctrinal standards, combined with a jealous protection of local church autonomy, gave the movement a fluidity and diversity as it expanded throughout the South and West.

Rejection of creeds as unwarranted intermediaries between the text and the believer would increasingly characterize restoration efforts in America. Hostility toward creeds would become a central theme among later Landmark Baptists and in the "Christian" movements led by Alexander Campbell and Barton W. Stone in the early nineteenth century. In general, most restorationists agreed that creeds and interpretive systems were nothing but human inventions that forced the truths of first times into artificial, time-bound moulds. The irony lay in the fact that restorationists typically refused to recognize for what they were the creeds and interpretive schemes they themselves inevitably developed. They often sought, therefore, to press on others their "freedom of understanding," but in the process they both particularized and absolutized the universal for which they had plumbed. This is the heart of the story as one moves from the Separate Baptists, for whom creeds impeded freedom, to the

Landmark Baptists, for whom creeds undermined a highly particularized orthodoxy.

IV

Southern Separate Baptists transplanted their fluid biblical primitivism to the western frontier in the early 1770s. The fierce Regulators' War in the region around Sandy Creek dispersed the mother congregation, reducing it from 606 members to 14. According to Morgan Edwards, · fifteen hundred families left the region about 1771–72, many of them migrating into eastern Tennessee.[35] The westward migration increased sharply after 1780, bringing many Separate Baptists from Virginia and the Carolinas into south central Kentucky and the upper Cumberland region of Tennessee.[36] Though many of the Separates blended into Regular Baptist congregations, many others maintained the separation, forming in 1787 the South Kentucky Association of Separate Baptists. There were repeated attempts at union, but the Separates resisted until 1801.

The main issue, as in the East, was the Regulars' insistence on subscription to the Philadelphia Confession. The biblical primitivism of the Separates caused them to reject all confessional authority and to seek to constitute their churches on the authority of the Bible alone.[37] They feared the centralizing tendencies of the Philadelphia Baptists and guarded jealously the autonomy of the individual congregation. In forming their own associations, the Separate Baptists refused to employ any confession or written rules; associational meetings served simply as occasions for preaching, inspiration, and discussing disputed issues. By the early nineteenth century, the churches of two large Kentucky Separate Baptist associations had rejected creeds and even the simplest official rules of decorum for associational life, adhering instead to the Bible alone "without note or comment."[38]

The uneasy union of Separate and Regular Baptists in Kentucky in 1801 furthered the complex sifting and blending of the two traditions that had begun in the first frontier settlements. Tensions, controversies, and schisms continued almost unabated. In 1803 the fragile union was broken, and many Separates withdrew to continue their existence as a distinct group. But the reciprocal influences continued, so much so that the Baptist faith emerging in the early nineteenth-century South and West must be seen as an amalgam of the two traditions. The influence of the Separate Baptists appears especially in the stress on evangelism and on the pure church ideal, the suspicious attitude toward creeds and confessions, and a heightened emphasis on the primacy of the local church.[39]

The Separates, in short, heightened the biblical primitivism that had characterized the Baptist tradition from its beginning, thus helping give the Baptists their amazing vitality among the other primitivist sects on the western frontier.

In view of the Separate Baptists' primitivism, it is hardly surprising that when Barton Stone, leader in the great Cane Ridge revival, and Alexander Campbell, editor of the *Christian Baptist,* began calling for a simplified Christianity based on a "restoration of the ancient order," rejecting all creeds and human societies, many defected from the Baptist ranks in Kentucky, Tennessee, Ohio, and western Pennsylvania. By 1811, according to a contemporary observer, there were thirteen thousand "Christians" in the West associated with the Stone movement, many of them from Separate Baptist background, and the number grew until 1832 when Stone officially joined forces with Campbell.[40] The restoration movement of Campbell also drew heavily from Separate Baptist ranks, especially in Kentucky. Between 1824 and 1832, for example, eleven churches and nearly five hundred members of the South Kentucky Association joined Campbell's movement. Feeling vindicated by the spread of Campbell's anticreedal, anti-institutional views, this Separate Baptist association considered corresponding with the "reformers" in 1826, and in their minutes wrote: "We hope and believe the day will come when the Gospel in its ancient simplicity and purity will be preached." In Tennessee the Stone-Campbell movement also took a heavy toll. R. B. C. Howell, early leader in the Southern Baptist Convention and archenemy of James R. Graves in the 1850s, wrote with chagrin that "destruction reigned supreme. . . . Out of the ruins of our churches theirs sprung up everywhere, like mushrooms on a summer night."[41]

As the Baptist ranks were depleted, the Separate Baptist associations joined other Baptists in opposing the "reformers," particularly their doctrine of conversion. Despite the rapid recoil of the Baptists to Stone's and Campbell's ideas, however, this much is clear: the Baptists in south central Kentucky and the upper Cumberland region in the late eighteenth century, and especially the Separate Baptists, plowed the ground in which Stone's "Christian" movement and Campbell's "restoration" took root. And in the same soil, as we shall see, the Landmark Baptist movement took root, flourished, and reaped its harvest thirty years later.

Baptist primitivism in the West, with its deep concern for freedom from human constraints, its strong objection to drawing up or enforcing standards of ecclesiastical orthodoxy, and its stress on local church autonomy, had other, more far-reaching reverberations in the early nineteenth century. The primitivist impulse contributed greatly to the Baptists' central role in the vast and complex antimission crusade that swept across the nation after 1818.[42] Though rooted in the hyper-Calvinism that had emerged among the English Baptists of the early eighteenth century, the antimission sentiment in America spread far beyond its original bounds and was whipped up into a crusade by the rise of the great Protestant missionary societies in the early nineteenth century. The Baptist phase of the crusade was the most spectacular and influential, but antimissionism was not solely a Baptist phenomenon. A variety of unlikely allies emerged as leaders in the movement, including "Christians" such as Elias Smith and Alexander Campbell, Methodists such as Peter Cartwright and Lorenzo Dow, Deists such as Elihu Palmer, and Baptists such as John Leland, John Taylor, and Daniel Parker. The diverse movement was welded together by a common fear that the proliferating missionary and benevolent societies were becoming tools through which the eastern churches could control the nation in the wake of legal disestablishment.

Primitivist rhetoric became a powerful tool of dissent against the emerging societies. Everywhere throughout the literature of the crusade, polemicists contrasted the organizational simplicity and freedom of the primitive church with the greedy and cumbersome societies of the eastern churches, the simple ordinances of Christ with illicit "human inventions." In the East, Elias Smith, the most prominent propagandist in New England, rested his case on "the simplicity that is in Christ," which for him meant the abandonment of everything—including human societies—for which one could not find an exact prescription in the New Testament.[43] Gilbert Beebe, leader in the breakaway Antimission or Primitive Baptists, wrote in 1832 that "popular creeds are substituted in the place of the faith once delivered to the saints—the commandments of men instead of the gospel of Jesus Christ—human inventions take the place of divine ordinances—the work of the Holy Ghost, in gathering in and quickening the elect of God, is superceded by human contrivances." The flood of "innovations" was symbolized, for Beebe, by the many parachurch organizations, including seminaries, Sunday schools, and "protracted meetings," all of which he dismissed as "unscriptural nurseries for the church."[44] The vituperative Joshua Lawrence of North Carolina saw the societies as blatant attempts to "make gain by godliness" and responded that "the scripture speaks not one word" authorizing them; he added that all such things are "contrary to the church, in her virgin beauty . . . when ministers of the gospel suffered the loss of all things, and were counted the filth and offscouring of society."[45]

In the West, where such primitivist appeals resounded in the writings of men such as former Separate Baptist John Taylor of Kentucky and implacable Calvinist Daniel Parker of Tennessee, the antimission cause swept through the Baptist churches bringing bitterness and division.[46] Not surprisingly, antimissionism found fertile soil in the regions where Separate Baptists long had defended the freedom and sufficiency of the single congregation. By 1820 most Baptist churches in Tennessee, North Carolina, and northern Alabama had embraced the antisociety position, and, between 1836 and 1838, many of these churches officially withdrew to form the Antimission or Primitive Baptist church.[47]

The primitivism that pervaded the Baptist element of the antimission movement served various theological agendas. The Primitive Baptists used it to oppose all human effort and thus to uphold hyper-Calvinistic doctrinal standards. A larger number of Baptists, especially those influenced by the intense revivalism of the Separates, used primitivist appeals against the societies out of a more direct concern for New Testament precedent, biblical simplicity, and the immediate dangers they saw to religious and political freedom. Undergirding these more or less explicit theological concerns were less explicit social and economic factors. Students of the movement have pointed to such things as sectional tension arising out of fear of northern imperialism, deep cultural resentment expressed in hostility to eastern, well-educated missionaries, and concern for ministerial status.[48] Whatever the web of factors that helped shape it, the antimission crusade left a deep mark on the Baptists of the South and West in the early nineteenth century, keeping in place the vigorous primitivist impulse and heightening the partisan spirit that was to provide a favorable milieu for the dramatic spread of Landmarkism.

V

The Landmark movement began in Nashville, Tennessee, in the late 1840s under the leadership of James Graves. In the decades that followed, Landmarkism enjoyed an enormous influence in the Baptist churches across the South and Southwest.[49] Though it became a movement of large proportions, its beginnings were small and its founder obscure. Graves arrived in Nashville in 1845, a young man of twenty-five, and the following year became assistant editor of the *Baptist* (later the *Tennessee Baptist*). In 1848, after becoming sole editor, Graves began publishing a flury of articles attacking non-Baptist denominations and especially the validity of infant baptism and all "alien" immersions. He became embroiled, as a result, in a heated exchange with fellow Baptist John L. Waller, editor of the *Western Baptist Review,* an exchange that effectively began the Landmark movement.[50]

As the movement gained momentum, Graves enhanced his position as prophet and leader by organizing a mass meeting of Baptists at Cotton Grove, Tennessee, in 1851, and there introducing what became known as the Cotton Grove Resolutions. Based on the premise that only Baptist churches were true churches, the five resolutions sought to erect standards by which the true churches could be kept free from doctrinal compromise. The first resolution denied the Baptists should "recognize those societies not organized according to the pattern of the Jerusalem church, but possessing a different *government,* different *officers,* a different class of *membership,* different *ordinances, doctrines,* and *practices,* as the Church of Christ." The other resolutions followed logically: unscriptural "societies" must not be called "Gospel Churches," their ministers must not be recognized as "gospel ministers," especially by inviting them to preach in Baptist pulpits, and their members should not be addressed as "brethren."[51] As the first official pronouncement of the movement, the Cotton Grove Resolutions focused the doctrinal issues that comprised the heart of Landmarkism.

With his commanding personality, great platform skill, and tremendous drive, Graves soon made Landmarkism a growing influence throughout the Southwest and a major force in the Southern Baptist Convention (established in 1845). Two men—James M. Pendleton (1813–1891) and Amos C. Dayton (1811–1865)—came to share his views and aided his campaign to restore the New Testament pattern of the church. Pendleton, a Baptist pastor in Bowling Green, Kentucky, came under Graves's influence in 1852 and soon became associate editor of the *Tennessee Baptist.* He wrote extensively for Landmark papers, but he made his greatest impact on the movement when, at Graves's request, he wrote a tract elaborating on and defending the Cotton Grove Resolutions. Graves published the tract in 1854 under the title *An Old Landmark Reset,* a title suggested by the admonition of Proverbs 22:28, "remove not the ancient Landmark which thy fathers have set." In this case, the "old landmark" that had been removed and needed restoring was Baptist refusal to recognize non-Baptists as true gospel ministers and thus non-Baptist churches as true churches. A bald and unwincing polemic, Pendleton's tract created a stir throughout the denomination and did much to place Landmark concerns at center stage.[52]

Amos C. Dayton converted from Presbyterianism to the Baptist fold in 1852 and a short time later became a strict follower of Graves. Both in his key positions with the Southern Baptist Bible Board and other denominational organizations, and in his work as an editor and writer, he was a powerful force in the spread of Landmark views. His book entitled *Pedo-Baptist and Campbellite Immersions* provided perhaps the most in-depth attack on "alien immersions" produced by the movement, and his religious novel entitled *Theodosia Ernest* was a great polemical success.[53] Although James Graves was the genius and driving force behind Landmarkism, Pendleton and Dayton played important roles in its success.

Without question Graves was the master polemicist of the movement. Belligerent, rigorous, sometimes vindictive, and always supremely confident that his views were unassailable, he excelled during a time when, as a middle Tennessee Baptist remarked in 1851, "theological champions meet with burnished swords and cut and hew each other to the wondrous gratification of their respective partisans, who gather in hundreds for successive weeks to these scenes of religious combat." Graves displayed his gladiatorial prowess in about a dozen oral debates with representatives of the major western denominations and gained great status as "a fearless, peerless and successful champion of Baptist and New Testament orthodoxy."[54] Early in his career he gained particular fame and notoriety for his written debate with the aging Alexander Campbell, published first in 1854 in the *Tennessee Baptist* and the *Millennial Harbinger,* then by Graves under the title *Alexander Campbell and Campbellism Exposed.* Other vigorous polemics against the denominations followed: against Methodism he wrote *The Great Iron Wheel* (1856) and *The Little Iron Wheel* (1857); against Presbyterianism he wrote *The Trilemma* (1860); and against Puritan intolerance for Baptists he wrote *Trials and Sufferings for Religious Liberty in New England* (1858).[55] In addition, he filled the pages of the *Tennessee Baptist* with unremitting attacks on the spurious "religious societies" that had sprung up around the Baptists.

The constant invective against man-made or invented churches was an expression of Graves's deep anxiety over the religious pluralism that had been intensified in the young nation's westward expansion. With an array of denominations all competing in a great free market of souls, the questions about the true church became the focus of bitter debate and exalted claims. To Graves this was the great question of the age. He lamented the "sad and paradoxical spectacle of Christian Churches (admitting the title they claim) divided, and warring against themselves." Before this spectacle the "friendly alien is astonished and offended— sceptics laugh and devils rejoice." It should be plain to every logical person, Graves thought, that "all the ten or twelve so called evangelical, yet conflicting denominations cannot be the churches of Christ, equally scriptural in doctrine, policy, and practice." One must be true and the others false, one Christian, the others antichristian. "Two, much less a dozen, contradictory propositions cannot be equally true." If the great task of evangelization was to proceed, he concluded, the conflict over

"Church legitimacy" must be resolved "and all united upon the original and divine New Testament model, taking the Testament alone for our Liturgy, our Book of Common Prayer and Psalter, our Confession of Faith and our Discipline."[56]

The resolution of this conflict was the driving force of Landmarkism. With its doctrinal complexities, overwhelming invective, and astonishing array of arguments, the Landmark system, at root, put forth a resounding claim about the true church set out on profoundly primitivist grounds. Graves and his comrades-in-arms battled the Protestant "societies" in the unbending belief that they had established an exact line of demarcation between the true church and all pretended churches and that this dividing line was unmistakable and inviolable. They worked from the conviction that all claims to be the true church must be tested by three fundamental principles: (1) Christ "visibly set up" the true church before his ascension and gave it "a definite organization, laws, [and] ordinances" as a model for all time; (2) the true church has existed in an unbroken line since the first century; and (3) the true church always exhibits a "structural identity" fully identical with the original church set up by Christ.[57] Much of the Landmark system grew out of these three principles.

VI

Most basic to the system was a stress on the precise New Testament blueprint for the church. Though Baptists from their inception had been marked by a search for bare New Testament forms, and the Landmarkers stood in this tradition, Graves gave those forms an unprecedented rigidity, making each element of equal importance in the constitution of an authentic church. In Graves's view, Christ was the only lawgiver and the New Testament the only law for the church. "[Christ] has given to the Church all its laws," Graves wrote. "We have therefore no right to abolish, change, or add to, the laws of the Church, for he is the only King-Lawgiver. He has enjoined all Christian duties, connected with the Church, and we have no right to add to, or take from them."[58] The first Jerusalem congregation embodied Christ's complete set of laws for the church, and all other authentic churches have been patterned after it. According to Graves, Christ commanded his people "for all time to come, to construct all organizations that should bear his name according to the pattern and model he 'built' before their eyes; and those who add to or diminish aught, do it at their peril." If Moses dared not vary the divine pattern for the tabernacle, Graves asked, "may we dare to build churches altogether different from the pattern Christ has given?"[59]

For Graves the pattern Christ had legislated for his "model church" consisted of at least eight distinct and unmistakable elements, all of which must be present in a true church. First, the church was of "divine institution," containing nothing added by any mere mortal and missing nothing ordained by God. Second, it was a "visible institution," with a "specified organization, officers, faith, laws and ordinances, and a living membership." Third, it was a "visible *earthly* organization," for Christ never had and never would have a church in heaven. Fourth, the "primitive model was a single congregation, complete in itself, independent of all other bodies . . . amenable only to Christ, whose laws alone it receives and executes." Fifth, the "primitive and apostolic church" was constituted only of those persons professing an experience of regeneration by the Holy Spirit, and thus had no infant membership. Sixth, the first church practiced baptism after Christ's design: it baptized by immersion only those who had experienced regeneration. Seventh, it observed the Lord's Supper not as a sacrament but strictly as "a *local church ordinance*," thus forbidding intercommunion with members of other Baptist churches who might be present. Eighth, it was a church that Christ promised would never "cease from the earth" until he returned to reign over it.[60] Graves believed that Christ himself had enacted these features into law and that they must characterize the true church for all time and in every place.

The Landmark system particularly stressed that the church was nothing more than a visible and local institution. In this emphasis, the Landmarkers were shaped powerfully by the Separate and Antimission Baptists, notably the Separates' jealous guardianship of congregational autonomy against the centralizing tendencies of the Particular Baptists and the Antimissionists' crusade against monolithic Protestant societies. The Separate and Antimission Baptists, however, despite their overwhelming concern for the local church, generally did not reject the notion of a universal church; indeed, most Baptists of the time, influenced by the Philadelphia Confession, affirmed the local, visible church as an instrument of the universal spiritual church. Graves repudiated the Philadelphia Confession and all doctrines of a universal or invisible church. Christ "has no invisible kingdom or church, and such a thing has no real existence in heaven or earth." He charged that such a doctrine "is only an invention employed to bolster up erroneous theories of ecclesiology." According to Graves, every term used in the Bible in reference to the church "is a term necessitating *form,* and therefore visibility"; Christ "visibly set up" his church, and therefore its one proper form, its unique ordinances, and its prescribed government must be visible to all. The universal church theory, he charged, was "preposterously absurd" because it drew many conflicting sects into one church, thus denying Christ's original "model and pattern for all his churches."[61]

Inextricably tied to the insistence on a detailed New Testament pattern was Graves's claim that true churches conforming to the pattern have existed in an unbroken succession since the days of the apostles. Taking his cue from Jesus' assertion that the "gates of hell shall not prevail against" his church (Matt. 16:18), Graves believed that in all ages a group of people existed who held "just the doctrines and order of Christ's house, in some good degree, in conformity with the model of the primitive church," and that through this historical chain of faithful witnesses the true doctrines and ordinances "have been transmitted to us in their primitive integrity and purity." The study of this history, he urged, would reveal, amid the "present distracted state of Christendom," which of all the competing denominations comprised the "true Churches of Christ"; furthermore, it would enable faithful Baptists to confound all "human traditions, and mutilated and profaned church ordinances, and those who impiously presume to enact laws in place of Christ, and to change the order of his church."[62] In Graves's view, the doctrine of "church successionism" made the Landmark system impregnable to all assaults, establishing once and for all the claim to primitive purity.

Eager to substantiate his view with historical evidence, Graves seized on G. H. Orchard's *A Concise History of Foreign Baptists* and reprinted it in 1855. Orchard had written that "all Christian communities during the first three centuries were of the Baptist denomination, in constitution and practice," and that from the fourth century onward one could trace the Baptist lineage through various dissenting, persecuted groups.[63] The copious documentation gave Orchard's work an impressive scholarly appearance, and it served Graves's cause well. The successionist doctrine as a result became a mainstay in the polemical arsenal of the Landmarkers.

The polemical power of the doctrine can be seen especially in the way Graves used it to dissociate Baptists from the whole stream of Protestantism. Baptists, according to Graves, are not and never have been Protestants, for they always stood apart from Roman Catholicism and thus never had any need to break in "protest." Graves asserted: "Baptists never dissented from anything but sin—and are not Protestants, but have been, in all ages, the Repudiators of Popery."[64] All Protestants, in Graves's view, were simply offspring of Rome, still related to that "mother of harlots" in doctrine and practice. Protestants, for example, despite their claims, followed Rome in denying the "ALL SUFFICIENCY of the Word of God," Graves charged, for one has only to point to the "Books of Common Prayer, Rubrics, . . . Confessions of Faith, and authenticated

Disciplines, that in every Protestant meeting-house are placed either on top of the Bible or by its side."[65]

By grouping Protestantism together with Catholicism, Graves drew one massive battle line between the true church (the Baptist) and the false (Roman Catholicism and her offspring), thus forcing Protestants onto the horns of a dilemma. Protestants, he believed, must either "carry out their principles and be Catholics, or purge their creeds and disciplines of their popery, and become Baptists. . . . There is no middle ground."[66] The choice was urgent, for Graves set the conflict in a chiliastic framework: history was moving swiftly toward its climax, toward the time when God would destroy "a corrupt Protestantism and Popery" and establish his kingdom (the Baptists). The successionist doctrine played a pivotal role in supporting such expectations. Graves attempted, using successionism as a lever, to lift the Baptist church entirely out of the stream of profane ecclesiastical history and position it within a lofty, sacred history, making it all one piece with the church in her first and freshest hour.

The triumphalism that Graves here employed illustrates two propensities of the restoration posture. First, it illustrates the ease with which the gap between primordium and present—so evident among the Separate Baptists—could be closed. Instead of eternal judgment on the present, the primordium had become, in Graves's thinking, eternal justification for a particularized perspective. That this could occur within the Baptist heritage is all the more striking. Indeed, Graves turned traditional Baptist primitivism on its head and likely discredited the restoration theme for later generations of Baptists, especially in the twentieth century.

Second, Graves's triumphalism illustrates the extent to which primordial visions often provide both content and justification for millennial expectations. In Graves's case, the millennial kingdom would be a Baptist kingdom, based squarely on the patterns of first times, and destruction of Catholicism and Protestantism would be fully justified since both, Graves thought, rejected primordial patterns. The dependence of millennialism on primitivism is a relationship not often noted by scholars, though it has appeared in Christian history with significant regularity.[67] This relationship will be especially apparent later in this book in discussions dealing with Churches of Christ and the Mormons.

Though Graves and his lieutenants believed that the big gun of successionism could destroy all of Protestantism with one mighty blast, the Landmarkers fought much of their war in the trenches with smaller weapons. If the big gun fired over the heads of the enemy, the smaller ones—fired at point-blank range—would complete the job. Thus, it was adequate, Graves believed, to insist simply that every true church demonstrate an "identical structural organism" to that of the first Jerusalem church.[68] If a church did not—if it was missing a *single one* of the many elements Christ made essential to his church—then it was disqualified automatically from being a New Testament church. A sure way to expose such fatal dissimilarities, the Landmarkers believed, was to inquire about a group's date of origin: if it did not originate with Christ himself and thus did not bear all of the primitive marks, it must be rejected. On this basis, Graves charged in 1855 that "Methodism cannot justly be called a Church of Christ because [it is] too young by 1747 years—it being only 68 years old."[69]

Amos Dayton used this tactic with particular force in the second volume of *Theodosia Ernest*, subtitled *Ten Days Travel in Search of the Church*. In the novel, Dr. Thinkwell, a recent convert to Christianity who is searching eagerly for the true church, encounters the Reverend Percy and the learned classical scholar Professor Courtney, both Baptists. A Methodist minister and an Episcopal bishop join them in the discussions. After searching the New Testament and finding nine marks of a true church, the Baptists lead the group in measuring the existing Protestant denominations against these marks. One by one they find each to be of too recent origin. Finally they apply the biblical marks to the Baptist church, and it, of course, measures up exactly at each point.[70] The conclusion is obvious to all: any person who thinks well will be compelled finally to join the Baptist ranks.

Wielding the powerful weapons of "church successionism" and "structural identity," the Landmarkers claimed to "unchurch" all non-Baptist denominations, thereby resolving the troublesome question of religious pluralism in the American nation. The exclusivism of the Landmark claim was tempered only by an individualistic view of conversion: Landmarkers granted that the illicit Protestant societies contained some converted or regenerate people. "We may unchurch an organization," Graves wrote, "without unchristianizing its members." By refusing fellowship with all non-Baptists, he continued, we are "not declaring . . . that we believe their ministers and members are unregenerate, but that they are not members of scriptural churches."[71] Before Graves, the common Baptist view of non-Baptist churches was that they were true Christian churches but were "irregular and unscriptural in their ordinances and polity." The Landmark theologians ruled out such a possibility, for in their view it was absurd "to say that the Scriptures provide for the existence of *unscriptural* churches."[72]

In an age of intense sectarian strife and widespread anxiety over religious pluralism, such logic proved compelling indeed. With its bold, sweeping claims, it pushed Baptist sectarianism to new heights. It gave beleaguered and demoralized Baptists a quick infusion of denominational pride and self-respect. It inspired the heady conviction that, though often cast down and abused by the world, the Baptists comprised the Lord's one chosen body and, as a result, soon would take their rightful place of preeminence.

With Graves's inflammatory writing and constant agitation, Landmarkism became a dominant force in the Southern Baptist Convention by the outbreak of the Civil War. Thereafter, its influence continued to spread, so much so that by the 1880s the historian J. H. Spencer could observe that "at present" the tenets of Landmarkism "prevail, in whole or in part, in nearly all the southern churches." Regarding Graves himself, it may not be an exaggeration to conclude, with a contemporary Baptist scholar, that "he influenced Southern Baptist life of the nineteenth century in more ways, and probably to a greater degree, than any other person."[73]

VII

With the emergence of the Landmark movement, this study of Baptist primitivism can be concluded, for in this movement the tensions inherent in the primitivist impulse become clearly visible. As we have seen, the primitivist drive among the early Separate Baptists was primarily for freedom from all civil and ecclesiastical control so that God could work directly in individuals. Landmarkism, however, drastically transformed that concern into a drive for rigid doctrinal uniformity based on the delineation of the one true church in the midst of religious pluralism. The concern for individual liberty in understanding the Bible fell away and was replaced, in the theology of James Graves, by the elevation of a precise model or blueprint of the primitive church, a blueprint from which a person could not vary and still consider herself a member of God's true church. Graves, as a result, presented the religious world with two choices: become a member of the Baptist church—God's one true church preserved without interruption since the days of the apostles— or remain in sinful human societies that by their very nature undermine the American republic.

With this stark dichotomy, the profound shift is unmistakable: the primitivist rhetoric so often enlisted in the service of disestablishment and liberty became, paradoxically, a powerful tool for promoting a new establishment in which dissenters could have no legitimate place. In the Landmark movement, the *right to seek the truth* and follow its dictates wherever they led—a right won by the Baptists after nearly two centuries of struggle—was transformed into the *duty to follow the truth* as defined and championed by Graves. The freedom to dissent was transformed into the duty to conform. The primitivist protest against constricting human laws and traditions itself became a means of coercion and exclusion.

Not only did Separate Baptists provide substance and content for the later Landmark Baptists. They also exerted a profound impact on the "Christian" movements of Barton W. Stone and Alexander Campbell, as we have already seen in this chapter. Further, both of these latter movements in their early years embraced the restoration perspective as a means to freedom from ecclesiastical and creedal control over faith and practice. In this they shared a common commitment with the Separates. But like their cousins, the Landmark Baptists, many in the "Christian movement" at an early date transformed their freedom from coercion into a coercive system in its own right. This is the story that emerges in the following chapter.

FIVE

From Freedom to Constraint: The Transformation of the "Christians in the West"

When the Baptist Jeremiah Jeter wrote *Campbellism Examined* in 1855, he recalled asking a young girl belonging to the restoration movement of Alexander Campbell "whether she was satisfied that her new views were correct. She replied, 'I can't be wrong—I follow the Book.' "Jeter agreed that "the Bible is an infallible guide," but told the lass, "I am not quite certain that you are an infallible interpreter of it." Jeter recalled that "our conversation continued for some time, and I could not, by any argument or appeal, extort from her the confession that she might possibly misinterpret the Scriptures. 'I follow the Book, and can't be deceived,' was her unchanged reply."[1]

In 1811 the "Christian" preacher Joseph Thomas was returning from Kentucky to his home in North Carolina. Along the way, a Presbyterian clergyman asked to see his preaching credentials. "I then pulled out my Bible," Thomas recalled, "and told him that was my credential. He asked me if that was all I had? I told him that this *credential* had the signature of the great head of the church, and was sealed with his own blood, and I thought that was sufficient."[2]

In 1860 the Kentucky "Christian" preacher John Rogers admonished his cohorts in the Churches of Christ not even to speak of themselves as another denomination. "When we speak of other *denominations,* we place ourselves *among them,* as one *of them.* This, however, we can never do, unless we abandon the distinctive ground—the apostolic ground—the anti-sectarian ground, we have taken."[3]

These three episodes typify the profoundly ahistorical worldview of the "Christians in the West"—those followers first of Barton W. Stone and then of Alexander Campbell—who called themselves "Christians" and their congregations "Churches of Christ," and who won numerous converts in the first half of the nineteenth century in northern Alabama, middle Tennessee, Kentucky, and southern to middle Ohio. By the 1840s these people had become, at least in the eyes of their neighbors, a separate denomination called the Church of Christ—or sometimes the Christian church[4]—though they themselves stoutly denied their denominational status and claimed instead to be the one true church of the apostolic age, from which all others had departed. Indeed, some leaders in the Church of Christ by the early 1840s even threatened their religious neighbors with divine retribution if they refused the truth and continued in the errors of their way.

That this spirit of exclusivism and even coercion surfaced so soon is deeply ironic when one considers that the Churches of Christ were born of a passion for freedom and that their earliest leaders drank deeply of the spirit of the American Revolution. But, then, the soul of this tradition was the conviction of its people that they had bypassed history with its constraints and limitations, that they were heirs to no cultural presuppositions, that their spiritual sights were clear and unclouded, and that they therefore stood squarely on the firm ground of the first Christian age. This sentiment was the two-edged sword with which these Christian soldiers could, on the one hand, proclaim freedom from the housetops or, on the other, de-Christianize their neighbors and consign them to the wrath of God. How the restoration theme could sustain both these perspectives in the same movement is the focus of this chapter.

I

Five dissident Presbyterians set the agenda for the initial phase of the "Christian" movement in the West. Following the great Cane Ridge Revival in 1801, the Synod of Kentucky sustained the Washington (Ky.) Presbytery's charge that Richard McNemar, through his participation in the revival, had compromised the doctrines of the Westminster Confession of Faith. At that, four other Presbyterian ministers—knowing that McNemar's fate soon would be their own—joined McNemar, and all five quickly formulated a protest and withdrew from the synod's jurisdiction. Their protest fairly rang with affirmations of freedom.

> We claim the privilege of interpreting the Scriptures by itself according to Section 9 Chapter 1st of the confession of faith, and we believe that the Supreme Judge by whom all controversies of religion are to be determined . . . can be no other but the Holy Spirit speaking in the Scriptures. —But from the disposition which the Synod manifests it appears to us that we cannot enjoy this privilege, but must be found up to such explanations of the Word of God as preclude all farther advances after truth.[5]

The document was signed by Robert Marshall, John Dunlavy, Richard McNemar, Barton W. Stone, and John Thompson, and dated September 10, 1803.

Having determined to recognize no authority but the Bible alone, these five dissidents then formed themselves into the Springfield Presbytery. By the summer of 1804, however, they judged that their new-formed presbytery was potentially as oppressive and divisive as was the Synod of Kentucky, and by all accounts was merely a human organization standing between the people and the word of God. They therefore formally dissolved that body on June 28, 1804, with the publication of "The Last Will and Testament of the Springfield Presbytery."

This document made even bolder claims for freedom than had the earlier apology. Recognizing that religious bondage finally was rooted in the creeds and accumulated traditions of human history, this document simply dismissed creeds and traditions and appealed beyond history to the pure word of God.

> We *will,* that the people henceforth take the Bible as the only sure guide to heaven; and as many as are offended with other books, which stand in competition with it, may cast them into the fire if they choose; for it is better to enter into life having one book, than having many to be cast into hell.
>
> We *will,* that our weak brethren, who may have been wishing to make the Presbytery of Springfield their king, and wot not what is now become of it, betake themselves to the Rock of Ages, and follow Jesus for the future.
>
> We *will,* that the Synod of Kentucky examine every member, who may be *suspected* of having departed from the Confession of Faith, and suspend every such suspected heretic immediately; in order that the oppressed may go free, and taste the sweets of gospel liberty.[6]

Under the influence of Rice Haggard, these dissidents adopted the simple name of "Christian."[7] They never claimed in those early years to be the only Christians, but they did claim to be Christians only. Here again, they scuttled the traditions of history, including its denominating and confining labels. They sought escape from the bondage of human systems, and to them the surest path to that goal was the path that led directly to the first Christian age.

Their zeal for freedom was so intense that Richard McNemar wrote of the early "Christian" movement that "it is difficult to paint the zeal for liberty, and just indignation against the old aristocratic spirit, which glowed through every member of this new confederacy."[8] Indeed, from their perspective the American Revolution was only half won. Despotic political powers had been silenced, but religious despots continued to coerce the consciences of the faithful. The task of these "Christians," therefore, was to complete what the American Revolution had only begun. One correspondent wrote to Barton W. Stone, the acknowledged leader of the "Christian" movement in the West before 1823, that "the present conflict between the Bible and party creeds and confessions . . . is perfectly analogous to the revolutionary war between Britain and America; liberty was contended for on the one side, and dominion and power on the other."[9] Jacob Creath, a Kentucky preacher influenced chiefly by Alexander Campbell, argued in 1830 that creeds and historic traditions were "the faith of the clergy . . . not of the people" and "anti-republican in soul, body, and spirit."[10] John Rogers, an early and important leader of the "Christians in the West," linked the "Christians'" struggle with the Revolution when he proclaimed on July 4, 1828, that "the motto of the patriot and the Christian is, Liberty or death."[11] These "Christians" even employed Jefferson's phrase "certain unalienable rights," but expanded its meaning to include the "inalienable rights of free investigation, sober and diligent inquiry after [religious] truth. . . ."[12]

It is hardly surprising, then, to find these "Christians" contending that the primitive church was fundamentally democratic, while the creeds and traditions of history were essentially un-American. Thus, J. and J. Gregg argued in 1826 that the primitive church was characterized by "equality of privileges, and mutual enjoyment of equal rights, by every member of each church," and Joseph Thomas wrote that the primitive church was essentially republican and sustained "a perfect *equality* as it related to power."[13] Similarly, T. M. Allen argued that creeds and confessions of faith "were forged in a period of darkness" and were now, under the bright light of American liberties, "liable to be exposed and broken." It made no more sense, Allen said, to "go back to old England . . . for confessions of faith, catechisms, and church articles, in a religious point of view" than it did to return to the Old World "for a constitution, laws, and form of government, in a civil point of view."[14] Racoon John Smith, another Kentucky preacher who gave allegiance chiefly to Campbell rather than Stone, made the same point regarding the clergy: Americans had learned that "a nation could exist without a king on its throne," and soon would learn that a church could exist "without a clergyman in the *sacred desk*."[15]

These "Christians" rarely linked the fall of the church to the adoption of false or erroneous doctrine. Rather, they almost unanimously agreed that the church fell from its ancient purity when 318 "luxurious clergymen" enforced creedal uniformity at Nicaea during the reign of

Constantine. John Rogers's assessment was typical: "as soon as she [the church] established a human Creed as a test of truth & Union, she made rapid strides into Babylon . . . : The Man of Sin, & Son of Perdition was soon revealed, & seen clambering into the temple of God . . . ; [then] the reign of priestly terror began."[16] J. and J. Gregg agreed: coerced uniformity launched "those swarms of creeds and confessions, which have ever since deluged the world in confusion and darkness." But the remedy was plain: "disannul all their . . . Popish idols, creeds and confessions, which enslave the consciences of Christ's disciples" and "organize every worshipping assembly upon primitive principles . . . of self government."[17]

This they proceeded to do. Among many examples, one will suffice. On the fourth Sunday in October 1830, a Baptist congregation meeting at Roberson Fork, Giles County, Tennessee, "resolved that we consider ourselves as no more belonging to the Richland Creek association" since that association had engaged in "Despotic Conduct" toward the congregation. Almost two years later, in June of 1832, this congregation "unanimously agreed" to "take the word of God alone contained in the Old and New Testaments to be our rule of faith and Practice and Particular the latter as our rule for Practice." Along with many other Baptists in the early nineteenth century, the members of this congregation simply heeded the advice common in the "Christian" movement to "shake off that yoke of ecclesiastical despotism, and burst those fetters of degrading tyranny."[18] As early as 1810–11, Joseph Thomas found that the "Christians" in Kentucky, Tennessee, and Ohio "have unanimously rejected and laid aside all doctrinating books, and have laid hold on the scriptures . . . and every thing respecting doctrine that they cannot find expressed there, they with all boldness spurn at it, and hoot it out of conversation."[19]

So committed were these "Christians" to achieving freedom by returning to the first Christian age that they celebrated this theme in song.

> Many follow men's inventions,
>   And submit to human laws,
> Hence divisions, and contentions,
>   Sully the Redeemer's cause:
>
> Some of Paul, some of Apollos,
>   Some of Cephas, few agree;
> Jesus, let us hear thee call us,
>   Help us, Lord, to follow thee.

Or again:

> Lay aside your party spirit,
>   Wound your Christian friend no more,

All the name of Christ inherit,
    Zion's peace again restore.

We'll not bind our brother's conscience,
    His to God alone is free,
Nor contend with one another,
    But in Christ united be;

Here's the Word, the grand criterion,
    This shall all our doctrines prove,
Christ the centre of our union,
    and the bond in christian love.[20]

With one voice these "Christians" agreed on what impeded their freedom: the traditions of Christian history embodied in creeds, synodical decisions, and clerical decrees. They therefore proclaimed their liberty by ignoring Christian history altogether and taking their stand instead on the Bible and the primitive church. As John Thompson observed, "We are not personally acquainted with the writings of John Calvan [*sic*], nor are we certain how nearly we agree with his views of divine truth; neither do we care." An anonymous correspondent wrote to Lexington's *Christian Examiner* in 1830 that "the primitive christian never heard of the five points of Dort, nor of Calvinism."[21] And Jacob Creath observed that "the Bible came from Heaven," while "human creeds came from London, Westminster, and Philadelphia." Therefore, he warned his brothers and sisters "not to be tossed about with such contradictory jargon as Calvinism, Fullerism and Arminianism. But stand fast, cast your anchor upon the foundation of the Apostles and Prophets, and New Testament ground." Accordingly, these "Christians" labored to remove the rubbish of history "with which the seed has been choked; that the . . . bare word of the Almighty may have free course."[22]

These "Christians" simply sidestepped history for the sake of freedom. Accordingly, they routinely conceived of the restoration task as one of pruning and negation. They feared that any attempt on their part to require particular articles of faith or ordinances might introduce again the bondage from which they so recently had escaped. They viewed their task, therefore, not as one of positive construction, but rather as one of elimination: they would prune the traditions of history and remove the encrustations of time until the primitive church in all its effulgent purity emerged once more. In actual practice, this meant, for example, a great hesitation to ordain ministers since they "had too fresh a remembrance of the sufferings they had underwent, in obtaining liberty from the reputed viceregents of Christ acting in his room and stead."[23] Or again, it meant a refusal to insist on immersion of adults, though most in the "Christian" movement had come voluntarily to this position. When Joseph Thomas visited the Kentucky "Christians" in 1810–11, he found that

> those that have, and those that have not been 'buried with Christ in baptism,' do not divide and contend about the subject; but they continue upon the plan which they set out upon—to let nothing divide them but Sin, and all search the scriptures for themselves, and act according to their understanding in the fear of God.[24]

As late as 1830, Barton Stone criticized Alexander Campbell, who, it seemed to Stone, increasingly made immersion a requirement for Christian identity. He protested:

> Should they make their own peculiar view of immersion a term of fellowship, it will be impossible for them to repel, successfully, the imputation of being sectarians, and of having an authoritative creed (though not written) of one article at least, which is formed of their own opinion of truth; and this short creed would exclude more christians from union than any creed with which I am acquainted.[25]

Further, the "Christians in the West," at least prior to Alexander Campbell's appearance in Kentucky in 1823, developed no systematic understanding of church government. At the same time, they rigorously opposed clerics, bishops, synods, and councils as impediments to Christian liberty. Stone later recalled that their enemies "represented us as disorganizers, having no form of government, and aiming a destructive blow at all church government."[26] Their enemies were right. If anything, the early "Christians in the West" were theologically and organizationally vacuous. But after all they simply did not concern themselves with organizations, new or old, or with systematic theological construction. Their concern, instead, was for freedom.

II

In some respects, the early "Christians in the West" had a great deal in common with their rivals in Kentucky and Ohio, the Shakers. If one asks, for example, how the Shakers could rest content to leave no children in this world, one might also ask how the "Christians" could rest content with a theological and organizational vacuum. The answer in both instances is the same: both expected the millennial dawn. Indeed their eager anticipation of the millennial age lent urgency and power to the

"Christian" enterprise and made their highly idealistic expectations seem both realistic and attainable.

What were those expectations? The early "Christians" believed, in brief, that if all Christians in the United States could be liberated from creeds and historic traditions and all return to the platform of the primitive, apostolic church, they then would unite, the denominational structures would simply cease to exist, and the millennium would have begun.

These early "Christians" shared with most Americans in the new nation deep misgivings regarding religious pluralism. The various religious denominations with their claims and counterclaims bewildered many and prompted that peculiarly American question, Which of all the churches is the true church? A case in point, as we shall see in the next chapter, was the Mormon prophet, Joseph Smith, who launched his career when he put that simple question to the Lord in the spring of 1820. According to Smith, the Lord responded that none of the existing churches was his, and Smith in due time sought to retrieve the one true church from the debris of the ages.

While the early "Christians" shared with Smith a restorationist response to religious pluralism, there also were differences. Thanks partly to the experiential ecumenism of the revivals which gave them birth, these "Christians" recognized that there were Christians in all the Protestant denominations. However, they denied institutional legitimacy to the denominations themselves. In this, they held precisely the position that James R. Graves and the Landmark Baptists would hold later in the century. The denominations, after all, were born of history and tradition and, taken together, comprised "Babylon" and "a wilderness of confusion." As Barton Stone was fond of saying, "Now Babylon signifies confusion, and O what a wilderness of confusion are the many divisions and subdivisions of the christian professors in the world!" But Stone and his colleagues were consoled by their conviction that "in this wilderness—in this Babel of confusion, is the true church of Christ, concealed and protected from the furious rage of the Dragon." The task of the "Christians in the West," therefore, was to cry aloud, "Come out of her my people." As Christians heeded this call and deserted their human habitations for the house of God, the denominational structures would simply crumble into the dust and be no more. This was the ground of their millennial anticipation. As Stone wrote, "In every division, with which we are acquainted, there appears to be an uncommon stir; and christian liberty, fellowship, and union is the theme. The division-walls, which are human authoritative creeds, are falling, fast falling in America and in Europe. Who does not see the signs of the times?"[27]

Their conviction that Christians resided in all the sects facilitated substantial dialogue between the "Christians" and their rivals in those early days. Typical was Joseph Thomas, who was interrogated in Columbia, Tennessee, in 1810, concerning, as Thomas put it, "what profession I was of": "I answered I was a professor of religion. But of what denomination? I said, of the religious denomination. Ah! but presbyterian, methodist, baptist, or what? I said I am of each. Are you a turn coat? (said he.) No, but I consider there are good people among all these denominations, and inasmuch as they were of God, I was of them."[28] As late as 1827, reports circulated of "Christians" sharing in fellowship and worship with members of other denominations. John Jones, for example, wrote to Barton Stone about the common worship experienced in Casey, Green, and Adair counties, Kentucky, in the summer of that year. "At the meetings appointed for worship, may be seen the Baptist, the Methodist, the Presbyterian, with the Christian Brethren all united; and if a stranger were looking on, he would not hesitate to say, they were all of one society."[29] Through all of this, however, the "Christians" firmly expected the dissolution of the sects at an early date. Thus, when accused of disorganization and of destroying all church government, Stone admitted that their enemies "evidently saw if we prevailed all parties must be dissolved."[30] This admission, after all, was only to state what seemed obvious in the context of his millennial expectations.

Millennial excitement had been building in America ever since the Great Awakening of the 1730s and 1740s, but the success of the Revolution convinced many Americans that the millennium was dawning or perhaps already had dawned. After all, the United States was a new nation in a new and virgin land whose citizens were experiencing liberties hitherto unknown. As the founding fathers put it, America was a *novus ordo seclorum*.

John Boles has suggested, however, that these millennial sentiments were not significantly awakened among southerners until the revivals beginning in 1801 "revolutionized thinking about the present time and the age to come."[31] And revolutionize their thinking the revivals certainly did. Indeed, Richard McNemar wrote that "the late revival was not sent to RE-FORM the churches. It did not come with a piece of new cloth to patch the old garment . . . , but to prepare the way for that kingdom of God, in which all things are new." Following the Cane Ridge Revival, John Dunlavy recalled that many people confidently thought that "the day of the Lord, or Millennium, was at hand, and that that revival would never cease until that day should commence." And Levi Purviance wrote that in the midst of the Kentucky revivals, "many were fully persuaded that the glorious Millennial Day had commenced, and that the world would soon become the Kingdom of our Lord Jesus Christ." "In these sublime figures," wrote McNemar, "was couched the whole purport of the Schismatic ["Christian"] vision, viz.: the coming of the Lord's kingdom with power."[32]

The aspect of the revivals that especially triggered millennial speculation among the "Christians" was their visible demonstration of Christian unity. Many fully expected the erection of a "dome of the king of kings," as McNemar put it, "in which the groanings of Presbyterians, Methodists, Baptists, and—Christians, for the wounds of their petty party cause would not be heard." All would be one, united in "a pure gospel church." Only then, the "Christians" contended, would "Zion shake herself from the dust . . . and shake terribly the nations . . . for God is now about to take the earth."[33]

The ecumenism implicit in these revivals was intimately bound up with primitivism as well, and the "Christians" frequently spoke of unity and restoration in the very same breath. As late as 1826, for example, on the first page of the first issue of his newly launched *Christian Messenger,* Barton Stone pled for "the restoration and glory of the ancient religion of Christ—the religion of love, peace, and union on earth."[34] After all, a united church capable of inaugurating the millennium would not be built on historic creeds and traditions, but rather on the platform of the apostolic age—a platform all Christians shared. The themes of restoration and unity were so intertwined in the thinking of the "Christians" that insistence on the one almost always involved insistence on the other. The dynamic that gave urgency to both was the eager expectation of the millennium, though the millennium was itself contingent on the restoration of the apostolic church and the realization of Christian unity. Clearly, restoration, unity, and millennialism were interrelated and mutually reenforcing themes.

The intimate connection of millennial, ecumenical, and primitivist themes in "Christian" thought appears in literally hundreds of their assertions. An article in the *Christian Examiner* in 1830 stated flatly that "the Apostolic Churches all had one Lord, one faith, and one immersion, and so will his 'Millennial Church.'" In the same year, Jacob Creath contended that "Christ can never be the universal King of Zion, until these artificial barriers [creeds] are broken down, and his people will then be governed by one code of laws, as they were in the primitive times." The close relation of all three of these themes—primitivism, ecumenism, and millennialism—to Christian liberty was suggested by one "Christian" who longed for the time when "the anti-christian clergy may be *dethroned,* . . . all dogmas . . . may be cast to the moles and the bats, and . . . the Lord Jesus alone may be exalted as head and King of

111

Zion." Then, he judged, there would be "one Lord, one faith, and one immersion . . . 'and the leopard shall lie down with the kid . . . and a little child shall lead them.'"[35] The "Christians" even celebrated these themes in their hymns. After singing of freedom, union, and the ancient faith, they then swelled the last refrain:

> Now the world will be constrained
>   To believe in Christ our King;
> Thousands, millions be converted,
>   Round the earth his praises ring;
> Blessed day! O joyful hour!
>   Praise the Lord—his name we bless.
> Send thy kingdom, Lord, with power,
>   Fill the world with righteousness.[36]

Clearly, these "Christians" sought to transmute the bondage of sectarianism into the freedom of Christian union by planting one foot squarely in the primitive church and striding boldly with the other into the millennial dawn. In the process, they essentially straddled and ignored the centuries of Christian history that had shaped them.

No wonder, then, that the "Christians" strongly dissented from the popular notion implicit in the great seal of the United States and echoed by such church leaders as Lyman Beecher, namely, that the American experiment itself would in some way hasten the millennial age.[37] If a new order of the ages was imminent, it would not be inaugurated by any tradition-bound, history-laden institution, but only by God's own institution which eclipsed time and tradition altogether: the primitive church. No government, no nation, no sect or mere denomination, no Bible society or missionary society—no creation of humankind whatsoever—possessed the power to transform and rejuvenate the world. Only the restored primitive church, whose perfections stood outside the bounds of time and tradition, could inaugurate an equally perfect millennial age.

Armed with these convictions, the "Christians" and their heirs stoutly resisted ecclesiastical societies of all kinds on the grounds that they both destroyed Christian freedom and arrogantly usurped the millennial role of the primitive church of God. When some suggested that the benevolent and religious societies not only would save the West from barbarism but usher in the millennium as well, Stone could only scoff, concluding that they were "too weak to bind Satan."[38]

III

The greatest tyrant with whom these "Christians" had to deal, however, was not that of societies, ecclesiastical structures, or creedal inventions. It rather was the sovereign God of Calvinistic predestination. According to the terms of this God, no one could approach either faith or salvation unless God both called and empowered her. Ironically, after asserting their freedom from kings, clerics, and creeds, the "Christians" now faced the ultimate bondage of the will.

The "Christians'" struggle with this God was writ large in practically all their autobiographies. Barton Stone wrote of being tossed for a year "on the waves of uncertainty—laboring, praying, and striving to obtain saving faith—sometimes desponding, and almost despairing of ever getting it." Nathan Mitchell recalled how he "would most fervently pray in secret, by day and by night, seeking, as I never sought for any thing before, to obtain 'the blessing.'" His prayers, however, were in vain. "The heavens were brass over my head, and for me there seemed to be no mercy. God was not willing in my case to be reconciled. . . . I was so much afraid of death, that I often wondered in the mornings that I was still alive." John Rogers spoke of a period during which "my prayers seemed to get no higher than my head." And in 1820, seventeen-year-old B. F. Hall sought God "back of the field, near a hollow, in a briar thicket. . . . I knelt for some moments in silence, for words came not to my lips. I could think of nothing to say. My pent-up grief was intence [*sic*]. . . . Tears gushed unbidden from my eyes. I sobbed aloud." When Hall finally reached conversion, his mother marveled "how Benjamin got through so soon. He was only about four weeks under conviction; and it was seven years before I obtained comfort, and I was all the while earnestly seeking the Lord." Joseph Thomas, after a long and bitter struggle, retired to the woods in May of 1807 to inform the Lord that "if this mercy was not for me I wished it to be made known to me by the vengeance of the almighty being let loose on me, to drive me down to hell and let me know the worst of my final state." No wonder John Dunlavy shrank from returning to Calvinism and being "beset with the distressing apprehensions of eternal death."[39]

These struggles raised the fundamental question Who would be sovereign, God or his subjects? As Stone observed, the Kentucky revival partly answered that question as the preachers largely "omitted the doctrines of Election and Reprobation."[40] But Stone himself addressed the question in a systematic way, beginning in 1803. Since God is unchangeable, Stone reasoned, God cannot be reconciled to human beings; however, human beings can and must reconcile themselves to God through rational belief of scriptural testimony and through righteous behavior. Christ did not die, Stone argued, to atone God to human beings but human beings to God, and his life and death in part provided an example that we should follow in his steps.[41]

According to McNemar all the schismatics who broke from the Synod of Kentucky in 1803 shared Stone's judgments. They taught, McNemar wrote, that "no one could be justified or accepted of God, but they that forsook their sins, and became personally righteous, . . . that there could be no . . . atonement to God, until the evil spirit . . . was overcome, and rooted out of God's creature." They even taught, McNemar continued, that "all that were born of Christ, and united to him, were true Christ, as much as fire produced by fire, is very fire, of fire." But this union between the believers and Christ, he added, clearly depended on the strength of their faith. No wonder McNemar judged that this doctrine "threatened the total subversion of the Calvinist system, at one blow."[42]

Once freed from the strictures of Calvinism, the "Christians" scorned its decrees as unchristian. One of their hymns told of a Christian who had tasted free grace but who returned to the chains of Calvinistic bondage.

The free love of Christ was my joy and my song,
    Till some did persuade me, my views were all wrong;
Such strong consolation they deemed a bad mark,
    That christians were safest when most in the dark. . . .

A Sinner, they said, had no right to believe,
    Till some special gift he from heaven receive,
And when he received it, to doubt and repine,
    Were needful to prove that the gift was divine. . . .

Can this be religion, I thought with a sigh,
    But surely the Levites know better than I.
Then founded my faith on the wisdom of man,
    And soon was induc'd t' embrace the whole plan. . . .

The spirit was grieved and soon did withdraw—
    I let go the gospel and turned to the law;
The spirit of bondage soon brought me to doubt,
    And under this bushel my candle went out. . . .[43]

Once freed of Calvinism, however, and committed to freedom as they were, the "Christians" simply could not provide sinners any means of certainty or assurance. "The Last Will and Testament of the Springfield Presbytery" urged that "the people henceforth take the Bible as the only sure guide to heaven" and simply left the matter there. John Dunlavy soon left the "Christians" for the Shakers; he charged that his former comrades in the faith, having deserted the sovereignty of God, simply had "left the people without any clear ground of justification." The Shakers' ground of justification, he urged, was celibacy by which they might "live free from sin" in the millennial age. But if celibacy was the Shakers' door to salvation, the "Christians'" primitivism provided no such opening.[44]

Here, then, is a portrait of the "Christians in the West"—a people so drunk on the wine of freedom that they spurned history with all its inherent constraints and limitations. They supposed instead that they might live their lives in those majestic temples that bracketed human time—the primordial age of the gods and the millennial dawn. Organizationally and theologically vacuous, they vigorously rejected the claims of tradition as "inventions of men," resisted structure of all kinds, and lived in simple faith that the approaching new world would both consummate and vindicate their radical insistence on a free church of God.

Many people, however, found the freedom of Christian primitivism a burden too great to bear. Robert Marshall and John Thompson, two of the five seceders from the Synod of Kentucky in 1803, complained by 1811 that the "Christian" movement provided no firm ground on which to stand. They charged, therefore, that the "Christians" engaged in endless speculation on a variety of theological topics and that "some of those men we have seen run entirely wild." John Rogers concurred, recalling in later years "our unprofitable strifes about untaught questions" wherein no one knew the difference "between saving truth and mere human speculation." In this atmosphere of freedom and unbridled speculation, distressed by the lack of structure and order of their churches and chagrined by the defection of colleagues to the Shakers, Marshall and Thompson finally judged "The Last Will and Testament" to be "a mischievous engine of disorganization" and returned to the Presbyterians.[45]

Theological vacuity and disorganization would not last long, however, for in 1823, "a new and very brilliant Star," as John Rogers put it, appeared in Kentucky in the person of Alexander Campbell.[46] Campbell had come to Kentucky to debate the Presbyterian W. L. McCalla on the mode of baptism—immersion versus sprinkling—but in the process of that debate he developed the theme that immersion is for forgiveness of sins.[47] For the "Christians in the West," this message was a godsend, for it provided what they wanted most: immediate certainty of salvation and an end to waiting and mourning. No longer would a sinner anxiously wait for months or even years, seeking an experience that might ratify his or her election. Instead, the sinner simply would hear the gospel and submit to immersion for the forgiveness of sins. Immediately all doubts would be erased; the sinner would know that he or she was now saved. As John Rogers explained, the early Christians were immersed and were thereby "pardoned, & knew it, & rejoiced in it . . . & never spoke in the language of doubt or fear upon the subject."[48] For many, this newfound certainty was not only liberating but even exhilarating. Nathan Mitchell recalled that he had once been "bound hand and foot in the chains forged by philosophizing metaphysicians." But on hearing this message of immediate certainty, "I bounded as a roe and leaped as an hart." B. F. Hall first discovered the gospel of immediate certainty in a crude Kentucky cabin when he found there the printed text of Campbell's debate with McCalla. On reading that text,

> I sprang to my feet in an ecstacy, and cried out, "Eureka! Eureka! I have found it! I have found it!" And I had found it. I had found the key-stone in the gospel arch, which had been set aside and ignored by the builders. I had found the long lost link in the chain of gospel obedience. . . . I now saw the evidence of remission, which I had never seen before.[49]

Even outsiders discerned that for these "Christians" baptism had become the sure and firm door to salvation that had replaced the uncertainties of Calvinism. The Presbyterian historian Robert Davidson told how "they sing, '*Since* I can read my title clear,' instead of '*When* I can read my title clear,' because a believer who has been immersed can have no doubt of his title."[50] No wonder an unsympathetic Methodist bard ridiculed this position with a piece of doggerel, "The Gospel in Water":

> Ho, every mother's son and daughter,
> Here's the "gospel in the water,"
> Here's the ancient gospel way,
> Here's the road to endless day,
> Here begins the reign of heaven,
> Here your sins shall be forgiven.
> Every mother's son and daughter,
> Here's the "gospel in the water."[51]

IV

In addition to immediate certainty of salvation, Campbell also provided the "Christians" with a theological certainty that eclipsed speculation. In the first place, both Campbell and his father, Thomas, viewed the New Testament essentially as a law book, a kind of divine constitution for the church. The Campbells shared with many of their contemporaries in the Reformed tradition the notion that scripture was fundamentally a legal document. But they differed with their peers when they affirmed that the law for the church is the New Testament alone. Thomas Campbell wrote in the *Declaration and Address,* the cornerstone of the Campbell movement, that "the New Testament is as perfect a constitution for the worship, discipline, and government of the New Testament Church, and as perfect a rule for the particular duties of its members, as the Old Testament was for the worship, discipline, and government of the Old Testament Church, and the particular duties of its members."[52] And Alexander Campbell argued in 1823 that Christ's "will published in the New Testament is the sole law of the church." If the Bible was a constitution, Campbell's next argument followed logically from the first: biblical examples were as binding as express commands, and the silence of scripture was always prohibitive.[53] Thus the Christian could know the law of God with certainty, and have confidence that he or she had obeyed that law, simply by reading the New Testament, attending to its commands and examples, and observing its silence.

But there was more. Influenced deeply by Common Sense Realism, Campbell taught the "Christians" that "the Bible is a book of facts, not of opinions, theories, [or] abstract generalities." To know the truths of scripture, therefore, one simply proceeds in an inductive manner to collect and classify all Bible facts on a given topic. Since these facts are uniform in their meaning, they bring uniformity of belief and undermine all theorizing and speculation. In this way, all Christians could understand the Bible alike.[54]

Since the "Christians" were deeply committed already to ancient and apostolic norms, this interpretive tool had great appeal. After all, it promised to illumine the teachings of the apostles with clarity and scientific precision. But further, the method itself, so simple and so clear, seemed to transcend time, custom, and culture and to be universally applicable in all times and ages. As George Jardine, Campbell's teacher at the University of Glasgow, put it, "All men, the savage, the farmer, and the huntsman all make use of this mode of Reasoning by induction." And Robert Richardson, a colleague of Campbell's, argued that even the apostles "began with facts and drew from these by induction the proper inferences and rules of action."[55]

Already convinced that creeds and statements of faith were engines of tyranny, the "Christians" further siezed on Campbell's suggestion that they confine themselves not just to Bible facts but even to Bible words. Campbell argued in 1827 that if all Christians simply would "abandon every word and sentence not found in the Bible on this subject [in this case, the Trinity], and without explanation, limitation, or enlargement, quote with equal pleasure and readiness, and apply on every suitable occasion, every word and sentence found in the volume, to the Father, to the Son, and to the Holy Spirit," divisions in Christendom simply would cease to exist. This insistence made sense to the "Christians." John

Rogers typified most when he expressed regrets over earlier days when "I indulged in speculations. . . . [But now] I . . . most heartily accept & endorse bro: A. Campbell's plan of settling all those controversies, viz: By letting them alone." By 1860, Rogers was advising the Church of Christ in Carlisle, Kentucky, to "be more and more scrupulous to call scriptural thoughts or ideas, by scriptural names; to abjure the language of Ashdod, and use the pure language of Canaan, especially in regard to all questions of doubtful disputation."[56] No wonder that in 1832, most of the "Christians in the West" formally united themselves with Campbell and his Disciples.

Here was the root and core of the perspective that so bewildered Jeremiah Jeter: the conviction that "I can't be wrong—I follow the Book." And here lies the irony in the "Christian" movement. From an early date, the "Christians" rejected the creeds and traditions of history and took their stand instead on the Bible and the first Christian age. In this way they meant to protect their freedom to think, to dialogue, and to search for fuller understanding of scripture and the ancient order of things. They simply rejected those explanations of the Bible that had crystallized in the course of time and that, as they complained to the Synod of Kentucky in 1803, "preclude all farther advances after truth." Clearly, then, the "Christians'" commitment to the first age was at one and the same time a commitment to the task of theologizing, with the single qualification that no one's theology or interpretation would ever be accepted as equivalent to the word of God. Put another way, their search for the ancient order was just that: a search. It was process, not accomplished fact. For them, restoration would sustain liberty only so long as the first age stood in judgment on "the inventions of men."

This posture, however, proved difficult to sustain. In the first place, its inherent uncertainties could make life terribly insecure. And in the second place, theirs was an age of scientific discovery on the one hand and sectarian competition on the other, and in such an age, certainty meant standing, stature, and even power. The temptation, therefore, to exchange their birthright of freedom for intellectual and spiritual certainty could be overwhelming.

The temptation came when Campbell pressed them to restrict themselves to "gospel facts" and to Bible words "without explanation, limitation, or enlargement." To confine themselves to Bible words without explanation would be to speak where the Bible speaks and to be silent where the Bible is silent and, in so doing, to identify with the Christian primordium in the fullest sense possible. Or so it seemed. But in accepting this seductive posture, the "Christians" engaged in a profound but subtle transformation that would have lasting and even devastating effects. In the first place, restoration became no longer a means to an end—that end being freedom—but rather an end in itself. In the second place, confining themselves to Bible "facts" and Bible words allowed the "Christians" to believe that while others interpreted the Bible they did not. And in the third place, if their understandings were identical with the Bible's intent and purpose, there was really, then, no reason for any further search.

The transformation of the restoration ideal among the "Christians" paralleled that wrought by the Landmark Baptists in the same region, as we saw in chapter 4. Ironically, the restoration theme, which had served the cause of freedom so well in the "Christians'" early years, now was poised to become freedom's foe. After all, the "Christians" now possessed complete certainty. They were certain of salvation since they had been immersed, and they were certain that their perspectives were identical with those of scripture. They had thrust the God of Calvinism largely out of doors, leaving little sense either of the radical sovereignty of God or of the fallenness and frailty of humankind. At this point, it perhaps was inevitable that some would claim that the Church of Christ had fully restored the ancient order and now was the one true church outside of which there was no salvation. These claims would come in due time.

V

One further step, however, faced the "Christians" if they were to exclude completely the sovereign God of Calvinism. That step was to confine the activities of the Holy Spirit to a rational and manageable sphere. In the early years of the nineteenth century, the "Christians in the West" regularly claimed the power of the Spirit in their services, pointing to such ecstatic exercises as dancing, jerking, falling, and barking as evidence of that power. McNemar noted that their belief that "God and Christ had their abode in the soul of man" tended to increase "whatever exercise was congruous to that inward feeling." Stone himself spoke warmly of the exercises and, according to Dunlavy, both approved and practiced the dancing exercise which began in the spring of 1804.[57] Joseph Thomas, who toured the "Christian" congregations of Tennessee, Kentucky, and Ohio in 1810 and 1811, provides evidence that these exercises persisted for several years among these "Christians." Thomas wrote that the "Christians" "have an exercise . . . amongst them called the JIRKS. It sometimes throws them into the fire, into the mud, upon the floor, upon the benches, against the wall of the house, &c." Thomas recorded numerous instances of these exercises, especially the jerks, among the "Christians" in Kentucky and Tennessee.[58] In January of 1811,

119

he visited the "Christians" in Mount Tabor, Kentucky, where he "saw dancing going on for the worship of God," and in Concord, Kentucky, where he saw the laughing exercise in "a large congregation."[59] Isaac Jones, born in east Tennessee in 1822, recalled from his boyhood days

> the customs of praying for mourners, shouting and clapping of hands (chiefly among the ladies), and the telling of experiences as to how the Holy Spirit brought them from death to life, etc. Especially in east Tennessee were many affected by that whirl-wind of excitement called "The Jerks." The writer has seen more than a dozen under its influence at the same time.

But Jones also recalled that "by degrees . . . these all passed away, and people began to do things 'decently and in order.' " And he added: "Many were the hard-fought battles necessary to get the *brethren* to see the simple teachings of God's word, and to break loose from the doctrine of abstract operations of the Spirit in converting the sinner."[60]

The general who directed those battles was, once again, Alexander Campbell. As early as 1824, in his first volume of the *Christian Baptist*, Campbell declared that "since those gifts (of the Spirit) have ceased, the Holy Spirit now operates upon the minds of men only by the word." Over the years, he would sound this refrain time and again. "Whatever the word does, the Spirit does; and whatever the Spirit does in the work of converting men, the word does." He even argued that "if the Spirit of God has spoken all its arguments" in scripture, then "all the power of the Holy Spirit which can operate on the human mind is spent."[61] By 1827, Barton Stone concurred: "To say that the Scriptures are not the cause nor foundation of our faith, but some immediate, mysterious operation of the spirit on the mind, involves so many insurmountable difficulties, that we are obliged to reject it."[62] By the decade of the 1830s, the position that the Spirit was shackled to the word had become orthodoxy. B. F. Hall typified most "Christians" when he wrote in 1837: "I believe that the Holy Spirit exerts no influence on the heart of sinners over and above the word: that his influences are in the facts he has revealed in the gospel, the evidences by which he has confirmed these facts, and in the motives to obedience presented in the Scriptures of Truth."[63] The Presbyterian historian Robert Davidson perhaps understated his case when he wrote of the "Christians" that "the noble and animated hymn, 'Come, Holy Spirit, Heavenly Dove!' is never permitted to vibrate on their tongues, because they deny that the Spirit is a personal agent or anything more than a mere influence."[64] He perhaps should have added, "a mere influence shackled to the word."

In this way, the early "Christians in the West" gradually rendered the primordium both reasonable and manageable. Further, the Christians had institutionalized the first age, and on their own terms. They had taken the time of the gods—that expansive and universal epoch which sustained all times, structures, and cultures—and slowly, even imperceptibly, transformed it into a nineteenth-century Anglo-American creation. They had particularized the universal, though they imagined that they had recovered the universal in their particular perspectives and institutions. What seemed to them entirely natural, universal, and transcendent of times and cultures was in fact their own small world of laws and constitutions, of scientific facts, and of Common Sense philosophy applied to the scriptures of the Christian faith.

What sustained this irony in those transitional years was the "Christians'" profound sense of historylessness—a sense of living not in the profane and precarious present, but rather in those strong and certain times of primordial beginning and millennial end. For one thing, they had convinced themselves that by abjuring all human traditions and confining themselves to biblical terminology they had re-created the first Christian age. For another, they firmly believed that they stood at the very edge of a new heaven and a new earth and that their own efforts hastened the millennial dawn. Fully identifying with first times and last times, they thought they saw the present age, with all its frailties and imperfections, passing away before their very eyes. Barton Stone proclaimed in 1827 that "the signs of the times are visible to such as are observant. The Christians in this wilderness of confusion are beginning to see and lament . . . the evils of partyism, of human authoritative creeds and party names." Later that year he urged that "the spirit of reform" would "in a little time . . . break every human fetter which has long bound and enslaved the Christian world."[65] Nor was Stone alone in this conviction. In 1829, J. Norwood began publication in Lexington, Kentucky, of the *Christian Examiner*. Norwood had intended to call this journal the *Christian Examiner and Millennial Herald,* but found his title preempted by Alexander Campbell's plans to launch his own *Millennial Harbinger* in 1830. In that journal and in that year, Campbell proclaimed his own conviction that his "*Ancient Gospel*" was "long enough, broad enough, strong enough for the whole superstructure called the Millennial Church—and [that] . . . it will alone be the *instrument* of *converting* the whole human race, and of *uniting* all christians upon one and the same foundation."[66]

By 1835, millennial excitement and anticipation were unabated. Stone and several colleagues wrote in that year that "the church of God is the great moral engine to revolutionize the world; that on this lever rests the mighty arm."[67] But Stone well knew by then the terrible, haunting question that threatened to smash the lever and release the mighty arm.

That question was simply Which church? Would it be the universal church of God embracing all Christians in all times and all cultures? That had been the original ideal. Or would it be a new denomination called the "Church of Christ"—a particular creation of the nineteenth-century American frontier cloaked in universal garb? It was this question that troubled Stone when he wrote in 1836 that "some among ourselves were for some time zealously engaged to do away with party creeds, and are yet zealously preaching against them—but instead of a written creed of man's device, they have substituted a non-descript one, and exclude good brethren from their fellowship, because they dare believe differently from their opinions."[68] But Stone had every confidence that the drive toward first times had released the millennial impetus and would soon crush the sectarian spirit everywhere, even among his own people. He warned that his own sectarian brethren who had particularized the universal, creedalized the absence of creeds, and turned the rhetoric of freedom into an instrument of oppression—he warned that these people soon would be crushed. "These brethren will find that their non-descript creed and sectarian spirit will break them in pieces. Floods of light are rolling from the book of God, which are sweeping away all refuges of lies, and will clear the world of the trash which has been accumulating for ages. In vain they try to establish another sect. It is too late."[69]

VI

But it was not too late. In fact, the process of particularizing the universal and then cloaking those particulars in the rhetoric of the ancient faith had begun in earnest in 1823. The man chiefly responsible for this development was not so much Alexander Campbell as Walter Scott, one of Campbell's close associates. Scott and Campbell had become friends in 1821, and in 1823 Scott began to write in Campbell's *Christian Baptist* concerning the "one uniform and universal plan of teaching the [Christian] religion." This plan was simply to proclaim the single rational assertion made popular by John Locke years before, namely, that Jesus is the Messiah. Scott felt that he had discovered the very "plan of God" and held in contempt "the various stupid schemes, all different and all wrong, pursued by Roman Catholics, Socinians, Arians, Covenanters, Seceders, Presbyterians, High-Churchmen, Baptists, Independents, and so forth."[70]

By 1827, the Mahoning (Ohio) Baptist Association, with which the Campbell movement was still affiliated, prevailed on Scott to serve as its missionary in the Western Reserve. By this time Scott had engrafted other elements onto his plan which he both conceived and preached as a covenant between God and humankind. Humankind's obligation to God was threefold, Scott argued: to believe, to repent, and to submit to immersion for the remission of sins. In response, God would grant forgiveness of sins, the gift of the Holy Spirit, and eternal life.[71] Preaching this simple and rational message on the Western Reserve, Scott met with astounding success and won that year close to one thousand new converts.

The following year Scott reported his successes to the Mahoning Association meeting in Warren, Ohio. This report was a pivotal document, due both to its content and to the wide circulation it received. It was less a factual accounting of his work than an exhilarating statement of his own primordial/millennial anticipations. His success in preaching the "ancient gospel" had convinced him that the nineteenth century was "a sublime eminence" from which the Christian could "look backward upon nearly the whole train of events leading to the *Millennium*." Scott then made an important claim: the true method of preaching the ancient gospel had been restored in 1827. For the first time in either the Stone movement in the South or the Campbell movement further north, restoration was now heralded as an accomplished fact, and even tied to a definite date. Scott seemed astounded, even stunned, when he asked the delegates, "but who would have thought it remained for any so late as 1827, to restore to the world the manner—the primitive manner—of administering to mankind the gospel of our Lord Jesus Christ! . . . Yet these things have actually occurred." Scott was almost ecstatic with the anticipation that "the ancient gospel and ancient order of the church must prevail to the certain abolition of all those contumacious sects which now so woefully afflict mankind," and concluded this portion of his report with the declaration that "the Millennium—the Millennium described in Scripture—will doubtless be a wonder, a terrible wonder to ALL."[72]

Scott's speech was printed in Lexington's *Christian Examiner* and thereby circulated among the "Christians in the West." Further, Scott's influence grew enormously from that time on. He baptized perhaps one thousand persons per year for the next thirty years—far more than anyone else in the movement. And much of his work was in Kentucky. In 1831 the *Christian Examiner* announced Scott's proposal to launch a new journal called the *Evangelist*. Beginning in 1832, it enjoyed a wide circulation in Kentucky and was moved from Cincinnati to Georgetown (Ky.) in 1837 where Scott coedited the paper with John T. Johnson. In this way, Scott exerted an enormous influence over the hearts and minds of the old "Christians in the West."

If the extent of Scott's influence was important, the nature of his message was even more so. Increasingly, he believed that the true gospel had been restored in 1827 and that he was the agent of its restoration. In 1836 he published a volume entitled *The Gospel Restored* and claimed in the preface that "in 1827 the True gospel was restored."[73] Then, in 1838, he enlarged the title of the *Evangelist* to the *Evangelist of the True Gospel.*

What enabled Scott to make such bold and stirring claims was, at least in part, his reliance on the Baconian method. For Scott, as for Campbell, the gospel was essentially a collection of facts. The preacher's task was arranging those facts in their proper order and then supporting them with appeals to evidence. Scott defined the gospel as "a rational advocacy . . . [that] pleads the faith in its saving proposition from evidence"; he argued that "the Christian faith . . . belongs to the science of inference—reason—logic, and depends for its reception in society on proof." In this scheme of things, the task of the Spirit was not to "enter the soul of the sinner" but rather to convince "us as we convince one another—by truth and argument."[74] To Scott's mind, the Baconian method entirely precluded interpretation; it simply laid bare the plain facts of the ancient gospel—facts that should be perfectly clear and compelling to any rational mind.

Campbell shared the Baconian perspective, but he refused to join Scott in claiming the gospel had been restored. This became clear in 1838 when a Francis Emmons rendered his judgment that both Campbell and Scott had claimed the honor of having restored the ancient gospel—Campbell in 1823 and Scott in 1827. Scott was deeply hurt and rushed into print to set the record straight. Campbell, he admitted, clearly proclaimed immersion for the forgiveness of sins in 1823. But, Scott argued, "the restoration of the whole gospel in 1827, can never be confounded with the definition of a single one of its terms in 1823, or in any year preceding it."[75] Campbell was appalled at Scott's bold and pretentious claim. He denied ever claiming, for his own part, "that 'the gospel was restored' in 1823," and registered his protest "against this invidious style of fixing dates, places, and persons, and instituting comparative claims for the restoration of the original gospel." He admitted that he himself had published a book with the title *Christianity Restored,*[76] but claimed embarrassment at the title which was, he said, the work of his printer and not himself. *"To restore the gospel,"* Campbell urged, "is really a great matter, and implies that the persons who are the subjects of such a favor once had it and lost it"—a pronouncement that Campbell, at least at this late date in his career, was unwilling to make.[77]

Scott's confidence that he had restored the ancient gospel persisted, however, in spite of Campbell's reservations. Two factors sustained his belief—and that of the many "Christians" who followed his lead—that the gospel, now restored, would soon "prevail to the certain abolition of . . . [the] sects." One was the presumed clarity of scripture when read through the Baconian perspective. The other was their confidence that they stood at the very edge of the millennial dawn. The ancient truths, so long obscured, now were clear and surely would triumph in history's final years. These convictions were especially easy to hold during the great revivals when the gospel seemed so potent and the unity of Christians so promising.

This original vision, however, became more and more difficult to sustain as the "Christians" increasingly encountered the stubborn and persistent fact of religious pluralism in the United States. Indeed, when the revival fires cooled, as Levi Purviance later recalled, "sectarianism raised its hydra head, and 'made war upon the saints of the most High God and overcame them,' and the fair prospects of Zion were in some degree blasted."[78] The harsh reality of pluralism had now particularized the "Christian" movement and thrust it rudely and abruptly into the sea of finite history which the "Christians" had thought to escape. When this happened, many of the "Christians" rejected the dilemmas that confronted them, denied the finitude of their own movement, and insisted that while others may be caught in the web of history, they were not. Their church belonged to the first age, not to time or tradition. Those who adopted this posture turned a critical corner in their movement as they relinquished the original ideal of restoration as process. Instead, restoration became for them an accomplished fact. In this way, the "Christians" developed a tradition whose very substance was a denial of their tradition and a history that, ironically, would be characterized for many years by a keen sense of having no history at all.

The dilemma of being a people with neither history nor tradition in a fundamentally finite and historic world emerged early in the movement. An almanac published in Cincinnati in 1806 correctly assessed the problem. The "Christians," it noted, "believe and declare that they are not a church separate from other christians," and "desire to have no other name than that of CHRISTIAN." Yet, the almanac reported, "it is manifest that this common name will distinguish them so long as others hold their peculiar distinguishing names."[79] Others, however, were hardly so mild in their assessment. Isaac Jones recalled the difficult times experienced by his father, Rees Jones, who preached the "Christian" message in east Tennessee in the early years of the movement. For admonishing his neighbors to "come out of Babylon," "vile personal abuse was heaped upon him, sticks were shaken over his head, rewards were offered for his lynching, and he was threatened with the law, etc." In the same region, a local bell maker named Dodge had embraced the "Christian" cause and soon found circulating in his neighborhood the following lines:

> Against old Dodge we're bound to lodge
> A heavy accusation;
> He clinks the bell that tolls to hell,
> Sad victims of damnation.

In the same region, a sign posted to a tree proclaimed, "Twenty dollars reward for any man or set of men that will whip old John Mulkey and Rees Jones." Joseph Thomas, after visiting the "Christians" in Kentucky, Tennessee, and Ohio, returned to his native North Carolina where he found that

> meeting-house doors were shut against me; several private families would not suffer me to speak of religion in their houses for fear I might *warp* their minds from Presbyterianism, Metodism [*sic*], or some other *ism:* and one man ordered me out of his house and to begone off his plantation, and for no other reason that that he said *I preached the Devil's doctrine, and was an imp of hell.*

Thomas returned the compliment, however, noting that in one town in South Carolina "I found the moschetos and gnats to be exceedingly troublesome, the sectarians very bitter, and the water extremely bad and insalubrious."[80]

All these events transpired in the early years when restoration was still viewed as process, when boundaries had not been drawn, and when no one had even thought to claim that the ancient gospel had been fully restored. Barton Stone, therefore, was understandably troubled by the charge that the "Christians" were "laboring to establish a party. I deny the charge," Stone declared, and then added:

> We have publicly and sincerely professed the spirit of union with all christians—We have neither made nor adopted any party-creed, but have taken the Bible only as our standard—We have taken no party-names by which to distinguish ourselves from others, but the general name *christians*—We have raised no bars from our communion, but what the Bible has raised before us—And yet we are accused of partyism![81]

But when Walter Scott claimed in 1827 that the gospel had been fully restored, when he particularized the gospel on his rational grid, and when his understandings circulated and gained popularity among the

"Christians" farther south, opposition became even more intense. The Methodist *Gospel Herald* stated the issue bluntly:

> A loud cry against the use of Confessions of Faith, is made by a large body of professing Christians in the West, who assume to be the only people that acknowledge the Bible as the only infallible rule of faith and practice: a truth which is the very foundation of Protestantism, and a prominent article in the creed of every Protestant Church.

Opponents argued that the "Christians" no more belonged to the first age than anyone else, that they too were children of history, and that all their claims to the contrary were both arrogant and pretentious. Thus they increasingly fastened on the "Christians" the label "Campbellite." But the "Christians" rejected these labels and simply reaffirmed their identity with the first age. Alexander Reynolds typified most when he wrote in 1838,

> I will now say to all those who seem to intend to neutralize the gospel we preach by giving it a human name, that they had better first convict us of a departure from the Apostolic gospel, at least in some prominent instance. Until this is done all their attempts to fix the name Campbellite upon us cannot be regarded in any other light than the foulest slander.

By 1830, John Rogers surveyed the "slander" and the "Christians'" response, projecting utter confidence concerning the rightness of the "Christians'" position. "We therefore, as might have been expected, met with powerful opposition from every quarter. We were denounced as damnable heritics [*sic*], schismatics, Anti-Christs, &c. But unmoved by all this sectarian clamor, we pursued 'the even tenor of our way.'"[82]

Pursuing the "even tenor" of their way, the "Christians" soon began counting heads to determine precisely how many had gathered to their fold. In so doing they abanoned the early position so clearly stated by Barton Stone when he wrote that "we have publicly and sincerely professed the spirit of union with all christians." Now reports like the following began appearing in the "Christian" periodicals.

> There are seven congregations of Christ in this county. One of 20 members, one of 22, one of 35, one of 45, one of 65, one of 100 and one of 135. And 1 should have planted the eighth . . . had my health permitted, with eight members; making in all, the No. of *four hundred and thirty* members who have united with the church of God in this county.

Then the reporter added, "From what I can ascertain there are more who have taken their stand on apostolic ground to believe what God has said and do what he has commanded, in this county than all the sects put together."[83]

The millennial ship of the Churches of Christ had struck the rock of pluralism running full speed ahead. In the context of religious pluralism in America and in the eyes of their peers, the Churches of Christ became thereby a denomination among other denominations. Many "Christians," however, continued to claim that they constituted no denomination in any sense at all, but rather comprised the one true church of the apostolic age.

VII

In the late 1830s and early 1840s, two new periodicals made their debut and circulated widely among the "Christians" in Ohio, Kentucky, Tennessee, Alabama, and even Mississippi. These journals were Arthur Crihfield's *Heretic Detector,* begun in Middleburgh, Ohio, in 1837, and John R. Howard's *Bible Advocate,* launched from Paris, Tennessee, in 1842. While not as influential as Campbell's *Millennial Harbinger* or Scott's *Evangelist,* both papers nonetheless claimed substantial numbers of readers, featured articles by the most influential preachers among Churches of Christ, and exerted an immense influence on the hearts and minds of the "Christians" in the old Southwest. Crihfield became so popular that the "Christians" in Kentucky invited him to leave Ohio and settle in Harrodsburg, to edit his paper there and to increase its frequency from a monthly to a weekly.[84]

One finds in these papers a rhetoric similar to the rhetoric that characterized the "Christians" in their earliest years. Terms such as *freedom, unity,* and *primitive Christianity* occured over and again. But one also finds that these terms had undergone a subtle but profound change in meaning. The concern for a primitive church of Christ that would embrace all Christians and thereby inaugurate the millennial age had all but disappeared. Instead, the task that preoccupied these papers was that of defending the Church of Christ as the one true church in a sea of false churches. Further, the "Christians'" confrontation with religious pluralism—or as they put it, with the "sects"—lay behind the change. Crihfield said as much when he justified the existence of the *Heretic Detector.* "A work of this character is loudly called for, at this crisis," he wrote, since "from the one end of this vast country to the other, the cry of 'heresy' has been raised against the Disciples of Jesus Christ." Crihfield therefore set out to expose the real heretics by wielding "the sword of the Spirit, which is the word of God," and he was quite certain that "the proper use of it . . . will make an impression not easily obliterated or forgotten."[85]

To a substantial degree, both papers adhered to the same ideological starting point that had served Alexander Campbell and Walter Scott. The Bible was a book of facts and the Spirit was confined to its pages. But Crihfield and Howard divorced these themes from their original ecumenical intent and used them instead to fortify the boundaries of the Church of Christ. Accordingly, a writer in Howard's paper contended that "the church of Jesus has for its foundation, facts and truths, . . . while, very frequently, the foundation of the sects is some trifling opinion at which an apostle would blush!" And Crihfield made it clear that the gospel "facts" were precisely those announced by Walter Scott years before: faith, repentance, and immersion, followed by remission of sins, the Holy Spirit, and eternal life.[86] The Spirit, however, was shackled to the word, and the "Christians" ridiculed their charismatic competitors. One correspondent informed the *Heretic Detector* that

> there has recently been a three-day meeting of the Episcopal Methodists in this vallage [*sic*]; and it was all spirit from beginning to end. They sung holy ghost, and prayed holy ghost, and preached holy ghost, and felt holy ghost. The holy ghost convicted, converted, and pardoned. In short, he did every thing, and did it all without words. . . . This may be emphatically styled the 'day of ghosts.'[87]

Having laid their foundation in gospel "facts," Howard and Crihfield then proceeded to assail their foes and prove beyond any doubt that the Church of Christ was the one true church outside of which one could not be saved. Numerous articles appeared in both papers on the identity of the one true church.[88] Aylette Raines informed readers of the *Bible Advocate* that there was "no church in the world, in which Peter the apostle would be an acceptable preacher, but that vulgarly nick-named Campbellite!" And John Howard proclaimed that there is a true church and a false church, and "he who is not in one must be in the other. There is no neutral ground."[89]

More than anyone else, John Howard supplied the identifying marks of the true Church of Christ. It originated, he said, at Pentecost; is called "Church of Christ" or "Christian Church"; has no creed but the Bible; admits members upon faith, repentance, confession, and immersion; is organized into independent congregations, each with elders, deacons, deaconnesses, and evangelists; and worships by preaching, praying, and partaking of the Lord's Supper weekly. It was this church, he said, that "originated . . . in the days of the Apostles, and was founded by them;

while all others began in after ages, and were founded by uninspired men." Howard then pressed far beyond Stone, Campbell, or Scott and simply unchristianized everyone not in his own Church of Christ. He readily admitted that "it may . . . be said of us, 'You have unchristianized every Church in the land but one—but your own—and consigned them all alike to the disapprobation of God, disownment by the Lord Jesus Christ, and utter extinction and annihilation!'" But Howard was assured—and here is the critical point—that "it is not *we* who have done it, but it has been done by the New Testament, by the WORD of God."[90] To Howard and his colleagues, there was simply no difference between the Bible and their interpretation of the Bible. In fact, they were quite certain that they were not involved in the interpretation process in any sense at all. Their implicit reliance on Baconianism had convinced them that they had escaped the constraints of history, culture, and tradition and simply stood with the apostles in the first Christian age.

Both Crihfield and Howard, therefore, addressed to "sectarians" the appeal the "Christians" had used since the early ministry of Barton W. Stone: "Come out of her my people." But the intent was no longer an ecumenical intent, sustained by anticipations of a glorious millennial dawn when all Christians would be one. Instead, the intent had become sectarian and coercive as Crihfield, for example, threatened those who "will not 'come out'" with "the plagues of Babylon when she falls." Crihfield even recited a poem that captured this theme:

People and Priests, from Babel's smoke
  And darkness, now retire:
'Come out of her,' as Jesus spoke,
  And leave the town on fire.[91]

The motif of fire held much more than metaphorical significance, for both Howard and Crihfield embraced in 1843 a radically premillennial posture inspired by the Millerite excitement of that year. However, they turned the Millerite fervor to their own ends when, for example, Howard urged "sectarians"

to cast away all your unscriptural names, forms and practices; and return back to the true faith—the pure, original Gospel. . . . The coming of the Lord, in vengeance to destroy his enemies, cannot . . . be very far off, . . . And should *you* not be found among his true people—his genuine disciples—but arrayed in opposition against them, he will "destroy" you "with the *breath* of his *mouth,* and with the *brightness* of his *coming.*"[92]

The premillennial vision vanished among the "Christians" almost as soon as it began. But the fact that it appeared at all indicates that the earlier postmillennial vision of Stone, Scott, and Campbell had collapsed among many of the "Christians" in the old Southwest. The cause for its collapse was simply the strong, stubborn, and immovable rock of religious pluralism. By the late 1830s, it became increasingly clear to the "Christians" that pluralism would not vanish and that proclamation of the ancient gospel would not hasten the millennial dawn. Arthur Crihfield candidly admitted this fact:

> deaf to the calls of thousands of their fellows who, with the Bible poised in their hands, are urging a return to duty and to unity, sects still presume to multiply. . . . And yet we are dreaming that this miserable condition of Christendom is to be cured by the therapeutics of moral suasion? Be not deceived, reader! The hour is past for such means to avail. Slight topical ameliorations will be effected by the reproclamation of the gospel; a few from the different parties will be induced to leave; but the Sects, as such, will never become extinct till "the sign of the Son of Man is seen in the heavens."

Crihfield simply despaired. The postmillennial dream now appeared as sheer illusion. "We are dreaming of the success of the gospel . . . , while a systematic priesthood must be supported by division," he wrote. "And still we dream of a millennium brought about by science and theology, while money without stint is appropriated to sectarian purposes." But at one level, Crihfield rejoiced, for he felt confident that "the Nobleman will return to reckon with his servants—to reorganize his Residence, and take up his abode with us."[93]

By 1845 the die was cast. In that year, Tennessee's Tolbert Fanning—the man who would be the most influential leader among Churches of Christ in the Southwest in the mid-years of the nineteenth century—spoke for most when he categorically rejected a suggestion that Churches of Christ originated with Alexander Campbell on Brush Run Creek in 1810. "No modern system or church is of God," he proclaimed, "and he who professes to believe a system, formed since the Apostolic age, or to be a member of a church founded since the memorable Pentecost . . . must be in great error. . . . We claim to be members of the Church of Christ, which had its origin in Jerusalem on the day of Pentecost, and not on Brush Run Creek, in 1810."[94]

VIII

What had happened to the "Christians" in the short span of forty years? More than anything else, the collapse of the original postmillennial vision helped turn them from affirmations of freedom to threats of coercion. The road along which this transformation occurred had taken many turns, to be sure. The "Christians" began their journey with the simple intent of restoring first times in the interest of liberty, unity, and the millennial age. Along the way, they embraced the Common Sense perspectives of Baconianism, rejected the radical sovereignty of God, and confined the Spirit to the pages of Holy Writ. Their encounter with the persistent fact of pluralism, however, finally shattered their postmillennial vision. When this vision disappeared, they found themselves relentlessly hurled into the abyss of history which they thought they had escaped. At that point, some of the "Christians" turned in upon themselves, intensified their claim to apostolic origins and identity, and threatened with divine retribution those who refused the wisdom of their way.

History had obtruded on the "Christians" in spite of themselves. Their original vision of the primitive church, with its promise of liberty and union, became for many of their heirs only a rhetorical hedge against the terrors of history. The millennium did not dawn, unity did not transpire, and freedom from the constraints of history and tradition proved illusory. Some continued to struggle against the forces of history to keep alive the original ideal of restoration as process, grounded in hope. But for many "Christians," restoration became an accomplished fact. For them, history emerged victorious, leaving only the rhetorical husks of a grand vision of liberty and union for all.

SIX

Soaring with the Gods:
Early Mormons and the Eclipse of
Religious Pluralism

The Mormon commitment to restoring first times was no less intense than that of the "Christians," though it took a radically different form. Indeed, Mormons rejected two central "Christian" premises, namely, that Baconian rationalism was the only proper lens through which the Bible should be viewed, and second, that the New Testament was the only legitimate guide to the restoration task. Mormons looked instead to a constellation of sacred times, claiming that in Joseph Smith, their prophet, God had communed with earth again just as in the days of Adam, Abraham, Moses, and Jesus. Further, if the "Christians" took almost forty years to transform the lure of first times into a radically antipluralistic posture, that posture was inherent in the restoration vision of early Mormons from the very start. This chapter seeks to explain how and why this was so.

I

Sidney E. Mead observed in *The Lively Experiment* that one of the defining themes of American Christianity during the nation's early years was a profound sense of "historylessness," a perspective shaped by three assumptions: "the idea of pure and normative beginnings to which return was possible; the idea that the intervening history was largely that of aberrations and corruptions which was better ignored; and the idea of building anew in the American wilderness on the true and ancient foundations." Reinforcing this restoration perspective was the radical newness of the American experiment, which worked to erase continuity not only with Europe but also with the historic churches. Thus, many Christians imagined they were beginning again "at the point where mankind had first gone astray—at Eden, the paradise of man before the fall."[1]

Alongside this theme lay another that Mead developed in much greater detail, namely, the persistent refusal of many religionists in America to accept either the legitimacy or the premises of religious pluralism. Indeed, Mead argued that antipathy toward pluralism was especially strong in the early nineteenth century when the religious premises for pluralism were "drowned in the great tidal wave of revivalism that swept the country" at that time.[2]

Mead noted the close connection between pluralism and primitivism in early nineteenth-century America. Thus, each sect competed with all the others by claiming that it "most closely conformed to the Biblical patterns."[3] But the relation between pluralism and primitivism was more intimate even than that. In the first place, while practically every sect and denomination may have used the appeal to biblical patterns as an effective weapon in denominational rivalry, some groups took upon themselves the restoration ideal as a defining characteristic, in many instances a raison d'être. This was the case, for example, with Mormons, Separate Baptists, Shakers, Disciples, and New Light "Christians" of both the West and the East. And in the second place, restoration among these sectarians often became the basis for not just rivalry and competition, but for also opposing both the fact and premise of religious pluralism itself. Accordingly, many restorationists argued that a return to the ancient order of things would bring not only Christian unity but also civil unity under the lordship of Jesus Christ. Alexander Campbell, for example, argued that "there is now a scheme of things presented, in what is called the *Ancient Gospel,* which is long enough, broad enough, strong enough for the whole superstructure called the Millennial Church—and . . . it will alone be the *instrument* of *converting* the whole human race." Campbell added that this conversion finally would "subvert all political government," including that of the pluralistic American nation.[4] Or again, the Mormon missionary Parley P. Pratt foresaw in 1851 that through the progress of the Mormon restoration, all governments, kingdoms, and tribes would be "dissolved—destroyed—or mingled into *one*—one body politic—*one* peaceful empire—*one* Lord—*one* King—*one* interest all."[5]

How does one account for this radically ecumenical thrust with its antipluralist dimension? From a theological perspective, restorationists commonly appealed to Jesus' prayer for the unity of believers. But what prompted them to heed that prayer so devoutly, it seems, was the radical newness of the religious situation in America during that period. After all, early nineteenth-century Americans were not far removed in time from the established churches of the nations from which they had come. Whatever else one might choose to say about those Old World environs, they at least provided *cosmos.* One knew where one stood, and one stood invariably in the bosom of *the* church. In contrast, the "brave new world"[6] launched on these shores was religiously chaotic. Clearly, one compelling way to bring order and cosmos to a messy, disorderly, and chaotic pluralism was to present the "ancient order of things" as a firm ecumenical foundation. Thus, as Mead observes,

> it is notable that the most successful of the definitely Christian indigenous denominations in America, the Disciples of Christ, grew out of the idea of a "new reformation" to be based, not on new insights, but on a "restoration" of the practices of the New Testament church—on which platform, it was thought, all the diverse groups of modern Christianity could unite as they shed the accumulated corruptions of the Church through the centuries.[7]

While the Disciples may have been the most successful of the indigenous American traditions for their time, none presents to the historian a more richly textured restorationist-ecumenical perspective than does the Church of Jesus Christ of Latter-day Saints in its early years. And no single Mormon spokesperson more clearly explained the restorationist premises for Mormon antipluralism than did Parley P. Pratt, one of the original twelve apostles of the Latter-day Saints. It is therefore to the early Mormon understanding of restoration and its relation to the problem of pluralism, and especially to Parley Pratt's understanding of these themes, that we now turn.

II

The intimate connection between the early Mormon understanding of restoration and the problem of religious pluralism becomes apparent in the event that prompted the beginnings of this faith: the first vision of Joseph Smith. Profoundly distressed by the competing claims of America's frontier sects, fifteen-year-old Joseph retired to the woods in the spring of 1820 to ask the Lord which of the churches he should join. The Lord replied that he "must join none of them, for they were all wrong" and that "all their creeds were an abomination in his sight."[8] Following that vision, Joseph became a seeker, earnestly searching for the one true church which once had flourished but now had disappeared from the face of the earth.

As a seeker, Joseph was hardly unique. Seekerism as a religious phenomenon abounded in America in the 1820s and especially in New York where the Smith family lived. Typical was Solomon Chamberlain of Lyons who had long been convinced that "faith was gone from the earth" and that "all Churches were corrupt," or Wilford G. Woodruff who became convinced in 1830 that Christ's church no longer existed on the face of the earth.[9] Joseph's own parents reflected the same perspective. His father, Joseph Smith, Sr., dreamed of a barren earth which signified "the world which now lieth inanimate and dumb, in regard to the true religion, or plan of salvation." And Lucy Mack Smith, his mother, concluded that all the churches were "unlike the Church of Christ, as it existed in former days," and that there was not, therefore, "then upon the earth the religion I sought." Both Joseph and Lucy refused to "subscribe to any particular system of faith, but contended for the ancient order as established by our Lord and Saviour Jesus Christ, and his Apostles."[10]

For most of these seekers, religious pluralism clearly was the source of their despair. George Burnham of Greenville, New York, bewailed the "multitude of sectarian divisions" which for him provided proof that American Christianity "is not the *house of God,* while thus divided against itself—and is not the *body of Christ* which cannot be divided."[11] And Joseph Smith himself in later years recalled the days of his youth when "the different religious parties . . . created no small stir and division amongst the people, some crying, 'Lo here!' and others, 'Lo, there!'" Indeed, he wrote in his *History of the Church* concerning those early years that

> so great were the confusion and strife among the different denominations, that it was impossible for a person young as I was, and so unacquainted with men and things, to come to any certain conclusion who was right and who was wrong. . . . In the midst of this war of words and tumult of opinion, I often said to myself, what is to be done? Who of all these parties are right; or, are they all wrong together?[12]

Like Roger Williams two hundred years before, Smith concluded that they were "all wrong together." Indeed, the similarities between Smith and Williams are profound. Both concluded that the true apostolic and primitive church had vanished from the face of the earth. Both concluded that the church had grown so completely corrupt over the centuries that no human being or group of human beings could possibly restore it to its original purity. And both longed eagerly for a latter-day prophet or apostle, bearing authority from the throne of God, who would restore the church to its first state.

But there the similarities break down, for Smith and Williams differed profoundly in two major respects. Most obvious is that Williams died a seeker, still longing and searching for the prophet and the restoration. In contrast, Smith himself became that prophet and by 1830 claimed that God, through Smith, had restored the Church of Christ once again to the earth. The other difference pertains to motivation. Williams found the church of his day a corrupt abomination and a gross departure from the primitive model precisely because it compelled and coerced the consciences of men and women. For Williams, therefore, the premise of religious freedom was essential to recovery of the apostolic church. Put another way, true religion, for Williams, was religion born of persuasion, not of coercion.[13] Ironically, however, it was the prevalence of persuasion in the competitive free market of souls that convinced Joseph Smith and a host of other seekers in the new American nation that the true church had disappeared. As Mother Smith had said, the claims and counterclaims of the various sects made "them witnesses against each other." In this context of vacuous relativity, people needed authority—a clear word from God that would subdue the confused and errant words of men and women.[14]

Nowhere was the quest for authority more evident than in the conversion of Parley P. Pratt. Living in Ohio in 1829, Pratt heard Sidney Rigdon, a follower of Alexander Campbell, proclaim faith in Jesus Christ, repentance toward God, baptism for remission of sins, and the gift of the Holy Ghost. "Here was the ancient gospel in due form," Pratt later wrote in his autobiography. Yet he was not content. By what authority could Rigdon establish this ancient gospel? He was neither prophet nor apostle. "Who is Mr. Rigdon?" Pratt asked. And "Who is Mr. Campbell? Who commissioned them?" On what basis could one determine that their ancient gospel was any more authentic than the ancient gospel of, say, the Baptists or of some other group with a primitivist orientation? What Rigdon and Campbell lacked, in Pratt's view, was "the *authority* to minister in holy things—the apostleship, the power which should accompany the form." After reading the *Book of Mormon,* however, and after learning that God had anointed Joseph Smith as his prophet in the latter days, Pratt exulted that "I had now found men on earth commissioned to preach, baptize, ordain to the ministry, etc., and I determined to obey the fulness of the gospel without delay."[15]

Indeed, for Pratt and for other early Mormons, the fact that God had restored to earth the ancient gospel through the agency of a latter-day prophet rendered entirely irrelevant the tumult of words, the contentions of preachers, and the strife of the sects. Campbell, Rigdon, the Baptists, and others might preach their *opinions* concerning the ancient gospel. But God had bestowed on Joseph Smith, Jr., the authority of the priesthood both to baptize and to confer the gift of the Holy Ghost in the latter days. Further, God had communicated with Smith in visions and revelations, had called him to translate the *Book of Mormon* from the Golden Plates buried by ancient American Christians, and had anointed him both prophet and apostle. In this way, to the Mormon mind, God had established once again the true Church of Jesus Christ on the earth, sanctioned not by human opinion, or by the inventions of men, but by the authority of heaven itself.

This notion of restoration made it abundantly clear that God had sanctioned one, true church, and that others were false. This dichotomy, which allowed no room for abstractions, ambiguities, or shades of gray, found clear expression in the *Book of Mormon,* which asserted that "there are save two churches only; the one is the church of the Lamb of God, and the other is the church of the devil; wherefore, whoso belongeth not to the church of the Lamb of God belongeth to that great church, which is the mother of abominations; and she is the whore of all the earth." From this premise it was only a short step to the notion that God's wrath would be "poured out upon . . . the great and abominable church of all the earth."[16]

Fundamental to this antipluralist posture was the peculiarly Mormon understanding of restoration. If Puritans, Baptists, and "Christians," for example, sought simply to emulate the faith and practices of the ancients, Mormons embraced a scheme of restoration that was cosmic in its scope, that penetrated space to the ends of the earth and the outer bounds of the universe itself, and that encompassed time from its very beginning to its end. Indeed, Mormons referred to their vision as the "restoration of all things."[17]

III

In the annals of the Latter-day Saints, no one has articulated this vision more cogently and vividly than Parley P. Pratt. Born in Burlington, Otsego County, New York, on April 12, 1807, Pratt moved in 1827 to Ohio where he made common cause with Sidney Rigdon and the Campbellite "restoration movement" which Rigdon espoused. Returning to New York in 1830 on a preaching mission, Pratt discovered the *Book of Mormon,* converted, and was baptized by Oliver Cowdery on September 1, 1830, in Seneca Lake. From that initiation into the fellowship of Latter-day Saints, Pratt would become one of its most significant proponents. Ordained one of the twelve apostles on February 1, 1835, Pratt essentially was a missionary throughout his life. He preached throughout the United States, and in England, Canada, the Pacific Islands, and South America. On May 13, 1857, he was murdered while on a preaching tour near Van Buren, Arkansas.[18]

Pratt made his most lasting contribution through numerous pamphlets written in defense of the Mormon faith. In fact, many consider him the "Father of Mormon Pamphleteering."[19] Beyond this, scholars generally acknowledge that two of his pamphlets in particular furnished the most cogent, noncanonical expressions of the Mormon faith to appear in the nineteenth century. His 1837 work, *A Voice of Warning,* has been judged "the most important of all noncanonical Mormon books" and "the most important missionary pamphlet in the early history of the church."[20] Peter Crawley argues that while this was not the first Mormon tract, "it was the first systematic statement and defense of the fundamentals of Mormonism. More than this it erected a standard for all future Mormon pamphleteers, setting down a formula for describing the tenets of Mormonism as well as biblical proof-texts, arguments, examples and expressions that would be used by others for another century."[21] *A Voice of Warning* went through at least eight editions by 1860. The *Times and Seasons* reported that by 1842 both a first edition of three thousand copies and a second edition of twenty five hundred copies had been exhausted. The editor of the most recent edition suggests that this book "undoubtedly contributed to the conversion of thousands of seekers to Mormonism."[22]

Pratt's other major work was *The Key to the Science of Theology.*[23] Published in Liverpool, England, in 1855, this work was one of the earliest attempts to systematize the disparate elements of Mormon theology. Clearly, it was among the most successful attempts, for the book was in great demand and remained through the early twentieth century "one of the leading statements of Church doctrine."[24]

Throughout his writings Pratt consistently cast Mormon theology in a restorationist mould. But what did he mean by this term *restoration?* Pratt addressed this question frequently and forthrightly. "Now we can never understand what is meant by restoration," he wrote, "unless we understand what is lost or taken away."[25] What had been lost, he made clear, was dialogue with God and communion with heavenly beings. Thus he contrasted the ancients and the moderns in this regard: "Witness the ancients, conversing with the Great Jehovah, learning lessons from the angels, and receiving instruction by the Holy Ghost, in dreams by night, and visions by day, until at length the veil is taken off. . . . Compare this intelligence, with the low smatterings of education and worldly wisdom, which seem to satisfy the narrow mind of man in our generation."[26] The key to the science of theology, then, was for Pratt precisely "the key of divine revelation," and it was this key Mormons claimed to have restored.[27]

From this perspective, Pratt and his Mormon colleagues could only view as extraordinarily deficient the restoration efforts of Disciple leaders, Thomas and Alexander Campbell. For Pratt, these "restorers" were part of the problem, not part of the solution. After all, these men maintained that the gifts of the Spirit had expired with the original apostles. In their view, the object of restoration therefore was not recovery of the gifts of the Spirit or of divine revelation but rather recovery of the forms and structures the Spirit had inspired.

Armed with these convictions both Thomas and Alexander Campbell attacked Mormon claims to have restored the gifts of the Spirit. When Sidney Rigdon converted to the Latter-day Saints, Thomas Campbell challenged him to debate, claiming that he would demonstrate that "imposition of hands for communicating the Holy Spirit, is an unscriptural intrusion upon the exclusive prerogative of the primary apostles."[28] And Alexander simply ascribed Rigdon's claims to spiritual gifts to insanity: "Fits of melancholy succeeded by fits of enthusiasm accompanied by some kind of nervous spasms and swoonings which he has, since his defection, interpreted into the agency of the Holy Spirit, or the recovery of spiritual gifts, produced a versatility in his genius and deportment which has been increasing for some time."[29]

Whether Pratt ever read these specific attacks is unknown, but he clearly responded to the common claim that spiritual gifts had ceased with the deaths of the apostles. To him, miraculous gifts partook of the essence of the Christian faith, and to claim that these gifts had ceased was tantamount to admitting that the church had ceased to exist. "When the miracles and gifts of the divine Spirit ceased from among men, Christianity ceased, the Christian ministry ceased, the Church of Christ ceased," he argued. Then he launched an attack of his own. "That ministry which sets aside modern inspiration, revelations, prophecy, angels, visions, healings, &c., is not ordained of God; but is Anti-Christian in spirit. In short, it is that spirit of priestcraft and kingcraft, by which the world, for many ages, has been ruled as with a rod of iron."[30]

From Pratt's perspective, the central defect of Protestant restorers such as Campbell was a narrow fixation on the Bible. For Pratt and his Mormon colleagues, the Bible was not the ultimate authority in religion, nor was it the final source of power or knowledge. Rather, the Bible simply pointed beyond itself to the God who was the final arbiter of ultimate things. While the scriptures are true and good and useful, Pratt argued, "they are not the fountain of knowledge, nor do they contain all knowledge, yet they point to the fountain, and are every way calculated to encourage men to come to the fountain and seek to obtain the knowledge and gifts of God."[31] The chief function of the Bible, Pratt argued, was not to provide guidelines or blueprints for forms, structures, or static institutions, but rather to demonstrate the divine power behind all forms, structures, and institutions. By this power, Pratt contended, Enoch was translated, Moses freed a nation, Joshua conquered the Canaanites, David excelled the wisdom of the East, and Jesus Christ himself conquered death and hell. And by this same divine power, "a Joseph in modern times has restored the fullness of the gospel; raised the church out of the wilderness; restored to them the faith once delivered to the saints."[32]

It was precisely because early Mormons pointed not to a book but to the divine power behind all books that Mormon theology could grow and evolve. Accordingly, Joseph announced many revelations that continued from the First Vision until his death in Carthage, Illinois, in 1844. Those early Mormons who resisted theological change and defected to a more static tradition simply never understood the premises of the Mormon restoration ideal.

Indeed, Pratt specifically excluded from the Mormon faith the authority of a particular antiquity, even Christian antiquity. Mormons had no interest in patterning their faith and practice after a particular time, but looked instead to the God who had worked wonders in all times. "[Mormons] claim no authority whatever from antiquity," Pratt proclaimed; rather, "the Lord uttered his voice from the heavens, an holy angel came forth and restored the priesthood and apostleship, and hence has arisen the church of the Saints."[33] In contrast, traditional restorers had fixed their gaze on a particular age or institution—the church of the first century, for example—and had missed the divine reality that had inspired not only the primitive church but also the patriarchs, the prophets, and Christ himself. Pratt therefore criticized those traditional restorers as having "fallen into this one inconsistency, viz., of patching new cloth on to old garments; and thus the rent has been made worse." Alexander Campbell, for example, had "attempted to restore the ordinances without the priesthood, or gifts of the spirit."[34] In contrast, Pratt described the Church of Jesus Christ of Latter-day Saints as

> a NEW "TREE"—NEW "FRUITS,"—"NEW CLOTH," and "NEW GARMENTS,"—"NEW WINE" and "NEW BOTTLES"—"NEW LEAVEN" and a "NEW LUMP," "A NEW COVENANT" and spirit; and may it roll on till we have a new heaven and a new earth, that we may dwell for ever in the new Jerusalem, while old things pass away, and all things are made new, even so. Amen.[35]

Pratt maintained that neither Campbell nor any other human being was capable of restoring the divine power and initiatives unless God had chosen him for the task. Like Roger Williams before him, Pratt believed that once the priesthood and spiritual gifts had been lost from the earth, they could be restored only at God's own initiative. Thus, "the man or men last holding the keys of such power . . . [must] return to the earth as ministering angels, and select . . . certain individuals of the royal lineage of Israel, to hold the keys of such Priesthood, and to ordain others, and thus restore and reorganize the government of God, or His kingdom upon the earth."[36] But this restoration would take place only in the fullness of time or, as Mormons liked to say, "the times of restitution of all things." Indeed, this latter phrase was part of the text by which Mormons typically justified their restoration efforts, Acts 3:20–21 (KJV): "And he shall send Jesus Christ, which before was preached unto you: whom the heaven must receive until the times of restitution [restoration] of all things, which God hath spoken by the mouth of all his holy prophets since the world began."

God alone, Pratt believed, had determined this extraordinary time of restoration. Reformations, protests, and religious revolutions had failed time and again because their leaders had acted on their own, apart from the initiative of God. In a particularly cogent passage, Pratt wrote:

> Protests upon protests! reforms and re-reforms; revolutions, and struggles, exertions of every kind, of mere human invention, have been tried and tried in vain. The science of Theology, with all its keys and powers, once lost, could never, consistent with the ancient Prophetic testimony, be restored to either Jew or Gentile, until the full time should arrive—"*The times of restitution of all things. . . .*" Then, and not till then, could the science, the keys, the powers of Theology, be restored to man. No individual or combined human action could obtain or restore again these keys—this science. A mighty angel held the keys of this science for the last days.[37]

Pratt was convinced that he lived in these last days—"the times of restitution of all things"—and that God had anointed Joseph Smith as apostle and prophet in order to begin the restoration. Further, Pratt was convinced that the Mormon restoration was radically dissimilar to all other restoration attempts. If other would-be restorers focused on particular books, persons, or ancient times, Mormons treated all particular, sacred manifestations as transparencies that pointed beyond themselves to ultimate reality. If other restorers, on their own initiative, sought to recover mere finite forms, God had called and enabled Mormons to recover communion with the infinite itself.

When viewed from this perspective, early Mormonism may well be understood as a romantic rejection of the Common Sense rationalist perspective so prevalent in America in the early nineteenth century.[38] The respective movements led by Alexander Campbell and Joseph Smith were both restoration movements, but there were differences. Campbell's restoration movement was rational to the core, calling for the application of human reason to the biblical text and limiting authentic religion to that sphere. In so doing, the Campbell movement was as clear an expression of the spirit of Common Sense rationalism as one could hope to find in American religion in the early nineteenth century. On the other hand, Mormonism sought to transcend the cognitive and the rational and to soar with the gods in the realm of the infinite and the eternal. In this sense, Mormonism was an expression of romanticism in revolt against the constrictions of Common Sense.

The numerous defections from Campbell's Disciples to the Latter-day Saints illustrate well the nature of this revolt. In each instance, the converts despaired of Common Sense rationalism and longed instead to experience the Holy Ghost with power and authority from on high. Elizabeth Ann Whitney reports, for example, that "my husband, Newel K. Whitney, and myself were Campbellites. We had been baptized for the remission of our sins, and believed in the laying on of hands and the gifts of the spirit. But there was no one with authority to confer the Holy Ghost upon us." When the Mormon gospel arrived in Kirtland, Ohio, therefore, the Whitneys readily converted. Or again, Eliza Snow "heard Alexander Campbell advocate the literal meaning of the Scriptures—listened to him with deep interest—hoped his new life led to a fulness—was baptized." But she soon discovered that Campbell had not been empowered by God and determined that "my baptism was of no consequence." In April of 1835, therefore, she "was baptized by a 'Mormon' Elder, and in the evening of that day, I realized the baptism of the Spirit as sensible as I did that of the water in the stream."[39]

The case of John Murdock holds particular interest. A Seceder Presbyterian, Murdock had determined independently that baptism was for remission of sins. "I kept searching the Scriptures and looking to find a people that lived according to them," he wrote, "but could not find such a people." At last, however, he learned of Alexander Campbell whose baptismal teaching struck Murdock as not only rational but extraordinarily mechanistic. The Campbellites, he wrote, "promised any person remission of sins that would be baptized and that they had caught a whole Baptist Church in Mentor, and they would receive a drunkard or any profane person." Murdock found it "impossible that they should have caught that whole Baptist Church in such a gross error all at one haul," but he nonetheless submitted to immersion and joined the Disciples. Within three years, however, "finding their principal leader, Alex Campbell, with many others, denying the gift and power of the Holy Ghost, I began to think of looking me a new home." On November 5, 1830, he found his new home when Parley Pratt baptized him in the Chafrin River, "and the spirit of the Lord sensibly attended the ministration." At his confirmation several days later, Murdock wrote, "the spirit rested on me as it never did before and others said they saw the Lord and had visions." The following summer Barton Stone visited a meeting of the Saints where Murdock was preaching "and tried to put us down by his learning." But Murdock proclaimed "the first principles of the gospel— Repentance and baptism for the remission of sins and the laying on of the hands for the gift of the Holy Ghost. . . . Priest Stone trembled, but would not yield."[40]

Many commentators on Mormonism have noted the literalism of the Mormon tradition. But literalism took second place to their romantic visions of the Spirit. Put another way, the Saints took quite literally a romantic theology that came to them in visions, dreams, and revelations, mediated through a latter-day prophet. But this was a very different sort of literalism from the rational, New Testament–oriented literalism that characterized Campbell and his Disciples of Christ.

With this singular restoration vision, Mormons addressed the problem of religious pluralism which they found so disconcerting. In fact, religious pluralism, they thought, simply would not exist if the "science of theology"—communion with angels and gods—had not been lost. In their view, pluralism was merely the symptom of the human confusion that inevitably resulted when divine authority disappeared. Pratt wrote that "the reason for all the division, confusion, jars, discords, and animosities; and the reason of so many faiths, lords, baptisms, and spirits . . . is all because they have no Apostles, and Prophets, and other gifts, inspired from on high . . . , for if they had such gifts . . . they would be built up in one body, . . . having one Lord, one faith, and one Baptism."[41] Indeed, the final objective of the Mormon restoration was recovery of the one body, the one faith, and the one baptism.

This quest for *ultimate* power and *ultimate* authority, descending from the very heavens themselves, was the genius of the Mormon restoration ideal. Yet, it is undeniably true—and fundamentally important— that early Mormons sought recovery of infinite and ultimate authority precisely through recovery of the finite forms inspired by God in all ages past. Here was the meaning, then, of the phrase "restitution of all things": Mormons would restore "all things" in all God's epochs since the creation itself. We now turn, therefore, to this other side of Mormon primitivism, the recovery of finite structures and forms, and the implications of this concrete, tangible restoration for Mormon attitudes toward religious pluralism in America.

IV

If Parley Pratt condemned Alexander Campbell for attempting to restore the outward ordinances without the gifts of the Spirit, he also condemned the Quakers for attempting to restore the gifts of the Spirit apart from outward ordinances.[42] Pratt's dual judgment in this regard is highly significant, for it symbolized the extent to which the finite and the infinite were inseparably related in the early Mormon imagination. Indeed, to encompass sacred, finite forms *was* to encompass the infinite precisely because, as Joseph Smith revealed in May of 1843, "there is no such thing as immaterial matter. All spirit is matter."[43] Conversely, early Mormons argued that all matter is eternal. Thus Parley Pratt simply rejected creation ex nihilo. He asserted that "the original elements of matter are eternal" and "uncreated and self-existing." The very term *creation,* Pratt argued, is misleading: God no more created the world than he created himself; he simply organized preexisting elements into a coherent whole or universe.[44]

If inanimate matter was uncreated, Pratt contended, then obviously the same was true for humanity. Pratt scoffed at the Genesis notion that God made man from the dust of the ground and Eve from Adam's rib. Moses knew better, he said. But because humankind, immature as it was, could not view the Almighty face to face, Moses "was forced again to veil the past in mystery, and . . . assign to man an earthly origin." In so doing, Moses resembled a watchful parent who "would fain conceal from budding manhood, the mysteries of procreation . . . by relating some childish tale of new born life, engendered in the hollow trunk of some old tree." The real truth, however, which Moses refused to tell was that "man is the offspring of Deity."[45]

As the "offspring of Deity," humankind possessed the power to restore the divine original from which it had sprung. Pratt therefore exhorted his readers to "burst the chains of mortality which bind thee fast; unlock the prison of thy clay tenement which confines thee to this groveling, earthly sphere of action; and robed in immortality, wrapped in the visions of eternity, with organs of sight and thought and speech which cannot be impaired or weakened by time or use; soar with me amid unnumbered worlds which roll in majesty on high."[46] Pratt even suggested that God's saints would, "like the risen Jesus, ascend and descend at will, and with a speed nearly instantaneous."[47]

This constellation of ideas—that spirit is matter, that matter is eternal, and that human beings sprang from God and can become gods themselves—constitutes the philosophic foundation for the early Mormon understanding of restoration. If the Saints ultimately would "ascend the heights" and "descend the depths" and "explore the lengths and breadths of organized existence"—something the gods themselves had done in the primordium—should not the Saints embrace this cosmic perspective in their restoration?[48] Unwilling therefore to confine themselves to a single book or to a single sacred epoch as did traditional restorationists, early Mormons sought "the restoration of all things." Like bees sucking nectar first from this flower and then from the next, early Mormons moved at ease from the primitive church to Moses to the prophets to Abraham to Adam and finally to the coming millennium. Many interpreters of Mormonism have commented on this amalgamation of sacred times, an amalgamation so complete that it appears as sheer confusion. To early Mormons such as Parley Pratt, however, it was far from confusion, resting instead on an inner logic that simply baffled those whose gaze was riveted to the finite particulars of religious faith.

To early Mormons, after all, the finite ordinances of every sacred age equally partook of the infinite. Nothing, therefore, could be more consistent than to practice Christian baptism in a baptismal font resting on twelve oxen symbolizing the twelve tribes of Israel. Likewise, Mormons saw no inconsistency whatever in restoring at one and the same time the ancient Christian rite of baptism for the remission of sins and the patriarchal practice of polygamy; nor did they see inconsistency in their intention to worship in a restored "Jewish" temple built on the site of the Garden of Eden. One must remember what motivated Mormons in the first place, namely, their quest for the infinite and therefore ultimate authority. To saturate themselves, therefore, with the infinite by sucking the nectar of the infinite from the various finite blossoms of every sacred age only made sense.

Granted, this perspective made no sense to those whose restoration premises were governed by the rationalism of Common Sense. Alexander Campbell, for example, was appalled that Jews in the *Book of Mormon* were "called Christians while keeping the law of Moses, the holy sabbath, and worshipping in their temple at their altars and by their high priests," and that "the Nephites . . . were good christians, . . . preaching baptism and other christian usages hundreds of years before Jesus Christ was born!"[49] Likewise, Walter Scott, Campbell's colleague in their New Testament–oriented restoration, criticized the *Book of Mormon* for confounding "history with prophecy, . . . putting in the mouths of his fictious seers the language of the apostles."[50] From the Mormon perspective, however, neither Smith nor Pratt would have winced at these critiques, for to them these critiques failed entirely to speak to the heart of the Mormon faith. For Smith and Pratt, patriarchal polygamy,

Jewish temple rites, and Christian baptism were all finite and material ordinances ordained by God during some sacred epoch. They all shared one common function: to bring the power and authority of the infinite into the world of the Latter-day Saints. To Common Sense restorationists such as Campbell and Scott, this perspective was spiritual gibberish and religious nonsense.

It all made wonderfully good sense to early Mormons, however, for one fundamental reason—their conviction that they lived in the last days and on the threshold of the millennial dawn. Indeed, their millennial awareness lent both purpose and meaning to the Mormon restoration ideal. Pratt argued that "God has sent us . . . to prepare his way, and to make straight his paths—by gathering in the children of God from all the jarring systems in which they are now organized, and planting them in one fold by the ministration of the ordinances in their ancient purity." When that task was accomplished, Pratt proclaimed, "then shall the Lord Jesus Christ, the great Messiah and King, descend from the heavens in his glorified, immortal body, and reign with his saints, and over all the kingdoms of the earth, one thousand years."[51]

Further, this final age was not just one dispensation among others. Rather, as the last age, it would embrace all the others, tying together with cords of infinity the perfections of all previous sacred times. The twelve apostles therefore made it clear that "this [present] dispensation comprehends all the great works of all former dispensations."[52] Standing on the threshold of the age of infinite perfections, Mormons sought to reenact the sacred dramas of all prior ages and to saturate themselves with the infinite as it had manifested itself throughout the course of time. All of this made wonderfully good sense to those who stood in the shadow of the end.

To understand the early Mormon approach to religious pluralism, it is important to understand how Mormons consistently tied restoration of the infinite to restoration of particular, finite forms, rites, and institutions. Indeed, Mormons found in Zion and its temple an institutional complex that embraced all rites and ordinances of all sacred epochs, that encompassed time from beginning to end and earthly space from pole to pole, that obligated all men and women of all ages and nations to receive the Mormon gospel, and that provided means for their inclusion into the Mormon fold.

The city of Zion provided the link between heaven and earth and between primordium and millennium. Zion was no mere human concoction, but a city that literally would descend from heaven itself. According to the *Book of Moses* in the *Pearl of Great Price,* Enoch built the city of Zion, which the Lord took with Enoch unto himself, and which one day would descend to the earth as New Jerusalem, the center of the millennial kingdom. According to Joseph Smith in 1831, this heavenly city would be restored and rebuilt in Jackson County, Missouri, adjacent to the site of the primordial Garden of Eden in Davies County, Missouri, though in 1844 Smith proclaimed that "the whole of America is Zion."[53] Parley Pratt argued further that Zion served as the hinge between the ancient order of things and the millennial dawn and that restoration of this city must precede Christ's second coming. "When this city is built the Lord will appear in his glory, and not before," Pratt announced. "So from this we affirm, that if such a city is never built, then the Lord will never come."[54]

Further, Joseph Smith in 1833 envisioned the construction of city after city, all modeled after New Jerusalem and built in adjacent plots; in this way, he told the Saints, they would "fill up the world in these last days." Parley Pratt reflected this charge when, writing on behalf of the apostles, he declared that God "has commanded us to . . . build up holy cities and sanctuaries—And we know it."[55] Thus, a British brother reported a dream in which he saw a conference of the Saints wherein

it was motioned by Joseph Smith and seconded by John the Revelator, "That forty-eight new cities be laid out and builded, this year, in accordance with the prophets which have said, 'who can number Israel? Who can count the dust of Jacob? Let him fill the earth with cities.' "[56]

While these visions all seem millennial, one must not forget their fundamentally restorationist underpinnings rooted in Enoch's Zion of old. Even in ancient times this Zion had stood opposed to religious pluralism and had symbolized unanimity rather than diversity, for, as the *Book of Moses* put it, "the Lord called his people ZION, because they were of one heart and one mind, and dwelt in righteousness; and there was no poor among them" (7:18).

Finally, during the Nauvoo period of Mormon history, Joseph Smith introduced into Mormon practice and theology two ordinances that would make Mormonism more expansive still. Significantly, both ordinances could be performed only in the temple. The first was the doctrine of baptism for the dead, included in a revelation of January 19, 1841, in which Joseph also announced the Lord's command to build the Nauvoo Temple.[57] Not content to extend their restored, millennial kingdom through space, the Mormons by this doctrine might also extend the kingdom backward through time and thereby erase whatever religious pluralism existed in ages past. Regarding this doctrine Pratt proclaimed that "in the world of spirits . . . are . . . Catholics, and Protestants of every sect. . . . There is also the Jew, the Mohametan, the infidel. . . . All these must be taught, enlightened, and must bow the knee to the eternal king." In this way, as Klaus Hansen has noted, the living and the dead would be linked together "in one gigantic chain of family and kinship that would ultimately bind together the entire human race."[58]

If baptism for the dead might potentially erase religious pluralism from ages past, the doctrine of celestial marriage promised the rule of the Saints on other worlds in ages to come. In a sermon of May 16, 1843, Joseph Smith declared that if "a man and his wife enter into an everlasting covenant and be married for eternity . . . , they . . . will continue to increase and have children in celestial glory." In the revelation of this doctrine, Joseph announced that those males who take a wife "by the new and everlasting covenant . . . shall inherit thrones, kingdoms, principalities, and powers, dominions, all heights and depths. . . . Then shall they be gods, because they have no end."[59]

Clearly, through this expansive, cosmic theology, early Mormons addressed the problem of religious pluralism not only for their own age but also for ages past and future. Their posture in this regard rested squarely on the issue of authority. Other reformers, even restorers, acted on their own, apart from divine authority, guidance, and direction. But the Latter-day Saints responded to God himself, who spoke to them through his prophet in dreams, visions, and revelations, as he had to saints of old. Restoration among Mormons, therefore, essentially meant soaring with the gods while others groveled on the earth. It meant appealing to the sacred while others could appeal only to the profane. It was only appropriate, therefore, that the particular rites and ordinances that Mormons chose to restore were rites and ordinances that would bring heaven to earth, collapse both primordium and millennium into their own time and place, and tie the Saints to God's work in all time past. This perspective ultimately provided the theological basis for the political rule of the Saints.

V

In 1841, Parley Pratt addressed a dire warning to Queen Victoria of England. He told the queen that the world was "on the eve of a REVOLUTION," that a "new nation will be established over the whole earth, to the destruction of all other kingdoms," that if the rulers of England would "hearken to this message, they shall have part in the glorious kingdom," but "if they will not . . . they will be overthrown with the wicked, and perish from the earth."[60] Earlier, in 1836, Pratt had incorporated these themes into his widely influential missionary tract, *A Voice of*

Warning, which was intended to be just that: a voice of warning. There Pratt proclaimed that the Mormon restoration "is the gospel which God has commanded us to preach. . . . And no other system of religion . . . is of any use; every thing different from this, is a perverted gospel, bringing a curse upon them that preach it, and upon them that hear it." Indeed, all who refused the Saints' message "shall alike feel the hand of the almighty, by pestilence, famine, earthquake, and the sword: yea, ye shall be drunken with your own blood . . . until your cities are desolate . . . until all lyings, priestcrafts, and all manner of abomination, shall be done away."[61]

How can one account for the fact that the Saints could entertain such violent, coercive visions? This question is both underscored and complicated by the fact that Mormons consistently proclaimed their faith in religious freedom. For example, a general assembly of the Saints voted unanimously in Kirtland, Ohio, in 1835 that governments should "secure to each individual the free exercise of conscience" and that human law has no right "to bind the consciences of men." That same declaration affirmed the total illegitimacy of mingling "religious influence with civil government, whereby one religious society is fostered and another proscribed." Further, as a candidate for the presidency of the United States in 1844, Joseph Smith promised to "open the prisons, open the eyes, open the ears, and open the hearts of all people, to behold and enjoy freedom—unadulterated freedom."[62]

Here, then, are two dominant threads in the intellectual garment of the early Saints: a coercive, sometimes even violent antipluralism, alongside a ringing affirmation of the right of all people to freedom of conscience in matters of religion. How can one reconcile these two themes?

Several observations are in order. First, Mormons themselves suffered intense persecution, including physical violence, at the hands of other Americans, and therefore took steps to defend their lives and property. Thus, the Kirtland Declaration of 1835 affirmed that "all men are justified in defending themselves . . . from the unlawful assaults and encroachments of all persons in times of exigency, where immediate appeal cannot be made to the laws, and relief afforded."[63] It would be fair to suggest that the persecutions they suffered and the steps they took for defense at the very least made violence, and the possibility of violence, a factor in their perspective. But how did they cross the line from the rhetoric and reality of defensive violence to a rhetoric of coercion?

The second observation: early Mormons such as Parley Pratt were missionaries whose task was made urgent by what they perceived as an imminent end to a profane and fallen world. In this apocalyptic context, it was God, not they, who would avenge the wicked and stiff-necked of this earth. Accordingly, many interpreters of Mormonism have rooted the coercive visions of the Saints precisely in their apocalypticism. Thus, for example, Klaus Hansen viewed the creation of the Council of Fifty as a consequence of Mormon millennialism. And Grant Underwood, while faulting Hansen for rooting millennial perspectives in social deprivation, nonetheless concurred with Hansen on the point at issue and argued that "Mormon millennialism disposed the Saints to a . . . conspiratorial view which . . . leagued the whole sectarian world with Lucifer."[64]

But even these explanations, as helpful as they are, leave much unexplained. For what reason would God smite the wicked and exalt the Saints? To what final court would Pratt appeal for the legitimacy of his apocalyptic vision? And why would the God of a freedom-affirming people smite those of different faiths at all?

The fact is that the ideological basis for the coercive rhetoric of early Mormons was their restoration sentiment, not their millennialism. After all, early Mormons hardly could claim to differ from other religious groups on the basis of a millennium that was yet in the future. But they could—and did—put an infinite distance between themselves and their religious neighbors by identifying themselves with a constellation of sacred and primordial pasts while others were confined to the finite realm of history and time. Put another way, early Mormons, by rooting themselves in the primal past, simply removed themselves from history and the historical process and claimed instead that they had sprung full blown from the creative hands of God. In April of 1830, they said, their prophet had restored to earth the ancient church with all its gifts, miracles, and visions.

This perspective spoke decisively to the Saints regarding the dilemmas posed by religious pluralism in American life. In the first place, the Saints at one level were committed fully to freedom of conscience for all human beings so long as this fallen and profane world should last. But religious pluralism, as with other childish things, would be put away in the age of millennial perfection. In this scenario, millennialism was the source of neither Mormon perfectionism nor coercive rhetoric. The role of the millennium, instead, was simply to provide a stage on which the great cosmic drama, pitting the "church of the Lamb" against "the church of the devil," could be brought to its final conclusion.

In the meantime, the Saints could anticipate the coming age when, as Pratt predicted, "a universal Theocracy will cement the whole body politic. One king will rule. One holy city will compose the capitol. One temple will be the centre of worship. In short, there will be one Lord, one Faith, one Baptism, and one Spirit."[65] And in anticipation of that golden

151

age, they could proceed to establish the political kingdom of God which one day would rule with Christ. As Orson Pratt, Parley's brother, wrote in 1851, "The kingdom of God . . . is the only legal government that can exist in any part of the universe. All other governments are illegal and unauthorized."[66]

One might argue that the doctrine of degrees of salvation, announced in a revelation of February 16, 1832, was in some sense an accommodation to religious pluralism. According to this doctrine, the Saints would inherit celestial glory; the "honorable men of the earth, who were blinded by the craftiness of men," would inherit a lesser, terrestrial glory; and those "who received not the gospel of Christ" would inherit a still lesser, telestial glory.[67] Here, to be sure, non-Mormons would be saved, but hardly on equal terms with Mormons. One finds a similar hierarchic vision in Parley Pratt. According to Pratt, the millennial kingdom would encompass the "heathen nations," but these nations would "be exalted to the privilege of serving the Saints. . . . They will be the ploughmen, the vine-dressers, the gardners, builders, etc. But the Saints will be the owners of the soil, the proprietors of all real estate, . . . and the kings, governors, and judges of the earth."[68] One finds in these visions evidence of the tension that plagued a people who, at one level, valued religious pluralism but who, at another level, anticipated its final collapse. In any event, the pluralism inherent in these visions is hardly the kind of pluralism implicit in the First Amendment and plowed into the history of the American experience.

The fact is that early Mormons ultimately rejected the ideal of religious pluralism as that ideal has been understood by most Americans. Further, that rejection finally rested on the notion that through their restoration, early Mormons had burst the bounds of time, history, and finitude that for centuries had imprisoned humankind. As Parley observed, they had "burst the chains of mortality" and now soared with the gods "amid unnumbered worlds which roll in majesty on high." Here indeed was a radical form of that common nineteenth-century vision which Mead described as "building anew in the American wilderness on the true and ancient foundations."

SEVEN

Freedom from Dogma:
James S. Lamar and
the Disciples of Christ

The profound differences between the restoration movements of Alexander Campbell and Joseph Smith, as the previous two chapters have shown, can be explained to a significant degree by reference to Common Sense or Baconian rationalism. If Campbell's movement exalted rationality and shackled the Spirit to the "facts" and propositions of scripture, Smith's movement exalted the Spirit and revolted against the stark, earth-bound premises of the Disciples. But despite such revolt, the "Baconian philosophy" held sway over a sizable segment of Protestant theologians in the first half of the nineteenth century and must figure prominently in any assessment of the period. Indeed, theologians commonly supposed that Baconianism would be the tool to free Americans from the centuries-old accretions of dogma and tradition.

Especially noteworthy was the use of this philosophy in the Disciple tradition, for there theologians placed Baconianism most strikingly in the service of recovering first times. Campbell, James Lamar, and many others believed that with such a method they could complete the task they supposed Martin Luther had begun in the Reformation. As this chapter shows, however, the breathtaking promise of freedom from human dogma and of unity among believers soon proved illusory, for new dogmas and new traditions emerged, all justified by their proponents on the grounds of "common sense." The new dogmas, clad in the garb of scientific induction and indisputable truth, turned out to be, if anything, more divisive than the dogmas they replaced. No wonder then that toward the century's end, some Disciples, like the Mormons, began to enshrine the Spirit above the stark and rational "facts" of scientific religion.

I

Many scholars have observed that during the first half of the nineteenth century Scottish Realism, or the philosophy of Common Sense, dominated American philosophy, science, and education. Howard Mumford Jones remarked that it was "the official academic belief of the period." Its first significant influence emerged with John Witherspoon, an Edinburgh-trained minister who became president of the College of New Jersey in 1769. Thereafter, especially after 1800, Realist texts were introduced gradually into American colleges and by the 1820s generally had replaced the older texts. Through use in numerous American colleges, the works of Thomas Reid, Dugald Stewart, George Campbell, James Beattie, William Hamilton, and others exercised a pervasive influence.[1]

The rise of Scottish Realism to prominence in America was made possible, to a large degree, by a growing awareness that the Lockean philosophy, which dominated America during the revolutionary period, had been undermined by new philosophical challenges. To counter the "metaphysical heresies" of Hume and Berkeley and the "infidelity" of the French philosophers, Americans—especially Calvinist and Unitarian clergymen—seized on the Common Sense philosophy as a firm foundation for scientific and religious knowledge.[2]

The Scottish Common Sense teachings were originated by Thomas Reid (1710–1796), who held the chair of moral philosophy at Glasgow; Reid's work was restated and embellished by Dugald Stewart (1753–1828) at Edinburgh, the most important early popularizer of the Scottish philosophy. The antidote to the skeptical philosophy of the age, Reid and Stewart believed, was to begin with the assumption that all normal people were endowed with the ability to reach common sense conclusions on which all human life was founded. Every sane person believed, for example, in the existence of an external world, the reality of the self and of other minds, and the reliability of the senses in causation and memory. Reid and Stewart built their philosophical system on these assumptions. They rejected the position that the object of human perception is not the object in itself but only the "idea"; rather, they construed perception as a dynamic activity through which the senses intuitively seized on the real existence of an object. In this way, Reid and Stewart upheld the common sense assumptions of the day and gave perplexed Americans the much-needed assurance that "the evidence of sense is a kind of evidence which we may securely rest upon."[3]

Along with the appeal to intuited "first principles," the Scottish philosophers often appealed to Francis Bacon and the inductive scientific method. Dwight Bozeman has documented this appeal in his important work *Protestants in an Age of Science,* arguing that "both Reid and Stewart considered their entire philosophical program to be an enactment of the inductive plan of research set forth in Bacon's *Novum Organum.*"[4] Bozeman argues further that it was through the veneration by Reid and Stewart of Bacon and his methods that the "Baconian philosophy," as it came to be called, took America by storm in the first half of the nineteenth century. Bozeman isolates four principal elements of "Baconianism" as refracted through the lens of Scottish Realism: a "spirited enthusiasm for natural science"; a "scrupulous empiricism" built on Realist confidence in the senses; deep suspicion of abstract concepts and speculation, and insistence on an inductive accumulation of "facts"; and a celebration of "Lord Bacon" as the founder of the inductive method. This pattern, according to Bozeman, was "engrafted wholesale into the main structure of nineteenth-century ideas."[5] It rose to such prominence that Edward Everett could remark in 1823 that "at the present day, as is well known, the *Baconian* philosophy has become synonymous with the true philosophy."[6]

Theologians quickly and widely perceived the "Baconian philosophy" as a means of advancing theology. Anxious for the certainties this scientific approach might provide, they quickly concerned themselves with examining evidence, ruthlessly focusing on "facts," and systematically classifying those facts. With this method many Protestant theologians sought to restore and reinforce the essential harmony between natural science and Christian faith. They sought to resolve the dilemmas of epistemology and ethics and to prove the reasonableness of faith. By this means they believed that they could place all knowledge—whether scientific, theological, or moral—on a sure foundation.

Beyond this common concern, however, Baconianism proved itself a deft and flexible tool that could be employed in the service of numerous antebellum theologies, as several recent studies have shown.[7] This flexibility resulted from the fact that Baconianism was not so much a set of conclusions as it was a method of thinking that stressed empirical observation and an antitheoretical attitude. As a result, the invocation of Bacon or Baconianism easily became in practice simply a means of legitimating whatever cause one wished to support and a tool for attacking the views one disliked. Baconian rhetoric, that is, sometimes had little to do with the actual theological or scientific method.[8] But whether rhetoric or reality, Baconianism made a great impact on Protestant thought in antebellum America. Many viewed it as the product of Protestantism itself and as a prime factor responsible for the triumphant spread of the Protestant faith. One writer claimed that "Protestant Christianity and the Baconian philosophy originate in the same fountain." Others argued that Bacon had begun his career in deep study of the Bible and that, by this means, he had discovered the principles he later formed into the inductive method. Benjamin Palmer, a southern Presbyterian considered later in this book, could remark: "There never could have been a

Bacon without the Bible. . . . Francis Bacon was the offspring of the Reformation."[9] Significant sectors of American Protestantism during this period elevated Baconianism as the true method for study of both the natural world and the Bible.

II

This chapter explains the development of Baconianism among Alexander Campbell and the Disciples of Christ and shows the distinct way in which they employed the Baconian method in interpreting the Bible. The focus is on James S. Lamar's book *The Organon of Scripture: Or, the Inductive Method of Biblical Interpretation* (1859). Appearing near the end of the hegemony of the Baconian method, Lamar's work can be seen as the height of attempts by evangelical theologians to develop a "scientific" or inductive biblical theology. It was published near the end of three decades of effort by Presbyterians, Congregationalists, Episcopalians, Disciples, and those of other traditions to establish the claim that proper theological method should be an exact imitation of the method of the natural sciences.

Lamar's stated purpose was to demonstrate that "the Scriptures admit of being studied and expounded upon the principles of the inductive method; and that, when thus interpreted they speak to us in a voice as certain and unmistakable as the language of nature heard in the experiments and observations of science."[10] Theology, Lamar claimed, should be viewed as a science virtually identical in method to the natural sciences. In this way theology could establish the precise meaning of scripture and make its laws the "objects of *precise and certain knowledge.*"[11] Then, by means of such certainty, people could be persuaded to give up their theories and embrace scriptural "facts," and the sinful divisions of Protestantism, which had turned masses of people into religious skeptics, could be healed. In short, the church would be restored to its primitive purity and strength.

In making such an argument, Lamar was repeating—albeit in more explicit and systematic Baconian form—the basic appeal made by the "Christians" and Disciples of Christ from their inception. As chapter 5 already has shown, this movement emerged between 1790 and 1815 as a loose network of religious radicals arguing for rejection of religion dominated by creeds and the power of the clergy and calling for a return to the unadorned text of scripture as the norm for doctrine and church order. The central figures in the early movement were James O'Kelly in Virginia, Elias Smith in New England, Barton Stone in Kentucky, and Thomas and Alexander Campbell in Pennsylvania, all of whom moved independently to similar conclusions within a fifteen-year period.[12] In general, these leaders expressed their primitivism in the call to scuttle the elaborate, authoritarian structures of the ecclesiastical establishment and to erase and transcend all the corruptions of history and start once again at the beginning, the time of Christianity's greatest purity. The polluted stream, they believed, should be abandoned for the pure spring.

As we have seen in earlier chapters, this appeal for a restoration of pristine biblical Christianity free from all human additions was widespread in America during the first half of the nineteenth century. The slogan "No Creed but the Bible" resounded throughout numerous denominations, sects, and movements. A legacy from Reformed Protestantism and Puritanism, this attitude was stimulated further by the democratic revolution of the age and by the application of the notion of popular sovereignty to the church.[13] In this atmosphere the "Christian" reformers denounced the clergy as "tyrannical oppressors," called for the abolition of the traditional clergy-laity distinction, and pressed for "the inalienable right of all laymen to examine the sacred writings for themselves." Only by renouncing oppressive clerical authority and, in fact, organizational restraints of any kind could "the oppressed . . . go free, and taste the sweets of gospel liberty."[14]

Rejection of all humanly devised theological systems constituted an integral part of this program for "gospel liberty." All systematic theologies were suspect, for they all allowed unscriptural speculations to cloud the plain text of scripture. Further, the various systems, when established as "orthodoxy" and enforced by the clergy, perpetuated division and strife and deprived the church of much of its spiritual power. Alexander Campbell sought, therefore, to provide deliverance from "the melancholy thraldom of relentless systems." Toward this end, these restorers virtually dismissed the history of Christianity. For restoration and unity to be achieved, Thomas Campbell, for example, advocated "clearing the way before them [Christians] by removing the stumbling blocks—the rubbish of ages, which has been thrown upon it [scripture], and fencing it on each side." Pure doctrine, these restorers urged, could be established only by confining religious discourse to the direct propositions of scripture—without any additions whatsoever "of human authority, of private opinion, or inventions of men."[15] Campbell spelled out what this attitude meant in his approach to scripture. "I have endeavored to read the Scriptures as though no one had read them before me," he said, "and I am as much on my guard against reading them today, through the medium of my own views yesterday, or a week ago, as I am against being influenced by any foreign name, authority, or system whatever." In order to bring about "a restoration of the ancient order of things," one must reject systematic theology and confine religious discussion to the "plain declarations recorded in the Bible."[16]

The rich veins of Common Sense rationalism undergirded this primitivistic and egalitarian appeal as it gathered momentum in the first two decades of the nineteenth century. Under the influence of John Witherspoon at Princeton, students from Princeton had flooded the South, forming scores of academies, colleges, and seminaries that became centers for the dissemination of Scottish ideas.[17] However, for the "Christian" and Disciple movements, Alexander Campbell, steeped in Scottish philosophy through his father Thomas and a brief career at the University of Glasgow, provided the chief influence. Through the vehicle of his periodical the *Christian Baptist,* published from 1823 until 1830, Campbell gained a tremendous following in western Pennsylvania, western Virginia, Ohio, and Kentucky. And when in 1832 the "Christians" who had rallied around Barton Stone agreed to unite with Campbell's Disciples of Christ, Cambell's influence spread, quickly overshadowing Stone and transforming the early primitivism into a more rational and explicitly Baconian form. Campbell's influence continued to be enormous up until his death in 1866. By that time, the movement claimed over two hundred thousand adherents, making it the fifth largest Protestant body in the United States.[18]

If interpreters have agreed that Campbell exerted immense influence on the movement and that he promulgated a staunchly empiricist theology, they have not agreed on the philosophical sources of his thought. Clearly the figure of John Locke looms large, and many scholars have understood Campbell primarily as a Lockean. Others have argued, with varying degrees of emphasis, for the influence of Thomas Reid and Scottish thought.[19] But most interpreters of Campbell, whatever their position, have failed to see his thought in the context of the wholesale transfer of "Baconianism" to the American intellectual scene in the first decades of the nineteenth century. By 1820 Lockean philosophy had been crowded out of American colleges by Scottish texts and was hardly taught at all. When invoked, Locke was most often viewed through a Scottish lens.[20]

The evidence is strong that Alexander Campbell appropriated Scottish Baconianism to a considerable degree and employed it in the service of his primitivist theology. Both Alexander and his father were educated at Glasgow University which was saturated with Reid's and Stewart's modifications of Locke. They both studied logic under George Jardine whose favorite textbook was the *Novum Organum* of Bacon.[21] In his famous debate with the skeptic Robert Owen, Campbell often appealed to "Lord Bacon" as the one who "laid the foundation for correct reasonings" upon "the subject of human experience and knowledge." Citing five of Bacon's aphorisms, Campbell asserted that he would "make the principles of the inductive philosophy . . . my rule and guide in this investigation." Any argument, he insisted, should "be examined by the approved principles of the inductive philosophy, by those very principles which right reason and sound experimental philosophy have sanctioned as their appropriate tests."[22]

Throughout his writings Campbell demonstrated the revulsion to speculation and the insistence on an inductive accumulation of "facts" that typified the Baconian pattern. Accepting Bacon's definition of a "fact" as "something said" or "something done," he asserted: "The Bible is a book of facts, not of opinions, theories, abstract generalities, nor of verbal definitions. It is a book of awful fact, grand and sublime beyond description. . . . The meaning of the Bible facts is the true biblical doctrine. . . . History has, we say, to do with facts—and religion springs from them."[23] The facts of nature and the facts of revelation were to be studied using the same method: one inductively gathers the facts, then through reason extracts the truths contained in them. If such a method had brought harmony and certainty in the natural sciences, then the same method could do the same for religion. In his discussion of "Principles of Interpretation," Campbell made the connection explicit:

> Great unanimity has obtained in some of the sciences in consequence of the adoption of certain rules of analysis and synthesis; for all who work by the same rules, come to the same conclusions. And may it not be possible that in this divine science of religion, there may yet be a very great degree of unanimity of sentiment, and uniformity of practice amongst all its friends?[24]

In the same way that Bacon wanted to abolish the medieval scholastic theories of science and place science on an inductive basis, so Campbell wanted to abolish the dogmatic creeds and systems of religion and place Christianity on an inductive basis.

In an atmosphere where the "Baconian philosophy" had "become synonomous with the *true* philosophy," other early Disciple leaders followed Campbell in employing the Baconian method. Walter Scott, one of the most powerful early preachers of the movement, heartily endorsed the inductive method. Concerned to find an easier evangelistic method for the Disciples, he developed through his own inductive study of the Bible an influential "five-finger" method of salvation: believe, repent, confess, be baptized, receive the remissions of sins and the Holy

Spirit. This schema constituted "the True Gospel," which, as already noted in chapter 5, Scott claimed he had restored.[25] Scott later helped establish Bacon College, founded in 1836 "in honor of Lord Francis Bacon, father of the inductive method of reasoning and the new science." When Scott was elected president of the college, his inaugural address consisted largely of an overview of the *Novum Organum.*[26]

Tolbert Fanning of Nashville was another early proponent of the Baconian method. Deeply influenced by Campbell and formally educated under the Presbyterian Philip Lindsley (an 1807 graduate of Princeton), Fanning became the most influential Disciples preacher in the South prior to the Civil War. He devoted most of his time to Franklin College, which he founded, and to his journal, the *Gospel Advocate,* but he also edited several scientific journals and in other ways pursued a lifelong interest in science. Throughout his career Fanning opposed the inroads of speculation or "spiritualism." He feared the new transcendentalism because, he argued, it "necessarily" excluded "knowledge from observation, or the Baconian philosophy, and all revelations through the Bible." He warned: "Lot's wife was philosophical, so is Theodore Parker."[27]

The influence of Alexander Campbell's appropriation of the Baconian method can be seen clearly in prominent second-generation Disciples—men such as Robert Richardson, Robert Milligan, and J. W. McGarvey.[28] James Lamar's *Organon,* however, provides without doubt the most explicit case of the entrenchment of the Baconian ideal. The book was published when he was just thirty years old, only a few years after his graduation from Campbell's Bethany College. Convinced that sectarian division was caused primarily by the "uncertainty of Biblical interpretation," Lamar believed that the Baconian method could usher in Campbell's great program for Christian unity.

III

In his early twenties Lamar, through conversations with a young man who had studied under Tolbert Fanning at Franklin College, had become acquainted with the Disciples' plea for a return to the "Ancient Order." After his conversion Lamar enrolled at Campbell's school in early 1853; he graduated in July 1854 as valedictorian of a class of seventeen. The same year, on Campbell's recommendation, he began preaching for First Christian Church in Augusta, Georgia, and throughout the rest of his life he ministered to Christian churches in Georgia. In 1869 he became associate editor of the influential *Christian Standard* and wrote extensively in its columns. After the *Organon,* Lamar's other major work, published in 1893, was a two-volume biography of Isaac Errett, longtime editor of the *Standard.*[29]

With the publication of *The Organon of Scripture* in 1859, Lamar's reputation spread throughout the Disciple movement. The book received favorable review and strong recommendation from Alexander Campbell, from W. K. Pendleton, associate editor of the *Millennial Harbinger,* from Tolbert Fanning, editor of the influential *Gospel Advocate,* and from others.[30] "Lamar takes the true ground in regard to reading the scriptures of truth," Fanning remarked, but then proceeded to criticize the phrase "Biblical Interpretation" in the title. It "seems to imply," he wrote, "that the Bible needs interpretation; whereas, in strictness, the book of God is but a transcript of the mind of our Heavenly Father, and the New Testament particularly, is a full and complete will of our Lord Jesus Christ." "The Scriptures fairly translated," he concluded, "need no explanation."[31] Lamar almost would have agreed with him, but would have insisted that the true method must be found and employed to dispel the "fogs of mystical or metaphysical obscurities" and "all manner of crude and pernicious deductions."[32]

At the outset Lamar claimed to present to the public "a New Method of Biblical Interpretation," a method that has been "satisfactorily tried in other departments of study, but which . . . has never been presented and urged as *the* Method of Biblical Interpretation." He believed he was presenting "radically and essentially" a new departure in Christian theology.[33] In this claim Lamar was amazingly naïve, for just such a program of inductive theology had been underway among British and American theologians for over three decades. Lamar's work, rather than presenting a new method, represents the peak, the most explicit and systematic effort, of this trend.[34]

Lamar began with a problem: the great masses of people in Christendom, he believed, were "Skeptics," though they had been reared under the influence of the Bible. It was not the skepticism of Voltaire or Hume, but rather the skepticism induced by "the conflict of opposing creeds and contradictory doctrines" and based on "*the uncertainty of biblical interpretation.*" Such uncertainty was caused not by the Bible itself, the perversity of its interpreters, or the lack of "many excellent principles" of interpretation, but rather by the lack of an "all-comprehensive and pervading method" able to apply the principles and laws. Exegetical laws, Lamar explained, usually have supplied theological builders with the proper "materials or individual facts of revelation," but confusion arises when they begin to put the materials in place in "the great temple of truth." Each theologian builds skillfully and claims indeed to have built the house of the Lord. But all of them need not only the correct materials and engineering skill but also the correct blueprint. Not until then will they erect the proper building and see the masses of people unite within it. Unity would not be found, Lamar asserted, "by singing hosannas to union once a year in our Tract Societies," but by finding the method enabling people to "ascertain with certainty what is *the faith* and what [are] *the requirements* taught in the Bible." Until that method was found, skepticism would run rampant: "church will be arrayed against church, and Christian against Christian."[35]

Discovery of the true method, Lamar believed, required exposure of the false methods used over the centuries. He grouped all of these into two categories—the "Mystic Method" and the "Dogmatic Method." By mysticism he meant "any system which professes to see more in natural and revealed phenomena than is cognizable by common sense," that is, any course pursued to make the facts of nature support ideas arising from contemplation or speculative deduction. Tracing its origins from Neoplatonism through Justin Martyr, Clement, and Origin, Lamar asked incredulously how such "wonderful phantasmagoria [could] be generated out of the plain and simple truths of revelation?" This stream of mysticism had poured into the whole of the Western world in the Middle Ages, then after the Reformation had been carried on by the Quakers, Swedenborg, and a host of other "spiritualists." And despite the widespread repudiation of mysticism by Protestants, Lamar argued, it nonetheless lurked just beneath the surface of Protestant hermeneutical methods. It came to the surface whenever Protestant theologians attempted "to reconcile revelation with their favorite system of religious philosophy": whenever the literal meaning of scripture fit the system, they accepted that meaning, but when it did not fit, they resorted—most often unconsciously—to the mystic method of spiritualizing.[36]

Far more potent as an "instrument of error and perversion" was the dogmatic method, which used mysticism as a tool to serve its purposes. This method could be seen most clearly in medieval scholasticism with its "fondness for the subtleties of the Aristotelian logic and metaphysics." Scholasticism's "essential evil" was that it employed logic "solely in support of the doctrines of the Romish Church," and that its "theology was the result of a *dominant ecclesiastical authority,* imposed without mercy and received without examination." When Luther appeared on the scene he saw that reform would be impossible without abolishing scholastic theology and logic, philosophy, and all other false methods of interpretation. He determined to "burst the bonds of ecclesiastical authority, separate the Bible from its unholy and unnatural alliance with philosophy, . . . and leave the Bible in the hands of responsible men in the exercise of common sense."[37]

The success of Luther and his colleagues in the reformation of religion, Lamar claimed, had been equaled only "by the reformation of science which was superimposed upon it." But when the Reformers "abandoned their own ground," the influence of Aristotle had been reestablished until, in the physical sciences, "Lord Bacon" finally destroyed it. In religion, however, the influence of dogmatic Aristotelianism had not yet been abolished. Lamar therefore thought that by extending the methods of inductive science to religion he would complete the tasks begun by Luther on the one hand and Bacon on the other.[38]

Lamar illustrated the entrenchment of the dogmatic method after the Protestant Reformation by a lengthy discussion of creeds.[39] He stressed the themes—prominent since the early years of the Disciple movement—of liberty, clerical oppression, and a return to the unadorned text of scripture. The Reformation had begun, he argued, with two fundamental principles: the Bible as *"the only rule of religious faith and practice"* and the universal right of *"private judgment or interpretation."* But such principles, embraced in theory, seldom were carried out in practice. Going beyond the "express language of the Bible," people composed creeds and summarily imposed them as tests of orthodoxy. People began looking to "great names" and to Geneva, Augsburg, and Westminster; on such authority, they began excluding people from membership in the churches. Claiming to occupy "broad catholic ground," Lamar asked why a person "should be ruled at all except by the plain authority of the word of God?" Though a person was free to draw up any creed he wished, he could not hold it up *"as* Christianity, either in whole or in part," and proceed to compel its adoption, for he then invaded the liberty of others. The Protestant had no reason to fear the exercise of this liberty, for by means of "the dictates of common sense" and a "strictly inductive exegesis" of scripture drawn from Bacon, he could attain a faith grounded on "facts." He could free himself from the dictates of confessional theologians and from the dogmatic method. All theoretical debates—for example, as to whether the ability to obey God was a gift of nature or of grace, or as to how humanity became sinful—could be dismissed as *"practically* unimportant." The whole library of creeds, confessions, and other human speculations could be jettisoned, for they contained "nothing which is not more plainly, precisely and justly taught" in the Bible. The true Protestant, in short, "could not look to any age subsequent to the first for a single element of the true, divine and complete Christian religion."[40]

<h1 style="text-align:center">IV</h1>

With plentiful invocation of "Lord Bacon," Lamar turned finally to a systematic analysis of the "true method" of interpretation—the "Inductive Method." His starting point was scripture as a body of "natural fact." Bacon had wrought wonders in science by inducing people to "abandon their theories . . . and consult nature for *truth,* not for *proof.*" With this method, as a result, "ten thousand subjects of controversy" had all been settled because "everything is reduced to one single point—*Are these the facts?*"[41] The same wonders could be wrought, Lamar believed, and numerous controversies settled by extending this focus on "natural fact" to scripture and theological method.

The common analogy between God's two books of knowledge provided the ground for this extension. "God has spread before his children," Lamar wrote, "two great volumes—the Book of Nature, and the Book of Revelation." Both were produced by the same mind, and if they were produced uniformly, they must be interpreted uniformly. In both volumes one could see without contradiction "the will and wisdom of God written upon facts." The facts are of a different sort in the two volumes, but *"the method observed in their communication is precisely similar."* Like nature, *"the Bible is not an abstraction,"* and "the comprehension of its revelation of law and truth is just as dependent upon the facts it contains as a knowledge of the laws of nature upon the facts of nature." Nature and revelation were congruous because both were composed of "facts." On this basis, Lamar's central thesis is that "the same method should be pursued in the interpretation of both volumes."[42]

One of Lamar's basic assumptions was that all truth rests on empirically observable facts. "A fact is produced," he believed, "and then truth springs spontaneously and immediately into being." Founded on this basis, truth was eternal and unchangeable. For this reason, Lamar could exult that *"the whole Bible is founded upon facts!"* It was "a record in all respects analogous to that of a competent scientific observer; a record containing, like his, rules, laws, incidents, circumstances, influences, modifications, and everything necessary to enable us to rise to the clear, full, and joyful comprehension of the truth."[43]

The scriptural scientist could rise to this "joyful comprehension of the truth" when he used the proper inductive method to classify the facts of the Bible. But simple induction alone would not suffice. The induction

Bacon advocated, Lamar said, involved not only careful induction—the collection and study of facts—but also deduction, or the descent from the general to the particular. Induction and deduction should function in reciprocal correction and adjustment. "Thus we go up and down the ladder," Lamar advised, "from particulars to generals, and from generals to particulars. . . . Everything has its place and its use, and unites with everything else in proclaiming that *truth must be consistent with fact,* upon which it rests."[44] As a guide to the process, Lamar borrowed eight "Canons of the Inductive Method" from Sir John Herschel's *Preliminary Discourse on the Study of Natural Philosophy* (1830). Using these as "the key," every person would find truth easily accessible.[45] In fact, whenever people had worked "strictly upon the inductive method" they had without exception "perfectly agreed"; they had achieved as much "uniformity as can be found in any branch of physical science." With this method, a person could "perceive the exact place and the precise force of every fact, incident, circumstance, precept, doctrine, and communication" and could "assign every sentence to its proper place, and give to every word its legitimate force." Application of the method was sure because "it is founded upon the eternal principles of common sense."[46]

Throughout the book Lamar repeatedly illustrates the inductive method using the doctrine of conversion, a teaching he ranked as crucial above all others, yet widely perverted. To find the truth on this subject, a person first must dismiss all prejudice from his mind, then use the rules that were "plainly the dictate of common sense" to collect the relevant scriptural facts. In this process he must eliminate scripture's "highly-colored imagery and bold hyperboles" and retain the "real facts and unadorned doctrine remaining as residual phenomena after those things are excluded." To be classified with the *"simple* facts," the "poetic element" must be *"rendered* simple."[47] Then one must classify the facts according to their bearing on the topic. The biblical doctrine of conversion, Lamar said, was a generalization made from a certain class of facts—"the cases of actual conversion" in the New Testament, especially in Acts of the Apostles. When studied inductively, all the cases of conversion agreed in one central point: "the exhibition of an *obedient faith."* Though faith and obedience did not cause salvation, they were the *"conditions* necessarily precedent to the effectual operation of the true cause," which was God's love. A vital part of this obedient faith was baptism, which the "uniform analogy of Scripture" shows to be "for the remission of sins." As to the "proximate cause of faith," the same analysis shows that the degree of faith was "measured by the amount of testimony" received; thus "faith is produced by testimony" or evidence.

Lamar's conclusion: "every human being who has capacity to enable him to appreciate the force and meaning of ordinary language, *will reach precisely the same conclusion as to what is scriptural conversion.*"[48]

By laying such a secure foundation for precise agreement on all aspects of biblical teaching, Lamar believed that he had cleared the way for overthrowing all human sects and the creeds around which the sects rallied. The stranglehold of the dogmatic and mystic methods could be broken and Bacon's great revolution in method completed. Through Common Sense all rational persons, no matter how humble, could throw off the shackles of clerical oppression and exercise their democratic right to interpret the Bible for themselves. Through strict use of the inductive method, as set out by Bacon and refined by others, the simple truth of scripture would prevail, the "great temple of truth" would be constructed according to God's original design, and in the free air of America people could unite within its walls. Campbell's vision of Christian unity through a "restoration of the ancient order of things" could be furthered and even brought to a glorious fulfillment.

V

Lamar's Baconian agenda, along with that of the many other evangelical theologians who placed their hopes in Baconianism, soon faced serious challenges, however. After 1845 scientists increasingly recognized the limits of Baconianism, the inability of the inductive method to explain the rapidly accumulating "facts." And after 1860, the Protestant consensus based on the harmonious interrelationship of the Bible, natural science, and morality began to weaken and crumble under the impact of Darwinism and a changing cultural climate. By the end of the nineteenth century, the United States had shifted considerably from a nation more or less united by British Protestant values to a nation greatly diversified by waves of immigration and rapid social change. Baconianism lost much of its intellectual and social base.[49]

In the Disciple movement itself, Baconian confidence in the perspicuity of scripture proved insufficient to hold the movement together. After the Civil War the Disciples slowly assimilated to a diversifying culture. While theological seeds of division were present much earlier, the movement began to fracture following the Civil War—in part along North-South, rural-urban, and socioeconomic lines, and in part over long-standing theological tensions.[50] The tensions produced discernible conservative, moderate, and liberal elements. The conservative Disciples, commonly known as Churches of Christ, adopted a dissenting sectarian position as early as the 1830s and thus maintained a social and intellectual milieu supporting the Baconian worldview. Led by men such as Tolbert Fanning and David Lipscomb, both editors of the *Gospel Advocate* in Nashville, conservative Disciples heightened the Baconian emphasis on biblical "fact" and inductive precision, leaving little room for honest disagreement in matters of scriptural interpretation. The resulting sectarian emphasis appears starkly in the remark of one Tennessee preacher in 1901: "I doubt if there is a section in the world that holds more ernestly and faithfully to the truth . . . than Middle Tennessee."[51]

Including perhaps three-fourths of the Disciple movement, the moderate element—commonly known as the Christian Churches—adopted a more open stance to the changing culture. The conservatives often attacked them as "liberal Christians . . . always contending for the 'Spirit,' and not the letter."[52] Moderates such as J. H. Garrison and Isaac Errett responded that the "literalism and legalism" of the conservatives and their ongoing "crusade against mystery" had robbed the movement of its heart and could no longer meet the needs of the time. The moderates turned toward a more pietistic, less precise hermeneutic and away from the Baconian primitivism of earlier years; they placed increasing stress on Christ in the heart, in contrast to the "nice doctrinal points, fine spun distinctions, . . . and creeds and rulers" of the sects.[53] At the same time, however, the moderates firmly resisted theological liberalism and the strong currents of evolutionary thought and higher criticism of the Bible. Only in the last decade of the century did a liberal element gain strength and forge a new division within the Disciple ranks.[54]

The moderates' more open stance toward culture can be traced clearly in the career of Lamar himself, who by 1900 had moved a considerable distance from the Baconianism of the *Organon*. As early as 1872 Lamar could write that the Disciple plan for Christian union "needed no carefully drawn formularies or rigid standards of doctrine, because it was not a union in doctrines." The only test for a person was "How did he stand related to Christ?" Lamar still had confidence, however, in knowing what the Bible "*expressly* taught" and "*expressly* commanded." It is still a "plain book," he wrote, and "means just what it says—neither more nor less."[55] By the early 1890s Lamar's emphasis on "vital religion" had grown more pervasive and his rejection of a rigid Baconianism more pronounced. It was possible, he observed, to present the Christian message "simply as logical propositions" and as "mainly intellectual," and in earlier years such an approach had been necessary to dislodge the exorbitant claims and emotionalism of the competing religious groups. But what once had been the right way "is so no longer"—now it was "distasteful, jangling, rasping." Churches were tired of "our cold, heartless, clamping, clinching, invincible logic," he concluded; what they wanted was "the primitive gospel with the sweet fragrance of the primitive spirit." Thus Lamar said that "first principles" should be presented "simply as great vitalizing and organizing elements of the truth."[56]

By 1900, modernism and the new science clearly had shaped Lamar's outlook. In a series of articles in 1901, for example, he expressed doubts that "highest truth can ever be *indubitably* brought home to the mere intellect." Rather, he wrote, truth must be impressed upon a person's "inmost heart"; there must be "an intuition of the soul—a deep sympathetic feeling so that with his inner eyes he can *see* God." Faith, he concluded, must be supported "by something much more than logic."[57] Later in the same series, Lamar affirmed a form of theistic evolution, denied the facticity of the Eden story, calling it "a divine formulation of deepest truth," and accepted the possibility that the earth may be "billions" of years old.[58] Despite the liberal ring of such pronouncements, Lamar at the same time could attack the young scholars enamored with higher criticism who, with their "drills and dynamites," threatened the "supernatural elements" in Christianity.[59] Clearly for Lamar the Baconian "temple of truth" needed a thorough remodeling, though he insisted that some of its foundation pillars must be kept firmly in place.

VI

The intellectual and spiritual odyssey of James S. Lamar from the 1850s to 1900 reflects his increasing disillusionment with the Baconian method as a tool to bring about Alexander Campbell's goal of Christian union through restoration of the "ancient order." He saw to his dismay that the freedom from constricting human systems and traditions sought by early Disciple leaders quickly had given way to a new orthodoxy as firmly set and as narrowly defended as the Old Protestant creedalism they had sought to transcend. As the conservative Disciples hardened the Baconian hermeneutic that his own writings had done so much to promote, Lamar pulled back in an effort to preserve the ideal of Christian unity and tolerance of theological diversity that had marked the movement's earlier years.

Though forced into some theological retooling as a result, Lamar seems never to have been struck by the deep irony that marked the movement almost from its inception—the irony of claiming to overturn all human traditions and interpretive schemes while at the same time being wedded to an empirical theological method drawn from early Enlightenment thought. By virtually denying the necessity of human interpretation of the Bible and the inevitable impact of extrabiblical ideas and traditions, the Disciples simply allowed their interpretive traditions to become all the more entrenched for being unrecognized. Lamar and his brethren never quite saw that in addition to being Disciples of Christ they also had become disciples of Baconian empiricism.

Among conservative Disciples the inductive method continued to exercise enormous influence, though they quickly forgot the name of Bacon and pared to a more plebian and practical form the elaborate hermeneutical strictures of Lamar. David Dungan tersely expressed the prevailing view in 1888: "nothing more respecting the Scripture method need be said, for it is everywhere apparent that when the Lord would conduct an investigation on any subject, He did it by the inductive method."[60] For Dungan and many other Disciples, the inductive method, like the Disciples movement itself, was born not of profane history but of the sacred primordium, the time of Jesus and the apostles. With this method, therefore, they believed they could stand above the shifting sands of human speculation and the dangerous currents of modernity. But in a movement long marked by theological and cultural rifts, the outcome finally was a bitter fundamentalist-modernist controversy and permanent division.[61] Caught in the middle was the aging James Lamar, his vision of restoration, liberty, and unity chastened by time, the glorious promise of Baconianism unfulfilled.

EIGHT

From Primitive Church to Protestant Nation: The Millennial Odyssey of Alexander Campbell

In the next three chapters, we shift our discussion from the restoration of primitive Christianity in the context of the church to the restoration of the primal, natural order of things in the context of the nation. The previous chapters have demonstrated (1) the long history of the restoration ideal in the Anglo-American experience, (2) the great appeal of restoration ideology in the American context, (3) the way restoration ideology undergirded claims to freedom and innocence, and finally, (4) the persistent tendency of restorationists to close the gap between primordium and present and to claim that their particular situation is a virtual replication of first times to which all should conform. In other words, previous chapters, by focusing on sectarian dissenters, have demonstrated the way restoration ideology has actually worked in the context of American religious pluralism.

In these last three chapters, we focus not on religious pluralism in America but rather on America's role in a pluralistic world. Typically, Americans have sought to justify their existence and their expansion in the world by appealing to the same restoration ideology employed by sectarians. The fact that most Americans have appealed not to primitive Christianity but to nature for national justification should not obscure the restorationist perspective at work in the life of the nation. After all, American Enlightenment thinkers who laid the legal and theoretical basis for the nation did not view nature as a mere abstraction. Instead, nature symbolized for them the way God intended things to be from the beginning. Nature *was* the primordium, and to the standards of this primordium they sought to conform the nation.

When Americans have sought through the years to conform the nation to nature's standards, however, the notion of nature has functioned in two dramatically different ways. Domestically, most Americans have rejected particularized religious traditions as standards for the nation. Instead, they have recognized at least in some sense—though sometimes grudgingly—the concept of "Nature and Nature's God" as a universal standard of religious faith and values, and this concept has worked relatively well as a safeguard for domestic religious freedom. In the world order, however, the reverse often has been true. In the world context, Americans persistently have exhibited great reluctance in allowing the notion of nature to function in a way consistent with domestic ideals. Instead of acknowledging nature as a symbol pointing to the primordial and the universal—categories that ideally stand in judgment on every present and every particular—Americans typically have employed nature as a construct absolutizing the nation and its cultural particularities. This tendency appeared early in the national experience. As we have seen, for example, Thomas Paine argued that when one viewed the new United States government, "we are brought at once to the point of seeing government begin, as if we had lived in the beginning of time."

This suggests that in the pluralistic world community the American nation has functioned in much the same way that sects have functioned within the pluralistic national community. Ironically, while the construct of nature has undermined sectarian claims to absolute and universal status, that same construct has supported national claims to absolute and universal status—a tendency we will explore especially in chapter 10. In foreign affairs, therefore, the nation often has not so much possessed the soul of a church as the soul of a sect that has been nourished and sustained by restoration ideology.

In the context of the Judeo-Christian heritage, a reliable measure of the extent to which a given household of faith has universalized the particular (or particularized the universal) is the extent to which the faithful ascribe to themselves a key role in bringing about the millennium or new world order. We already have encountered the tendency of restorationists to assume that their own restoration of first times will lead inevitably to the millennial kingdom. In previous chapters we have seen this perspective at work among "Christians in the West," Mormons, and Landmark Baptists. In this chapter we shall see the same perspective at work in the thinking of Alexander Campbell.

We focus on Campbell, however, not to illustrate yet once again the close connection between primitivism and millennialism. That much is already apparent. Rather, Campbell is significant because he provides a classic example of the shift from denominational sectarianism to national and cultural sectarianism. In his early days, Campbell fully believed that his movement would inaugurate the millennial dawn when human governments would be abolished and Christ alone would rule. But like James S. Lamar, Campbell grew disillusioned with aspects of his own movement. His disillusionment occurred for two reasons. First, men such as Arthur Crihfield, John R. Howard, and Tolbert Fanning had turned a sizable portion of Campbell's movement in the direction of sectarian conformity, thereby undercutting Campbell's own ideal of unity in diversity. Second, it struck Campbell that, in any event, the nation simply had beaten his movement at its own game. While many in his movement were taking exclusive rather than universal positions, the nation was forging unity from diversity, thereby hastening the millennial dawn, or so it seemed to Campbell by the 1840s and 1850s. But even when Campbell reached these conclusions, he absolutized the particularities of his culture and argued that the blessings of liberty and diversity flowed not from "Nature and Nature's God" but instead from Protestant Christianity. Nature's nation, therefore, was a Protestant nation, and assurance of both freedom and the coming millennium rested squarely, Campbell thought, on this "natural" Protestant foundation. In reaching these conclusions, Campbell was far from unique. Hosts of Americans in the midyears of the nineteenth century shared his convictions.

The irony emerges when one remembers that Campbell moved to this "broader" perspective when he saw how narrow and oppressive the restoration ideal had become in the hands of at least some in his movement. The nation, he assumed, was different. After all, it had been built, Campbell imagined, on the broad and universal foundation of "natural Protestantism" and therefore was able to encompass the whole human race and launch the millennial dawn. But when Campbell finally voiced these convictions in 1849, the nation already had dispossessed and even killed hundreds and thousands of both native Americans and Mexicans, all for the sake of extending the domain of freedom which the natural order of things, embodied in "Protestant America," guaranteed to all humankind.

We do not know if Campbell ever fully perceived the ironies that haunted his millennial pursuits in their various shades and hues. But we can at least trace the nature of those changes and the inner logic that accompanied them. This chapter explores how for Alexander Campbell, Protestant America steadily displaced the primitive church as midwife for the millennial age.

I

From the early years of his movement until almost the end of his life, Campbell anticipated a millennium of earthly bliss when justice would triumph, tyranny would be abolished, and the Christian faith would hold sway over the world.[1] However, until at least the mid-1830s, Campbell's vision differed from the popular, Protestant millennial vision in one critical respect. The more prevalent vision hinged the millennium on the spread and influence of both the Christian religion and American social and political institutions, and generally perceived no real tension or opposition between the two.[2] Campbell, on the other hand, did not base the millennium on the influence of America but rather on the success of his movement to unite Christendom through the restoration of the primitive, apostolic church. He proclaimed in the *Christian Baptist* in 1825 that "just in so far as the ancient order of things, or the religion of the New Testament, is restored, just so far has the Millennium commenced." And in 1829, in the debate with Robert Owen, he heralded his "sanguine anticipation" of a "restoration of the ancient order of things, and a state of society far superior to anything yet exhibited on earth."[3]

> Fancy to yourselves, my friends, a society in which such [good] characters shall have the rule, and then you want no poet to describe the millennium to you. Peace, harmony, love and universal goodwill, must be the order of the day. There wants nothing—believe me, my friends, there wants nothing—but a restoration of ancient christianity, and a cordial reception of it, to fill the world with all the happiness, physical, intellectual, and moral, which beings like us in this state of trial could endure— shall I say?—yes, endure and enjoy.

And Campbell rejoiced "to know that this period is nigh at hand."[4] In 1830, Campbell betrayed the same presuppositions in the prospectus of his new journal, the *Millennial Harbinger*:

> This work shall be devoted to the destruction of Sectarianism, Infidelity, and Anti-christian doctrine and practice. It shall have for its object the development, and introduction of that political and religious order of society called THE MILLENNIUM, which shall be the consummation of that ultimate amelioration of society proposed in the Christian Scriptures.

And Campbell now often spoke of the "Millennial Church."[5]

One of the chief reasons Campbell based the millennium on primitive Christianity was that only the restored church, he thought, could produce the unity in both church and society that the millennial age required.[6] "We assume it for a principle," he wrote in 1830, "that the union of christians, and the destruction of sects, are indispensable prerequisites to the subjection of the world to the government of Jesus, and to the triumphant appearance of Christ's religion in the world." But at the same time, he argued, "there is no platform in any of the great sects of christendom on which to rear this glorious superstructure. They are all *too narrow* and too weak."[7] On the other hand, Campbell claimed, "there is now a scheme of things presented, in what is called the *Ancient Gospel,* which is long enough, broad enough, strong enough for the whole superstructure called the Millennial Church—and . . . it will alone be the *instrument* of *converting* the whole human race, and of *uniting* all christians upon one and the same foundation."[8] A universal return to the clear, self-evident "gospel facts" would secure the unity Campbell sought.

In all of this, however, Campbell did not seek a rigid uniformity. Instead, he sought unity through a restoration of essentials while extending liberty on all nonessential matters. "There is but 'one faith,'" he argued, "but nowhere is it written that there is but *one opinion.*"[9] For this reason, he asserted that "we do not ask them [Christians] to give up their opinions—we ask them only not to impose them upon others."[10] But how might one determine those core essentials on which both unity and the millennium depended? In good Baconian fashion, Campbell answered simply, "by abandoning opinions, and founding all associations upon the belief of gospel facts. Let every sect give up its opinions as a bond of union, and what will remain in common? The gospel facts alone."[11]

While Campbell had every confidence that his own program for recovering "gospel facts" would inaugurate the millennium, he was equally certain that the American nation was impotent in this regard. After all, the founding fathers inclined toward Deism, and that was enough to convince Campbell of the nation's deficiencies. "Our fathers . . . imagined that government without any religion, a government purely deistical, skeptical or political, was the *summum bonum*—the very maximum of social bliss," Campbell complained. "They went as far as mortals, stung by the fiery dragon, could go, to devise a government without a single religious institution." To be sure, Campbell had only praise for these "political institutions which have hitherto secured . . . the greatest amount of political and temporal happiness hitherto enjoyed by any people." But he made it clear that the happiness introduced by the Republic would be far surpassed when "Christianity conquers the world."[12] And when *"Jesus Christ will yet govern the world by religion only,"*

> . . . then shall they literally "beat their swords into ploughshares and their spears into pruning-hooks, and learn war no more." Christianity, rightly understood, cordially embraced, and fully carried out in practice, will . . . certainly subvert all political government, the very best as well as the very worst. . . . The admirers of American liberty and American in-

stitutions have no cause to regret such an event, nor cause to fear it. It will be but the removing of a tent to build a temple—the falling of a cottage after the family are removed into a castle. . . . The American Revolution is but a precursor of a revolution of infinitely more importance to mankind . . . —the emancipation of the human mind from the shackles of superstition, and the introduction of human beings into the full fruition of the reign of heaven.[13]

Campbell firmly believed that the natural theology on which the founders had erected the Republic lacked the self-evident qualities so many thought it possessed. This, to Campbell, rendered ridiculous the claim that allegiance to "Nature and Nature's God" would bring the millennial age. If the volume of nature was as apparent and intelligible as Deists and skeptics claimed, Campbell argued, then "one would expect to find a remarkable conformity and coincidence of sentiment among the students of this one volume, which needs neither translation nor commentary." But to the contrary,

There are more versions of the volume of nature, then of the volume of revelation. Though, they say, it wants no *written* commentary, it certainly requires some prophet or interpreter to explain it. How else came it to pass that all the ancient nations, and all the modern without revelation, have, from the same premises, come to so many different conclusions![14]

In reality, however, Campbell declared, nothing of God can be known from nature at all. "You might as reasonably expect a person born deaf to have all the ideas of harmony, as a man destitute of supernatural revelation to have the ideas of God and spiritual system" since the notion of God is simply "not derivable through any of his senses."[15] Thus Campbell ridiculed both Deism and its seventeenth-century father, Lord Herbert of Cherbury.

When I hear a Deist talking about 'the light of nature' and 'the great God of nature,' I am reminded of the school-boy, who stole a penknife; and when charged with the fact, said, he found it growing upon an apple-tree. This was equivalent to a confession of the theft, since we all know penknives do not grow upon apple-trees. In like manner the reasonings of the Deists, upon their own premises, show that their conclusions do not logically follow. You might as well look for penknives growing upon apple-trees as for Lord Herbert's doctrine in the mind of a savage. There is no stopping-place between Atheism and Christianity.[16]

As late as 1859–60, Campbell still sought to stop "the mouths of those who are continually saying, we look up through nature to nature's God."[17]

Not only did Campbell criticize the Deists, whom he commonly called "skeptics" and "Infidels," but he refused to ascribe to "Nature and Nature's God" the primary credit for American civil and religious liberties, crediting Christianity instead. "We are indebted for all the great improvements in society to the philosophy of christians," he proclaimed, "and not to the philosophy of skeptics. . . . The labors of the Reformers, and the more recent labors of Milton, the poet, and Locke, the philosopher, have done more to create the free institutions of Europe and America, than the labors of all the skeptics." Contrasting Locke with the founders, Campbell called him the "Christian philosopher to whom we are more indebted than to . . . our revolutionary heroes and statesmen" for "cause of civil and religious liberty," for it was Locke's "Essay on Toleration [that] first burst the chains that held England and Europe fast bound under a religious and civil despotism."[18] Presumably Campbell would have granted the founding fathers equal acclaim had they predicated their efforts to secure liberty on the Christian revelation.

When the Deists, however, rejected revelation and held instead to their "flimsy sophistry" of nature, Campbell supposed they did so on the basis of distorted information. The Christianity they knew, he thought, was corrupted and was hardly the religion of the primitive, apostolic age. "We are assured," he said, "that the progress of skepticism is neither owing to the weakness nor the paucity of the evidences of christianity; but to a profession of it unauthorized by, and incompatible with, the christian scriptures."[19] He accused Robert Owen of reacting not to authentic, New Testament Christianity but rather to "papal enormities" or "the state-religions of Europe." Thus, "many of the skeptics, and even Mr. Owen himself, have been attacking antichrist and thought they were opposing Christ."[20]

But if the Republic and its theology could neither inaugurate the millennium nor sustain the unity on which the millennium was contingent, Campbell was assured that "the restoration of the ancient order" of the Christian faith could spark these great and final changes.

> To introduce the last and most beneficial change in society, it is only necessary to let the gospel, in its plainness, simplicity and force, speak to men. Divest it of all the appendages of human philosophy, falsely so called, and of all the traditions and dogmas of men, and in its power it will pass from heart to heart, from house to house, from city to city, until it bless the whole earth.

176

Campbell asserted his opinion that "more new churches have been formed within twelve months, where the primitive gospel has been proclaimed with clearness and power, than the twelve preceding years can count under the humanized gospel of the sects."[21] Because of his great faith in the power of the primitive gospel, rather than in the power of the Republic, to introduce the millennium, Campbell often taught that Christians should neither hold political office nor engage in war and that there was "nothing more antipodal to the gospel than politics."[22] He was not always consistent, however, with his own advice.[23]

That Campbell would make the millennium contingent on recovery of the primitive Christian faith is striking. But, then, in Campbell's thought, as in the thinking of Parley Pratt, Arthur Crihfield, and James R. Graves, the primordial age and the millennial age were but opposite and congruent ends of the same historical continuum. What made them congruent was simply that the former gave to the latter its texture and shape. Further, with Campbell, the continuum closed full circle and the congruent ends embraced and interlocked.[24] That Campbell could attach such revolutionary expectations to his restorationist program at a time when others attached the same expectations to the American state belies the sheer power the notion of the primitive church exercised over the minds of its nineteenth-century adherents. The apostolic church was *ontos*. Its recovery would unite Christendom and regenerate the world.[25]

II

In spite of such grand expectations, Campbell's movement faltered on the question of defining the essentials. This problem became a major obstacle in Campbell's path for the simple reason that he constructed his ecclesiastical platform out of two intellectual traditions that themselves had been at odds over this very issue. Campbell derived his emphasis on restoration from Puritanism, mediated to him through the Seceder Presbyterian church in Ireland and several secessionists from the Church of Scotland.[26] His emphasis on unity he derived from the British rationalists, especially John Locke, who sought a means to societal unity in the aftermath of Calvinism, sectarian disputes, and religious wars.[27] Campbell and the rationalists differed not in intention or theological model but in content. The intention in both instances was pluralism and unity. The theological model in both instances was the reduction of religion to a set of self-evident essentials on which all reasonable persons could agree. The Deists, however, specifically excluded revelation as content for the model since they judged revelation, individually interpreted, as the basic source of societal division. John Locke accepted revelation as content for the model, but reduced that content to one essential only: the belief that Jesus is the Messiah. Ironically, Campbell, being a child of the Puritans as well as of the rationalists, filled the rationalists' model with the Puritans' restorationist content which the rationalists already had rejected as divisive. And by predicating unity on the restoration of an institution—the primitive, apostolic church—rather than on a religion of nature, or a single revealed doctrine as with Locke, he elevated the problem of essentials-nonessentials to critical significance. Campbell himself, in fact, provided thereby a fundamental source for the theological tension that would plague his movement for its duration.

The tension in Campbell's thought between restoration and unity appears most clearly in the early years of the movement when Campbell edited and published the *Christian Baptist* (1823–30).[28] Campbell, for those years, could be classified as a radical restorationist since he claimed that a New Testament precedent or example was as binding as an express command and that what was not commanded in scripture was necessarily forbidden.[29] Campbell's father, Thomas, employed the argument from silence at an early date, and Alexander subsequently used it to show that missionary and Bible societies, creeds, and fellowship with the unimmersed were all unscriptural and thus prohibited.[30] In taking these positions, Campbell stood squarely in the restoration tradition marked out by Heinrich Bullinger and Thomas Cartwright in the sixteenth century.

The hermeneutic of silence and example, however, lacked the clarity Campbell desired and gave rise to the problem of essentials—the issue that stood at the very heart of Campbell's theological struggles during those years. People pressed him from a number of sides to define the essentials, and he had great difficulty complying consistently and satisfactorily. On the one hand, he was reluctant to define them at all since that would impair his plea for unity. On the other hand, he had to define in some way the institution he wished to restore.

Campbell clearly stated his basic principle in 1826: "We are always to distinguish what is merely circumstantial in any institution from the institution itself."[31] And he proposed two methods by which this could be done. First, a practice employed by only one congregation rather than universally in the New Testament church was obviously only circumstantial and thus nonessential. Second, he affirmed that "all instituted acts of religion are characterized by the definite article, as, *the* Lord's table, *the* Lord's day, &c."[32] In 1826, a German Baptist (Dunkard) wrote to the *Christian Baptist* asking Campbell, in effect, why he refused to extend the concept of restoration to certain obvious New Testament practices such as the Lord's Supper at night, foot washing, and the kiss of charity. Campbell's handling of the kiss of charity provides a good example of the problems he encountered. He argued unconvincingly, and somewhat counter to his earlier stated principles, that since the kiss of charity was commanded five times in the Epistles, it therefore was not an essential ordinance. Essential practices, he said, were *assumed* by the New Testament writers, not commanded.[33] A year earlier, Campbell addressed the question of communitarian living and asserted that this practice was both circumstantial and nonessential. In this case his primary evidence was that "no other christian congregation [except that at Jerusalem] held a community of goods."[34] Significantly, an actual division occurred over this issue among Campbell's followers. Sidney Rigdon, who believed that consistent restorationism required communitarian living, clashed with Campbell at Austintown, Ohio, in 1830 and shortly thereafter broke with Campbell over that issue and associated himself with the Mormons.[35]

The issue of baptism was a particular problem for Campbell since he believed, after 1812, that immersion of believers was the only valid form of the ordinance.[36] But to require believers' baptism as an essential ordinance would seriously impede his efforts toward unity. We already have seen, for example, that Barton W. Stone vigorously protested the imposition of adult immersion as "a term of fellowship." That short step, Stone complained, "would exclude more christians from union than any creed with which I am acquainted."[37] In his debate with W. L. McCalla in 1823, therefore, Campbell worked out a position enabling him in effect to affirm both the necessity and the non-necessity of believers' baptism at one and the same time. Campbell argued that baptism was essential for remission of sins and salvation, but then distinguished between *formal* and *real* remission of sins. Real remission of sins, he said, was by the blood of Christ, while baptism was "a *formal* proof and token of it [forgiveness]." Real remission of sins, in fact, might well occur prior to baptism in point of time.[38] This distinction enabled Campbell to affirm the necessity of believers' baptism while at the same time recognizing as forgiven Christians those believers who had not submitted to this rite. In this way, he preserved both the restoration of believers' baptism and his thrust toward Christian unity which an unqualified insistence on believers' baptism might have impaired.

Campbell, however, did not always utilize this distinction and sometimes engaged in a great deal of theological double-talk concerning baptism. For example, in April of 1827 he wrote that both Baptists and pedobaptists "wear different regimentals, rally round different standards, and flight [*sic*] under different captains; but neither the flag nor the cockade makes a difference in the soldiers." He added that among both pedobaptists and Baptists, "he that feareth God and worketh right- eousness is accepted of him."[39] Nevertheless, in that very same issue, Campbell reversed himself and affirmed that without both belief and baptism a person was "not in the kingdom of Jesus Christ" and was worthy of condemnation.[40] Examples could be multiplied, but this brief survey demonstrates the tension in Campbell's thinking that emerged from his attempt to combine unity and restoration into a single platform.

Abundant evidence indicates that by the mid-1830s, Campbell's con- cern for Christian unity had modified and even undermined his earlier concern for a radically restorationist posture based on the hermeneutic of example and silence.[41] In 1830 Campbell discontinued the icono- clastic *Christian Baptist* and introduced a new, more constructive journal, the *Millennial Harbinger;* in 1832, Campbell's "Disciples" merged with the "Christians" of Barton W. Stone; and in 1831, Campbell began to relax his argument from the silence of scripture concerning missionary societies. He now argued that the New Testament both com- mands Christians to preach the word and suggests the principle of church cooperation. But since it is silent on the details of cooperation, churches are free to proceed in ways they deem expedient.[42] By 1849 Campbell was arguing not only for cooperation but for organization, significantly basing his argument on the silence of scripture. "Matters of prudential arrangement for the evangelizing of the world . . . are left without a single law, ordinance, or enactment in all the new Testa- ment. . . . I see no necessity for any *positive Divine statutes* in such matters." That same year, largely at Campbell's prodding, the Disciples organized the American Christian Missionary Society, and Campbell served as president from 1849 until his death in 1866.[43] Further, Camp- bell took an unequivocal stand in his famous Lunenburg Letter of 1837 when he argued that baptism is not essential to one's status as Christian. He claimed there that he would give "the preference of my heart" to a loving, devoted pedobaptist over someone who was neither loving nor spiritual but who had been immersed.[44]

Clearly, the growing spirit of exclusivism in Campbell's own ranks— a development traced in some detail in chapter 5—provided one of the chief reasons for Campbell's shift. Deeply rooted in Baconian perspec- tives but alienated from the postmillennial hopes that sustained Campbell, men such as Arthur Crihfield and John R. Howard determined with precision the form and shape of the true Church of Christ and argued that it alone comprised the kingdom of God. Such sectarianizing of the restoration ideal was more than Campbell could bear, and as early as 1826 he remonstrated.

This plan of making our own nest, and fluttering over our own brood; of building our own tent, and of confining all goodness and grace to our noble selves and the "elect few" who are like us, is the quintessence of sublimated pharisaism. . . . To lock ourselves up in the bandbox of our own little circle; to associate with a few units, tens, or hundreds, as the pure church, as the elect, is real Protestant monkery, it is evangelical nunnery.

In 1837 Campbell defended Protestantism in a debate with Bishop John Baptist Purcell of Cincinnati. Anticipating a rebuke from some of his brethren for including Protestants within the bounds of the kingdom, Campbell explained in clear and certain terms the motives for his shift.

Some of our brethren were too much addicted to denouncing the sects and representing them *en masse* as wholly aliens from the possibility of salvation—as wholly antichristian and corrupt. . . . Therefore, we have been always accused of aspiring to build up and head a party. . . . On this account I determined the more readily to defend Protestantism.

And when some of those same critics accused Campbell of too broad a stance in his Lunenburg Letter, Campbell turned their own rhetoric back on themselves.

Why should we so often have quoted and applied to apostate Christendom what the Spirit saith to saints in Babylon—"Come out of her, my people, that you partake not of her sins, and that you receive not of her plagues"—had we imagined that the Lord had no people beyond the pale of our communion![45]

III

In the mid-1830s, Alexander Campbell made two important shifts. First, he steadily lost faith in a radical restoration of the primitive church to produce the ecclesiastical and societal unity required by the millennial age. At the same time, he recognized more and more that the nation, not the church, had secured unity, equality, and pluralism to an unprecedented degree. Further, while Campbell, with marginal success, had sought to unify Christendom by restoring the essential doctrines of the primitive church and by permitting but rendering harmless a plurality of religious opinions, the founders, with considerably greater success, had sought to unify the Republic by restoring the essential doctrines of nature and by permitting but rendering harmless a plurality of religious sects. And by 1854 Campbell judged that the United States in effect possessed a civil religion established by law. This religion, he contended, did not consist in any specific form of worship, but in the rights of conscience, in the administration of oaths, or appeals to God, on the part of all the organs of government, from the President of the United States down to a common magistrate, and in the administration of oaths to all witnesses, according to conscience. In these we have a solemn recognition of the being and perfections of God, of a day of judgment, of future and eternal rewards and punishments.

Campbell's understanding of civil religion, as reflected in this passage, clearly appealed to the existence of God, to the rights of conscience that God guarantees, and to the notion that God stands in judgment over human behavior—themes central to American civil religion from Jefferson to Kennedy, as Robert Bellah has pointed out.[46]

Ironically, however, while Campbell now recognized the existence of a theological perspective that legitimated religious pluralism in America, he, like the "religious 'mind diseas'd'" of which Sidney Mead speaks,[47] consistently refused to recognize the deistic premises on which that theology rested. He argued, therefore, that "*the Christian religion, but no sectarian form of it, is by law established and recognized in the institution of marriage, in the inhibitions of bigamy, adultery, fornication and incest,*" and by the cessation of secular and legal business on the "Christian Sabbath."[48] And as early as 1841 he had argued that

> notwithstanding all our sectarian differences, we yet have something called a *common* Christianity;—that there are certain great fundamental matters—indeed, every thing elementary in what is properly called piety and morality—in which all good men of all denominations are agreed; and that these great common principles and views form a common ground on which all Christian people can unite, harmonize and co-operate in one great system of moral and Christian education.[49]

And that this common Christianity was Protestant and not Catholic, Campbell left no doubt at all.[50]

Thus, while throwing the blanket of Protestant Christianity over "Nature and Nature's God," Campbell argued that the establishment of this common, national faith provided the strongest provisions for religious pluralism that could be desired. Indeed, he argued that Protestant Christianity was absolutely "essential to political and religious liberty." Hence, he claimed in 1854 that "the Jew and Gentile are alike protected in the practice and enjoyment of all the religious dictates of their consciences towards God. . . . This is a very broad and rational provision in behalf of . . . all religious faith and worship."[51]

The shift that occurred in Campbell's thinking from the mid-1820s to the mid-1830s was subtle but profound. Campbell always, throughout his career, ascribed civil and religious liberties to Christianity rather than to Deism or "infidelity." In this he remained consistent. The change, rather, involved his recognition of a common religion. Earlier in his career, Campbell recognized no common religion at all, anticipating instead the day when primitive Christianity would become the common religion, thus securing liberty, unity, and pluralism to the highest degree. When he realized that America did have a common religion which, indeed, had secured liberty, unity, and pluralism, he acknowledged it but refused to call it by its proper name. In this way, the primitive Christian who once had made war on the Protestant sects now joined the Protestant forces since he had come to believe that the Protestant faith was "essential to political and religious liberty."

For Campbell, Protestantism now represented a clear expression of the primordial, universal faith. The man, therefore, who in 1829 and 1830 had opposed national Sabbath legislation on the grounds that it tended toward an established church,[52] by 1848 wished to enthrone Protestant Christianity in the government itself. Neither the United States nor England are really Christian nations, he argued, for their governments "are yet deistical in form, rather than Christian." Where they ought to have inscribed, *"In the name of the Lord,"* they have, written only, " *'In the name of God.'* " Indeed, Campbell said, the two notions that " 'all *authority'*. . . is given to Jesus Christ" and that "God has . . . anointed him Sovereign of the universe" are the "two grand declarations that ought to revolutionize our whole views of civil government as respects its ultimate authority, and change some of our forms of legal justice."[53] In this perspective, Campbell foreshadowed those defenders of the Confederacy whom we shall meet in chapter 9—men such as George Foster Pierce and Benjamin M. Palmer who sought to ground the Confederacy in "God in Christ—ruling the world by the double right of creation and redemption."

By 1850, Campbell stood before a joint session of Congress for an hour and a half, preaching to them of "the Divine *Philanthropy*." And by 1853, Campbell judged that the United States government reflected the Christian faith more clearly than did any other because, he said, it was the most "Protestant."[54] Nevertheless, he still was not entirely satisfied, and in 1854, he urged that congressional and legislative proceedings be preceded not only by a prayer but also by "the reading of at least one chapter [of scripture] previous to these intercessions and thanksgivings. It would, I conceive, greatly tend to smooth the troubled waters of legislative strife, could our lawmakers hear God speak to them before their orator addresses him."[55]

But there was no institution in society that Campbell more diligently wished to Protestantize than the schools. After all, the schools he regarded as "the palladium of our free government and the true nurse and cradle of both civil and ecclesiastic liberty. Without them, indeed, we would have either a tyrannical oligarchy, an absolute autocracy, or a fierce democracy, in both church and state."[56] But since "the Bible in any school in America is the palladium of all our rights," he contended, "we [therefore] want the Holy Bible of Protestant Christendom to be consecrated in the heads, the hearts, the consciences and the lives of our sons and daughters. We therefore, plead with . . . the curators, the superintendents, the presidents, the professors, the teachers, of all seminaries of learning, to *permit* their pupils, if not to cause them, duly to listen to God."[57]

Campbell made it clear, however, that he did not want opinions and interpretations of the Bible taught in the schools. Rather, the schools should teach only those "prominent Christian facts, precepts and promises" stated in scripture "so plainly, so perspicuously and so fully that all Christendom admits them." These, of course, were those same "gospel facts" on which Campbell had sought to restore the primitive Christian faith. Clearly, Protestantism was now the bearer of the primitive Christian faith, and Campbell had chosen Protestant America and its schools as agents for the restoration. If the schools succeeded in this task, then "we, as a nation and people, shall stand among the nations of the earth great and happy and powerful—fair as a morning without clouds, 'bright as the sun, and terrible as an army with banners.' "[58] In this way, the school, for Campbell, assumed the traditional catechetical function of the established church, and the catechetical core, Campbell imagined, was simply America's common religion.[59]

Armed with these convictions, Campbell now lifted his gaze beyond America itself to the larger world. How might America's "common faith" enlighten those beyond its borders? Campbell found the most obvious answer in the immigrants pouring into America's harbors in the mid-nineteenth century. "We will," he therefore proclaimed, "by common schools and common ministrations of benevolence, dispossess them of the demons of priestcraft and kingcraft, and show them our religion by pointing to our common schools, our common churches, our common colleges, and our common respect for the Bible, the Christian religion and its divine and glorious Founder—the Supreme Philanthropist."[60]

But Campbell was not content to enlighten immigrants. Like so many in mid-nineteenth-century America, he turned also to the theme of expansion. Further, American expansion, spreading America's "common religion" around the globe, would now be the agent through which the millennium would come.[61] By 1849, therefore, in the aftermath of wholesale and continuing dispossession and extermination of native Americans, of the annexation of Mexican territories, and of John L. O'Sullivan's proclamation regarding America's "manifest destiny," Campbell confidently trumpeted that

> the Lord Almighty, who has now girdled the earth from east to west with the Anglo-Saxon people, the Anglo-Saxon tongue, sciences, learning and civilization, by giving a colossal power and grandeur to Great Britain and the United States over the continents and oceans of the earth, will continue to extend that power and magnificence until they spread from north to south, as they have already from east to west, until, in one vernacular, in one language and with one consent they shall, in loud acclaim and in hallowed concert, raise their joyful and grateful anthem, pealing over all lands and from shore to shore, from the Euphrates to the ends of the earth. Then will "they hang their trumpet in the hall, and study war no more." Peace and universal amity will reign triumphant. For over all the earth there will be but one Lord, one faith, one hope and one language.[62]

The last sentence in this passage is particularly significant. With his phrase "one Lord, one faith, one hope," Campbell apparently intended to point to the primitive Christian faith—the nation's "common faith"—now embodied, he supposed, in Anglo-American Protestantism. This would be the faith of the millennial kingdom, and English would be its language.

Then, in 1852, Campbell described again the grand station to which God had summoned Protestant England and the United States in the millennial scheme of things. "To Britain and America," he asserted,

> God has granted the possession of the new world; and because the sun never sets upon our religion, our language and our arts, he has vouchsafed to us, through these sciences and arts, the power that annihilates time and annuls the inconveniences of space. Doubtless these are but preparations for a work which God has in store for us,—a great, a mighty, a stupendous work, that will bring into requisition the arts, the sciences and resources with which he has so richly, so simultaneously and so marvellously endowed England and America.[63]

A few paragraphs later, he defined that work when he argued that it was the special task of "Protestant America and Protestant England" to shine the light of freedom and liberty into all the world, thus emancipating the world "from the most heartless spiritual despotism that ever disfranchised, enslaved and degraded human kind. This is our special mission into the world as a nation and a people; and for this purpose the Ruler of nations has raised us up and made us the wonder and the admiration of the world."[64] But, to America, especially, Campbell argued, "[God] has given the new world and all its hidden treasures, with all the arts and sciences of the old. Europe, Asia, and Africa look to Protestant America as the wonder of the age, and as exerting a preponderating influence on the destinies of the world. We have, then, a fearful and a glorious responsibility."[65]

IV

By 1860, however, when civil war loomed on the horizon, the unity of the Republic was fragmenting and Campbell's millennial hopes were fading. Moreover, he no longer pinned his few remaining hopes on the nation. He admitted in 1860 that "the long cherished and yet unsatisfied inquisitiveness, as to the unaccomplished promises and prophecies, concerning the career of the Christian Institution . . . has not been, is not now, nor is it likely soon to be, perfectly satisfied." Indeed, he now returned to his earlier position that "before the *Christocracy,* or the actual reign of the Messiah over all the nations, kindreds, tongues, and people, can culminate in all glory and grandeur, the gospel must be announced to all the nations and peoples on this earth." And he stated with considerable sobriety that "we need to be reminded, in tones of tenderness, coming as from the world-renouncing agonies of the cross, that *we, the people of the living God, are not of the world.* . . . Let us not forget the weapons of our warfare, nor distrust the wisdom and power of our Leader."[66]

But his Civil War–related rhetoric should not obscure the extent to which Alexander Campbell, in the 1840s and 1850s, typified the ironies inherent in nineteenth-century American expansionism. In Campbell's view, God had called America to make the world free. But Campbell soon attached the theme of freedom—primordial and universal in its own right—to the particularized contents of American culture. This constituted for Campbell no problem since for him primitive Christianity, the Protestant faith, and American culture were all equally primordial and universal at their core, and therefore perfectly compatible with the theme of freedom. For Campbell, therefore, to make the world free was only to conform the world to Protestant and American ideals and, through those ideals, to the primitive Christian faith. The accomplishment of these objectives was no longer the exclusive task of the Disciples movement. In fact, this task now fell chiefly to the nation and its schools. Ernest Tuveson, therefore, was not far from the mark when he wrote of

Campbell that "no other preacher more completely fused the religious and secular elements of the millennial utopia. . . . One could say that for Campbell . . . 'Americanizing' the world, in the right sense, is almost identical with millennializing it."[67] What Tuveson missed was that "the right sense" for Campbell meant Protestant Christianity and simple "gospel facts." Here was the ground—and the only ground—for true freedom and the grand millennial age.

NINE

A Civic Theology for the South:
The Case of Benjamin M. Palmer

As we have seen, although Alexander Campbell finally concluded that Protestant America was a clear expression of pure beginnings and therefore would hasten the millennial dawn, the Civil War shattered his faith in the primordial dimensions of the Republic. There were others in the South, however, who identified the Confederacy, slavery, and the southern way of life with the purity and rectitude of first times. For these southerners the Civil War became, as this chapter shows, essentially a struggle between God's primordial people, on the one hand, and the threatening legions of time, history, and tradition, on the other.

I

When H. L. Mencken used the phrase "Bible Belt" to describe the American South, he pointed to the essential core of southern identity which had deep roots in the white South's defense of slavery between 1830 and 1865. Southerners not only displayed a ruthless allegiance to the Bible in defense of their "peculiar institution." They also expelled from their region the notion of "Nature's God" and attached themselves almost exclusively to Jehovah, God of the Bible. In attaching themselves so firmly to biblical religion to the exclusion of the Enlightenment heritage, southerners effectively drove a wedge down the middle of the national civic theology, dividing and isolating its two principal symbols.

By the dawn of the nineteenth century, popular imagination in America had thoroughly synthesized the notions of "Jehovah" and "Nature's God" to form the bedrock of America's civic theology. The synthesis of these two concepts resulted from two earlier developments, one philosophical and one experiential, that coalesced and intertwined in the eighteenth century. Rationally oriented philosophers and theologians throughout the eighteenth century had cloaked Jehovah in the garb of reason and nature in an effort to make him more rational and more palatable. Then, with the intense quest for liberty, first in the Great Awakening and later in the Revolution, theologians tended to invert God and his apparel so that the old garb often became the new substance and vice versa: many apologists for civil and religious liberty now staked their claim to freedom on "Nature's God" whom they dressed and adorned in the apparel of the biblical Jehovah. In turn, Baconian thinkers of the Common Sense tradition rendered the biblical Jehovah increasingly rational.[1] Eventually "Nature's God" became biblical and Jehovah became both natural and rational, and a theological synthesis was erected that would form the basis of America's civic theology from the Revolution to the Civil War.

The synthesis, however, was contrived and somewhat awkward, since "Nature's God" presided over a kingdom of supposed universal values while Jehovah ruled in a realm of explicitly Christian particularities. One certainty that almost all shared, however, obscured these fundamental differences. That certainty was the near universal conviction that the new nation was a virtual recovery of an ancient primordium, pristine and pure, standing at the fountainhead of time. Christ's particularities and Nature's universalities blended together to facilitate the conviction that both expressed the first age. From this perspective, there was little difference between proclaiming liberty and egalitarianism, on the one hand, and Christ, the Bible, and the church, on the other; all, in one way or another, reflected the natural order that was thought to exist at the time of creation.[2]

This synthesis was well developed and firmly in place by the early nineteenth century. By the early 1830s, however, the white South's enthusiasm for liberty, with respect to one segment of humankind, dramatically and abruptly waned and focused instead on slavery, liberty's antagonist. No god who ruled over Nature's universal kingdom of "life, liberty, and the pursuit of happiness" for "all men" could possibly be the patron-deity of this new commitment to human bondage. Nor were white southerners fooled by the fact that "Nature's God" was dressed in Jehovah's apparel. He was still the God of liberty for all men and, as such, would never do for their region. No wonder then that Robert Lewis Dabney, a Presbyterian theologian at Hampden-Sydney College, took his stand squarely on the Bible and wrote in 1851: "Here is our policy then, to push the Bible continually, to drive Abolitionism to the wall, to compel it to assume an anti-Christian position."[3] In this strategy, Dabney typified many southern clerics.

The task of the white, southern clergy was essentially threefold: to strip "Nature's God" of his Christian clothing, leaving him naked in his infidelity; to bring the biblical Jehovah south of the Potomac to rule over his new, latter-day Israel; and finally, to establish this grim God of the South as far older than "Nature's God," who was simply a modern-day invention of northern skeptics, atheists, and infidels, and therefore not God at all.

White southerners therefore effectively dissolved for their region the natural rights–biblical synthesis that had formed the basis for America's civic theology since the Revolution. Essentially, the white South took its stand on the biblical strand of that tradition, virtually excluding Deism and the natural rights tradition. Clement Eaton noted that "deism was dying a natural death in the South in the first quarter of the nineteenth century," and Brooks Holifield observed that during the 1830s, "the South's nascent liberal movements were on the verge of collapse." This is all the more significant since, as Holifield notes, "the Old South in post-Revolutionary America was no Bible Belt" and was rife with skepticism, indifference, and infidelity.[4] If, however, by the 1830s "Nature's God" was departing Dixie, the southern clergy nonetheless defended their biblical Jehovah with a new form of rationalism: the Baconian philosophy of the Scottish Common Sense Realists.[5] Consequently, Thomas R. Dew, president of the College of William and Mary, could report in 1836 that the case against infidelity had been closed:

> Avowed infidelity is now considered by the enlightened portion of the world as a reflection both on the head and heart. The Humes and Voltaires have been vanquished from the field. . . . The argument is now closed forever, and he who obtrudes on the social circle his infidel notions, manifests the arrogance of a literary coxcomb, or that want of refinement which distinguishes the polished gentleman.[6]

By 1860, as Eaton notes, "the profound orthodoxy of the South . . . was revealed by the virtual absence of liberal sects below the Potomac." Most telling was that, while free thought and Deism had done well in the South early in the nineteenth century, by 1860 the South could claim only 20 of the nation's 664 Universalist churches and only three of the nation's 257 Unitarian societies.[7] Clearly the white South had created its own civic theology embracing the mainstream southern denominations in a virtual evangelical consensus. Significantly, this development began in the 1830s, precisely when the South was becoming increasingly defensive over salvery.

II

As had been the case so often in the American experience, southerners attempted to legitimate their civic theology by rooting it in a primordial frame of reference. The striking dimension of the white southern primordium was its complexity: southerners constructed their primordium not be restoring one "strong time" but at least five "strong times" which they uncritically wove together to form one coherent pattern of meaning. In its eclectic dimensions, therefore, southern civic theology resembled the Mormon restoration. Even motivations were similar, for both Mormons and southerners sought to ground their respective causes in the power that flows from first times.

The "first times" important to southerners included the following: (1) the experience of ancient Israel, since many southerners increasingly regarded the South as God's new latter-day Israel; (2) the ancient Jewish patriarchs, and especially Noah, who became the pattern for the patriarchal dimension of plantation life and who legitimated "the curse of Ham"; (3) the primitive church, since many white southerners thought that the South alone preserved the church in its ancient purity and simplicity; (4) the Puritan fathers of New England from whose fidelity to God, according to many southerners, the founding fathers of the American nation had utterly departed; and (5) the political faith of the otherwise heretical American founding fathers. This constellation of primordial symbols—Jewish patriarchs, ancient Israel, primitive church, Puritan fathers, and founding fathers—became the lodestone of the white, southern identity worked out in defense of the "peculiar institution."

The white, southern clergy, wielding tremendous influence over southern hearts and minds during the Civil War period, articulated this complex mythology with astounding zeal. Various preachers emphasized some themes more than others, but no single preacher was more zealous in promoting all the themes than Benjamin Morgan Palmer (1818–1902). Palmer was the son of a Presbyterian minister in Charleston, South Carolina; a product of Amherst, the University of Georgia, and Columbia Seminary in Columbia, South Carolina; the first moderator of the General Assembly of the Presbyterian church in the Confederate States of America; and pastor of the First Presbyterian Church in New Orleans from 1856 until 1902. While no single preacher represented all the strands of the white southern civic theology during the war years, Palmer came as close as any.[8]

Any primordial theology must take seriously the notion of a fall from an original state of pristine purity. For Palmer, the North clearly had fallen from "all that is ancient and stable" and threatened to pull the South from her Edenic purity into the abyss as well. "We have seen," he observed in his famous Thanksgiving Day sermon of 1860, "the trail of the serpent five and twenty years in our Eden."[9] Determined to rid Eden of these vipers, Palmer launched on Thanksgiving Day, 1860, an intensive campaign to crush the head of the northern serpent. If his claim that "I have never intermeddled with political questions" ever had any credibility, the Thanksgiving Day sermon changed all that.[10] In ringing tones, he assailed the northern infidels and held up the cause of the South as the cause of God and the ancient traditions. The New Orleans *Daily Delta* published this sermon three times in the next four days. When it was published the third time, the publisher justified the repetition by citing "a demand which seems yet far from exhausted, although the supply from this office alone has exceeded thirty thousand copies.[11] Further, many other papers in New Orleans and across the Southwest published either summaries of the sermon or its complete text, and the sermon soon circulated throughout the South as a pamphlet under various titles. No wonder George Junkin, a northern writer, described Palmer in 1863 as one of "the leading spirits of the rebellion" who contributed immeasurably to the southern secession.[12]

Palmer further elaborated the theme of the fall and restoration in a sermon in 1861. The early Puritans in America, he argued, simply sought freedom to worship God. "After the lapse of a century and a half," however, when the Constitution was written, "there was a total ignoring of the divine claims and of all allegiance to the divine supremacy." This omission was not due, Palmer argued, "to the irreligiousness of the masses, for they were predominantly christian. But the public leaders of the time were largely tinctured with the free-thinking and infidel spirit which . . . brought forth at last its bitter fruit in the horrors of the French Revolution." Though faith in God characterized the earliest Puritan settlements, when the American nation was born she "stood up before the world a helpless orphan, and entered upon its career without a God."[13]

Though the masses had been "predominantly christian" in 1776, by 1860, the free-thinking infidel spirit had pervaded the entire northern region and had provided the undergirding ideology of abolitionism. "The abolition spirit," Palmer proclaimed, "is undeniably atheistic. The demon which erected its throne upon the guillotine in the days of Robespierre and Marat, which abolished the Sabbath and worshipped reason in the person of a harlot, yet survives to work other horrors." Southerners should not be fooled, he added, by the "old threadbare disguise of the advocacy of human rights." Indeed, the South must recognize deistic infidelity for what it is—a power that "blasphemously invades the prerogatives of God, and rebukes the Most High for the errors of his administration."[14]

While Palmer highlighted these themes in his Thanksgiving Day sermon of 1860, he had sounded the same themes as early as 1845 when he warned a University of Georgia audience of the "introduction of Infidelity by means of Pseudo-Reformations." He raised for his audience "a question for grave and deep thought, whether Satan under the disguise of a Reformer may not be playing a deep game with the destinies of men and of nations." He warned of an impending fall when he asserted that "no more fatal calamity can befall a people than to have false moral principles, substituted for the true."[15] Consequently, even when the war was over and the South had suffered humiliating defeat, Palmer still could argue that the purpose of the South had not been so much to defend slavery "as to oppose the subtle species of infidelity, which sought to accomplish its overthrow by assumptions which placed the whole Bible as an authoritative and final revelation, under the feet of profane scoffers."[16] Like most of his southern clerical colleagues, however, Palmer did not impugn all forms of rationalism. Quite to the contrary, he hailed Baconian philosophy as an essentially biblical and Protestant perspective that provided the only rational guide to interpreting scripture aright.[17] This Common Sense approach to scripture would serve Palmer well when he fashioned his biblical defense of slavery. In the meantime, however, the rationalism of the "infidels" was another matter altogether.

Palmer's depiction of a fall from the pristine purity of the early Puritan settlements into the apostasy of infidelity and atheism was by no means unique in the Civil War South. The Rev. Thomas Smyth, preaching before the Second Presbyterian Church in Charleston, South Carolina, on November 21, 1860, argued that the fall was due to "atheists, infidels, communists, free-lovers, rationalists, Bible haters, anti-christian levellers, and anarchists."[18] While Palmer impugned only the Constitution as godless and atheistic, Smyth impugned the Declaration of Independence as well. "The evil and bitter root of all our evils is to be found in the infidel, atheistic, French Revolution, Red Republican principle, embodied as an axiomatic seminal principle—not in the Constitution, but in the Declaration of Independence." The problem, Smyth explained, was the Declaration's doctrine of fundamental human equality. "All men are not born equal," he argued. "The only equality is, that all men are born in sin." God's name in the Declaration was simply window dressing. "Though God is introduced, the Declaration is Godless. God is introduced to give dignity and emphasis; to create man, and to ordain government; and then He is banished. The sceptre is torn from his hands, and fictions are substituted for facts."[19]

Southern preachers generally agreed that a fall from the American garden of Eden had occurred when the wily serpent offered the founding fathers the forbidden fruit of Deism and infidelity. Benjamin Palmer was not utterly dismayed, however, for a restoration of the God of Israel, of the church, and of the piety of early American Puritans was being accomplished in the Confederate South. He made this point unmistakably clear in 1861:

> Thanks be unto God, my brethren, for the grace given our own confederacy, in receding from this perilous atheism! When my eye first rested upon the Constitution adopted by the Confederate Congress, and I read in the first lines of our organic and fundamental law a clear, solemn, official recognition of Almighty God, my heart swelled with unutterable emotions of gratitude and joy. It was the return of the prodigal to the bosom of his father, of the poor exile who has long pined in some distant and bleak Siberia after the associations of his childhood home. At length, the nation has a God: Alleluia! "the Lord reigneth let the earth rejoice."[20]

III

Because of the restoration of pure and undefiled religion in the Confederate South, Palmer clearly depicted the South as a new Israel. He compared the South to the ancient Hebrews when they "pronounced the solemn Amen to the curses and blessings of the divine law as proclaimed by the Levites. Not less grand and awful is this scene today, when an infant nation strikes its covenant with the God of Heaven." He went on to affirm that "our whole people through eleven States are called to ratify the covenant, and to set up the memorial stone thereof."[21]

The New Israel motif was a theme to which Palmer returned again and again. In an 1862 funeral sermon for Gen. Maxcy Gregg, he compared the invasion of the South by northern troops to the invasion of Judah by Sennacherib's armies. When Sennacherib advised Hezekiah to cease trusting in God, "God answered, 'Because thy rage against me is come up into mine ears, therefore I will put my hook in thy nose, and my bridle in thy lips, and will turn thee back by the way by which thou camest.'" Then Palmer drew the parallel. The issue confronting the South was clear:

> Grand as the contest is when our firesides and our altars are the stake, it rises into the sublime and awful when the question is whether God shall reign, or take into his privy council the hypocritical and infidel fanatic of the North. . . . What [other] nation, save Judah alone, ever had such trusts committed to its hands? And what nation ever had such cause to spread its hands unto heaven, and to feel that the battle is not theirs, but God's?[22]

In an 1863 fast-day sermon delivered to the General Assembly of South Carolina, Palmer personified his legislative hearers as Israel herself and applied to the South words from Moses' farewell address (Deut. 33:27–28): Oh Israel, "the eternal God is thy refuge, . . . and He shall thrust out the enemy from before thee, and shall say, destroy them. Israel then, shall dwell in safety alone; the fountain of Jacob shall be upon a land of corn and wine; also His heavens shall drop [down] dew."[23] It would be surprising if the analogy of Israel leaving Egyptian bondage had escaped Palmer's imagination, and it did not:

> Eleven tribes sought to go forth in peace from the house of political bondage: but the heart of our modern Pharaoh is hardened, that he will not let Israel go. In their distress, with the untried sea before and the chariots of Egypt behind, ten millions of people stretch forth their hands before Jehovah's throne, imploring him to "stir up his strength before Ephraim and Benjamin and Manasseh, and come and save them."[24]

In Palmer's thought the South not only was a restoration of ancient Israel standing in a covenantal relation to God; it also was a haven for the restoration of the pure and ancient Christianity enshrined in the pages of the Bible, a Christianity that had been lost under the impact of northern, infidel apostasy. Pure Christianity meant for Palmer a reliance on God's sovereignty reflected through the Bible alone. In good restoration fashion, Palmer excluded all religious innovations and human inventions. Unlike Alexander Campbell, however, who focused on the worship and polity of the church, Palmer focused on God's will for the social order. In other words, the Bible became a constitution governing the behavior of society. Any lapse from the guidelines of this constitution was apostasy, and it was precisely apostasy into which the North had descended.

Palmer's Common Sense presuppositions compelled him to believe that the ancient, biblical constitution simply means what it says and says what it means. Interpretation was illegitimate. It followed that a godly society was static and continuous with godly societies throughout the ages, since all godly societies of all time simply conformed to the biblical constitution. A logical and divine continuity, therefore, ran from Israel to the ancient church, to the Puritan communities of New England, and finally to the South. It followed that preservation of the godly status quo was of first importance. So long as society followed the ancient, biblical constitution satisfactorily, pressure for change or reform—even from the church—was simply out of order. The church, instead, should simply encourage prayer, praise, and pious living. In this way, southern churches were estranged from the political sphere and sustained an almost pietistic irrelevance to the social order around them. In fact, the godly society became a kind of church to which the various denominations simply rendered allegiance and support. Further, the various denominations preserved their primordial purity to the extent that they supported the godly society. Political irrelevance, therefore, was the final measure of the true church.

This peculiar application of Scottish Common Sense philosophy to the social order helps explain why southern religion, as Samuel S. Hill pointed out, has been marked more by a pietistic satisfaction with the political status quo than by zeal for political and social reform.[25] It also explains why Benjamin Palmer could be extraordinarily involved in political pronouncements, while at the same time accusing northern churchmen who espoused political and social causes of apostasy from the ancient order. Palmer simply was preserving the primordial status quo while northerners were promoting human inventions. He therefore warned in 1858 that the American nation, while previously continuous with the primal status quo, was falling from the primordial to the merely historical sphere. He hailed the "eighty years [during which] the state has been free from . . . complication with the spiritual power" as a period in which Christianity had thrived as never before since the apostolic age. In these latter days, however, the pulpit had been "converted into a political rostrum, and the ambassadors of heaven degraded into jobbing politicians."[26] Only the South preserved the primordial purity of the church.

In a sermon delivered before the Georgia legislature in 1863, Palmer argued that preservation of a pure church, continuous with its primal beginnings, in turn preserved the nation. He claimed that never, in ancient or modern times, had a "nation been destroyed, holding in her bosom a pure and uncorrupted church." He added that "so long as with sound doctrine, and pure worship, and uncontaminated ordinances, she fulfills the mission to which she is appointed, just so long will the nation which enshrines and protects her be sheltered from destruction."[27]

Because, on the one hand, the South was itself a godly society, and because, on the other hand, it sheltered in its bosom a pure church, Palmer was certain that the South would prevail in her war for secession. In a clear and lucid rendition of southern civic theology, Palmer told the South Carolina General Assembly:

> The preeminent grandeur of this war is found in the fact that it centres upon a religious idea. On the one hand is a wicked infidelity, lifting its rebellious arm against the Ruler of the universe; and on the other, humble loyalty, receiving the blow, and offering itself a sacrifice to His insulted majesty. Patriotism is sanctified by religion, which from her sacred horn pours upon it the oil of consecration. Can we doubt the issue of such a conflict? . . . that in the end the wicked will be trampled in His fury.[28]

The North had ignored the judgments of God and the Bible on every hand. When Palmer observed in 1852 how infidels dominated science and philosophy, the northern locus of this academic infidelity was implicit. This unbelieving sort of science, Palmer charged, "simply handles its fossils and ignores the Bible. Putting on its wise spectacles, it reads off . . . the world's chronology in millions and billions of years, just as calmly as though God had never written a book, in which was set down the age of man."[29] Clearly, such a godless society could never prevail.

Palmer's implicit assumption that the ancient biblical constitution should govern society reached its zenith when he argued before the Georgia lesislature in 1863 that the house of the Confederate States of America would never be fully in order until brought under the dominion of Jesus Christ. He substantially amended his fast-day sermon of 1861 to argue that when the Confederacy had recognized God in its Constitution, it still had failed to acknowledge the whole truth. Clearly recognizing the distinction between the "God of Nature" and "Jehovah, God of the Bible," Palmer urged upon his hearers that "this national confession fails to define whether the God we invoke be 'Jehovah[,] Jove[,] or Lord,'— whether the God of the Pantheist, the Pagan, the Christian, or the Deist." He argued further that the Confederate Constitution did not really recognize that the ultimate "king, whose footsteps are seen in all the grand march of history, is God in Christ—ruling the world by the double right of creation and redemption." Therefore, he urged the legislators "to take this young nation as it passes through its baptism of blood, and to seal its loyalty to Christ at the altar of God."[30]

Only minutes before Palmer delivered this address to the Georgia legislature, George Foster Pierce, bishop of the Methodist Episcopal church, South, had urged the same point on the same assembly of lawmakers. Pierce contended that while common sentiment all along had supposed that America was a Christian nation, this was not the case at all. The foundational principles of American government and legislation, he said, ignored all reference to God and his universal law. In fact, the Confederate Constitution, "in its appeal to Almighty God, . . . uses the language of deism, or natural religion, rather than of christianity." Then, in a devastating paradox, Pierce argued that, while he did not wish to see the church established by law or a religious creed forced on the citizens, nonetheless, he did "believe that, in the organic law, God should be acknowledged in his being, perfections, providence and empire; not as the first great cause simply . . . but as the God of the Bible, Maker, Preserver, Governor, Redeemer, Judge, Father, Son and Holy Ghost." Pierce said that "to avoid controversy—to forestall objections, I would be content if the framers of our constitution in their appeal to God, would designate the Almighty as FATHER, SON and HOLY GHOST."[31] Clearly, to these southern minds, there could be no authentic "God of Nature" who was not the God of the primordial Christ.

It was precisely his inability to recognize this paradox that enabled Palmer in 1845 to proclaim, on the one hand, that "throughout this commonwealth of twenty-six States there is not one Protestant heart that desires an identification of the Church with the State," and then to proclaim, on the other hand, that if American principles are to be perpetuated, it will not be because "our people are religious after *some* sort but after the *true* sort."[32] It is not surprising, then, given the extent to which such notions abounded in the Civil War South, that the Rev. Thomas Smyth could proclaim of the South in 1860: "to you is given the high and holy keeping, above all other conservators, of the Bible, the whole Bible, and nothing but the Bible; and of that liberty of conscience, free from the doctrines and commandments of men. . . . Upon this rock let the South build her house, and the gates of hell shall not prevail against it."[33] Clearly, Mencken's "Bible Belt" was being born.

IV

Because of the South's deep commitment to slavery, a profound reliance on the Bible became a fundamental necessity. When the frontal attack from the abolitionists finally arrived, there were only two religious ideologies to which the South might turn for support of the "peculiar institution." The natural rights tradition, as articulated in the Declaration of Independence, would not serve the cause of slavery; that was beyond dispute.[34] The only option left was the Bible, nothing but the Bible, but not the whole Bible. Indeed, the southern clergy seized on a simple biblical narrative and transformed it into a world-defining myth. That narrative—the story of Noah and his three sons, Ham, Shem, and Japheth—became the soul of the civic theology of the South. Charles Wilson argues that race was not at the heart of the "religion of the Lost Cause," but it certainly was at the heart of southern civic theology both before and during the war years.[35]

Thomas Peterson, in his book *Ham and Japheth: The Mythic World of Whites in the Antebellum South,* has demonstrated the fundamental and mythical importance of the Ham narrative to many white Christians in the antebellum South. If it seems strange that white southerners would invest an obscure passage in Genesis 9, a passage only ten verses long, with mythic and world-preserving significance, two things must be remembered. First, southerners interpreted Noah as a prototype for the patriarchal structure of plantation life.[36] Thus, Thomas Cobb wrote in

1858 that "Southern slavery is a patriarchal, social system. The master is the head of his family. Next to wife and children, he cares for his slaves. . . . In return, he is revered and held as protector and master." Cobb here implicitly argued that plantation masters had restored God's own form of social organization first inaugurated with the "grand old patriarch, Noah." Further, Peterson significantly observes that "as long as planters could view themselves as presiding over a patriarchal family, they could also view the atrocities of slavery as rare."[37] Second, and even more important than the southern identification of Noah as primal patriarch, was Noah's identification as primal man. The Ham myth embodied primordial power for many white southerners simply because they viewed Noah as a virtual "new Adam" or, as one southern writer put it in 1860, "the father of the human family, the great representative of the race."[38] Further, it was through this primordial man and his sons, Ham, Shem, and Japheth, that God divided humankind into black, red, and white people, respectively. If, on the heels of this assumption, southerners could show that the primordial man/patriarch had pronounced the doom of perpetual bondage on the black race, they felt they possessed an invincible case for black slavery, a case rooted in the primordium itself.

Consequently, the Ham myth became a fundamental component of southern, white preaching during the antebellum period. Strangely enough, however, Peterson's fine analysis of the Ham myth during this period makes no reference to Benjamin Palmer's extensive use of this theme, in spite of Palmer's ministerial standing in the South. In 1861, Palmer stated the myth with exceptional clarity:

> Upon Ham was pronounced the doom of perpetual servitude— proclaimed with double emphasis, as it is twice repeated that he shall be the servant of Japheth and the servant of Shem. Accordingly, history records not a single example of any member of this group lifting itself, by any process of self-development, above the savage condition. From first to last, their mental and moral characteristics, together with the guidance of Providence, have marked them for servitude; while their comparative advance in civilization and their participation in the blessings of salvation, have ever been suspended upon this decreed connexion with Japheth and with Shem.[39]

In 1863, Palmer rooted both the myth and the South squarely in the patriarchal primordium. He told the South Carolina General Assembly that slavery had existed in many forms throughout the long course of human history. Palmer was astounded, however, that this particular time, of all times in human history, would be the occasion for a crusade against slavery. After all, he argued, it is only now in these latter days that slavery is "under precisely that patriarchal form in which it is sanctioned in the word of God, and in which it has never been found since the overthrow of the Hebrew empire, until now." Not only were northerners guilty, therefore, of "impeaching the Divine morality, and hurling their impious accusations against the integrity of God's rule"; they were also guilty of impeding the southern restoration of the patriarchal primordium.[40]

When he spoke before the Georgia legislature that same year, Palmer attempted to show that Jehovah, God of the Bible, who had spoken through the primordial patriarch and on whose side the South now fought, was far older than the more recent "God of Nature" who presided over northern abolitionism. "I base the vindication of the South," he declared, "upon a far older record than the Declaration of 1776, and assert her rights under a more authoritative charter than the Federal compact." This ancient, authoritative code will be discovered "if we ascend the stream of history to its source" where "we shall discover God dividing the earth between the sons of Noah." Palmer was all too happy to

> leave the Statesman to lay his hand upon the great instruments drawn up by our forefathers and from them to justify the South; but I ascend to that fundamental law, by which in the first organization of society God constituted civil government, and say that this law of separation is that "law of nature and of nature's God which entitles us to assume a separate and equal station among the powers of the Earth."

A further comparison between the Enlightenment perspective and the southern biblical perspective may be instructive at this point. As we have seen, Thomas Paine sought to push beyond "the intermediate stages" of antiquity "to the time when man came from the hand of his Maker." "The origin of man," Paine argued, provided "the origin of his rights," established the natural law, and legitimated the American nation.[41] Palmer, however, rejected this perspective altogether and found the "law of nature and of nature's God" in Noah's decree regarding Ham, Shem, and Japheth. But because northerners sought to subvert this decree, Palmer urged the Georgia legislators "to stand as sentinels around Jehovah's throne, and to strike against those who have openly impeached his morality and denounced as profligate his government of the universe."[42]

When the war was over, Palmer continued to cling to the Ham myth, to justify not slavery but segregation. In an address delivered at Washington and Lee University in 1872, he told his comrades in the lost cause that "it is indispensable that the purity of race shall be preserved on either side. . . . The argument for this I base upon the declared policy of the Divine Administration from the days of Noah until now." This meant for Palmer that blacks should "stand apart in their own social grade, in their own schools, in their own ecclesiastical organizations, under their own teachers and guides."[43] He was confident, however, that this new system of racial segregation in the now defiled southern Eden would be softened and tempered by "all the kindness and helpful cooperation to which the old relations between the races, and their present dependence on each other, would naturally predispose." The details of segregation would be worked out "through the gradual changes of time, in the exercise of practical Anglo-Saxon sense, and under the direction of a wise providence which still binds the destinies of the two together."[44]

If Palmer's transition from defending slavery to defending segregation seems too easy a resolution of the "lost cause," Charles Wilson reminds us that defense of segregation was part of a much larger "lost cause" posture. Fundamental to that posture was the virtue of the white South, even in defeat. While accepting God's judgment on southern pride or on failure to care adequately for slaves, southern ministers nonetheless defended the South's virtue on the issues of slavery and race. They were particularly concerned, as Wilson noted, about "the obstacle that postbellum blacks presented to the preservation of a virtuous Southern civilization."[45] Thus Palmer's apology for segregation did not represent an easy acceptance of what seemed to him second best or an evaporation of his civic theology. Rather, in the interest of preserving southern virtue, segregation simply adapted an older civic theology to a dramatically new situation. Consequently, the primordial patriarch became the patron saint of the South's new position as well as of the old.

V

In spite of Palmer's consistent attacks on the religious infidelity of the American founding fathers, he nevertheless praised their political wisdom and the republican institutions that they had established. The American model of republican government was, Palmer thought, a recovery of "primitive republicanism" that had been unknown since "the simplicity of patriarchal times."[46] Once again, however, a disastrous fall had occurred. Northerners first abandoned the creeds of the church; then, they perverted the Bible "into a sanction for all the utterances of an infidel philosophy"; and then the "transition was easy to a perverse criticism which should eviscerate the Constitution of all its meaning."[46] The gist of this political fall, Palmer contended, was the inability or unwillingness of the northern people to understand the true idea of a republic. "They have confounded it with democracy" and have made "the voice of the people the voice of God; in exalting the will of the numerical majority above the force of constitution and covenants."[47] In so doing, northerners had broken the sacred political covenant, and the South's only crime lay in "a peaceful withdrawal from those who would not agree to walk with us in the faith and according to the covenants of our fathers."[48]

When Palmer addressed the soldiers of the Washington Artillery in May 1861, he told the troops that they "contend today for the great American principle that all just government derives its powers from the will of the governed." This was the principle for which "eighty-five years ago our fathers fought," and "it is the corner stone of the great temple which, on this continent, has been reared to civil freedom." He told the soldiers that they were fighting in a holy war to prevent a total fall from primordial principles—"a war of civilization against a ruthless barbarism which would dishonor the dark ages."[49] Three years later, when Palmer addressed the confederate soldiers from South Carolina, he told them that "we are then contending for the very principles of our fathers." Then he elaborated:

> And when my thoughts have followed the soldiers of our armies on their lonely march and on the field of strife, it has seemed to me that the spectres of those who suffered at Valley Forge had risen from their revolutionary bed to hover around you, and testify to you that you were contending for the principles for which they fought, and for which they willingly surrendered their lives.[50]

Palmer sounded the theme of political restorationism in 1861 when he called on the South to "bring back the purer days of the republic." In those purer days, rule was by covenant rather than by mob, by Constitution rather than by party. Those days, however, were almost gone. Palmer observed that "when . . . party usurps the place of country [and] when public platforms become . . . higher than the constitution and the law . . . : then may be seen the handwriting upon the wall, and the glory has departed."[51]

The role of the South therefore was all the more significant, for it was the last, best hope for simple, primordial, republican government. "The last hope of self-government upon this Continent," Palmer proclaimed in 1860, "lies in these eleven Confederate States. We have retained the one, primary truth upon which the whole fabric of public liberty was reared by our fathers, and from which the North has openly apostacized."[52] In 1863, he contended that the Confederacy was "a last asylum for the genius of republicanism to work out, if possible, its promised blessings to the nations of the earth." The success of primordial republicanism clearly was yoked, in Palmer's mind, to the perpetuation of primordial patriarchalism as embodied in the institution of slavery. He made this point unmistakably clear in 1864 when he argued that "the only hope of republican institutions on this continent, is to be found in the perpetuation of that institution which has been made the occasion of this war."[53]

When the war was over, Palmer's last, best hope for republican government once again was being threatened, though this time by "appalling corruption," "lawless Radicalism," "the ascendency of a profligate Party, bestriding the neck of the nation," and "the secret suspicion . . . as to the impotency of Republican Institutions."[54] Once again, Palmer's prescribed cure was a return to the political faith of the founding fathers. In his address at Washington and Lee University in 1872, Palmer observed that "in every case alike, the existence of regulated liberty will depend upon the maintenance of our Ancestral Faith. My earnest prayer in reference to our country, is, that its institutions may be preserved exactly as they came to us from a wise and patriotic ancestry."[55]

VI

Since Benjamin Palmer believed that the South was the last, best hope for primordial, republican government, it is no wonder he viewed preservation of the South as a life and death issue of existential significance. He made this clear on a number of occasions. In 1863, he proclaimed: "Our country and our God! The two blend evermore in the Christian patriot's thought, and shall it be said there are no martyrdoms for the one, when the gibbet and the flame are welcomed for the other?"[56] In 1860, Palmer told his audience that the South "is in every sense my mother. I shall die upon her bosom—she shall know no peril, but it is my peril—no conflict, but it is my conflict—and no abyss of ruin, into which I shall not share her fall."[57]

Armed and sustained with this religious devotion to his homeland, Palmer articulated for the Civil War South a civic theology of extraordinary scope. Not content simply to identify the South with the purposes of God in the abstract, Palmer rooted his argument in the concrete details of history. When he had finished, he had created a mythical and illusory South that was the fulfillment of five different sacred histories: ancient Israel, the ancient Jewish patriarchs, primitive Christianity, the Puritan fathers, and the founding fathers. This South, for Palmer, was cosmos. Cosmos, however, trembled on the.brink of a chaos whose demonic agent was deistic infidelity. Here was civic theology that was even more than civic theology; it was cosmic drama with cosmic significance, acted out on a cosmic stage. If the illusions fostered by Palmer's vision seem particularly tragic in retrospect, they are only further testimony to the ironic power of the primitivist impulse that, beginning with the Puritans, has shaped the American experience. We turn now to examine the ironic side of the restoration theme in the larger American experience, especially in the nineteenth and twentieth centuries.

TEN

Nature, Innocence, and Illusion in American Life

If Benjamin Palmer imagined the American South a recovery of first times, he stood in a venerable American tradition. From an early date, Americans made a similar assumption about the larger nation. The chief difference between the southern vision and the American vision was that southerners wove various primal models into one complex myth, while many other Americans looked to a single primal model—the myth of nature. Americans first employed this myth to justify freedom from tyranny. But soon they began equating nature with particular dimensions of national life that seemed right or normal from their limited perspective. In this way they naturalized their particular culture and then heralded that culture as both universal and absolute.

Irony was inevitable. On the one hand, Americans exalted as natural and universal the freedom of all peoples to shape their own cultures and to determine their own destinies. On the other hand, however, they judged one particular culture to be natural above all others and therefore claimed the right to enforce this culture as the destiny of the world. In the process, they often redefined freedom to mean the right to conform to this most natural way of life. The tension between these two ideals—a natural and universal freedom and a natural and universal culture—has stood at the very heart of U.S. foreign policy dilemmas ever since. The tension could be resolved only by relinquishing the claim that freedom is a natural right or by abandoning the implicit assumption that conforming to American cultural norms is a natural obligation befitting all peoples. Seldom have Americans been prepared to do either.

I

The concept of nature as primal ground for the universal, at least in the modern period, descends from the eighteenth-century Enlightenment. In that period, nature lay at the heart of the climate of opinion pervading

205

the Western world. Many on both sides of the Atlantic simply assumed that nature reflected the truths of first times and would reveal the universal truths accessible to all human beings. In this context, the American founders sought "to plumb for the universal which is dressed and disguised in the particularities of doctrine and practice that distinguish one sect from another," as Sidney Mead so aptly described the situation.[1]

Carl L. Becker has provided the classic description of Enlightenment primitivism with its "sense of historylessness," its ironies, and its illusions. In *The Heavenly City of the Eighteenth-Century Philosophers,* Becker focused chiefly on the French Enlightenment to describe what he called "the eighteenth-century climate of opinion" that permeated France, England, and the American colonies. That climate clearly was primitivist, though Becker never used the term *primitivism* to describe the period. In *The Declaration of Independence: A Study in the History of Political Ideas,* actually written earlier than *The Heavenly City,* Becker explored the meaning of Enlightenment primitivism for the birth of the American nation. We turn, therefore, to a brief exposition of Becker's work.[2]

"In the eighteenth-century climate of opinion," Becker wrote, "whatever question you seek to answer, nature is the test, the standard: the ideas, the customs, the institutions of men, if ever they are to attain perfection, must obviously be in accord with those laws which 'nature reveals at all times, to all men.' "[3] But looking to nature as the universal standard for all people in all times also meant looking to creation as well. After all, from the perspective of that age, nature's God determined the laws of nature from the beginning of time. Their appeal to nature, therefore, placed most Enlightenment thinkers in a common restoration tradition with John Cotton, Roger Williams, James R. Graves, and Joseph Smith.

As soon as Enlightenment thinkers appealed to first times, however, they plunged into a dilemma of enormous proportions. That dilemma, as Becker put it, was simply this: "if nature be the work of God, and man the product of nature, then all that man does and thinks, all that he has ever done or thought, must be natural, too, and in accord with the laws of nature and of nature's God." How could these thinkers know what was born of nature and what of civilization? How could they determine what was the standard for all human beings in all ages and places, and what belonged merely to custom or tradition? As Becker put it, "George III, as well as Sam Adams, was presumably God's work; and if God's will was revealed in his work, how were you to know that the acts of George III, whose nature it was to be tyrannical, were not in accord with Natural Law, while the acts of Sam Adams, whose nature it was to be fond of Liberty, were in accord with Natural Law?"[4]

This dilemma was the classic restorationist problem. As we have seen, Alexander Campbell labored long and hard determining which aspects of primitive Christianity were cultural and "circumstantial" and which were "essential" and universally binding on all Christians. Mormons faced a similar quandry but quickly resolved it by embarking on a program of "restoring all things." Among the philosophers of the eighteenth century, Rousseau clearly perceived this problem and prescribed at least the outline for its resolution. He argued that unless philosophers "prescribe bounds to Nature, monsters, giants, pigmies and chimeras of all kinds might be specifically admitted into Nature. . . . We should *distinguish between the variety in human nature and that which is essential to it.*"[5] The call for such a distinction was easy enough to make. But how might it be done? What tools and methods would separate custom from nature, the temporal from the universal, the "variety" from the "essential"? "What the philosophers had to do," Becker wrote, "was to go up and down the wide world with the lamp of enlightenment looking . . . for 'man in general.' "[6]

At this point we reach the heart of restoration thinking: its sense of historylessness. For while the philosophers' search for "man in general" took them up and down the paths of human history, they often were uninterested in history for its own sake. As Becker observes, one should not ask the philosophers, "How did society come to be what it is?" for they often did not care. Their concern, rather, was for extrapolating from history the universal, natural man, a man who "did not exist in the world of time and place, but in the conceptual world, and who could therefore be found only by abstracting from all men in all times and all places those qualities which all men shared."[7]

Such attempts to traverse human experience in search of "man in general" resembled the Baconian methods employed by Alexander Campbell and James S. Lamar. For their task was to eliminate nature's "highly-colored imagery and bold hyperboles" and retain only the "real facts and unadorned doctrine remaining as residual phenomena after those things are excluded," as Lamar put it in *The Organon of Scripture*. And while Lamar laid out, side by side, the relevant biblical facts, abstracting from those facts the essential pattern of the primitive church, so the philosophers laid out, side by side, the relevant facts from all ages and climes of human kind, building from those facts the essential pattern of the natural human being.

In their search for the "real facts" and the fundamental truths of nature, however, no criterion guided the philosophers—indeed, no criterion could have guided them—other than their own limited, time-bound, provincial experience and perspective. This means, as Becker notes, that

> they are deceiving us, these philosopher-historians. . . . But we can easily forgive them for that, since they are, even more effectively, deceiving themselves. They do not know that the "man in general" they are looking for is just their own image, that the principles they are bound to find are the very ones they start out with. That is the trick they play on the dead.

Thus, even Jefferson expected that Unitarianism would finally be the universal and natural faith of the American people.[8]

One who is convinced, however, that he has surveyed human history and discovered nature's fundamental truths hardly perceives his judgment as trick or illusion. Instead, he raises the illusion to a higher level still, imagining that success in his restoration task will inaugurate the millennial dawn. Already we have traced among Puritans, Baptists, Mormons, and "Christians" that familiar trajectory which so often leads from first times to end times. Now we find the same trajectory among the philosophers of the eighteenth century. As Becker observes, the philosophers' "utopian dream of perfection, . . . having been long identified with the golden age or the Garden of Eden or life eternal in the Heavenly City of God, . . . was at last projected into the life of man on earth and identified with the . . . regeneration of society."[9] This final regeneration, moreover, would be faithful in every instance to the fundamental shape of human nature. Of all the eighteenth-century thinkers, perhaps none expressed this better than Joseph Priestley, whose profoundly restorationist treatise, *A History of the Corruptions of Christianity,* Thomas Jefferson so greatly admired. In another treatise, Priestley predicted that

> all knowledge will be subdivided and extended; and *knowledge* . . . being *power,* the human powers will, in fact, be enlarged; nature . . . will be more at our command; men will make their situation in this world abundantly more easy and comfortable; they will probably prolong their existence in it, and will grow daily more happy, each in himself, and more able (and, I believe, more disposed) to communicate happiness to others. Thus, whatever was the beginning of this world, the end will be glorious and paradisaical, beyond what our imaginations can now conceive.

And then, for those who might think his millennial optimism both far-fetched and ungrounded, Priestley hastened to ground his vision in nature: "extravagant as some may suppose these views to be, I think I could show them to be fairly suggested by the true theory of human nature, and to arise from the natural course of human affairs."[10] It was therefore nature on which the eighteenth-century philosophers erected their illusions of both first times and last.

II

The American experience grew from the widely held conviction that the nation's principles exemplified the natural human being, that universal "man-in-general" discerned in nature and ultimately in the creation. To hear these assumptions articulated most clearly, one need only attend to the Declaration of Independence, where Jefferson legitimated the Revolution by appealing to "the Laws of Nature and of Nature's God" and, from that sure foundation, proclaimed, "We hold these truths to be self-evident, that all men are created equal, that they are endowed by their creator with certain unalienable rights, that among these are Life, Liberty, and the pursuit of Happiness." Or we might hear John Adams declare that "the United States of America have exhibited, perhaps, the first example of governments erected on the simple principles of nature," or Tom Paine argue that "we have it in our power to begin the world over again. A situation, similar to the present, hath not happened since the days of Noah until now. The birthday of a new world is at hand."[11] The important point is simply this: from the beginning, Americans have viewed their nation as fundamentally natural, a virtual repristination of the way God intended things to be from the beginning.

Convinced that their nation had been "erected on the simple principles of nature," hosts of early nineteenth-century Americans firmly believed that America's example alone would inevitably extend free institutions throughout the world. Lyman Beecher typified this conviction when he argued in 1827 that the American Revolution would spark "revolutions and overturnings, until the world is free." To Beecher's mind, this was the inevitable conclusion to history. Tyrants might renew their efforts to drive again "the bolt of every chain," but they could not possibly extinguish "the rising flame" of freedom: "Still it burns, and still the mountain heaves and murmurs. And soon it will explode with voices and thunderings and great earthquakes. Then will the trumpet of Jubilee sound, and earth's debased millions will leap from the dust, shake off their chains, and cry, 'Hosanna to the Son of David.'"[12] Beecher's optimistic millennial vision was not unlike Alexander Campbell's expectation that "the *Ancient Gospel* . . . would alone be the *instrument* of *converting* the whole human race," or Parley Pratt's conviction that through the Mormon restoration, all governments, kingdoms, and tribes would be "dissolved—destroyed—or mingled into *one*—one body politic—*one* peaceful empire—*one* Lord—*one* King—*one* interest all."

We may easily dismiss such millennial optimism as eccentric or bizarre. By doing that, however, we fail to grasp the conviction of hosts of early nineteenth-century Americans that their nation had escaped the constraints of history, time, and finitude and stood shoulder to shoulder with the Almighty in the strong, first time. It was this conviction that lent substance to the ecumenical hopes of patriots that the American example was all that would ever be required to snatch "earth's debased millions" from the tyrannies of history and tradition and to restore them to "Nature and Nature's God."

Precisely here, however, irony disrupted the glorious American expectations. It was fine and good to view liberty and equality as natural and therefore universal principles, as grand, transcendent concepts, hovering in infinite judgment over their own developing civilization. In this way Americans would continually "plumb for the universal," always maintaining distance between the particular and the absolute. As it was, however, Americans quickly closed that gap, filling out their universal ideals with particularized assumptions based on historic traditions which they then judged to be fundamentally natural. Carl Becker shed considerable light on why this closure occurred when he wrote that the philosophy undergirding the Declaration of Independence was essentially unacceptable to the nineteenth century, both in Europe and America. After all, the natural rights philosophy "had been, and could again be, . . . effectively used as a justification of revolutionary movements." But this was precisely what no one in antebellum America wanted. Instead, "from the Revolution to the Civil War, the strongest political prepossession of the mass of men was founded in the desire to preserve the independence they had won, the institutions they had established, the 'more perfect Union' they had created." They persisted, therefore, in using the language of natural rights and ideals but quickly identified those ideals with the institutions and traditions they had created and were creating.[13]

Among the first and most powerful of the particular historic traditions that Americans confounded with "the simple principles of nature" was the Protestant faith. Lyman Beecher's millennial vision, for example, grew not only from his faith that America was natural, but also from his faith that America was biblical and therefore Protestant. "Our republic in its constitution," he trumpeted, "borrows from the Bible its elements, proportions, and power. It was God that gave these elementary principles to our forefathers."[14] In this connection, Sidney Mead has argued that orthodox Christians of the early nineteenth century, uncomfortable

with the Enlightenment, cosmopolitan premises of the new nation, casti-
gated those premises as "infidelity" which they then "drowned in the
great tidal wave of Christian revivalism."[15] But that tells only half the
story. When the orthodox realized that the "infidel" sentiments of universality had been plowed deeply into the American experience and
were there to stay, they invoked the old saw "If you can't whip them, join
them." In this way, they thereby adapted Enlightenment premises and
portrayed "Nature's God" as fundamentally Christian and their Protestant heritage as essentially natural and universal. Thus, as we saw in
chapters 1 and 9, the primordium of nature and the primordium of the
Christian story became so amalgamated as to be almost interchangeable
in the popular imagination. Because this perspective was so pervasive,
the United States became in the minds of many nineteenth-century Americans what it has continued to be in the thinking of millions of Americans
ever since—a fundamentally Christian nation.[16]

But that is not all. For the notion of "Christian" for many centuries
had conveyed to Europeans far more than mere concepts of religion; it
carried specific cultural meanings as well. As James Oliver Robertson
observes,

> Being "Christian," to Europeans, meant in the first place being
> fully human and civilized. . . . It was necessary that a person
> wear clothes of the proper kind. Native Americans were easy to
> recognize by their pagan dress. . . . It was also necessary that
> Christians live in houses—or at least acceptable huts—and till
> the soil. . . . A Christian was expected to attend a church—not a
> mosque or a synagogue, and certainly not a pagan temple or
> heathen grove. . . . The behavior of a Christian was also recog-
> nizable in the work assigned to each sex, in the household, in
> public, and in play.

Then Robertson makes the point so critical for America: "The Christianity
brought to the New World was perceived to be both an all-encompassing
ideology and a complete prescription for proper human behavior."[17]
Accordingly, Samuel Capen, president of the American Board of Commissioners for Foreign Missions and founder in 1906 of the New York–
based Laymen's Missionary Movement, argued, "When a heathen man
becomes a child of God and is changed within he wants his external life
and surroundings to correspond: he wants the Christian dress and the
Christian home and a Christian plow and all the other things which
distinguish Christian civilization from the narrow and degraded life of
the heathen."[18] Like Capen, many Americans confounded their religion,
their nation, and their civilization.

211

In this regard, the nation resembled Barton Stone's "Christian" movement in remarkable ways. If the "Christians" had thought themselves a primordial/millennial ark of liberty and ecumenism, only to emerge for some as the one true church in a sea of false churches, so the nation, perceived as a bastion of freedom for the world, became for some a haven of Christian civilization arrayed against the powers of darkness. And if "Christians" such as John R. Howard and Arthur Crihfield finally threatened with eternal destruction those who refused to return to the primitive church, so America moved against those who refused to conform to a way of life based on "the simple principles of nature." What we have already said of the "Christians," therefore, we may now say of the nation in the early nineteenth century: "the cosmic vision of liberty and unity had become, for some at least, a provincial vision of sectarian exclusivism, though ironically rooted and grounded in the well-worn primitivist ideology." As this occurred, Beecher's ideal of conversion-through-example steadily gave way to conversion-through-coercion as Americans sought, both at home and abroad, to compel others to be "free." This is the great irony of American history.

Coercion, however, was fully consistent with the logic of primitivism in American life. After all, how could a nation that had sidestepped history and that had become, in Fred Somkin's words, a "rebuke to time," coexist with nations and peoples whose allegiance to their own narrow histories and their own constricted traditions remained unabated and unabashed? This question grew especially acute as Americans increasingly committed themselves to highly particularized Anglo-Saxon, Protestant values which they then imagined fundamentally natural and universal. With such a commitment, Americans judged as perverse any nation or people who resisted these "natural" and "universal" values. When example and persuasion failed, therefore, the only option left was coercion.

In considering the coercive dimension in American life, our objective is not to rehearse a litany of American misdeeds, but to show instead how the coercive dimension consistently grew from America's identification of itself with the purity and rectitude of first times.

III

From an early date, few doubted the propriety of force in implementing nature's mandates. Samuel Adams, for example, wrote to James Warren in 1788 that "we never shall be upon a solid Footing till Britain cedes to us what Nature designs we should have, or till we wrest it from her."[19] Some thirty years later Rep. David Trimble made essentially the same argument when he spoke of "the natural limits of our country" which "the great Engineer of the Universe" has established. "To that boundary we shall go," Trimble proclaimed, " 'peaceable if we can, forcibly if we must.' "[20] Of all those who justified extending freedom by force, perhaps none waxed so eloquent as Sen. H. V. Johnson during the Mexican War. Johnson denied any intent on the part of the United States to "force the adoption of our form of Government upon any people by the sword." Nonetheless, it was clear to him that "the extension of the area of human liberty and happiness, shall be one of the incidents" of the war. Given that all-important consideration, Johnson told his colleagues in the Senate,

> War has its evils. In all ages it has been the minister of wholesale death and appalling desolation; but however inscrutable to us, it has also been made, by the Allwise Dispenser of events, the instrumentality of accomplishing the great end of human elevation and human happiness. . . . It is in this view, that I subscribe to the doctrine of "manifest destiny."[21]

Of the various "perverse" nations, the first to feel coercion's sword were the native Americans. Whites consistently justified the policy of Indian removal by appeals to the first age and claims of recovery and restoration. Specifically, white Americans contended that they had obeyed, and native Americans had refused to obey, that primal law which God himself had given at the time of creation: "Fill the earth and subdue it" (Gen. 1:28, RSV). In 1830, for example, George Rockingham Gilmer, later governor of Georgia, put the white Americans' case in the baldest possible terms: "Treaties were expedients by which ignorant, intractable, and savage people were induced without bloodshed to yield up what civilized people had a right to possess by virtue of that command of the Creator delivered to man upon his formation—be fruitful, multiply, and replenish the earth, and subdue it."[22] From the time of the New England Puritans to the end of the nineteenth century, proponents of Indian removal regularly employed this argument from the Genesis account of creation. John Winthrop had contended that "the whole earth is the Lord's garden & He hath given it to the sons of men, with a general condition, Gen. 1:28. Increase & multiply, replenish the earth & subdue it. . . . That which lies common and hath never replenished or subdued is free to any that will possess and improve it."[23]

The irony inherent in the nineteenth-century use of this argument, however, lay in the fact that "nature's nation" made ownership of land contingent not on a natural use of the land but on subjugation of the land in conformity with "civilization." Indeed, proponents of Indian removal specifically rejected the Indians' "state of nature" in favor of a "civilization" decreed by "Nature and Nature's God." William Henry Harrison, for example, asked,

> Is one of the fairest portions of the globe to remain in a state of nature, the haunt of a few wretched savages, when it seems destined by the Creator to give support to a large population and to be the seat of civilization, of science, and of true religion?[24]

Similarly, a treatise in the *North American Review* argued in 1830 that

> there can be no doubt . . . that the Creator intended the earth should be reclaimed from a state of nature and cultivated; that the human race should spread over it, procuring from it the means of comfortable subsistence, and of increase and improvement.

But native Americans, the article claimed, "depending upon the chase for support, . . . have a very imperfect possession of the country over which they roam."[25] Nineteenth-century white Americans altogether failed to see the irony in this line of reasoning, however, since they had thoroughly particularized "Nature and Nature's God" with a "civilized," Protestant, Anglo-Saxon content which they then assumed was primordial, eternal, and universal. Horace Greeley spoke perhaps for most white Americans when, on the grounds of obedience to the mandate of creation, he decreed extinction for native Americans in 1859:

> As I passed over those magnificent bottoms of the Kansas which form reservations of the Delawares, Potawatamies, etc., constituting the very best corn lands on earth, and saw their owners sitting round the doors of their lodges in the height of the planting season, and in as good, bright planting weather as sun and soil ever made, I could not help saying, "These people must die out—there is no help for them. God has given this earth to those who will subdue and cultivate it, and it is vain to struggle against His righteous decree."[26]

Appeals to nature and to the Genesis account of creation underpinned claims not only to Indian lands but also to Mexico and even to the Oregon Territory.[27] Thus John Quincy Adams argued that the United States' title to Oregon was unavoidable on the grounds that the Genesis account of creation "is the foundation not only of our title to the territory of Oregon, but the foundation of all human title to all human possession."[28] But the more common claim to Oregon rested on a complete dismissal of history and an appeal to the universal that lay behind all historic particularities. As we saw in chapter 1, John L. O'Sullivan rooted the United States' claim to the Oregon Territory squarely in America's sense of historylessness. He summarily dismissed "all these antiquated materials of old black-leather international law" along with "all these cobweb tissues" of finite, human history, and rested his case instead with "the Author of the Universe, Himself."[29] He might well have added, in the words of the Mormon proclamation issued that same year, that "the kingdom of God has come, . . . even that Kingdom which shall fill the whole earth and stand forever."

IV

By the last third of the nineteenth century, the American vision of nature embraced not just civilization and Protestant Christianity, but also industrial capitalism which flourished in the northern states especially following the Civil War. As it happened, the phenomenal growth of industrial capitalism occurred precisely during that time when Americans discovered that the new Darwinian notions of natural, evolutionary development provided a plausible explanation for American economic growth and progress. In this way, the new doctrines of evolution reinforced the American conviction that Yankee civilization—now including an expansive capitalist economy—had been decreed by "Nature and Nature's God."

Perhaps no one popularized this conviction more effectively than did Andrew Carnegie in his famous essay "Wealth," which appeared in the *North American Review* in 1889. There, he argued that

> while the law [of competition] may be sometimes hard for the individual, it is best for the race, because it insures the survival of the fittest in every department. We accept and welcome, therefore, as conditions to which we must accommodate ourselves, great inequality of environment, the concentration of business . . . in the hands of a few, and the law of competition between these, as being not only beneficial, but essential for the future progress of the race.

To Carnegie's mind, not only was "survival of the fittest" a primordial "law" which the Almighty had woven tightly into the very fabric of nature. It also was the harbinger of the millennium, "the true Gospel concerning Wealth, obedience to which is destined some day to solve the problem of the Rich and the Poor, and to bring 'Peace on earth, among men Good Will.'"[30]

Armed with such convictions, Americans encountered in the final decade of the nineteenth century the closing of the frontier, the end of the wilderness lands whose acquisition and development had fed the American economy for so long, and the collapse of Indian resistance. But white Americans were not done with Indians. Indeed, Richard Slotkin and Michael Rogin both have argued that native Americans, from an early date, provided white Americans with their paradigm for understanding the enemies of civilization.[31] James Oliver Robertson has carried this argument even further, suggesting that when the American wilderness disappeared, Americans projected the wilderness image onto the rest of the world.[32] According to this scenario, peoples of color in Africa, Asia, and Central and South America became manifestations of the "wretched savages" who should be taught the ways "of Nature and of Nature's God." Albert Beveridge therefore defended "liberation" of the Philippines on the grounds that God "has made us adept in government that we may administer government among savage and senile peoples."[33]

Through its military involvement in the Philippines, the United States proclaimed its intention to bring universal values, as Americans understood those values, to a people still shackled by the chains of history. Pres. William McKinley at least partly spelled out the nature of those supposed universal values when he explained that the United States sought "to educate the Filipinos, and uplift and civilize and Christianize them, and by God's grace do the very best we could by them, as our fellow-men for whom Christ also died."[34] But Sen. Orville Platt of Connecticut most effectively grounded America's Philippine involvement in the universal values that, he said, had guided white Americans since the days of the earliest Puritans. "I believe the same force was behind our army at Santiago and our ships in Manila Bay that was behind the landing of the Pilgrims on Plymouth Rock," he proclaimed, adding that "we have been chosen to carry on and to carry forward this great work of uplifting humanity on earth."[35]

Aside from the explicitly Protestant content of these "universal" objectives, American involvement in the Philippines was fraught with multiple ironies. In the first place, American motives in the Spanish-American War were essentially self-serving, though cloaked in the guise of altruism. After all, the Philippines would provide new markets and new lands for further economic expansion. Sen. James Henderson Berry of Arkansas made this charge explicit when he argued on the Senate floor that the United States was pursuing its Philippine policy "on the pretense, it may be, of humanity and Christianity, but behind it all . . . is the desire for trade and commerce."[36] Sen. Albert Beveridge of Indiana, perhaps the most effective propogandist for America's Philippine involvement, confirmed this judgment when he argued in 1902 that "the markets of the Orient are the Republic's future commercial salvation," and "the Pacific is the highway to these markets." Control of the Philippines, Beveridge judged, meant control of the Pacific, which in turn promised unbounded wealth for America. Beveridge therefore asked, "Does our fitness for the work prevent us from doing it? Or does the Nation's preparedness, the Republic's duty and the commercial necessity of the American people unite in demanding of American statesmanship the holding of the Philippines and the commercial conquest of the oriental world?"[37] But the conviction of most Americans that industrial capitalism manifested the natural, universal order, established by God himself, obscured from their eyes the degree to which self-interest governed national policy. Indeed, many Americans thought the Spanish-American War had nothing to do with exploitation or imperialism, but everything to do with extending the "Laws of Nature and of Nature's God." Charles Conant, one of the government's leading economic advisers in this period, affirmed that America's "irresistible tendency to expansion, . . . seeking new outlets for American capital and new opportunities for American enterprise" was simply "a natural law of economic and race development."[38]

The second paradox involved in this conflict was the American determination to compel the Filipinos to be free. Senator Platt unwittingly illumined this paradox when he argued that "God has placed upon this Government the solemn duty of providing for the people of these islands a government based upon the principle of liberty no matter how many difficulties the problem may present." When U.S. policy was criticized for what seemed to be imperialism, President McKinley asked, "Did we need their consent to perform a great act for humanity? We had it in every aspiration of their minds, in every hope of their hearts." This assumption governed U.S. policy in spite of the fact that Emilio Aguinaldo for more than two years led a bloody, popular revolution against American domination of the Philippines. In reflecting on all of this, Albert Weinberg remarked that it was "a paradoxical fact . . . indeed, that the same humanitarian ideal which had once been used to discredit conquest was now employed with equal confidence in its justification."[39]

There is, however, an explanation for this seeming paradox. It is found, we would argue, in the fact that America had rooted its historical particularities in the soil of nature and universality. Thus, Senator Beveridge, in his well-known defense of American involvement in the Philippines, argued in 1899 that God "has made us the lords of civilization that we may administer civilization." Retreat from the Philippines "would be the betrayal of a trust as sacred as humanity" and "a crime against Christian civilization."[40] From what now has been said, the particularities inherent in this vision of supposed universality are evident. But the extent to which the Anglo-Saxon, Protestant, and industrial-capitalist particularities of the American experience had undermined the very premises of that experiment became evident when Beveridge argued that Filipinos simply "are not yet capable of self government. How could they be? They are not a self-governing race; they are Orientals, Malays, instructed by Spaniards in the latter's worst estate."[41] Thus, the very ideal of freedom, which Jefferson had argued was a fundamentally unalienable right with which "all men" had been endowed, now was the right only of Anglo-Saxons and perhaps a few others who were "capable of self-government." In this way the United States was not only a rebuke to time; the nation also became, by the late nineteenth century, a rebuke to the universal and cosmopolitan ideals that, in the eighteenth century, had established its very reason for existence.

One might argue that Beveridge and people of his persuasion indulged in considerable hyperbole with such pronouncements. The fact nonetheless remains that they directed their rhetoric to a populace they judged to be fundamentally sympathetic. Further, many in the Senate took such language quite seriously. Sen. James Berry, for example, well expressed the extent to which America had betrayed its own ideals when he told his fellow senators

> that to-day every man who dares to raise his voice in the way of protest against this radical departure from our time honored beliefs, traditions, and professions is denounced as a traitor to his country, an ally, aider, and abettor of Malays, negroes, and savages. . . .
> And we are told that we must conquer these people in the interests of humanity and for their own good, . . . and kill and slaughter hundreds and, it may be, thousands of these people, in order that we may civilize and Christianize the remainder.[42]

When Berry spoke of "this radical departure from our time honored beliefs . . . in the interests of humanity," he underscored the ironies that had emerged from America's full identification with natural and universal values. If Berry knew the stories of particular religious movements in America's past, he might well have told the Senate of similar ironies that had emerged time and again in the nineteenth century and even before. Mormons and "Christians," for example, who had so thoroughly identified themselves with the purity of first times that they could threaten unbelievers with divine retribution, had been, in retrospect, paradigms for the national experience in the Spanish-American War.

While the Spanish-American War constituted perhaps the most obvious manifestation of American cultural imperialism in the 1890s, Americans of that decade also engaged in a far more subtle and seductive form of imperialism. This more subtle imperialism involved exporting American culture, civilization, and values abroad through private enterprise—a course of action that Emily Rosenberg, in her splendid volume *Spreading the American Dream,* has traced in substantial detail. For our purposes, two dimensions of American cultural and economic imperialism in this period deserve mention. First, many Americans believed that direct government involvement in economic and cultural expansion would undermine America's identity as a nation grounded solely on "Nature and on Nature's God." If America was fundamentally natural, it was obvious that American institutions would be naturally attractive to peoples around the globe. Expansion would occur, as Beecher had imagined, through the power of example, not through coercion. At the same time, however, an economy built on expansion demanded new markets, and demanded them now, especially given the demise of the American frontier. The situation, therefore, required a strategy that would facilitate American expansion, and even domination of recalcitrant and "backward" peoples, while at the same time preserving the myths of freedom, individualism, and innocence. The strategy adopted, therefore, placed the burden of expansion squarely on the private sector. Government's role was to assist those citizens, businesses, and corporations in their expansionist activities and to negotiate a reduction of foreign restrictions against U.S. activities abroad.[43]

By the end of World War II, this strategy had become what Rosenberg calls a "chosen instrument" approach: government "awarded a private group or corporation official blessing or monopolistic privileges in return for carrying out some element of American foreign policy."[44] With individuals, private agencies, and corporations implementing the United States' global mission, Americans could imagine that the nation itself pursued its course with clean hands, untainted by the world, undefiled by history, and true to its natural calling. Because government's role was only indirect, Americans could indulge themselves in the illusion that their cultural and economic expansion entailed no imperialist dimensions but simply preserved freedom and individualism on every hand.

This sort of imperialism by proxy has been a frequent feature of the restoration vision. The church or nation that has restored first times simply cannot engage in exploitive or imperialist behavior directly without subverting its primal identity and betraying its innocence. It therefore works indirectly through others, or on behalf of others, who can bear the blame. Thus, if early Mormons destroyed unbelievers, they would only be carrying out the will of God. Similarly, Andrew Jackson blamed destruction of the Indians entirely on the Indians themselves and on their advisers, thus preserving the innocence of the United States government. "I have exonerated the national character from all imputation," Jackson declared, "and now leave the poor deluded Creeks and Cherokees to their fate, and their annihilation, which their wicked advisors has [*sic*] induced."[45]

The theme of imperialism by proxy leads directly to the second important dimension of American cultural and economic expansion in this period. Americans clearly imagined that commercial expansion was somehow free from imperialistic overtones. What sustained this assumption was the common conviction that private enterprise was a fundamental manifestation of "Nature and of Nature's God." It followed that commercial expansion and even domination throughout the world in no sense constituted exploitation or imperialism, but simply extended the blessings of liberty around the globe. Albert Beveridge, therefore, could proclaim with no sense of irony at all that "we are enlisted in the cause of American supremacy, which will never end until American commerce has made the conquest of the world."[46] And one advocate of global commerce dominated by American values praised American railroad construction overseas as the very embodiment of civilization and freedom. Such global construction, he said, is

> the largest human calling. . . . We blow the whistle that's heard round the world, and all peoples stop to heed and welcome it. Its resonance is the diplomacy of peace. The locomotive bell is the true Liberty bell, proclaiming commercial freedom. Its boilers and the reservoirs are the forces of civilization. Its wheels are the wheels of progress, and its headlight is the illumination of dark countries.[47]

Robert Bellah has commented suggestively on the twentieth-century American confusion of free enterprise with individualism and freedom. "When capitalism in America did become ideologically self-conscious," Bellah writes, "it took shelter under the established categories of individualism, however incongruous that would turn out to be." It was incongruous, Bellah suggests, because the "vast hierarchical, bureaucratic corporations" in twentieth-century America enshrine hierarchic power, not individualism, and "are under even less popular restraint than state power."[48]

The oppressive dimension of American corporate power was especially apparent in the late nineteenth century. But this dimension went essentially unobserved by those Americans who benefited from the system. Indeed, the benefits were so great that one who shared its blessings could hardly doubt that industrial capitalism in America was the natural order of things, invented by God himself. But such verities were not so obvious to those dominated by American commerce. Rosenberg has nicely summarized the ironies involved in this situation.

> By pressing free flow, free enterprise, and open access on others, the American government, in effect, was prescribing a developmental process for foreigners quite unlike their own—a "development" dominated by strong American-based structures and organized by American capital and expertise. . . . Americans, in short, did not really seek a *free* marketplace but a *privately owned* marketplace which they mistakenly labeled "free."[49]

Or to place this irony in the context of this book, Americans did not really seek a natural marketplace, but instead inherited a historically particularized marketplace which they then imagined had simply derived from "Nature and Nature's God."

So natural did American civilization appear that American Protestant missionaries in the nineteenth century had a difficult time distinguishing their civilization from their faith. After all, Protestantism seemed rooted in the first Christian age while the nation's economic and political structures seemed rooted in the beginning of the world. Both, therefore, descended from the creative hands of God. From the missionaries' perspective, therefore, Protestantism, democracy, and capitalism all expressed the same primordial principles. As a result, a significant segment of the missionary movement of the nineteenth century proclaimed a gospel of Christian civilization, which became, as William R. Hutchinson has recently shown, "a moral equivalent for imperialism." Missionary theorists drew heavily on militant images of world conquest and empire. They denigrated foreign cultures, claiming at the same time that God through divine providence had readied those cultures for conquest by "Christian civilization." Across the theological spectrum—from premillennialist to postmillennialist, from Social Gospeler to conservative evangelical—missionary personnel in the latter half of the nineteenth century, Hutchinson notes, "shared a vision of the essential rightness of Western civilization and the near-inevitability of its triumph" throughout the world.[50]

In all these ways, the nineteenth century was for white, Anglo-Saxon, Protestant, and capitalist America a period of profound triumphalism. It was simply inconceivable to Americans who shared these values that the nation might not prevail. Their nation, after all, had recovered in all aspects of its civilization the truths of first times and now displayed those truths to the world.

221

V

Americans entered the twentieth century convinced of a national innocence still rooted in unswerving fidelity to the primordial principles of "Nature and of Nature's God." The perspective of Woodrow Wilson, in fact, was in many respects the epitome of American primitivist thinking to that time. Wilson imagined America the very embodiment of the purity of first times. He told the American people during World War I that "there is not a single selfish element so far as I can see, in the cause we are fighting for. We are fighting for what we believe and wish to be the rights of mankind and for the future peace and security of the world."[51]

At the same time, Wilson made it clear that the natural principles of humankind were "American principles" and "American policies," and that "we can stand for no other."[52] In spite of claiming to serve the universal good, Wilson administration policies often seemed transparently particularistic and even self-serving. The extensive activities of George Creel's Committee on Public Information during World War I is a case in point. Creel believed that his committee disseminated only scientifically objective and value-free information, completely lacking in prejudice. The CPI's presentations were not propagandistic, but only presentations of "facts." Creel easily made these assumptions since he shared Wilson's conviction that "American principles . . . are the principles of mankind."

How ironic, then, that CPI materials often were extraordinarily one-sided, that the CPI censored materials that disagreed with its own, and that the CPI launched a campaign to convince Americans of the truth and importance of the information it disseminated. Finally, under provisions of the Espionage Act, the government imprisoned some nine hundred people who remained unconvinced. One of those imprisoned was a man who produced a film, *The Spirit of 76*, which portrayed the United States' World War I ally, Great Britain, in a negative light. The irony of the entire episode was symbolized by the official name of this court case: *U.S. v. Spirit of 76*.

The particularities of America's "universal" principles also became evident in Wilson's campaign for a worldwide flow of information—a campaign traced in detail by Emily Rosenberg. Wilson, with most Americans of the time, believed that communication systems owned and operated by foreign governments were by definition prejudicial and disseminated partisan and contrived information, while American-owned communication systems presented only the "facts," the true "principles of mankind." The same attitude prevailed with respect to commerce, industry, and raw materials. Commerce controlled by other nations inevitably would be corrupt and unfair, but American-controlled commerce would be enlightened, operating in the interest of "all mankind."[53]

Following World War I, the aftermath of the Bolshevik Revolution impeded Wilson's dream that through American leadership and influence, the world would return to "natural and universal" principles and thereby be made "safe for democracy." In the first place, the Bolshevik Revolution launched in the world a massive force that held an entirely different vision of what was natural, universal, and therefore inevitable. Communism thereby became in American minds not only an enemy, but the very embodiment of evil—an artificial contrivance falsely cloaked in the guise of universality and historical inevitability. With this development, most Americans abandoned whatever hopes they still entertained that America, through the power of its example alone, would lead the world in the primordial paths of liberty and justice for all. Ironically, it now became clear that extention of liberty would require coercion, economic imperialism, and assorted covert operations, all designed to subvert the power of evil which opposed the progress of "Nature and of Nature's God." Partly for this reason and partly out of sheer economic self-interest, American business and government redoubled efforts to influence and even control those underdeveloped nations that might come under the sway of Communism.

As a direct result of these developments, the ironies of the American experience emerged in glaring relief following World War II. At the conclusion of that conflict, African, Asian, and Latin American nations, long under the domination of various colonial powers, declared their independence. Lyman Beecher, had he lived to see these events, might have hailed them as a fulfillment of his prediction that the American Revolution would spark "revolutions and overturnings, until the world is free." Indeed, in the case of Vietnam, Ho Chi Minh shaped his own proclamation of independence for the Democratic Republic of Vietnam with the words of Thomas Jefferson: "We hold these truths to be self-evident, that all men are created equal."

Instead of supporting these bids for national independence, however, America acted in most instances to subvert them. In the first place, the United States feared losing support of the European colonial powers whose aid was required in the ongoing struggle against Communism. And in the second place, the United States feared the loss of its own financial investments in the third world—investments that had expanded significantly since the 1890s when the United States launched its policy of economic colonialism.[54] While third world countries, therefore, sought to realize "the principles of mankind," as Wilson had put it years before, America pursued particular interests that undermined its own universal ideals. At the same time, Americans cloaked their particular interests in the garb of universality. American economic exploitation of third world nations, therefore, would make those nations both richer and freer than they might be without American involvement. From that time forward, American advocates of the "trickle-down theory" have assumed that policies that work in the interest of the rich also work to realize primordial and natural ideals.

In more recent years, confusion of particular national interests with universal ideals has led to still other ironies and illusions. Since the national mission was essentially redemptive, compromising with evil in any sense at all meant failing in the national task and losing the struggle. Here was a secularized version of Tyndale's covenant thelogy which demanded nothing less than inflexible righteousness and final victory. Accordingly, Pres. Richard Nixon confidently proclaimed that "any hope the world has for the survival of peace and freedom" depended on the United States' determination to emerge victorious in Vietnam.[55] An Indochina compromise was unthinkable for the nation that would yet redeem the world.

The dilemma of American identity deepened in the period Robert Bellah has called America's "third time of trial"—the 1960s and early 1970s.[56] Involved in coercion and exploitation both at home and abroad, the United States finally revealed its finitude for all to see. That tragic period presented an opportunity for the nation to admit at least its historic identity, its guilt, and its complicity in the structures of finitude. It was a chance for a new beginning: not a reaffirmation of primitive identity, but a realistic appraisal of America's finite role in a pluralistic world of nations.

But the myth of primordial innocence was too old and too powerful to be swept away by the mere events of history, and in the aftermath of Vietnam, Watts, and Watergate, it returned even stronger than before. Americans no longer wanted to hear of America's faults but of America's innocence and righteousness—a perspective that intensified throughout the 1970s and into the 1980s. Thus Pres. Ronald Reagan spoke to a receptive audience in his 1984 State of the Union message when he sounded a familiar myth: "Americans resort to force only when we must. We have never been aggressors. We have always struggled to defend freedom and democracy. . . . How can we not believe in the goodness and greatness of America? How can we not do what is right and needed to preserve this last, best hope of man on earth?" And then the president rooted this myth of innocence squarely in the nation's long-standing identity with pure, primordial beginnings. Quoting Carl Sandburg, he proclaimed: "I see America, not in the setting sun of a black night of despair. . . . I see America in the crimson light of a rising sun fresh from the burning, creative hand of God."[57] And the nation understood. For with this language, the president tapped a deep well of primitivist conviction which remained potent even in the closing years of the twentieth century.

Epilogue:
Beyond Innocence and Illusion in American Life

One measure of the appeal primitivist ideology continued to exert in the closing years of the twentieth century was the remarkable success of Allan Bloom's *The Closing of the American Mind.*[1] Many observers marveled that a fundamentally academic book could establish itself as the best-selling book in America during most of the summer of 1987. Doubtless much of its success was due to the skill with which Bloom tapped the continuing backlash against the 1960s, reflecting the values of the extraordinarily conservative decade in which this book appeared. Yet these kinds of appraisals miss the heart of Bloom's appeal.

Bloom's book was fundamentally a restorationist treatise, tapping deeply into the bountiful wellspring of American restorationist ideology. Like the early "Christians in the West," Bloom began with an impassioned appeal for the freedom to inquire and to search, contending that true liberal education requires "that no previous attachment be immune to examination and hence re-evaluation."[2] Like so many Americans before him, he legitimated both the freedom and importance of inquiry with appeals to the primordium of nature. Further, Socrates symbolized the natural and universal human being since he spent his life searching for universal truths and refusing to identify those truths with incomplete or partial answers. As Bloom noted, "conforming to nature is quite different from conforming to law, convention or opinion."[3] Therefore, "for those who wish to see, contemplation of Socrates is our most urgent task."[4]

This emphasis, so compatible with the philosophy of the Declaration of Independence, no doubt goes far to explain Bloom's tremendous popularity. But this dimension was only one side of Bloom's book. In fact, Bloom embraced the same irony that a host of sectarian primitivists had embraced over the course of American history. Like those forebearers, Bloom began with visions of freedom and openness rooted in the soil of a universal primordium. Then he, too, filled his primordial vision with all manner of cultural particularities. In spite of Bloom's avowed intentions, necessity finally overwhelmed freedom and closure conquered openness. Bloom finally imagined an unbroken "natural" tradition running from Socrates to the Declaration of Independence, and when he was finished he had thoroughly Americanized first times.

Bloom believed the American political tradition is "unambiguous, its meaning is articulated in simple, rational speech that is immediately comprehensible and powerfully persuasive to all normal human beings. America tells one story: the unbroken, ineluctable progress of freedom and equality." Bloom therefore dismissed those who criticized American imperialism, contending that the seemingly imperialistic behavior of the United States was carried out "in the name of self-evident truths that apply to the good of all men." Bloom's Americanization of the universal became especially apparent when he compared "rational Americans" with other peoples in other lands. Other peoples, he wrote, "were autochthonous, deriving guidance from the gods of their various places. When they too decided to follow the principles we pioneered, they hobbled along awkwardly, unable to extricate themselves gracefully from their pasts." On the other hand, America's "story is the majestic and triumphant march of the principles of freedom and equality, giving meaning to all that we have done or are doing."[5]

Yet Bloom's message in this regard was ambiguous. On the one hand, he often seemed to argue that American principles rather than American realities fully embodied the universal. One could argue, therefore, that Bloom was not really comparable to nineteenth-century sectarians. But on the other hand, sectarian dimensions appeared often in the book. For one thing, Bloom focused his search for the universal on the rational tradition of the West, essentially ignoring the collective wisdom of other parts of the world. For another, he particularized and even Americanized the universal in important ways. For example, he argued that those who insist that Americans know other cultures, learn to respect them, and even profit from them were "teachers of openness" who "had either no interest in or were actively hostile to the Declaration of Independence and the Constitution." He dismissed ethnic festivals in America as both "superficial" and "insipid," since they convey only the "decaying reminiscences of old differences that caused our ancestors to kill one another." Likewise, he rejected the feminist movement as "more a liberation from nature than from convention or society. . . . The women's movement," he pronounced, "is not founded on nature."[6]

For Bloom, appreciation for "cultures," ethnic festivals, and the women's movement had no place in the American Eden. Such things found a place only after the fall. The serpent who corrupted America, injecting poisonous notions into its natural consciousness, was Friedrich Nietzsche (1844–1900).[7] In the place of universal ideals, Bloom lamented, Nietzsche substituted the concept of particular cultures that generate particular values, legitimate only in particular cultural contexts. Max Weber and Sigmund Freud especially introduced these notions into American universities, and suddenly "good and evil . . . for the first time appeared as values, of which there have been a thousand and one, none rationally or objectively preferable to any other." The modern heresy of historicism, Bloom thought, perverted the good even further. But Bloom manifested no awareness that the term "historicism" has borne a variety of meanings. Accordingly, he fastened on the term a meaning with extremely relativistic connotations: "the view that all thought is essentially related to and cannot transcend its own time." The burden of the total book, however, suggested Bloom's objection even to a far milder form of historicism, namely, the assumption that thought is culturally conditioned and therefore grasps universal truths only partially. In any case, as an example of "relativizing" historicism, Bloom faulted especially Carl Becker's *Declaration of Independence,* which was important to our discussion in chapter 10. Under Becker's withering analysis, Bloom thought, the founding heritage of America "all began to seem like Washington and the cherry tree," devoid of universal truth. In all these ways, America became "corrupted by alien views and alien tastes" which promoted in this land a ruthless relativism. These views were especially repugnant to Bloom, who thought he saw in the Socratic tradition of the West only "pure mind, which is trans-historical."[8]

Bloom especially faulted American universities for sustaining these "alien views and tastes" by imposing on classic texts interpretive systems based on culture, value, and historicist perspectives. Bloom viewed interpretive systems the same way Alexander Campbell and James R. Graves had viewed creeds—as human inventions that obscured the universal truths of the primary text. As a result, Bloom argued, "there is no text, only interpretation." He therefore commended the Great Books tradition which thrived at the University of Chicago where Bloom taught for many years. The Great Books, after all, expressed natural and universal truths that transcended the constraints of particular times and places and therefore stood immune to historicist interpretations. Reading them, therefore, meant "*just* [italics ours] reading them, letting them dictate what the questions are and the method of approaching them—not forcing them into categories we make up, not treating them as historical products, but trying to read them as their authors wished them to be read."[9]

Bloom's intent seemed clear: if universal ideals do in fact exist, then the search for truth goes on; if, however, there is nothing but cultural values, produced by the accidents of time and place, then there is really nothing for which to search. Consequently, one finds in this relativized generation "the closing of the American mind." Bloom, however, though imagining the universal to be entirely transcultural, ironically tied the universal so firmly to particular cultural interests that he finally achieved just the reverse of his intent. In this, he shared with John Cotton, James R. Graves, Alexander Campbell, Parley Pratt, and a host of other American restorationists.

Bloom finally depicted an ideal America whose history was trans-historical, whose culture was transcultural, and whose values were rooted in the primal ground of first times. American values, therefore, were not "values" at all but simply universal ideals obvious and compelling "to all normal human beings." This ideal, "natural" world would be dominated by Great Books, good music, and traditional relationships, undefiled by feminism, interpretive systems, rock music, and ethnic festivals (if not ethnic traditions). Bloom began by calling for "a very great narrowness" toward relativism and openness toward universal truth. When he had finished, however, the narrowness he valued was little more than a defense of traditional Western values, cloaked in the garb of universal values and Socratic first times.[10] In this way, Bloom's book partook profoundly of the irony that has haunted and often subverted countless restoration traditions in the history of the West.[11]

Some argued that Bloom's book was a Straussian spoof, a put-on, not intended for serious consideration by serious readers, or perhaps containing one message for the elites and another for the conservative masses.[12] Such a view at least would explain the frequent ambiguity of language (e.g., "nature," "openness," "narrowness"). Whether Bloom intended the book as a spoof, however, is finally irrelevant to the fact that the great majority of Americans who read this book regarded it as a serious statement of American ideals. The fact that Bloom cast the book in the time-honored tradition of restoration rhetoric and the fact that the public response was so positive suggest that the restoration ideal continues to exert considerable sway in American public life.

The persistent tendency of Americans virtually to identify the nation with the purity and innocence of first times also predisposed Bloom's readers to view favorably another central thesis of the book: the view that others (in this case, Germans) were chiefly to blame for America's ills. Yet German thought was far less responsible for closing the American mind than the ahistorical bias so central to American primitivism. If

American ideals indeed embodied universal truths of nature, and if American traditions often expressed those ideals, then why should anyone be interested in other cultures, other religions, or other traditions of humankind? Clearly, many American students were not interested in other cultures, traditions, and religions precisely because they were convinced that their own was the highest, the noblest, and the most "natural" known to humankind—a prejudice to which Bloom lent substantial support.

This leads us to ask if there is a way to understand the American experiment without identifying the contents of its culture with first times and the particularities of its experience with the universals taught by nature. For a different vision we turn to Sidney E. Mead, another representative of the University of Chicago. But instead of representing the Great Books tradition at Chicago, Mead represents the "Chicago school" which dominated the divinity school at the University of Chicago during the early years of the twentieth century. Mead himself has expressed his debt to that "school" through which he passed, as he put it, in its "twilight years," and in which he taught from 1941 to 1960.[13] What distinguished that "school" was its pioneering attempt to take seriously the role of history and culture in the study of religion.[14]

Mead employed historical-critical methods throughout his long career, and his recognition of the power of history and culture gave him a theological perspective that informed all of his work. That perspective can best be described as a keen awareness of the finitude of human existence symbolized, as Mead put it, by "the emperor who kept beside him one whose sole responsibility was to say over and over again, 'Remember, you too are mortal.' "[15] Mead, like Bloom, also was driven by a profoundly restorationist spirit, recognizing in the Enlightenment's vision of "nature" something universal that partook of first times.[16] But Mead was an unusual sort of restorationist, resolutely refusing to identify the primordial with the historical and the universal with its particular manifestations. Like Roger Williams, Mead possessed a prophetic dimension that maintained a radical distance between the infinite and the finite. Further, this prophetic dimension was rooted squarely in Mead's awareness that all human beings are creatures of history and culture and, for that reason, cannot escape the constraints of time and place in their quest for the natural, primordial, or universal.

Mead made this point time and again, but perhaps nowhere more effectively than in his essay "The Nation with the Soul of a Church."[17] There, Mead refused to identify America with the universal; rather, he applied to America Paul Tillich's judgment that "a particular religion will be lasting to the degree in which it negates itself as a religion . . . [and] as long as it breaks through its own particularity." "Tillich's view," Mead observed, "seems to me implicit in the whole American experience with religious pluralism."[18] For this reason, the American experience pointed beyond itself to the universal, which always stood in judgment on the particularities, and especially on the pretentions, of that experience. The universal element in American life, therefore, did not obliterate ethnic traditions. Rather, it sought "to transcend and include all the national and religious particularities brought to it by the people who come from all the world to be 'Americanized.'"

For this reason, Mead severely criticized "sectarians . . . [and] all advocates who cannot disentangle their particular religious forms from the universal essence of religion." For Mead the cosmopolitan and universal principles drawn from nature's primordium shape American ideals but also stand in judgment on American life. Mead called this perspective the "religion of the Republic"—a perspective that finally rested on the bedrock foundation of history, culture, and human finitude. As Mead put it, "whatever 'God' may be, if indeed being is applicable to 'God,' a concept of the infinite seems to me necessary if we are to state the all-important fact about man: that he is finite."[19]

In Mead's view, this cosmopolitan, universal "religion of the Republic," which refused identification with particular finite forms, legitimated religious and cultural pluralism in American life. While all religious sects, therefore, expressed the infinite and the universal to one degree or another, none could claim to be identical with the infinite and the universal. It was this conviction, Mead suggested, that lay behind Thomas Jefferson's affirmation that there were sects "of various kinds, indeed, but all good enough; [because] all sufficient to preserve peace and order." And Mead often cited to similar effect Benjamin Franklin's judgment that he found the essentials (i.e., the universal) "in all the religions we had in our country."[20]

At this point a very fine but fundamentally important line separates Sidney Mead from Allan Bloom. For Bloom, history and culture obscured the universal. For Mead, in contrast, the universal manifested itself precisely within the context of history and culture. Culture did not obscure the universal; it rather enabled us to perceive the universal, cloaked and disguised in the particularities of various human religions, folkways, and ethnic traditions. To identify one particular human tradition with the universal to the exclusion of all other traditions was, therefore, for Mead idolatry.

With this perspective, Mead recognized that even the nation, like the sects it embraced, contained within itself the germs of sectarianism with respect to other nations and peoples. Mead clearly perceived this tendency in Josaiah Strong's *Our Country* with its ringing affirmation that "God with infinite wisdom and skill" is preparing our civilization to "impress its institutions upon mankind."[21] Indeed, the germs of sectarianism are perhaps more potent in American life than Mead realized. After all, the inclination to model our lives after primordial patterns is, as we suggested in the preface, a persistent habit of the American heart. Further, a razor-thin line separates, on the one hand, the vision that America points beyond itself to the universal from, on the other hand, the vision that America has encompassed the universal within itself. And, as we have seen time and again in this book, that line is extraordinarily easy to cross.

To understand America as pointing beyond itself to the universal is to view the American restoration as process rather than completion. Understood in this sense, our national experience continues the American Revolution as, through the course of human events and the power of rational debate, successive generations of Americans increasingly discern that the "unalienable rights" to "life, liberty, and the pursuit of happiness" belong not only to "all men" or to all Americans but to all humankind.[22] The alternative to this understanding of recovery as process is the grim vision Mead portrayed: "Sectarianism, religious or national, is a greater threat than secularism or outright atheism, because, as the story of religious persecution reminds us, when it comes in the guise of the 'faith once delivered to the saints' it may legitimate terrible tyrannies."[23] The only viable antidote to American sectarianism is the prescription issued by Reinhold Niebuhr when he wrote that American success in twentieth-century world politics "requires a modest awareness of the contingent elements in the values and ideals of our devotion, even when they appear to us to be universally valid; and a generous appreciation of the valid elements in the practices and institutions of other nations though they deviate from our own."[24]

Awareness of our own failures and appreciation of the traditions of others will not likely occur, however, so long as the luxuriant growth of pretentions to innocence remains unpruned. And that luxuriant growth will not likely be pruned so long as its roots go unexamined. This book has attempted to examine those roots in all their tangled complexity and to understand the illusory and ironic fruit the primitivist tree has borne and continues to bear in American religion, life, and culture.

Notes

•

Preface

1. Rhys Isaac, *The Transformation of Virginia* (Chapel Hill: University of North Carolina Press, 1982), p. 168; Gordon Wood, "Evangelical America and Early Mormonism," *New York History* (October 1980): 365; and Nathan O. Hatch, "The Christian Movement and the Demand for a Theology of the People," *Journal of American History* 67 (December 1980): 561 and 546.

2. Alexis de Tocqueville, *Democracy in America,* trans. George Lawrence, ed. J. P. Mayer (Garden City, N.Y.: Doubleday, 1969), p. 508.

3. Robert N. Bellah, Richard Madsen, William M. Sullivan, Ann Swidler, and Steven M. Tipton, *Habits of the Heart: Individualism and Commitment in American Life* (New York: Harper and Row, 1986), p. 84.

Chapter 1. Restoring First Times

1. J. Hector St. John de Crevecoeur, *Letters from an American Farmer, 1782* (New York: Penguin American Library, 1981), p. 70.

2. Charles Pinckney, address to the Constitutional Convention, June 25, 1787, in Charles Tansel, ed., *Documents Illustrative of the Formation of the Union of the American States* (Washington, D.C.: Government Printing Office, 1927), pp. 804–5; Guilian Verplanck, *The Advantages and Dangers of the American Scholar. A Discourse delivered . . . at Union College, July 26, 1836* (New York, 1836), p. 5.

3. "The Great Nation of Futurity," *Democratic Review* 6 (November 1839): 426–27.

4. For a sampling of the extent to which millennialism has been explored, see Leonard I. Sweet, "Millennialism in America: Recent Studies," *Theological Studies* 40 (September 1979): 510–31; and Hillel Schwartz, "The End of the Beginning: Millenarian Studies, 1969–1975," *Religious Studies Review* 2 (July 1976): 1–15.

5. Fred Somkin, *Unquiet Eagle: Memory and Desire in the Idea of American Freedom, 1815–1860* (Ithaca, N.Y.: Cornell University Press, 1967), p. 57.

6. Ibid., pp. 57, 61.

7. Ibid., pp. 60, 57.

8. Sidney E. Mead, *The Lively Experiment: The Shaping of Christianity in America* (New York: Harper and Row, 1963), pp. 108–13. Mead addressed in considerably more detail the theme of recovery in American life in "The Theology of the Republic and the Orthodox Mind," *Journal of the American Academy of Religion* 44 (March 1976): 105–13.

9. Martin Luther, "Against the Heavenly Prophets," in *Luther's Works: American Edition,* vol. 40, *Church and Ministry,* ed. Conrad Bergendoff (Philadelphia: Fortress Press, 1958), pp. 90–91.

10. Gordon Rupp, "Patterns of Salvation in the First Age of the Reformation," *Archiv für Reformationsgeschichte* 57 (Heftland 2, 1966): 60; George Yule, "Continental Patterns and the Reformation in England and Scotland," *Scottish Journal of Theology* 18 (1969): 305.

11. Mircea Eliade, *The Sacred and the Profane* (New York: Harcourt, Brace, 1959), pp. 20–113.

12. Mircea Eliade, *The Quest: History and Meaning in Religion* (Chicago: University of Chicago Press, 1969), p. 101.

13. Mircea Eliade, *The Myth of the Eternal Return* (Princeton: Princeton University Press, 1954), p. 129.

14. Cited in John C. Olin, ed., *Christian Humanism and the Reformation: Desiderius Erasmus* (New York: Harper and Row, 1965), pp. 104–5.

15. Abraham Friesen, "The Impulse toward Restitutionist Thought in Christian Humanism," *Journal of the American Academy of Religion* 44 (1976): 40–45.

16. William Clebsch, "John Colet and Reformation," *Anglican Theological Review* 37 (1955): 172.

17. John Colet, *An Exposition of St. Paul's Epistle to the Romans,* cited in Clebsch, "Colet and Reformation," p. 175.

18. *The Whole Works of W. Tyndale, John Frith, and Doct. Barnes* (London, 1573), p. 10.

19. "W. T. to the Reader," in *The New Testament* (Antwerp, 1534), p. 4. Michael McGiffert, "William Tyndale's Conception of the Covenant," *Journal of Ecclesiastical History* 32 (1981): 167–84.

20. Heinrich Bullinger, "Zuschrift an Frau Anna Roist," cited in Bernard Verkamp, "The Zwinglians and Adiaphorism," *Church History* 42 (1973): 495; *Heinrich Bullingers Reformationsgeschichte,* 1 (Frauenfeld, 1838–40), cited in Charles Garside, *Zwingli and the Arts* (New Haven: Yale University Press, 1966), p. 61.

21. Cited in John Opie, "The Anglicizing of John Hooper," *Archiv für Reformationsgeschichte* 59 (Heft 2, 1968): 155.

22. Martin Bucer, *De Regno Christi,* in Wilhelm Pauck, ed., *Melanchthon and Bucer* (Philadelphia: Westminster Press, 1969), pp. 194, 196, 209–11, 224, 225ff.

23. Dan G. Danner, "The Theology of the Geneva Bible of 1560: A Study in English Protestantism," Ph.D. diss., University of Iowa, 1969, pp. 67–68. See also

Judah J. Newberger, "The Law of the Old Testament in Tudor and Stuart England," Ph.D. diss., New York University, 1976, esp. pp. 127–32.

24. "To our Beloved in the Lord, the Brethren of England, Scotland, Ireland, &c.," in *The Geneva Bible,* pp. iiii.

25. Cited in Richard L. Greaves, "John Knox and the Covenant Tradition," *Journal of Ecclesiastical History* 24 (1973): 24.

26. Richard Vander Molen, "Anglican against Puritan: Ideological Origins during the Marian Exile," *Church History* 42 (1973): 49–56.

27. *The Second Replie of Thomas Cartwright: Agaynst Maister Doctor Whitgiftes second answer touching the Churche Discipline* (1575), p. 81; John K. Luoma, "Who Owns the Fathers? Hooker and Cartwright on the Authority of the Primitive Church," *Sixteenth Century Journal* 8 no. 3 (1977): 48–50. See idem, "The Primitive Church as a Normative Principle in the Theology of the Sixteenth Century: The Anglican-Puritan Debate over Church Polity as Represented by Richard Hooker and Thomas Cartwright," Ph.D. diss., Hartford Seminary Foundation, 1974.

28. Donald McGinn, *The Admonition Controversy* (New Brunswick, N.J.: Rutgers University Press, 1949), pp. 49–63; B. R. White, *The English Separatist Tradition* (Oxford: Oxford University Press, 1971), pp. 38–40. See James Spalding, "Restitution as a Normative Factor for Puritan Dissent," *Journal of the American Academy of Religion* 44 (1976): 47.

29. Leland H. Carlson, ed., *The Writings of Henry Barrow, 1587–1590* (London: Allen and Unwin, 1962), p. 126.

30. Robert Ashton, ed., *The Works of John Robinson, Pastor of the Pilgrim Fathers* (Boston: Jonathon Cape, 1851), 2:43.

31. William Ames, *The Marrow of Sacred Divinity drawne out of the holy scriptures* (London, 1642), p. 150.

32. Williston Walker, ed., *The Creeds and Platforms of Congregationalism* (New York: Charles Scribner's Sons, 1893), p. 203; William Bradford, *Bradford's History of Plymouth Plantation, 1606–1646,* ed. by William T. Davis (New York: Charles Scribner's Sons, 1908), 1:23.

33. Cotton Mather, *Magnalia Christi Americana: or, the Ecclesiastical History of New-England, from Its First Planting in the Year 1620 unto the Year of our Lord, 1698* (London, 1702), 1:26–27. Edward Winslow, *Hypocrisie Unmasked,* cited in Perry Miller, *Orthodoxy in Massachusetts* (New York: Harper and Row, 1970), p. 136.

34. Philip S. Foner, ed., *The Complete Writings of Thomas Paine* (New York: Citadel Press, 1945), 1:273. Henry F. May notes the primordialist dimensions of both the Jeffersonians and other participants in the phase of the Enlightenment that May terms "the Revolutionary Enlightenment": "Since the new order would be a natural order, there was usually some element of primitivism in adherents of the Revolutionary Enlightenment: the enlightened future would reproduce some golden age of simple goodness." *The Enlightenment in America* (New York: Oxford University Press, 1976), p. 153.

35. *Complete Writings of Thomas Paine,* 1:274.

36. Ibid., 1:274–75.

37. Ibid., 1:376.

38. Daniel Boorstin, *The Lost World of Thomas Jefferson* (Boston: Beacon Press, 1960), p. 169.

39. Thomas Jefferson to Thomas Whittemore, June 5, 1822, in Charles T. Cullen, series ed., *The Papers of Thomas Jefferson,* second series (Princeton: Princeton University Press, 1983), vol. 1: *Jefferson's Extracts from the Gospels, "The Philosophy of Jesus" and "The Life and Morals of Jesus,"* ed. Dickinson W. Adams, p. 404; Jefferson to Miles King, September 26, 1814, p. 361; and Jefferson to Benjamin Waterhouse, June 26, 1822, p. 405.

40. Thomas Jefferson, "Original Rough Draught" of the Declaration of Independence, in Julian P. Boyd, ed., *The Papers of Thomas Jefferson* (Princeton: Princeton University Press, 1950), 1:423.

41. Parley P. Pratt, "Declaration of Independence—Constitution of the United States," in *Journal of Discourses* (Liverpool and London, 1854), 1:139.

42. Sidney E. Mead, *The Nation with the Soul of a Church* (New York: Harper and Row, 1975), p. 60.

43. John Wise, *A Vindication of the Government of New England Churches* (Boston, 1717), pp. 10, 30. See Catherine Albanese, *Sons of the Fathers: Civil Religion in the American Revolution* (Philadelphia: Temple University Press, 1976), pp. 35–36.

44. Thomas Jefferson to Jared Sparks, November 4, 1820; Jefferson to Timothy Pickering, February 27, 1821; and Jefferson to Benjamin Waterhouse, July 19, 1822, in Adams, *Jefferson's Extracts from the Gospels,* pp. 401, 403, 407.

45. Boorstin, *Lost World of Thomas Jefferson,* p. 245.

46. Abraham Keteltas, "God Arising and Pleading His People's Cause, a sermon preached October 5, 1777" (Newburyport, Mass., 1777), pp. 29–32.

47. Jonathan Edwards, "Some Thoughts concerning the Present Revival of Religion in New England," in *The Works of President Edwards* (New York: S. Converse, 1830), 4:128–29.

48. Cf. Nathan O. Hatch, "The Origins of Civil Millennialism in America: New England Clergymen, War with France, and the Revolution," *William and Mary Quarterly* 31 (1974): 407–30.

49. Timothy Dwight, "A Valedictory Address . . . at Yale College, July 25, 1776" (New Haven, 1776), pp. 5–21.

50. Robert N. Bellah, "Civil Religion in America," *Daedalus* 96 (Winter 1967): 1–21; and idem, *The Broken Covenant: American Civil Religion in Time of Trial* (New York: Seabury, 1975).

51. *New York Morning News,* December 27, 1845, cited in Conrad Cherry, ed., *God's New Israel: Religious Interpretations of American Destiny* (Englewood Cliffs, N.J.: Prentice-Hall, 1971), p. 128.

52. Ibid., p. 129.

53. Reinhold Niebuhr, *The Irony of American History* (New York: Charles Scribner's Sons, 1954), p. 25.

54. Mead, *Nation with the Soul of a Church,* esp. pp. 48–77; and idem, *The Old Religion in the Brave New World* (Berkeley: University of California Press, 1977), pp. 1–57.

55. Allan Bloom, *The Closing of the American Mind: How Higher Education Has Failed Democracy and Impoverished the Souls of Today's Students* (New York: Simon and Schuster, 1987).

Chapter 2. The Constraints of "True Antiquity"

1. John Cotton, *Gods Promise to his Plantation* (London, 1630), pp. 11, 6, 19.

2. Theodore Dwight Bozeman, *To Live Ancient Lives: The Primitivist Dimension of Puritanism* (Chapel Hill: Published for the Institute of Early American History and Culture by the University of North Carolina Press, 1988), p. 140.

3. Geoffrey W. Bromiley, *Thomas Cranmer, Theologian* (London: Lutterworth Press, 1956), p. 22; John Jewel, *An Apology of the Church of England,* ed. J. E. Booty (Ithaca, N.Y.: Cornell University Press, 1963), p. 135.

4. Leonard J. Trinterud, ed., *Elizabethan Puritanism* (New York: Oxford University Press, 1971), pp. 3–4, 235.

5. "An Admonition to Parliament," in W. H. Frere and C. E. Douglas, *Puritan Manifestoes* (London: S.P.C.K., 1907), pp. 15, 19, 8. For a discussion of the restoration theme in "Admonition," see James C. Spalding, "Restitution as a Normative Factor for Puritan Dissent," *Journal of the American Academy of Religion* 44 (March 1976): 47–63.

6. Bozeman, *To Live Ancient Lives,* pp. 14, 49–50, 76, 345. Those who have interpreted Puritanism primarily as a progressive force in American civilization include Loren Baritz, *City on a Hill: A History of Ideas and Myths in America* (New York: John Wiley and Sons, 1964); Clifford K. Shipton, "Puritanism and Modern Democracy," *New England Historical and Genealogical Register* 101 (July 1947): 181–98; William G. McLoughlin, *Revivals, Awakenings, and Reform: An Essay on Religion and Social Change in America, 1607–1977* (Chicago: University of Chicago Press, 1979), pp. 25–39; and Sacvan Bercovitch, *The American Jeremiad* (Madison: University of Wisconsin Press, 1978).

7. Bozeman, *To Live Ancient Lives,* p. 9. For the origins and development of Puritan covenantal thought, see Leonard J. Trinterud, "The Origins of Puritanism," *Church History* 20 (March 1951): 37–57; William K. B. Stoever, *"A Faire and Easie Way to Heaven": Antinomianism and Covenantal Thought in Early Massachusetts* (Middletown, Conn.: Wesleyan University Press, 1978), pp. 81–118; and David A. Weir, *"Foedus Naturale:* The Origins of Federal Theology in Sixteenth-Century Reformation Thought," Ph.D. diss., University of Saint Andrews, 1984.

8. Bozeman, *To Live Ancient Lives,* p. 9. On the nature of Puritan piety see Charles E. Hambrick-Stowe, *The Practice of Piety: Puritan Devotional Disciplines in Seventeenth-Century New England* (Chapel Hill: Published for the Institute of Early American History and Culture by the University of North Carolina Press, 1982).

9. Bozeman, *To Live Ancient Lives,* p. 11.

10. Ibid., pp. 14, 50; Thomas Cartwright, *A Replye to An answere made of m. Doctor Whitgifte Agaynste the Admonition to the Parliament by T.C.* (1573), p. 79.

11. Bozeman, *To Live Ancient Lives,* pp. 53, 54.

12. Ibid., pp. 56–65. See also John K. Luoma, "Restitution or Reformation?

Cartwright and Hooker on the Elizabethan Church," *Historical Magazine of the Protestant Episcopal Church,* 46 (March 1977): 85–106; and idem, "Who owns the Fathers? Hooker and Cartwright on the Authority of the Primitive Church," *Sixteenth Century Journal* 8, no. 3 (1977): 45–60.

13. Bozeman, *To Live Ancient Lives,* pp. 72, 286.

14. Perry Miller, "Declension in a Bible Commonwealth," in *Nature's Nation* (Cambridge: Harvard University Press, 1967), pp. 14–49; idem, *Errand into the Wilderness* (Cambridge: Harvard University Press, 1956), pp. 1–15; Sacvan Bercovitch, "New England's Errand Reappraised," in John Higham and Paul Conkin, eds., *New Directions in American Intellectual History* (Baltimore: Johns Hopkins University Press, 1979), pp. 85–104. Bozeman surveys seventy-five discussions of the "errand" published since 1952, all of which assume an explicit world-redemptive mission as the conscious aim of the early colonists. *To Live Ancient Lives,* pp. 84–86.

15. See Larzer Ziff, *Puritanism in America: New Culture in a New World* (New York: Viking Press, 1973), pp. 35–45; Richard Waterhouse, "Reluctant Emigrants: The English Background of the First Generation of the New England Clergy," *Historical Magazine of the Protestant Episcopal Church* 44 (December 1975): 479–85; Timothy H. Breen, *Puritans and Adventurers: Change and Persistence in Early America* (New York: Oxford University Press, 1980), p. 17; Avihu Zakai, "Exile and Kingdom: Reformation, Separation, and the Millennial Quest in the Formation of Massachusetts and its Relationship with England, 1628–1660," Ph.D. diss., Johns Hopkins University, 1983, pp. 384–87; and David Grayson Allen, *In English Ways: The Movement of Societies and the Transferal of English Local Law and Custom to Massachusetts Bay in the Seventeenth Century* (Chapel Hill: Published for the Institute of Early American History and Culture by the University of North Carolina Press, 1981), pp. 89, 164–67, 171–73, 190–94.

16. Bozeman, *To Live Ancient Lives,* p. 92; idem, "The Puritans' 'Errand into the Wilderness' Reconsidered," *New England Quarterly* 59 (June 1986): 231–51.

17. Bozeman, *To Live Ancient Lives,* pp. 96–114. The key Puritan works include "General Observations for the Plantation of New England" and "General Conclusions and Particular Considerations," in *Winthrop Papers,* ed. Allyn Bailey Forbes and Steward Mitchell (Boston: Massachusetts Historical Society, 1929–47), 2:111–27; Richard Mather, "Arguments Tending to Prove the Removing from Old England to New to be not only lawful, but also necessary" (1635), in Increase Mather, *The Life and Death of Richard Mather* (Cambridge, 1670), pp. 12–19; Edward Winslow, *Good Newes from New-England* (London, 1624); and "John Cotton's Reasons for his Removal to New England" (1634), in Alexander Young, *Chronicles of the First Planters of the Colony of Massachusetts Bay, from 1623 to 1636* (Boston: Little and Brown, 1846), pp. 438–44.

18. John Allin and Thomas Shepard, *A Defence of the Answer made unto the Nine Questions or Positions sent from New-England* (London, 1648), pp. 4, 3, cited by Bozeman, *To Live Ancient Lives,* p. 108.

19. John Cotton, *The Way of the Churches of Christ in New-England* (London, 1645), p. 6; John Norton, *The Heart of New-England Rent at the Blasphemies of the*

Present Generation (London, 1660), p. 82; *New Englands First Fruits* (London, 1643), reprinted in Samuel Eliot Morison, *The Founding of Harvard College* (Cambridge: Harvard University Press, 1935), p. 443. See John Higginson, *The Cause of God and His People in New-England* (Cambridge, 1663), p. 13.

20. For biographical information on Cotton see the following: John Norton, *Abel Being Dead Yet Speaketh* (London, 1658); Cotton Mather, "Cottonus Redivivus: or, the Life of Mr. John Cotton," in *Magnalia Christi Americana: or, the Ecclesiastical History of New-England, from its First Planting in the Year 1620, unto the Year of our Lord, 1698* (London, 1702), 3:14–32; Samuel Whiting, "Concerning the Life of the Famous Mr. Cotton, Teacher to the Church at Boston, in New-England," in Young, *Chronicles,* pp. 419–31; Larzer Ziff, *The Career of John Cotton: Puritanism and the American Experience* (Princeton: Princeton University Press, 1962); Judith B. Welles, "John Cotton, 1584–1652, Churchman and Theologian," Ph.D. diss., University of Edinburgh, 1948; and Everett Emerson, *John Cotton* (New York: Twayne Publishers, 1965).

21: John Cotton, *Some Treasure Fetched out of Rubbish* (London, 1660), pp. 17, 20; G. B. Blenkin, "Boston, England, and John Cotton in 1621," *Historical and Genealogical Register* 110 (April–June 1874): 137–39.

22. "John Cotton's Reasons for his Removal," p. 441; Helen M. Alpert, "Robert Keayne: Notes of Sermons by John Cotton and Proceedings of the First Church of Boston from 23 November, 1639, to 1 June, 1640," Ph.D. diss., Tufts University, 1974, p. 195.

23. David D. Hall, ed., "John Cotton's Letter to Samuel Skelton," *William and Mary Quarterly* 22 (1965): 480–85; and John Cotton, *A Sermon Preached . . . at Salem, 1636; to which is Prefixed, a Retraction of his former Opinion concerning Baptism* (Boston, 1713).

24. John Winthrop, *Winthrop's Journal, "History of New England, 1630–1649,"* ed. James K. Hosmer (New York: Charles Scribner's Sons, 1908), 1:116.

25. See John Cotton, *Christ the Fountaine of Life* (London, 1651); idem, *A Treatise of the Covenant of Grace* (London, 1659); idem, *The Covenant of God's Free Grace* (London, 1645); and idem, *The Way of Life* (London, 1641). For analysis, see Stoever, *"A Faire and Easie Way to Heaven,"* pp. 34–57.

26. Thomas Shepard, *New Englands Lamentations for Old Englands Present Errours and Division* (London, 1645), p. 4.

27. For the key documents relating to the controversy, see David D. Hall, ed., *The Antinomian Controversy, 1636–1638: A Documentary History* (Middletown, Conn.: Wesleyan University Press, 1968). For Cotton's account, see *The Way of Congregational Churches Cleared* (London, 1648), in *John Cotton on the Churches of New England,* ed. Larzer Ziff (Cambridge: Harvard University Press, 1968), pp. 223–57. See also Norman Pettit, "Cotton's Dilemma: Another Look at the Antinomian Controversy," *Publications of the Colonial Society of Massachusetts* 59 (1982): 393–413; Philip F. Gura, *A Glimpse of Sion's Glory: Puritan Radicalism in New England, 1620–1660* (Middletown, Conn.: Wesleyan University Press, 1984), pp. 168–76, 237–75; and Ronald D. Cohen, "Church and State in Seventeenth-Century Massachusetts: Another Look at the Antinomian Controversy," *Journal of Church and State* 12 (Autumn 1970): 475–94.

28. Recent researchers have argued that Cotton's role in the Antinomian Controversy was not as pivotal as often supposed, that the crisis occurred more as a reflex of the volatile English Puritan movement in the 1630s than as a result of Cotton's doctrine. See Stephen Foster, "New England and the Challenge of Heresy, 1630–1660: The Puritan Crisis in Transatlantic Perspective," *William and Mary Quarterly,* 3d series, 38 (1981): 624–31, 643.

29. Cited by Darret Rutman, *American Puritanism: Faith and Practice* (Philadelphia: Lippincott, 1970), p. 107.

30. John Cotton, *A Practical Commentary upon the First Epistle General of John* (London, 1656), pp. 232, 77–79, 189, cited by Bozeman, *To Live Ancient Lives,* pp. 10–11.

31. For Perry Miller's classic study of the origins of congregational theory, see *Orthodoxy in Massachusetts, 1630–1650* (Cambridge: Harvard University Press, 1933), pp. 73–101. Cotton traced the pedigree of New England Congregationalism in *Way of Congregational Churches Cleared,* pp. 188–95. For primitivist themes see Ames, *Marrow of Sacred Divinity,* pp. 179–81; and Henry Jacob, *The Divine Beginning of Christ's Church* (Leyden, 1610).

32. The others were: "Questions and Answers upon Church Government," in *A Treatise* (Boston, 1713); *A Sermon Preached . . . at Salem, 1636; A Copy of a Letter of Mr. Cotton of Boston* (London, 1641); *The True Constitution of a Particular Visible Church, proved by Scripture* (London, 1642); and *The Keys of the Kingdom of Heaven* (London, 1644).

33. Cotton, *Way of the Churches of Christ,* pp. 6–10, 54–62.

34. Cotton, *True Constitution,* pp. 9, 5–6. Cf. Cotton, *Way of Congregational Churches Cleared,* p. 197; and idem, *A Modest and Cleare Answer to Mr. Balls Discourse of Set Formes of Prayer* (London, 1642).

35. John Cotton, *A Brief Exposition of the Whole Book of Canticles* (London, 1655), p. 92; idem, *Way of Congregational Churches Cleared,* p. 293.

36. John Cotton, "A short discourse of Mr. John Cotton touchinge the time when the Lordes day beginneth whether at the Eveninge or in the mourninge," in Winton U. Solberg, "John Cotton's Treatise on the Duration of the Lord's Day," *Publications of the Colonial Society of Massachusetts* 59 (1982): 510, 513, 518, 520, 514. See also idem, *Redeem the Time: The Puritan Sabbath in Early America* (Cambridge: Harvard University Press, 1977), p. 111.

37. *The Whole Booke of Psalmes Faithfully Translated into English Metre* (Cambridge, Mass., 1640), preface. See also Bozeman, *To Live Ancient Lives,* pp. 139–50.

38. John Cotton, *The Singing of Psalms a Gospel Ordinance* (London, 1650), pp. 19, 32, 29–30, 58, 5–6, 64–67. Cotton's position on instrumental music is reflected in Cotton Mather's report of disputed issues in the Cambridge Platform. "*Instrumental Musick* in the Worship of God," a number of ministers had concluded, "is but a very late Invention and Corruption in the church of the *New Testament.*" *Magnalia Christi Americana,* 5:55–56.

39. Cotton, *Way of Congregational Churches Cleared,* pp. 293–94, 301–2, 296. Cf. Allin and Shepard, *Defense,* pp. 31–32.

40. Thomas Shepard, *Works,* ed. John Albro (1853; reprint, New York: AMS

Press, 1967), 3:346; John Cotton, "Copy of a Letter from Mr. Cotton to Lord Say and Seal in the Year 1636," in Edmund S. Morgan, ed., *Puritan Political Ideas, 1558–1794* (New York: Bobbs-Merrill, 1965), p. 168.

41. For a summary of this doctrine, see Winthrop S. Hudson, "Fast Days and Civil Religion," in *Theology in Sixteenth and Seventeenth Century England* (Los Angeles: William Andrews Clark Memorial Library, 1971), pp. 3–24.

42. Cartwright, *Replye to An Answere,* preface.

43. Quoted in Roger Williams, *The Bloudy Tenent of Persecution, for Cause of Conscience, Discussed, in a Conference betweene Truth and Peace,* in *The Complete Writings of Roger Williams* (reprint, New York: Russell and Russell, 1963), 3:261. The Cambridge Platform of 1648 set out a similar view: magistrates must command or forbid things "respecting the outward man, which are clearly commanded or forbidden in the word." Williston Walker, ed., *The Creeds and Platforms of Congregationalism* (New York: Charles Scribner's Sons, 1893), pp. 190–91.

44. Winthrop, *Journal,* 1:219; Nathaniel B. Shurtleff, ed., *Records of the Governor and Company of the Massachusetts Bay in New England* (Boston: W. White, 1853–54), 1:197. Cotton was troubled by the 1637 law and for a time considered migrating to the Connecticut Valley with Thomas Hooker. Henry Vane, a former governor of the colony, also opposed the law. He debated Winthrop on the matter, arguing that the statute restricted the right of good Englishmen and thus violated the colony's royal charter. See Thomas Hutchinson, *The Hutchinson Papers* (Albany, N.Y.: Publications of the Prince Society, 1865), 1:79–113.

45. John Cotton, *The Bloudy Tenent, Washed, and made White in the Bloude of the Lamb* (London, 1647), pp. 41–42.

46. Norton, *Abel being Dead yet Speaketh,* p. 39; Perry Miller, "Thomas Hooker and the Democracy of Early Connecticut," *New England Quarterly* 4 (1931): 676.

47. John Cotton, *A Discourse about Civil Government in a New Plantation Whose Design is Religion* (Cambridge, Mass., 1663), pp. 14ff.; idem, *An Exposition upon the Thirteenth Chapter of the Revelation* (London, 1655), in Morgan, *Puritan Political Ideas,* pp. 175–76. Cf. also Cotton, *Keys of the Kingdom of Heaven,* p. 97; and idem, "Copy of a Letter to Lord Say and Seal," pp. 167–73.

48. *Records of Massachusetts Bay,* 1:174–75; Winthrop, *Journal,* 1:196.

49. For the complexities of Puritan covenantal theory, see Michael McGiffert, "Grace and Works: The Rise and Division of Covenant Divinity in Elizabethan Puritanism," *Harvard Theological Review* 75 (October 1982): 463–502.

50. John Cotton, *The Grounds and Ends of the Baptisme of the Children of the Faithful* (London, 1647), p. 159.

51. Paul D. L. Avis, "Moses and the Magistrates: A Study in the Rise of Protestant Legalism," *Journal of Ecclesiastical History* 26 (1975): 149–72; Bozeman, *To Live Ancient Lives,* pp. 160–70; Samuel Ward, *Jethro's Justice of Peace* (London, 1627), pp. 3, 4, 63 (with a dedicatory epistle by Nathaniel Ward).

52. John Cotton, *An Abstract, or the Lawes of New England, as they are now established* (London, 1641), pp. 10–13; Shepard, *Works,* 3:53; Worthington C. Ford, "Cotton's 'Moses His Judicials,'" *Proceedings of the Massachusetts Histor-*

ical Society, 2d series, 16 (1902): 284. See also Isabel M. Calder, "John Cotton's 'Moses His Judicials,' " *Publications of the Colonial Society of Massachusetts* 28 (1930–33): 86–94.

53. For the clerical discussion, see the text of "How Far Moses' Judicials Bind Massachusetts," in Ford, "Cotton's 'Moses His Judicials.' " For the rejection and later influence of the proposal, see George L. Haskins, *Law and Authority in Early Massachusetts: A Study in Tradition and Design* (New York: Macmillan, 1960), pp. 120ff.; and Bozeman, *To Live Ancient Lives,* pp. 174–81.

54. *Records of Massachusetts Bay,* 1:211.

55. John Cotton, *A Reply to Mr. Williams His Examination,* in *Complete Writings of Roger Williams,* 2:22; Peter Bulkeley, *The Gospel-Covenant; or the Covenant of Grace Opened* (London, 1646), p. 104.

56. See Gura, *Glimpse of Sion's Glory,* pp. 194–95, 280–82; and Robert E. Wall, Jr., *Massachusetts Bay: The Crucial Decade, 1640–1650* (New Haven: Yale University Press, 1972), pp. 121–47. Samuel Gorton recounted the trial in *Simplicities Defense against Seven-Headed Policy* (London, 1646), pp. 112–35.

57. Gorton, *Simplicities Defense;* Edward Winslow, *Hypocrisie Unmasked: By a true Relation of the Proceedings of the Governour and Company of Massachusetts against Samuel Gorton* (London, 1646).

58. Raymond P. Stearns, *Hugh Peter: The Strenuous Puritan, 1598–1660* (Urbana: University of Illinois Press, 1954), p. 183; Winthrop, *Journal,* 2:177; *Winthrop Papers,* 5:102. For the English developments, see William Haller, *Liberty and Reformation in the Puritan Revolution* (New York: Columbia University Press, 1967), pp. 143–88.

59. John Cotton, *The Controversie Concerning Liberty of Conscience in Matters of Religion* (London, 1646), pp. 7–14. Roger Williams included the portion of the Baptist tract and Cotton's answer to it in the opening section of *The Bloudy Tenent of Persecution.* For the complete tract, see *A Most Humble Supplication of Many of the King's Majesty's Loyal Subjects* (1620), in Edward Bean Underhill, ed., *Tracts on Liberty of Conscience and Persecution, 1614–1661* (London: Hansard Knollys Society, 1846), pp. 189–231.

60. Williams, *Bloudy Tenent,* pp. 41–53. Cf. also Cotton, *Bloudy Tenent, Washed,* p. 29.

61. For a full account of this incident, with focus on Obadiah Holmes, see Edwin S. Gaustad, ed., *Baptist Piety: The Last Will and Testimony of Obadiah Holmes* (Grand Rapids, Mich.: Eerdmans, 1978), pp. 22–41.

62. John Clarke, *Ill Newes from New-England: Or A Narrative of New-Englands Persecution. Wherein is Declared That while old England is becoming new, New-England is become Old* (London, 1652).

63. Thomas Cobbett, *The Civil Magistrates Power in matters of Religion Modestly Debated* (London, 1653); appendix entitled "A Brief Answer to a Scandalous Pamphlet called, Ill news from New-England, written by John Clarke of Rhode-Island, Physition." See also Gura, *Glimpse of Sion's Glory,* pp. 204–11, and Gaustad, *Baptist Piety,* pp. 36–41.

64. "Copy of a Letter from Sir Richard Saltonstall to Mr. Cotton and Mr.

Wilson," in Thomas Hutchinson, *A Collection of Original Papers Relative to the History of the Colony of Massachusetts Bay* (Boston, 1769), pp. 401–2.

65. "Copy of Mr. Cottons Answer to a Letter from Sir Richard Saltonstall," in Hutchinson, *Original Papers,* p. 406.

66. John Norton, *The Heart of New-England Rent at the Blasphemies of the Present Generation* (London, 1660), pp. 79, 84; Gura, *Glimpse of Sion's Glory,* pp. 212–13.

67. John Cotton, *A Letter of Mr. John Cottons, Teacher of the Church in Boston, in New England, to Mr. Williams a Preacher there,* in *The Complete Writings of Roger Williams* (New York: Russell and Russell, 1963), p. 28; idem, *The Churches Resurrection, or the Opening of the Fift and sixt verses of the 20th Chap. of the Revelation* (London, 1642), pp. 20, 21.

68. Richard Mather, *Church-Government and Church-Covenant Discussed,* p. 64, cited by David Kobrin, "The Expansion of the Visible Church in New England, 1629–1650," *Church History* 36 (June 1967): 207; John Higginson, *The Cause of God and His People in New-England* (Cambridge, Mass., 1663), p. 13.

69. See Timothy H. Breen and Stephen Foster, "The Puritans' Greatest Achievement: A Study of Social Cohesion in Seventeenth-Century Massachusetts," *Journal of American History* 60 (1973): 5–22.

70. See Henry W. Bowden, *American Indians and Christian Missions: Studies in Cultural Conflict,* Chicago History of American Religion (Chicago: University of Chicago Press, 1981), pp. 111–33; Charles M. Segal and David C. Stineback, *Puritans, Indians, and Manifest Destiny* (New York: G. P. Putnam's Sons, 1977), pp. 25–39 and *passim;* Neal Salisbury, "Conquest of the 'Savage': Puritans, Puritan Missionaries, and Indians, 1620–1680," Ph.D. diss., University of California, Los Angeles, 1972; and Alden T. Vaughn, *New England Frontier: Puritans and Indians, 1620–1675,* rev. ed. (New York: Norton, 1979), pp. v–xlv.

Chapter 3. The Quest for "Soul Liberty"

1. For the first exchange, see *A Letter of Mr. John Cottons, Teacher of the Church in Boston, in New-England, to Mr. Williams a Preacher there* (London, 1643), and *Mr. Cottons Letter Lately Printed, Examined and Answered: By Roger Williams of Providence* (London, 1644). Both works are reprinted in *The Complete Writings of Roger Williams* (Providence: Narragansett Club Publications; reprint, New York: Russell and Russell, 1963), 1:295–396. All of the references to Williams's published works will be to this edition of the *Complete Writings.*

2. See Elisabeth Hirsch, "John Cotton and Roger Williams," *Church History* 10 (1941): 38–51; Conrad Wright, "John Cotton Washed and Made White," in E. Forrester Church and Timothy George, eds., *Continuity and Discontinuity in Church History* (Leiden: E. J. Brill, 1979), pp. 338–50. W. Clark Gilpin gives some attention to the primitivist dimension of the exchange in *The Millenarian Piety of Roger Williams* (Chicago: University of Chicago Press, 1979), pp. 85–89 and *passim.*

3. Philip Gura, *A Glimpse of Sion's Glory: Puritan Radicalism in New En-*

gland, 1620–1660 (Middletown, Conn.: Wesleyan University Press, 1984), pp. 173–80; Gilpin, *Roger Williams,* pp. 167–73.

4. For full biographical treatment of Williams, see Samuel Brockunier, *The Irrepressible Democrat, Roger Williams* (New York: Ronald Press, 1940), a book flawed in its interpretation but solid in its facts; and Ola Winslow, *Master Roger Williams* (New York: Macmillan, 1957).

5. *Letters of Roger Williams,* in *Complete Writings,* 6:356; John Winthrop, *Winthrop's Journal: "History of New England," 1630–1649,* ed. James K. Hosmer (New York: Charles Scribner's Sons, 1908), 1:61–62.

6. See Hugh D. Spurgin, "Roger Williams and the Separatist Tradition: English Origins of His Religious and Political Thought," Ph.D. diss., Columbia University, 1985. On Separatist ecclesiology, see Champlin Burrage, *The Early English Dissenters in the Light of Recent Research (1550–1641)* (Cambridge: Cambridge University Press, 1912), 1:94–208; Edmund S. Morgan, *Visible Saints: The History of a Puritan Idea* (New York: New York University Press, 1963), pp. 20–63; and B. R. White, *The English Separatist Tradition: From the Marian Martyrs to the Pilgrim Fathers* (London: Oxford University Press, 1971).

7. For Winthrop's report see his *Journal,* 1:116–17, and his letter to John Endecott, printed in the *Proceedings of the Massachusetts Historical Society* (1871–73): 343–45; Roger Williams, *Bloody Tenent Yet More Bloody,* in *Complete Writings,* 4:461.

8. Winthrop, *Journal,* 1:154–55; John Cotton, *A Reply to Mr. Williams, His Examination,* in *Complete Writings of Roger Williams,* 2:76.

9. Nathaniel B. Shurtleff, ed., *Records of the Governor and Company of the Massachusetts Bay in New England, 1628–1692* (Boston: W. White, 1853–54), 1:160–61. For the debate between Williams and Cotton regarding the causes of the banishment, see Cotton, *Reply to Mr. Williams,* pp. 44–50, and Williams, *Cottons Letter Examined,* pp. 319–20. See also Henry M. Dexter, *As to Roger Williams, and His "Banishment" from the Massachusetts Plantation* (Boston: Congregational Publishing Society, 1876), pp. 58–80; and Brockunier, *Irrepressible Democrat,* pp. 66–81.

10. Winthrop, *Journal,* 1:168–69.

11. *Winthrop Papers,* ed. Allyn Bailey Forbes and Stewart Mitchell (Boston: Massachusetts Historical Society, 1929–47), 3:316–17; Williams, *Cottons Letter, Examined,* pp. 335, 384; *Letters of Roger Williams,* pp. 8, 10–11; Winthrop, *Journal,* 1:309.

12. John Smyth, "The Differences of the Churches of the Separation," in *The Works of John Smyth,* ed. W. T. Whitley (Cambridge: Cambridge University Press, 1915), 1:271.

13. Winthrop, *Journal,* 1:297, 309.

14. Ibid., 1:309; Roger Williams, *George Fox Digg'd out of his Burrowes,* in *Complete Writings of Roger Williams,* 5:102–3.

15. Roger Williams, *The Bloudy Tenent of Persecution, for cause of Conscience,* in *Complete Writings of Roger Williams,* 3:64; idem, *The Hireling Ministry None of Christs,* in *Complete Writings of Roger Williams,* 7:158.

16. *Letters of Roger Williams,* pp. 11–12.

17. Williams, *Bloudy Tenent,* p. 390, citing the Massachusetts ministers in "A Modell of Church and Civil Power."

18. Ibid., p. 369.

19. Perry Miller, in his influential work on Williams, argued that what made Williams unique among Puritans and got him into trouble was use of a typological method that the orthodox Puritans rejected as dangerous. This, Miller said, was "the open secret of [Williams's] radicalism": "Roger Williams was a 'typologist,' John Cotton and his colleagues were 'federalists.'" See Perry Miller, "Roger Williams: An Essay in Interpretation," in *Complete Writings of Roger Williams,* 7:5–25; and idem, *Roger Williams: His Contribution to the American Tradition* (Indianapolis: Bobbs-Merrill, 1953), pp. 33–38, 240. Recent studies, however, have proved Miller wrong; they have shown that the Puritans used typology widely in the attempt to establish the continuity of salvation history from the Old Testament to the New and down to their own time. See Sacvan Bercovitch, "Typology in Puritan New England: The Williams-Cotton Controversy Reassessed," *American Quarterly* 19 (Summer 1967): 166–91; John C. Crowell, "Perry Miller and Typology," *Andover Newton Quarterly* 17 (January 1977): 227–33; and Edmund S. Morgan, "Miller's Williams," *New England Quarterly* 38 (1965): 513–23.

20. Williams, *Bloody Tenent Yet More Bloody,* pp. 73, 43.

21. Ibid., pp. 450, 154.

22. John Cotton, *The Bloody Tenent, Washed, and Made White in the Blood of the Lamb* (London, 1647), pp. 68, 126, 180.

23. Williams, *Bloody Tenent Yet More Bloody,* p. 212.

24. Roger Williams, *Christenings Make Not Christians,* in *Complete Writings of Roger Williams,* 7:39; idem, *Bloudy Tenent,* p. 334; idem, *Bloody Tenent Yet More Bloody,* p. 241.

25. Williams, *Bloudy Tenent,* p. 200; idem, *Queries of Highest Consideration,* in *Complete Writings of Roger Williams,* 2:264.

26. Williams, *Bloudy Tenent,* pp. 324, 329; idem, *Bloody Tenent Yet More Bloody,* p. 447, cf. pp. 447–52.

27. Williams, *Cottons Letter Examined,* p. 330.

28. See John Foxe, *The Acts and Monuments of John Foxe,* ed. Josiah Pratt (London: Religious Tract Society, 1853–70), 7:49. These generalizations about Foxe are dependent on Richard Bauckham, *Tudor Apocalypse: Sixteenth Century Apocalypticism, Millenarianism, and the English Reformation* (Appleford, England: Sutton Courtenay Press, 1978), pp. 61–64, 132–33.

29. Williams, *Bloody Tenent Yet More Bloody,* pp. 79–80.

30. Ibid., pp. 403, 406, 408–9.

31. Ibid., pp. 243, 291, 74–75, 381, 404.

32. Williams, *Cottons Letter Examined,* pp. 33–34.

33. Williams, *Bloudy Tenent,* p. 127.

34. These tracts have been reprinted in Edward B. Underhill, ed., *Tracts on Liberty of Conscience and Persecution, 1614–1661* (London: Hansard Knollys Society, 1846). See also H. Leon McBeth, *English Baptist Literature on Religious Liberty to 1689* (New York: Arno Press, 1980), pp. 3–62. Aside from these works, most extended defenses of religious toleration and complete separation of

church and state before 1620 were found in the continental humanist traditions maintained by the followers of men such as Faustus Socinus and Sebastian Castellio.

35. Williams, *Bloody Tenent Yet More Bloody,* pp. 156, 158–59, 165.

36. Ibid., p. 446.

37. Williams, *Bloudy Tenent,* pp. 119–20.

38. Ibid., pp. 239–41.

39. "A Modell of Church and Civil Power," quoted in Williams, *Bloudy Tenent,* p. 247.

40. Williams, *Bloudy Tenent,* pp. 382, 388.

41. Ibid., p. 251; idem, *Bloody Tenent Yet More Bloody,* p. 170.

42. Williams, *Bloody Tenent Yet More Bloody,* pp. 179–80, 189,238.

43. Williams, *Bloudy Tenent,* pp. 207–8; idem, *Cottons Letter Examined,* p. 55.

44. William L. Sasche, "The Migration of New Englanders to England, 1640–1660," *American Historical Review* 53 (January 1948): 251–78; and Harry S. Stout, "The Morphology of Remigration: New England University Men and Their Return to England, 1640–1660," *Journal of American Studies* 10 (1976): 151–72.

45. Quoted in Carl Bridenbaugh, *Fat Mutton and Liberty of Conscience: Society in Rhode Island, 1636–1690* (Providence: Brown University Press, 1974), p. 5.

46. George Yule, *Puritans in Politics: The Religious Legislation of the Long Parliament, 1640–1647* (Appleford, England: Sutton Courtenay Press, 1981), pp. 118–22.

47. Ibid., pp. 119, 136–41.

48. Williams, *Bloody Tenent Yet More Bloody,* p. 103.

49. Thomas Goodwin, Philip Nye, Sidrach Simpson, Jeremiah Burroughes, and William Bridge, *An Apologeticall Narration, Humbly Submitted to the Honourable Houses of Parliament* (London, 1644), pp. 2–5.

50. Ibid., pp. 10, 12–14, 24.

51. Ibid., pp. 14, 17, 19.

52. David Walker, "Thomas Goodwin and Church Government," *Journal of Ecclesiastical History* 34 (January 1983): 90.

53. *Reformation of Church-Government in Scotland, Cleered from Some Prejudices* (London, 1644), pp. 5, 11–13, 4.

54. Williams, *Queries of Highest Consideration,* pp. 15, 20.

55. *A Paraenetick or Humble Adresse to the Parliament and Assembly for (Not Loose, but) Christian Libertie* (London, 1644), p. 14.

56. *The Ancient Bounds, or Liberty of Conscience* (London, 1645), pp. 27–28.

57. Williams, *Queries of Highest Consideration,* p. 23.

58. Williams, *Bloudy Tenent,* pp. 42–43, 68–70, 89.

59. Williams, *Queries of Highest Consideration,* pp. 17–18.

60. Ibid., p. 26.

61. lbid., pp. 27–29.

62. Ibid., p. 29.

63. Ibid., pp. 62–63; idem, *Cottons Letter Examined,* pp. 96–97, 102; idem, *Hireling Ministry,* pp. 158, 160–161, 167; idem, *Bloudy Tenent,* p. 63.

64. Williams, *Cottons Letter Examined,* pp. 62–63, 69; idem, *Hireling Ministry,* p. 166.

65. Williams, *Bloudy Tenent,* pp. 180, 186, 363; idem, *Bloody Tenent Yet More Bloody,* pp. 351–53.

66. Williams, *Cottons Letter Examined,* pp. 37, 41, 54, 42.

67. Williams, *Bloody Tenent Yet More Bloody,* p. 41; *Letters of Roger Williams,* pp. 8–9; cf. also *Winthrop Papers,* 3:315–36.

68. Williams's phrase reflects the distinctive and influential doctrine of the "middle advent" propounded by Thomas Brightman (1562–1607). Brightman believed that Christ had three "comings": the incarnation, the "coming in the brightness of the Gospel," and the "Second coming unto Judgment." By over-looking this doctrine, contemporary Puritan scholars often have misconstrued the nature and role of millennialism in the Puritan movement. See Theodore Dwight Bozeman, *To Live Ancient Lives: The Primitivist Dimension of Puritanism* (Chapel Hill: Published for the Institute of Early American History and Culture by the University of North Carolina Press, 1988), pp. 198–217; for the influence of this schema in early American Puritanism, see pp. 217–36.

69. Thomas Jefferson, "A Bill for Establishing Religious Freedom," in Julian P. Boyd, ed., *The Papers of Thomas Jefferson* (Princeton: Princeton University Press, 1950), 2:546.

Chapter 4. The Ancient Landmarks

1. See William G. McLoughlin, *New England Dissent, 1630–1833: The Baptists and the Separation of Church and State* (Cambridge: Harvard University Press, 1971), 2 vols.; Sidney Mead, *The Lively Experiment: The Shaping of Christianity in America* (New York: Harper and Row, 1963), pp. 16–37.

2. Isaac Backus, *Government and Liberty Described* (Boston, 1778), p. 4; idem, *A Seasonable Plea for Liberty of Conscience* (Boston, 1770), p. 12.

3. Isaac Backus to his wife, March 29, 1789, cited in McLoughlin, *New England Dissent,* 2:724.

4. Mead, *Lively Experiment,* p. 131.

5. James R. Graves, *Old Landmarkism: What Is It?* (Memphis: Graves, Mahaffy and Co., 1880), p. 25.

6. James R. Graves, *The Little Iron Wheel* (Nashville: Southwestern Publishing, 1857), p. 23; idem, *Old Landmarkism,* pp. xi–xii, 29–31; idem, *The Act of Christian Baptism* (Memphis: Baptist Book House, 1881), pp. 55f.

7. James R. Graves, *The Watchman's Reply* (Nashville: Graves and Shankland, 1853), p. 16.

8. John W. Nevin, "The Sect System," *Mercersburg Review* 1 (1849): 499. See also Sidney Mead, "Denominationalism: The Shape of Protestantism in America," in *Lively Experiment,* pp. 108–13; Nathan O. Hatch, "*Sola Scriptura* and *Novus Ordo Seclorum,*" in Nathan Hatch and Mark Noll, eds., *The Bible in America: Essays in Cultural History* (Oxford: Oxford University Press, 1982), pp. 59–78;

and R. W. B. Lewis, *The American Adam* (Chicago: University of Chicago Press, 1955), esp. pp. 1–10.

9. *An Admonition to Parliament* (1572), in W. H. Frere and C. E. Douglas, *Puritan Manifestoes* (London: S.P.C.K., 1907), p. 8; *An Apologeticall Narration, Humbly Submitted to the Honourable Houses of Parliament* (London, 1643), p. 3.

10. John Smyth, "The Differences of the Churches of the Separation," in *The Works of John Smyth,* ed. W. T. Whitley (Cambridge: Cambridge University Press, 1915), 1:271; Thomas Helwys, *A Short Declaration of the Mistery of Iniquity* (1612; reprint, London: Baptist Historical Society, 1935), p. 174. On the early Baptists see Champlin Burrage, *The Early English Dissenters in the Light of Recent Research (1550–1641)* (Cambridge: Cambridge University Press, 1912), 1:221–80; and James Leo Garrett, "Restitution and Dissent among Early English Baptists," Part I, *Baptist History and Heritage* 12 (October 1977): 198–210, and Part II, *Baptist History and Heritage* 13 (April 1978): 11–27.

11. On the "Philadelphia pattern" of Baptist life, see Robert T. Handy, "The Philadelphia Tradition," in Winthrop S. Hudson, ed., *Baptist Concepts of the Church,* (Philadelphia: Judson Press, 1959), pp. 30–52; A.D. Gillette, ed., *Century Minutes of the Philadelphia Baptist Association, 1707–1807* (Philadelphia, 1851); and David Spencer, *The Early Baptists of Philadelphia* (Philadelphia: W. Syckelmoore, 1877).

12. Benjamin Griffith, "Essay on the Power and Duty of an Association of Churches," in Gillette, *Century Minutes of the Philadelphia Baptist Association,* pp. 60–63. On this development, see Winthrop S. Hudson, "The Associational Principle among Baptists," *Foundations* 1 (January 1958): 10–23; and Walter B. Shurden, "The Associational Principle, 1707–1814: Its Rationale," *Foundations* 21 (July–September 1978): 211–24.

13. Morgan Edwards, *The Customs of Primitive Churches; or, A set of propositions relative to the name, materials, constitution, power, officers, ordinances, rites, business, worship, discipline, government, &c. of a church* (Philadelphia: Andrew Steuart, 1768).

14. Edwards, *Customs of Primitive Churches,* pp. 12, 13, 12–44.

15. Ibid., pp. 79–96, 84. In sermons, Edwards referred to the rites of a church "as an essential part of genuine obedience to Christ" (Manuscript Sermons 3:3, 11:4, 30:1, 35:7, in Ambrose Swasey Library, Colgate Rochester Divinity School, Rochester, N.Y.).

16. Edwards, *Customs of Primitive Churches,* pp. 46–47, 102, 105–7, 107–8.

17. For another example see Oliver Hart, *A Gospel Church Portrayed, and her Orderly Service Pointed Out* (Trenton, N.J., 1791). Among the many appeals to "Apostolick precedent" in this work, note the following: the church "subscribes to certain constitutional rules, drawn up by Christ, and engrossed in the archives of sacred truth. By these rules the church is governed, and ought never to deviate therefrom, an hair's breadth" (p. 28).

18. For accounts of this development, see C. C. Goen, *Revivalism and Separatism in New England, 1740–1800* (New Haven: Yale University Press, 1962); Edwin S. Gaustad, *The Great Awakening in New England* (New York: Harper and Brothers, 1957); McLoughlin, *New England Dissent,* 1:329–488; and William L.

Lumpkin, *Baptist Foundations in the South* (Nashville: Broadman Press, 1961).

19. Isaac Backus, *A Fish Caught in His Own Net* (Boston, 1768), p. 113.

20. Isaac Backus, *An Abridgment of the Church History of New England, from 1602–1804* (Boston, 1804), p. 192.

21. L. F. Greene, ed., *The Writings of the Late Elder John Leland* (New York: G. W. Wood, 1845), pp. 424, 114.

22. On the pietism and biblicism of the early Separate Baptists see Edwin S. Gaustad, "The Backus-Leland Tradition," in Hudson, *Baptist Concepts of the Church,* pp. 108–14; McLoughlin, *New England Dissent,* 1:421–39; and Goen, *Revivalism and Separatism,* pp. 208–13.

23. Alvah Hovey, *A Memoir of the Life and Times of the Reverend Isaac Backus* (Boston, 1859), p. 116.

24. Isaac Backus, *A History of New England with Particular Reference to the Denomination of Christians Called Baptists,* 2d ed. (Newton, Mass: Backus Historical Society, 1871) 2:v–vi; cf. idem, *A Fish Caught in His Own Net,* p. 253. See also Barrington R. White, "Isaac Backus and Baptist History," *Baptist History and Heritage* 5 (January 1970): 13–23; and Stanley Grentz, *Isaac Backus: Puritan and Baptist* (Macon, Ga.: Mercer University Press, 1983), pp. 226–32.

25. For detailed histories of Separatist Baptists in the South, see Lumpkin, *Baptist Foundations;* Robert B. Semple, *A History of the Rise and Progress of the Baptists of Virginia* (Philadelphia: American Baptist Publication Society, 1894), pp. 11–113; Paschal, *History of North Carolina Baptists,* 1:224–413; Leah Townsend, *South Carolina Baptists, 1670–1805* (Florence, S.C.: Florence Printing, 1935), pp. 122–271.

26. Morgan Edwards, "Materials toward a History of the Baptists in the Province of North Carolina," *North Carolina Historical Review* 7 (1930): 385; idem, "Tour of Morgan Edwards of Pennsylvania to the American Baptists in North Carolina in 1772–73," in George W. Paschal, *History of North Carolina Baptists* (Raleigh, N.C.: North Carolina Baptist State Convention, 1930), 1:227.

27. James Ireland, *The Life of the Rev. James Ireland* (Winchester, Va.: J. Foster, 1819), pp. 119–20, see p. 131.

28. Lewis P. Little, *Imprisoned Preachers and Religious Liberty in Virginia* (Lynchburg, Va.: J. P. Bell, 1938); Wesley M. Gewehr, *The Great Awakening in Virginia, 1740–1790* (Durham, N.C.: Duke University Press, 1930), pp. 119 and *passim*; David Thomas, *The Virginia Baptist: or, A View and Defense of the Christian Religion as it is Professed by the Baptists of Virginia* (Baltimore, 1774), p. 6; Richard J. Hooker, ed., *The Carolina Backcountry on the Eve of the Revolution* (Chapel Hill: University of North Carolina Press, 1953), pp. 98, 100–104, 113–17; Rhys Isaac, "Evangelical Revolt: The Nature of the Baptists' Challenge to the Traditional Order in Virginia, 1765 to 1775," *William and Mary Quarterly* 31 (July 1974): 351–62.

29. Ireland, *Life,* p. 189.

30. Morgan Edwards, "Materials toward a History of the Baptists in the Province of North Carolina" (1772), p. 16; idem, "Materials towards a History of the Baptists in South Carolina" (1772), pp. 35–36; idem, "Materials towards a History of the Baptists in the Province of Virginia" (1772), p. 56. See also James O.

Renault, "The Development of Separate Baptist Ecclesiology in the South, 1755–1976," Ph.D. diss., Southern Baptist Theological Seminary, 1978, pp. 106–10. For questions and debates about these rites that arose over the years, see George W. Purefoy, *A History of the Sandy Creek Baptist Association, from its Organization in A.D. 1758, to A.D. 1858* (New York: Sheldon, 1859), pp. 79, 84, 87, 90, and *passim.*

31. Semple, *History of the Baptists of Virginia,* p. 81.

32. Thomas, *Virginia Baptist,* p. 38. Whether the issue is baptism by immersion, laying on of hands, church covenants, church officers, or even associations, Thomas asserts that one "precept or example" from the divine record should remove all objection (p. 47). To the charge of novelty he answers that, though the Baptists may appear new, they are in reality as old as the apostles: "all the apostles were Baptists and all the churches they planted were Baptist-Churches" (p. 54). For his appeals to the "primitive Christians," see pp. 5, 6, 16, 19, 25, 26, 36, 38, 42, 47, 52, 62.

33. William Fristoe, *A Concise History of the Ketocton Baptist Association* (Staunton: W. G. Lyford, 1808), p. 21.

34. Gewehr, *Great Awakening in Virginia,* p. 177. See also Robert B. C. Howell, *The Early Baptists of Virginia* (Philadelphia: Bible and Publication Society, n.d.), pp. 89–99; and C. C. Bitting, *Notes on the History of the Strawberry Baptist Association of Virginia, 1776–1876* (Baltimore, 1879), p. 16.

35. Purefoy, *Sandy Creek Baptist Association,* pp. 71–72. For the tensions that sparked the Regulators' War and subsequent migration of many Baptists, see Jeffrey J. Crow, "Liberty Men and Loyalists: Disorder and Disaffection in the North Carolina Back-country," in Ronald Hoffman, Thad W. Tate, and Peter J. Albert, eds., *An Uncivil War: The Southern Backcountry during the American Revolution* (Charlottesville: University Press of Virginia, 1985), pp. 125–78.

36. See J. H. Spencer, *A History of Kentucky Baptists* (Cincinnati, 1886), 1:1–39; William Warren Sweet, *Religion on the American Frontier, 1783–1830,* vol. 1, *The Baptists* (New York: Henry Holt, 1931), pp. 1–57; David Benedict, *General History of the Baptist Denomination in America and Other Parts of the World* (New York: Lewis Colby and Co., 1848), pp. 790–92, 811–12, 820–24; and O. W. Taylor, *Early Tennessee Baptists, 1769–1832* (Nashville: Tennessee Baptist Convention, 1957), pp. 37–56. For the memoirs of one Separate Baptist settler, see Chester R. Young, ed., *Westward into Kentucky: The Narrative of Daniel Trabue* (Lexington: University Press of Kentucky, 1981), esp. pp. 128–33.

37. Minutes of the South Kentucky Association of Separate Baptists, 1793–98, 1803; Spencer, *Kentucky Baptists,* 1:108, 147, 175–76.

38. Spencer, *Kentucky Baptists,* 1:583.

39. Renault, "Separate Baptist Ecclesiology," pp. 200–205.

40. Joseph Thomas, *The Travels and Gospel Labors of Joseph Thomas . . . through Various Parts of the Western Country* (Winchester, Va.: J. Foster, 1812), p. 90. John Mulkey and Benjamin Lynn, both of Separate Baptist background, were two prominent preachers in Kentucky who, between 1800 and 1810, led a sizable group of Baptists into the Stone fold. See C. P. Cawthorn and N. L. Warnell, *Pioneer Baptist Church Records of South-Central Kentucky and the Upper Cum-*

berland of Tennessee, 1799–1899 (n.p., 1985), pp. 432–42 and *passim.* The continuing Baptist defections can be seen, for example, in Stone's report of 1826 that eleven preachers in Tennessee's Elk River Association withdrew in protest of "man-made Creeds, and doctrines." *Christian Messenger* 1 (November 25, 1826): 18.

41. Minutes of the South Kentucky Association, 1824–32; Spencer, *Kentucky Baptists,* 1:587, 615–16, 642–43; R. B. C. Howell, "A Memorial History of the First Baptist Church, Nashville, from 1820 to 1863," typescript, Dargan-Carver Library, Nashville, 1:76. See also Errett Gates, *The Early Relation and Separation of Baptists and Disciples* (Chicago: Christian Century, 1904), pp. 77–79.

42. For studies of this neglected episode, see Byron Cecil Lambert, *The Rise of the Anti-Mission Baptists: Sources and Leaders, 1800–1840* (New York: Arno Press, 1980); Larry Douglas Smith, "The Historiography of the Origins of Anti-Missionism Examined in Light of Kentucky Baptist History," Ph.D. diss., Southern Baptist Theological Seminary, 1982; B. H. Carroll, Jr., *The Genesis of American Anti-Missionism* (Louisville: Baptist Book Concern, 1902); Bertram Wyatt-Brown, "The Antimission Movement in the Jacksonian South: A Study in Regional Folk Culture," *Journal of Southern History* 36 (November 1970): 501–29; and Gaylord P. Albaugh, "Anti-Missionary Movement in the United States," in Vergilius Ferm, ed., *An Encyclopedia of Religion* (New York: Philosophical Library, 1945), pp. 27–28.

43. Elias Smith, *The Herald of Gospel Liberty,* 3:304; 7:614, 637. On Smith's radical biblicism, see idem, *The Life, Conversion, Preaching, Travels, and Sufferings of Elias Smith* (Portsmouth, N.H.: Beck and Foster, 1816), pp. 402–4.

44. Gilbert Beebe, *A Compilation of Editorial Articles Copied from the "Signs of the Times," Embracing a Period of Thirty-five Years; in which is Reflected the Doctrine and Order of the Old School, or Primitive Baptists* (Middletown, N.Y.: Benton L. Beebe, 1868), 1:11, iv–v.

45. Joshua Lawrence, *The North Carolina Whigs Apology for the Kehukee Association* (Tarboro, N.C.: North-Carolina Free Press, 1830), pp. 3–4; cf. "Declaration of Principles, by Elder Joshua Lawrence, 1826," Southern Historical Collection, University of North Carolina, Chapel Hill, where he stresses the sinfulness of anything "contrary to the express rule given by our Lord Jesus Christ" (p. 11). On the primitivism of the movement as a whole, see Lambert, *Anti-Mission Baptists,* pp. 405–9.

46. See John Taylor, *Thoughts on Missions* (1820), pp. 9–10, 25; Daniel Parker, *A Public Address . . . on the Principle and Practice of the Baptist Board of Foreign Missions* (Vincennes, Ind., 1820). For the Separate Baptists' rejection of organized missions, see the Minutes of the South Kentucky Association, 1815–17.

47. For the main documents of Primitive Baptist history, see Benton L. Beebe, comp., *The Feast of Fat Things* (Middletown, N.Y.: G. Beebe's Sons, 1890; reprint, Salisbury, Md.: Signs of the Times, 1980). See also Cushing B. Hassell and Sylvester Hassell, *History of the Church of God from the Creation to A.D. 1885, including Especially the History of the Kehukee Primitive Baptist Association* (Middletown, N.Y.: G. Beebe's Sons, 1886).

48. Wyatt-Brown, "Antimission Movement," pp. 501–29; T. Scott Miyakawa,

Protestants and Pioneers: Individualism and Conformity on the American Frontier (Chicago: University of Chicago Press, 1964), pp. 155–58; and Keith R. Burich, "The Primitive Baptist Schism in North Carolina: A Study of the Professionalism of the Baptist Ministry," M.A. thesis, University of North Carolina, Chapel Hill, 1973.

49. For treatments of Baptist Landmarkism, see the following works: James E. Tull, *A History of Southern Baptist Landmarkism in the Light of Historical Baptist Ecclesiology* (New York: Arno Press, 1980); idem, *Shapers of Baptist Thought* (1972; reprint, Macon, Ga.: Mercer University Press, 1984), pp. 129–51; Hugh Wamble, "Landmarkism: Doctrinaire Ecclesiology among Baptists," *Church History* 33 (December 1964): 429–47; John E. Steely, "The Landmark Movement in the Southern Baptist Convention," in Duke K. McCall, ed., *What Is the Church? A Symposium of Baptist Thought* (Nashville: Broadman Press, 1958); and Robert G. Torbet, "Landmarkism," in Hudson, *Baptist Concepts of the Church,* pp. 170–95.

50. John L. Waller, "The Validity of Baptism by Pedo-Baptist Ministers," *Western Baptist Review* 3 (March 1848): 267–72; *Tennessee Baptist* (June 29, 1848): 2; Waller, "The Administrator of Baptism," *Western Baptist Review* 3 (August 1848): 460–74.

51. Graves, *Old Landmarkism,* pp. xi–xii.

52. J. M. Pendleton, *An Old Landmark Reset,* 2d ed. (Nashville: Southwestern Publishing, 1857). Over forty thousand copies of this tract apparently were sold. Pendleton, *Reminiscences of a Long Life* (Louisville, Ky.: Baptist Book Concern, 1891), p. 104. On the life and thought of Pendleton, see also Leo T. Crisman and Harold Stephens, "James Madison Pendleton," *Encyclopedia of Southern Baptists* (Nashville: Broadman Press, 1958), 2:1082–83; and Torbet, "Landmarkism," pp. 182–86.

53. Amos C. Dayton, *Pedo-Baptist and Campbellite Immersions: Being a Review of the Arguments of "Doctors" Waller, Fuller, Johnson, Wayland, Broadus, and others* (Nashville: Southwestern Publishing, 1858); idem, *Theodosia Ernest; or, The Heroine of Faith,* 2 vols. (Nashville: Graves, Marks and Rutland, 1857). Volume 1 of the novel sold eighteen thousand copies the first year, and volume 2 reached its twenty-eighth edition in 1858. J. Clark Hensley and Homer L. Grice, "Amos Cooper Dayton," *Encyclopedia of Southern Baptists,* 1:351–52.

54. Reuben Jones in the *Biblical Recorder,* August 16, 1851, p. 1, cited by Tull, *History of Southern Baptist Landmarkism,* p. 145; James J. Burnett, *Sketches of Tennessee's Pioneer Baptist Preachers,* 1st series, 1 (Nashville: Marshall and Bruce, 1919), p. 188.

55. James R. Graves, *Alexander Campbell and Campbellism Exposed: A series of replies to Alexander Campbell's articles in The Millennial Harbinger* (Nashville: Graves and Marks, 1854); idem, *The Great Iron Wheel; or, Republicanism Backwards and Christianity Reversed,* 17th ed. (Nashville: Graves, Marks and Rutland, 1856); idem, *Little Iron Wheel;* idem, *The Trilemma; or, Death by Three Horns* (Memphis, 1860; reprint, Texarkana, Tex.: Baptist Sunday School Committee, 1928); idem, *Trials and Sufferings for Religious Liberty in New England* (Nashville: Southwestern Publishing, 1858).

56. Graves, *Great Iron Wheel,* pp. 23, 16, 24.

57. Ibid., pp. 25, 20–21.

58. Graves, *Little Iron Wheel,* p. 23.

59. Graves, *Old Landmarkism,* pp. 30–31; cf. idem, *Great Iron Wheel,* p. 550, and Dayton, *Theodosia Ernest,* 2:133.

60. Graves, *Old Landmarkism,* pp. 29–130. Earlier, in 1855, Graves had prepared a "Primitive Church Constitution" as a "first rude draft," setting forth the scriptural pattern for the church. In doing so he assumed that "the Church which Christ himself organized in Jerusalem, is an authoritative model to be patterned after until the end of time" (*Great Iron Wheel,* pp. 544–70). While agreed on the fact of a precise pattern, however, the leading Landmarkers disagreed on the elements of it. Amos C. Dayton, for example, enumerated nine marks of "a true church of Christ," only four of which match Graves's eight marks (see *Theodosia Ernest*).

61. Graves, *Old Landmarkism,* pp. 32, 18–20. Cf. Dayton, *Theodosia Ernest,* 2:93. For a response to Graves's position on this issue by a leading Baptist theologian, see John Leadley Dagg, *Manual on Church Order* (Charleston, S.C.: Southern Baptist Publication Society, 1858), pp. 113–14, 121, and *passim.*

62. James R. Graves, "Introduction," in G. H. Orchard, *A Concise History of Foreign Baptists: Taken from the New Testament, the First Fathers, Early Writers, and Historians of all Ages,* 13th ed. (Nashville: Graves, Marks, 1855), pp. iv, v, vi. Cf. idem, *Old Landmarkism,* pp. 121–30; idem, *Great Iron Wheel,* pp. 24–33; and idem, "Church History," *Southern Baptist Review and Eclectic* 1 (April–May 1855): 21ff. For in-depth, critical treatment of this issue, see W. Morgan Patterson, "A Critique of the Successionist Concept in Baptist Historiography," Th.D. diss., New Orleans Baptist Theological Seminary, 1956; and Tull, *Southern Baptist Landmarkism,* pp. 168–90, 287–321.

63. Orchard, *History of Foreign Baptists,* p. xiv.

64. James R. Graves, *Tennessee Baptist* (October 3, 1857): 2.

65. For Graves's most extensive formulation of this argument, see *The Trilemma; or, Death by Three Horns,* pp. 77–118.

66. Graves, *Watchman's Reply,* p. 59.

67. Grant Wacker, "Playing for Keeps: The Primitivist Impulse in Early Pentecostalism," in Richard T. Hughes, ed., *The American Quest for the Primitive Church* (Urbana: University of Illinois Press, 1988), pp. 205–6; and Richard T. Hughes, "On Recovering the Theme of Recovery," in Hughes, *American Quest,* pp. 12–14.

68. Graves, *Great Iron Wheel,* p. 25.

69. Ibid., p. 19.

70. Dayton, *Theodosia Ernest,* 2:257, 305, 417, 425, and *passim.* Another Landmark novel using similar arguments was Ambie White, *Leander Hall; or, the Investigation of Religious Truth, Comprehending the Origins and Nature of the Church of Christ* (Lexington, Ky.: Waller, Sherrill, 1865), esp. pp. 269ff., 570–71, 599–627.

71. Graves, *Old Landmarkism,* pp. 28, 143; also *Graves–Ditzler Debate* (Memphis: Southern Baptist Publication Society, 1876), p. 927.

72. Pendleton, *An Old Landmark Re-set* (1857 ed.), p. 45. On Baptist views

toward non-Baptist Protestant denominations during this period, see Tull, *History of Southern Baptist Landmarkism,* pp. 307–19.

73. Spencer, *Kentucky Baptists,* 1:716; Homer L. Grice, "James Robinson Graves," *Encyclopedia of Southern Baptists,* 1:576–78.

Chapter 5. From Freedom to Constraint

1. Jeremiah Jeter, *Campbellism Examined* (New York: Sheldon, Lamport, and Blakeman, 1855), p. 85.

2. Joseph Thomas, *The Life of the Pilgrim Joseph Thomas* (Winchester, Va., 1817), pp. 197–98.

3. John Rogers, *A Discourse Delivered in Carlisle, Kentucky, . . . 1860* (Cincinnati, 1861), p. 22.

4. The term "Christian," when used to designate the movement led by Barton W. Stone in Tennessee, Kentucky, and Ohio in the early nineteenth century, is placed in quotation marks throughout this chapter to distinguish this movement from other groups that also claimed the designation "Christian." The phrase, "Christians in the West," also is in quotes since this was a label commonly applied to the Stone movement in its early years.

"Church of Christ" was the typical designation of congregations affiliated with this movement. R. L. Roberts counted different designations used in a single volume (1835) of Barton Stone's *Christian Messenger* selected at random. In this volume, " 'church of Christ' (or with capital 'C') occurs 30 times (including 'congregations of Christ' once), while 'C. Church,' 'a Christian church,' and 'a Christian assembly' each appears one time only, a ratio of ten to one in a total of 288 pages." " 'Church of Christ': 1830 or 1889?" *Firm Foundation* 92 (September 30, 1957): 614.

At least prior to 1832, the "Christians in the West" typically rejected the label "Disciples of Christ," although Alexander Campbell preferred this designation and used it often to describe his movement whose geographical center lay further north and east, especially in Ohio and Virginia. In 1832, Barton Stone's "Christians" and Alexander Campbell's Disciples united, and following that date the three designations—Churches of Christ, "Christian" churches, and Disciples of Christ—were used often interchangeably in all regions of the country. Sectional, economic, and theological factors, however, precipitated division, and by 1906, the U.S. Bureau of the Census recognized that Churches of Christ and the Disciples of Christ, once a single movement, had become separate denominations. (For a sociological explanation of this division, see David Edwin Harrell, Jr., "The Sectional Origins of the Churches of Christ," *Journal of Southern History* 30 [August 1964]: 261–77.) In the twentieth century, Churches of Christ flourished in a belt running from Tennessee to Texas, growing out of the heartland of the old Stone "Christians," while Disciples of Christ maintained the center of their strength in the Midwest.

In later chapters, when dealing especially with Alexander Campbell and those he influenced (e.g., chaps. 7 and 8), we speak more of Disciples and less of "Christians."

5. Barton W. Stone, Robert Marshall, and John Thompson, *An Apology for Renouncing the Jurisdiction of the Synod of Kentucky* (Lexington, 1804), reprinted in Hoke Dickinson, *The Cane Ridge Reader* (n.p., n.d.), p. 148. This apology appears in William Warren Sweet, *Religion on the American Frontier, 1793–1840,* vol. II, *The Presbyterians* (Chicago: University of Chicago Press, 1936), pp. 317–19.

6. See Charles A. Young, ed., *Historical Documents Advocating Christian Union* (Chicago: Christian Century, 1904), pp. 19–26.

7. Rice Haggard had worked with James O'Kelly in Virginia and had suggested to O'Kelly in 1794 that his "New Lights" be known simply as Christians. Now he made the same suggestion to the Presbyterian dissidents in Kentucky and even wrote a pamphlet on this theme which was not known in modern times until 1953. That pamphlet—*An Address to the Different Religious Societies, on the Sacred Import of the Christian Name*—has now been reprinted under its original title as "Footnotes to Disciples History, Number Four," by the Disciples of Christ Historical Society, 1954. Regarding Haggard and his pamphlet, see Colby Hall, *Rice Haggard: The American Frontier Evangelist Who Revived the Name Christian* (Fort Worth, Tex.: Stafford-Lowdon, 1957).

There are two accounts of the meeting in Bethel, Kentucky, where Haggard suggested to the Presbyterian dissidents the name "Christian." Joseph Thomas specifically places this meeting prior to the dissolution of the Springfield Presbytery. See Thomas, *The Travels and Gospel Labors of Joseph Thomas* (Winchester, Va.: J. Foster, 1812), pp. 80–81; Barton Stone implies the reverse. See Barton W. Stone, "History of the Christian Church in the West—No. VIII," *Christian Messenger* 1 (September 25, 1827): 241–45.

8. Richard McNemar, *The Kentucky Revival* (New York, 1846), p. 59. This valuable document originally was printed in 1807.

9. T. S., "To the Editor of the Christian Messenger," *Christian Messenger* 1 (September 25, 1827): 249.

10. Jacob Creath, Jr., "Dr. Noel's Hollow Tree," *Budget and Clerical Index* 1 (April 26, 1830): 1; and idem, "Human Creeds and Confessions of Faith, Essay II," *Christian Examiner* 1 (January 1830): 53–54.

11. John Rogers, *A Discourse on the Subject of Civil and Religious Liberty, Delivered on the 4th of July, 1828, in Carlisle, Ky.* (Cincinnati, 1857), p. 10.

12. J. and J. Gregg, "An Apology for Withdrawing from the Methodist Episcopal Church," *Christian Messenger* 1 (December 25, 1826): 39–40. Cf. Rogers, *Discourse on Civil and Religious Liberty,* p. 9.

13. Gregg, "An Apology," pp. 39–40; and Thomas, *Life of the Pilgrim,* p. 206.

14. Milton (T. M. Allen), "For the Christian Messenger," *Christian Messenger* 1 (March 24, 1827): 102–5.

15. A Disciple, "Extract of a Letter to the Editor," *Christian Examiner* 1 (November 1829): 22. This quotation is attributed to John Smith in John Augustus Williams, *Life of Elder John Smith* (Cincinnati: Standard Publishing, n.d.), pp. 215–52.

16. John Rogers, "The Life and Times of John Rogers," in John Rogers Books, 1800–1859, Book I, p. 163, in Southern Historical Collection, Manuscripts Department, University of North Carolina at Chapel Hill. Cf. also Rogers, *Discourse*

Delivered in Carlisle, Ky., pp. 3–4; Jacob Creath, Jr., "Essay I. Human Creeds and Confessions of Faith," *Christian Examiner* 1 (December 1829): 33–34; and Barton W. Stone, *An Address to the Christian Churches In Kentucky, Tennessee, & Ohio* (Nashville, 1814), p. 95.

17. J. and J. Gregg, "An Apology," pp. 41–42.

18. Church Records, Roberson Fork Church of Christ, 1830–69, Tennessee State Library and Archives; and Milton (T. M. Allen), "To the Editor of the Christian Messenger," *Christian Messenger* 1 (March 24, 1827): 110.

19. Thomas, *Travels and Gospel Labors,* pp. 87–88.

20. Rice Haggard, comp., *A Selection of Christian Hymns* (Lexington, Ky., 1818), pp. 304 and 314.

21. Robert Marshall and John Thompson, *A Brief Historical Account of Sundry Things in the Doctrines and State of the Christian, or as it is Commonly Called, the Newlight Church* (Cincinnati, 1811), p. 17; and Archippus, "Calvinism and Arminianism. Review of Elder D's Letter—No. III," *Christian Examiner* 1 (May 31, 1830): 159.

22. Creath, "Essay I. Human Creeds and Confessions of Faith," p. 36; idem, "Mr. Chambers' Text Explained," *Budget and Clerical Index* 1 (April 26, 1830): 21; and idem, "Clearness of the Scriptures—No. I," *Christian Messenger* 1 (December 1829): 26.

23. McNemar, *Kentucky Revival,* p. 61.

24. Thomas, *Travels and Gospel Labors,* p. 88. Cf. also Stone, "History of the Christian Church in the West—No. VIII," p. 267. Robert Davidson, who chronicled the history of Presbyterianism in Kentucky, wrote that Stone came to his own conviction of immersion of believers "soon after the schism." *History of the Presbyterian Church in the State of Kentucky* (Pittsburgh, 1847), pp. 198–99.

25. Barton W. Stone, *Christian Messenger* 4 (August 1830): 201. See discussion of Stone's reluctance to require immersion, in Myer Phillips, "A Historical Study of the Attitude of the Churches of Christ toward Other Denominations," Ph.D. diss., Baylor University, 1983, pp. 34–37.

26. Stone, "History of the Christian Church in the West—No. VIII," p. 242.

27. Barton W. Stone, "Queries Answered," *Christian Messenger* 1 (October 25, 1827): 271–73. Cf. also idem, "Objections to Christian Union Considered," *Christian Messenger* 1 (March 24, 1827): 114; and idem, "Reply: To Elder Spencer Clack, Editor of the Baptist Recorder," *Christian Messenger* 2 (December 1827): 35.

28. Thomas, *Life of the Pilgrim,* pp. 128–29. Cf. also pp. 43, 207, 277, 305, and 321.

29. John Jones, "Extract of a Letter from Elder John Jones, to the Editor, dated Casey County, Ky., Aug. 10, 1827," *Christian Messenger* 1 (October 25, 1827): 275–76.

30. Stone, "History of the Christian Church in the West—No. VIII," pp. 241–42.

31. John B. Boles, *The Great Revival, 1787–1805* (Lexington: University Press of Kentucky, 1972), p. 102; see also pp. 34 and 101.

32. McNemar, *Kentucky Revival,* p. 3; John Dunlavy, *The Manifesto, or a Declaration of the Doctrine and Practice of the Church of Christ* (New York,

1847), p. 437; Levi Purviance, *The Biography of Elder David Purviance* (Dayton, 1848), pp. 248–49; and McNemar, *Kentucky Revival,* p. 69.

33. McNemar, *Kentucky Revival,* pp. 69–70; and Stone, Marshall, and Thompson, "Letter to the Synod of Kentucky," printed with *Reply to John P. Campbell's Strictures on Atonement* (Lexington, 1805), pp. 63–64.

34. Barton W. Stone, *Christian Messenger* 1 (November 26, 1826): 1.

35. Archippus, "Calvinism and Arminianism. Review of Elder D's Letter—No. III," pp. 159, 160–61; and Jacob Creath, Jr., "Essay III. Human Creeds and Confessions of Faith," *Christian Examiner* 1 (February 1830): 75.

36. Haggard, *Selection of Christian Hymns,* p. 304.

37. Cf. Lyman Beecher, "The Memory of Our Fathers," a sermon delivered at Plymouth, Massachusetts, December 22, 1827, abridged in Winthrop S. Hudson, ed., *Nationalism and Religion in America* (New York: Harper and Row, 1970), pp. 99–105.

38. Barton W. Stone, "Something New—Very New," *Christian Messenger* 9 (June 1853): 141–42.

39. *A Short History of the Life of Barton W. Stone, Written by Himself,* in Dickinson, *Cane Ridge Reader,* p. 9; Nathan J. Mitchell, *Reminiscences and Incidents in the Life and Travels of a Pioneer Preacher of the "Ancient Gospel"* (Cincinnati, 1877), pp. 25–26, 28; Rogers, "Life and Times of John Rogers," Book I, p. 4; B. F. Hall, "Autobiography of B. F. Hall," typescript, Center for Restoration Studies, Abilene Christian University, pp. 8, 22; Thomas, *Life of the Pilgrim,* p. 22; and Dunlavy, *Manifesto,* p. 444.

40. Stone, Marshall, and Thompson, *Apology,* p. 148.

41. The heart of Stone's arguments on the doctrine of God can be found in Stone, Marshall, and Thompson, *Apology* (1804); Stone, *Atonement: The Substance of Two Letters Written to a Friend* (Lexington, 1805); idem, *Reply* (1805); and idem, *An Address* (1814). See also the discussion of the issue in chapter six of William Garret West, *Barton Warren Stone: Early American Advocate of Christian Unity* (Nashville: Disciples of Christ Historical Society, 1954).

42. McNemar, *Kentucky Revival,* pp. 48–59, 59, and 57.

43. Haggard, *Selection of Christian Hymns,* pp. 360ff.

44. Young, *Historical Documents,* p. 21, and Dunlavy, *Manifesto,* pp. 420 and 437.

45. Marshall and Thompson, *Brief Historical Account,* pp. 4–5, 18–19, 22–23; and Rogers, *Discourse Delivered in Carlisle, Ky.,* pp. 15 and 18.

46. Rogers, *Discourse Delivered in Carlisle, Ky.,* p. 15.

47. Alexander Campbell wrote further in 1828 that "in, and by, the act of immersion, so soon, as our bodies are put under water, at that very instant our former, or 'old sins,' are all washed away, provided only that we are true believers." "Ancient Gospell—No. II," *Christian Baptist* 5 (February 5, 1828): 167. Cf. also idem, "Ancient Gospel—No. III," *Christian Baptist* 5 (March 3, 1828): 181–82; idem, "Ancient Gospel—No. VI," *Christian Baptist* 5 (June 2, 1828): 254–55; idem, "Query III," *Christian Baptist* 6 (February 2, 1829): 165; and idem, "Essays on the Patriarchal, Jewish, and Christian Ages—No. XV," *Christian Baptist* 7 (June 7, 1830): 277–78.

48. Rogers, "Life and Times of John Rogers," Book I, p. 8. Cf. also pp. 233 and 235; and idem, *A Discourse Delivered in Carlisle, Ky.,* p. 29.

49. Mitchell, *Reminiscences and Incidents,* p. 36; and Hall, "Autobiography," pp. 57–58.

50. Davidson, *History of the Presbyterian Church in the State of Kentucky,* p. 217.

51. Though this poem was published in the *Christian Standard* of October 21, 1871 (p. 333), John Rogers wrote that it was written by a Kentucky Methodist preacher, William Phillips, around 1833. Rogers also states that, according to Aylette Raines in the *Christian Teacher* (vol. 5), this doggerel " 'was circulated by thousands, if not tens of thousands.' " Rogers, "Life and Times of John Rogers," Book I, pp. 252–53. The poem has four additional verses.

52. Thomas Campbell, *The Declaration and Address,* ed. F. D. Kershner (St. Louis: Mission Messenger, 1972), p. 45.

53. Alexander Campbell, "The Clergy—No. II," *Christian Baptist* 1 (November 3, 1823): 72; idem, "A Restoration of the Ancient Order of Things—No. VII," *Christian Baptist* 3 (September 5, 1825): 29; and idem, "A Restoration of the Ancient Order of Things—No. II," *Christian Baptist* 2 (March 7, 1825): 153. Campbell's view of the New Testament as a legal document appears over and over again. See, e.g., Campbell, "To Bishop R. B. Semple—Letter IV," *Christian Baptist* 5 (June 2, 1828): 251, where Campbell writes that "almost the whole New Testament is engrossed with the regulations and rules and precepts which are to govern individuals." For discussion of this aspect of Campbell's theology, see Robert Earl Woodrow, "The Nature of Biblical Authority and the Restoration Movement," M.A. thesis, Abilene Christian University, 1983, pp. 65–74.

54. Alexander Campbell, *The Christian System* (Bethany, Va., 1839), p. 6. Cf. also idem, "The Confirmation of the Testimony," *Millennial Harbinger* 1 (January 4, 1830): 8–14; idem, "Essays on Education," *Millennial Harbinger* 6 (January 1835): 22–23; and idem, "Schools and Colleges—No. II," *Millennial Harbinger,* series 3, 7 (March 1850): 171–72.

On Baconian primitivism, see chapter 7. See also Theodore Dwight Bozeman, *Protestants in an Age of Science: The Baconian Ideal and Antebellum American Religious Thought* (Chapel Hill: University of North Carolina Press, 1977).

55. This statement appears in Campbell's notes on Jardines' logic class at Glasgow: "Lectures in Logic Delivered by Professor Jardan [sic] in the University of Glasgow, 1808." For Richardson, see "The Gospel—No. II." *Millennial Harbinger,* new series, 3 (April 1839): 149.

56. Alexander Campbell, "A Restoration of the Ancient Order of Things. No. XVII. Purity of Speech," *Christian Baptist* 4 (March 5, 1827): 154; Rogers, "Life and Times of John Rogers," Book I, pp. 113ff.; idem, *A Discourse Delivered in Carlisle, Ky.,* p. 21; cf. also pp. 28–29.

57. McNemar, *Kentucky Revival,* pp. 61–62; Rogers, "Life and Times of John Rogers," Book I, pp. 40–41 (cf. West, *Barton Warren Stone,* pp. 34–39); and Dunlavy, *Manifesto,* p. 463. McNemar described the beginnings of the dancing exercise: "At the spring sacrament at Turtle-Creek in 1804, Brother Thompson had been constrained just at the close of the meeting to go to dancing, and for an

hour or more to dance in a regular manner round the stand, all the while repeating in a low tone of voice— 'This is the Holy Ghost—Glory!' But it was not till the ensuing fall, or beginning of the winter, that the Schismatics began to encourage one another *to praise God in the dance,* and unite in that exercise" (*Kentucky Revival,* p. 63).

58. Thomas, *Life of the Pilgrim,* p. 186; cf. pp. 151, 175.

59. Ibid., pp. 140, 156.

60. Isaac N. Jones, "The Reformation in Tennessee," cited in J. M. Grant, "A Sketch of the Reformation in Tennessee," manuscript, Center for Restoration Studies, Abilene Christian University, pp. 31–34.

61. Alexander Campbell, "Address to the Readers of the Christian Baptist. No. IV," *Christian Baptist* 1 (March 1, 1824): 148; idem, *The Christian System,* 4th ed. (Bethany, Va., 1857), p. 48; and idem. *Christianity Restored* (Bethany, Va., 1835), p. 350. Cf. Thomas Olbricht, "Alexander Campbell's View of the Holy Spirit," *Restoration Quarterly* 6 (First Quarter 1962):1–11.

62. Barton W. Stone, "The Christian Expositor," *Christian Messenger* 1 (April 25, 1827): 127.

63. B. F. Hall, "The Operation of the Spirit," *Heretic Detector* 1 (July 1837): 179.

64. Davidson, *History of the Presbyterian Church in the State of Kentucky,* p. 217.

65. Barton W. Stone, "Objections to Christian Union Considered," *Christian Messenger* 1 (March 24, 1827): 114; and idem, *Christian Messenger* 1 (October 25, 1827): 270.

66. J. Norwood, *Christian Examiner* 1 (November 1829): 23; Alexander Campbell, "Millennium—No. 1," *Millennial Harbinger* 1 (February 1830): 58.

67. Barton W. Stone, J. Hewit, J. T. Jones, A. Reynolds, J. Kingdom, and M. Elder, "The Brethren Appointed for that Purpose Report the Following Address," *Christian Messenger* 9 (July 1835): 145.

68. Barton W. Stone, "Desultory Remarks," *Christian Messenger* 10 (December 1836): 181–83.

69. Ibid.

70. Philip, "On Teaching Christianity—No. I," *Christian Baptist* 1 (September 1, 1823): 30–32. Walter Scott often wrote under the pen name Philip.

71. For a discussion of the covenant theme in Walter Scott's thought, see William Austin Gerrard, "Walter Scott: Frontier Disciples Evangelist," Ph.D. diss., Emory University, 1982, pp. 126–30.

72. Walter Scott, "From the Minutes of the Mahoning Association. Report," *Christian Examiner* 1 (November 1829): 5–8.

73. Walter Scott, *The Gospel Restored* (Cincinnati, 1836), p. v.

74. Walter Scott, *To Themelion: The Union of Christians, on Christian Principles* (Cincinnati, 1852), pp. 78–79; idem, "Address Given before the American Christian Missionary Society" (Cincinnati, 1854), p. 26; and idem, *A Discourse on the Holy Spirit* (Bethany, Va., 1831), pp. 20–21. In this context, two items deserve note: (1) Scott's immense admiration for "Lord Bacon" reflected in his inaugural address as the first president of Bacon College, the first institution of higher

learning among the "Christians"/Disciples of Christ (cf. idem, "United States' System. An Address," 1837, in *College of the Bible Quarterly* 23 [April 1946]: 4–44); and (2) the revealing subtitle of Scott's *The Gospel Restored: A Discourse of the True Gospel of Jesus Christ, in Which the Facts, Principles, Duties, and Privileges of Christianity Are Arranged, Defined, and Discussed.* See chapter 7 of this volume.

75. Walter Scott, *Evangelist of the True Gospel,* new series, 6 (August 1, 1838): 180.

76. *Christianity Restored* was the first edition of what became *The Christian System.* See n. 61 above.

77. Alexander Campbell, "Events of 1823 and 1827," *Millennial Harbinger,* new series, 2 (October 1838): 466ff.

78. Purviance, *Biography of Elder David Purviance,* p. 249.

79. Robert Stubbs, *Browne's Western Calendar, or, the Cincinnati Almanac for . . . 1807* (Cincinnati, 1806), pp. Eff.

80. Jones, "Reformation in Tennessee," pp. 73–74, also pp. 37–38; Thomas, *Life of the Pilgrim,* pp. 245–47; and idem, *Poems, religious, moral and satirical, by Joseph Thomas . . . : to which is prefixed a compend of the life, travels and gospel labors of the author* (Lebanon, Ohio, 1829), p. 44.

81. Stone, *An Address,* pp. 99–100; cf. p. 105.

82. *Gospel Herald* statement cited in "Creeds and Confessions," *Christian Examiner* 1 (March 1830): 98; Alexander Reynolds, "Campbellite—Not the Name," *Heretic Detector* 2 (April 1838): 118–19; and Rogers, "Life and Times of John Rogers," Book I, pp. 120–21.

83. "Items of Ecclesiastical Intelligence," *Heretic Detector* 3 (February 1839): 35.

84. See Alexander Campbell, "Various Notices," *Millennial Harbinger,* new series, 5 (August 1841): 384.

85. Arthur Crihfield, "New Arrangement—Prospectus, &c.," *Heretic Detector* 1 (July 1837): 169–70.

86. Aylette Raines, "Christ's Church Identified. No. IV," *Bible Advocate* 2 (November 1843): 51, from the Christian Palladium; and Arthur Crihfield, "Preface," *Heretic Detector* 3 (January 1839): 8.

87. J. Winans, "The Day of Ghosts!!!" *Heretic Detector* 2 (January 1838): 24.

88. Cf. Aylette Raines, "Christ's Church Identified. No. 1," *Bible Advocate* 2 (August 1843): 2–4; and idem, "Christ's Church Identified. No. IV," *Bible Advocate* 2 (November 1843): 51, both from *Christian Palladium;* William E. Mathews, "The Body of Christ," *Bible Advocate* 1 (March 1843): 113–14; and Arthur Crihfield, "Letters to Elisha Bates—Letter 1," *Heretic Detector* 3 (October 1839): 259–60.

89. Raines, "Christ's Church Identified. No. 1," pp. 2–4; and John R. Howard, "Friendly Aliens," *Heretic Detector* 2 (April 1838): 119.

90. John R. Howard, "The Beginning Corner: or, the Church of Christ Identified," in *Biographical Sketch and Writings of Elder Benjamin Franklin,* ed. John F. Rowe and G. W. Rice (Cincinnati, 1880), pp. 208–27. This sermon is a much

fuller version of the same sermon called "Identification of the Church of Christ," published in *Christian Magazine* 1 (September 1848): 267ff.

91. Crihfield, "Letters to Elisha Bates—Letter 1," pp. 259–60, 262.

92. John R. Howard, "A Warning to the Religious Sects and Parties in Christendom," *Bible Advocate* 1 (January 1843): 82.

93. Arthur Crihfield, "Coming of the Lord—No. III," *Orthodox Preacher* 1 (February 1843): 25–31.

94. Tolbert Fanning, "The Origin of the Church of Christ Is Not Modern," *Christian Review* 2 (January 1845): 5–6.

Chapter 6. Soaring with the Gods

1. Sidney E. Mead, *The Lively Experiment* (New York: Harper and Row, 1963), pp. 108, 111, 110. On this theme, see also idem, "The Theology of the Republic and the Orthodox Mind," *Journal of the American Academy of Religion* 44 (March 1976): 105–13.

2. See, for example, Sidney E. Mead, *The Nation with the Soul of a Church* (New York: Harper and Row, 1975), pp. 49, 74; and idem, *Lively Experiment,* p. 53.

3. Mead, *Lively Experiment,* p. 110.

4. Alexander Campbell, "Millennium—No. 1," *Millennial Harbinger* 1 (February 1830): 55–56; idem, "An Oration in Honor of the Fourth of July" (1830), in *Popular Lectures and Addresses* (St. Louis: John Burns, 1861), pp. 374–75.

5. Parley P. Pratt, "The Millennium," in *Millennial Star,* reprinted in *Writings of Parley Parker Pratt,* ed. Parker Pratt Robison (Salt Lake City: Parker Pratt Robison, 1952), pp. 259–60.

6. Sidney E. Mead, *The Old Religion in the Brave New World* (Berkeley: University of California Press, 1977).

7. Mead, *Lively Experiment,* p. 111.

8. Joseph Smith, *History of the Church of Jesus Christ of Latter-day Saints* (Salt Lake City: Deseret Book Co., 1927), 1:6.

Marvin Hill also has observed the close and intimate connection between primitivism and antipluralism in the Mormon experience. In his 1968 Ph.D. dissertation, Hill wrote that most interpreters have "failed to see that within the primitive gospel beliefs was an anti-pluralistic tendency, largely resulting from a reaction to the fiercely divisive and strife promoting effects of sectarian revivalism." "The Role of Christian Primitivism in the Origin and Development of the Mormon Kingdom, 1830–1844," Ph.D. diss., University of Chicago, 1968, p. 4. Hill also recognized the antipluralistic dimensions of the "first vision," observing that through this vision Joseph "in effect turned his back upon the prevailing religious pluralism in the United States, rejecting it as the source of confusion and religious doubt in his own mind" (p. 55). Hill's dissertation was written under the direction of Sidney E. Mead.

Arguing along similar lines, Gordon Pollock saw early Mormonism as a response to the social, economic, and religious chaos that characterized early nineteenth-century America. "In Search of Security: The Mormons and the Kingdom of God on Earth, 1830–1844," Ph.D. diss., Queen's University, 1977, pp. 6ff. Regarding the Mormon response to religious pluralism, Pollock wrote: "The intense competition between sects was the application to religion of the free market system which characterized the American economy. . . . In the face of quarrelling and competing sects those who became Mormons did so because they accepted its claim to be the one, true and authoritative religion in the world" (pp. 22–23).

For other assessments of the restoration theme in early Mormonism, see Richard Bushman, *Joseph Smith and the Beginnings of Mormonism* (Urbana: University of Illinois Press, 1984), esp. pp. 179–88; Peter Crawley, "The Passage of Mormon Primitivism," *Dialogue* 13 (Winter 1980): 26–37; Marvin Hill, "The Shaping of the Mormon Mind in New England and New York," *Brigham Young University Studies* 9 (Spring 1969): 351–72; Jan Shipps, *Mormonism: The Story of a New Religious Movement* (Urbana: University of Illinois Press, 1985), esp. pp. 67–85; and F. Mark McKiernan, Alma R. Blair, and Paul M. Edwards, eds., *The Restoration Movement: Essays in Mormon History* (Lawrence, Kans.: Coronado Press, 1973).

9. Bushman, *Beginnings of Mormonism,* pp. 149–50; Thomas G. Alexander, "Wilford Woodruff and the Changing Nature of Mormon Religious Experience," *Church History* 45 (March 1976): 2. For a more expansive delineation of seekerism in the Smith milieu, see Hill, "Role of Christian Primitivism," pp. 49–61.

10. Lucy Smith, *History of the Prophet Joseph* (Salt Lake City: Improvement Era, 1902), pp. 55, 33, and 45.

11. George L. Burnham, *Voice of Truth,* July 27, 1844, cited in David L. Rowe, "A New Perspective on the Burned-Over District: The Millerites in Upstate New York," *Church History* 47 (December 1978): 415.

12. L. Smith, *History,* pp. 1, 3–4. The statistics of Laurence Yorgason point further to the pervasiveness of seekerism among early Mormons. He found that 62 percent of those who became Mormons earlier had changed their church affiliation at least twice. Yorgason, "Some Demographic Aspects of One Hundred Early Mormon Converts, 1830–37," M.A. thesis, Brigham Young University, 1974, pp. 49–50, cited in Alexander, "Wilford Woodruff," p. 3.

13. On the restoration vision of Roger Williams, see C. Leonard Allen, " 'The Restauration of Zion': Roger Williams and the Quest for the Primitive Church," Ph.D. diss., University of Iowa, 1984.

14. Mario S. De Pillis has argued fhat the quest for authority was from the beginning the fundamental issue in Mormonism. "The Quest for Religious authority and the Rise of Mormonism," *Dialogue* 1 (March 1966): 68–88.

15. Parley P. Pratt, *The Autobiography of Parley Parker Pratt* (Chicago: Law, King and Law, 1888), pp. 32, 42.

16. 1 Nephi 14:10, 17.

17. Jan Shipps has argued that Mormonism was not, like the "Christians" or Disciples, a mere imitation of primitive Christianity but rather a radical tear "across history's seamless web to provide humanity with a new world wherein

God is actively involved" (*Mormonism,* p. 72). It is largely for this reason that she describes Mormonism as a "new religious movement."

18. See Pratt, *Autobiography;* and Andrew Jenson, *Latter-Day Saint Biographical Encyclopedia* (Salt Lake City: Andrew Jenson History Company, 1901), 1:83–85. Pratt had converted Elenore McLean, who became convinced that Gentile marriages were illegitimate since they lacked priesthood authority. She therefore left her husband, Hector, and became Pratt's wife. Hector murdered Pratt on May 13, 1857. See Richard S. Van Wagoner, *Mormon Polygamy: A History* (Salt Lake: Signature Books, 1986), pp. 43–44.

19. David J. Whittaker, "Early Mormon Pamphleteering," Ph.D. diss., Brigham Young University, 1982, p. 58. Whittaker cites as the source of this designation of Pratt an unpublished essay by Peter Crawley, "Parley P. Pratt: The Father of Mormon Pamphleteering."

20. Parley P. Pratt, *A Voice of Warning and Instruction to All People, Containing a Declaration of the Faith and Doctrine of the Church of the Latter Day Saints, Commonly Called Mormons* (New York: W. Sanford, 1837); Crawley, "Passage of Mormon Primitivism," p. 33; and Introduction" to *Key to the Science of Theology/A Voice of Warning* (Salt Lake City: Deseret Book Co., 1978), pp. i–ii.

21. Crawley, "Passage of Mormon Primitivism," p. 33.

22. Whittaker, "Early Mormon Pamphleteering," p. 59, n. 30; "Introduction" to *Key* (1978 edition), p. i.

23. Parley P. Pratt, *Key to the Science of Theology: Designed as an Introduction to the First Principles of Spiritual Philosophy; Religion; Law and Government; as Delivered by the Ancients, and as Restored in this Age, for the final Development of Universal Peace, Truth and Knowledge* (Liverpool, England: F. D. Richards, 1855).

24. "Introduction" to *Key* (1978 edition), p. ii; and Whittaker, "Early Mormon Pamphleteering," pp. 62–63.

25. Pratt, *Voice of Warning,* p. 147.

26. Ibid., pp. 154–55.

27. Pratt, *Key to the Science of Theology,* pp. 26–27.

28. Thomas Campbell, "Open Letter to Sidney Rigdon," Painesville, Ohio, *Telegraph,* February 15, 1831, in Francis W. Kirkham, *A New Witness for Christ in America: The Book of Mormon* (Independence, Mo.: Press of Zion's Printing and Publishing, 1951), 2:93.

29. Alexander Campbell, "Sidney Rigdon," *Millennial Harbinger* 2 (February 7, 1831): 100.

30. Pratt, *Key to the Science of Theology,* pp. 108–9.

31. Pratt, "The Fountain of Knowledge," in *Writings,* pp. 20–21.

32. Ibid., pp. 19–20.

33. Parley P. Pratt, *Late Persecution of the Church of Jesus Christ, of Latter Day Saints. Ten Thousand American Citizens Robbed, Plundered, and Banished; Others Imprisoned, and Others Martyred for Their Religion. . . . Written in Prison* (New York: J. W. Harrison, 1840), p. iii; idem, "Grapes from Thorns, and Figs from Thistles," reprinted from *Millennial Star,* in *Writings,* p. 303.

34. Pratt, "Grapes from Thorns," p. 303.
35. Ibid., pp. 303–4.
36. Pratt, *Key to the Science of Theology,* p. 70.
37. Ibid., pp. 18–19.
38. This is a very different argument from that made by Robert N. Hullinger in *Mormon Answer to Skepticism: Why Joseph Smith Wrote the Book of Mormon* (St. Louis: Clayton Publishing House, 1980). Hullinger argues that Mormonism was essentially a response to skepticism and deism.
39. Edward Wheelock Tullidge, *The Women of Mormonism* (New York: Tullidge and Crandall, 1877), pp. 41–42; *Eliza R. Snow: An Immortal: Selected Writings of Eliza R. Snow* (n.p.: Nicholas G. Morgan, Sr., Foundation, 1957), 1:5ff.
40. John Murdock, *An Abridged Record of the life of John Murdock, taken from his Journal by himself,* pp. 4–10; copy loaned by Milton V. Backman, Brigham Young University.
41. Pratt, *Voice of Warning,* pp. 118–9.
42. Pratt, "Grapes from Thorns," p. 303.
43. *Doctrine and Covenants* 131:7.
44. Parley P. Pratt, "Immortality and Eternal Life of the Material Body," in *Writings,* p. 28; idem, "The World Turned upside Down," in *Writings,* pp. 28, 65; idem, *Key to the Science of Theology,* pp. 47–48. Likewise, Joseph Smith himself had declared in 1833 that "the elements are eternal" (*Doctrine and Covenants* 93:33).
45. Pratt, *Key to the Science of Theology,* pp. 49–50.
46. Pratt, "Fountains of Knowledge," p. 18. Cf. idem, *Key to the Science of Theology,* pp. 32–33.
47. Pratt, *Key to the Science of Theology,* pp. 155–56.
48. Pratt, "Fountain of Knowledge," p. 18.
49. Alexander Campbell, "Delusions," *Millennial Harbinger* 2 (February 7, 1831): 93, 87.
50. Walter Scott, "Mormon Bible—No. I," *Evangelist,* new series, 9 (January 1, 1841): 18–19.
51. Pratt, *Late Persecution,* p. 171; Pratt, "Proclamation of the Gospel," in *Writings,* p. 163.
52. "An Epistle of the Twelve Apostles, to the Brethren Scattered Abroad on the Continent of America," in J. Smith, *History of the Church,* 4:437.
53. *The Book of Moses* 7, esp. verses 21, 23, and 62–65. *The Book of Moses* is included in the Mormon scripture, *The Pearl of Great Price.* For Jackson County, Missouri, as Zion, see J. Smith, *History of the Church,* 1:189; and idem, *Doctrine and Covenants* 57:1–3. For America as Zion, see J. Smith, *History of the Church,* 6:318–19. For Davies County as Garden of Eden, see J. Smith, *Doctrine and Covenants* 107:53–57, 116.
54. Pratt, *Voice of Warning,* p. 177.
55. J. Smith, *History of the Church,* 1:358; Parley P. Pratt, "Proclamation of the Twleve Apostles," in *Writings,* p. 13.
56. *Millennial Star* 6 (1845):140–42, cited in Robert Flanders, "To Transform History: Early Mormon Culture and the Concept of Time and Space,"

Church History 40 (March 1971): 111–12. Flanders's article is a seminal statement of early Mormon attempts to collapse both space and time into their restored millennial kingdom.

57. J. Smith, *History of the Church,* 4:277; Idem, *Doctrine and Covenants* 124:27–39. Cf. Robert Flanders, *Nauvoo: Kingdom on the Mississippi* (Urbana: University of Illinois Press, 1965), pp. 190–91.

58. Pratt, *Key to the Science of Theology,* pp. 128–29; Klaus J. Hansen, *Mormonism and the American Experience* (Chicago: University of Chicago Press, 1981), p. 103.

59. J. Smith, *History of the Church,* 5:391–92; idem, *Doctrine and Covenants* 132:19–20. The revelation on celestial marriage was never made public by Joseph Smith during his own lifetime, but only in 1852 by Brigham Young. See Flanders, *Nauvoo,* pp. 274–75.

60. Parley P. Pratt, "A Letter to the Queen," in *Writings,* pp. 97, 100, and 108.

61. Pratt, *Voice of Warning,* pp. 140–42. This chapter, which is the pivotal "warning" section of *Voice of Warning,* has been deleted from the modern 1978 edition.

62. J. Smith, *Doctrine and Covenants* 134; idem, *History of the Church,* 6:208–9.

63. J. Smith, *Doctrine and Covenants* 134:11.

64. Klaus J. Hansen, *Quest for Empire: The Political Kingdom of God and the Council of Fifty in Mormon History* (Lincoln: University of Nebraska Press, 1974), p. 23. Grant Underwood faults Hansen's social deprivation perspective, in "Early Mormon Millenarianism: Another Look," *Church History* 54 (June 1985): 222f. But see also idem, "Millenarianism and the Early Mormon Mind," *Journal of Mormon History* 9 (1982): 45.

65. Pratt, *Key to the Science of Theology,* p. 135.

66. Orson Pratt, *The Kingdom of God* (Liverpool, England, 1851), p. 1. The antipluralism implicit in the early Mormon vision of the kingdom of God should not be surprising, expecially given the Old Testament, theocratic roots of this vision. Indeed, Richard Bushman has argued effectively that the "templates for Book of Mormon politics" were biblical, not American. Bushman notes that "Book of Mormon government by Jacksonian standards was no democracy. . . . Looking at the Book of Mormon as a whole, it seems clear that most of the principles associated with the American Constitution are slighted or disregarded altogether." Bushman concluded that "Book of Mormon political attitudes have Old World precedents, particularly in the history of the Israelite nation." Bushman, "The Book of Mormon and the American Revolution," *Brigham Young University Studies* 17 (Autumn 1976): 16–19.

67. J. Smith, *Doctrine and Covenants* 76.

68. Pratt, *Key to the Science of Theology,* p. 134.

Chapter 7. Freedom from Dogma

1. Howard Mumford Jones, "The Influence of European Ideas in Nineteenth-Century America," *American Literature* 7 (1935): 251; Richard J. Petersen, "Scottish Common Sense in America, 1768–1850: An Evaluation of Its

Influence," Ph.D. diss., American University, 1963; Sydney E. Ahlstrom, "The Scottish Philosophy and American Theology," *Church History* 24 (1955): 257–72; D. H. Meyer, *The Instructed Conscience: The Shaping of the American National Ethic* (Philadelphia: University of Pennsylvania Press, 1972); idem, *The Democratic Enlightenment* (New York: Putnam, 1976); Douglas Sloan, *The Scottish Enlightenment and the American College Ideal* (New York: Teacher's College Press, Columbia University, 1971); Thomas Edward Frank, "Conserving a Rational World: Theology, Ethics, and the Nineteenth Century American College Ideal," Ph.D. diss., Emory University, 1981; Herbert Schneider, *A History of American Philosophy* (New York, 1946), pp. 238–40, 246–50; J. David Hoeveler, Jr., *James McCosh and the Scottish Intellectual Tradition: From Glasgow to Princeton* (Princeton: Princeton University Press, 1981).

2. Ahlstrom, "Scottish Philosophy," pp. 267–68.

3. Thomas Reid, *Essays on the Intellectual Powers of Man,* ed. Baruch Brody (Cambridge: Harvard University Press, 1969), essay 2, chap. 5, p. 114. Essay 6, entitled "Of Judgment," contains a summary of Reid's first principles. For summary and analysis of Reid's views, see James McCosh, *The Scottish Philosophy, Biographical, Expository, Critical, from Hutcheson to Hamilton* (New York: Robert Carter and Bros., 1875); S. A. Grave, *The Scottish Philosophy of Common Sense* (Oxford: Oxford University Press, 1960); and Olin McKendree Jones, *Empiricism and Intuitionism in Reid's Common Sense Philosophy* (Princeton: Princeton University Press, 1927).

4. Theodore Dwight Bozeman, *Protestants in an Age of Science: The Baconian Ideal and Antebellum American Religious Thought* (Chapel Hill: University of North Carolina Press, 1977), p. 7.

5. Ibid., pp. 4–21, 160. See also George H. Daniels, "The Reign of Bacon in America," in *American Science in the Age of Jackson* (New York: Columbia University Press, 1968), pp. 63–85; and Herbert Hovenkamp, *Science and Religion in America, 1800–1860* (Philadelphia: University of Pennsylvania Press, 1978), pp. 19–36.

6. Edward Everett, "Character of Lord Bacon," *North American Review* 16 (1823): 300, quoted by Bozeman, *Protestants in an Age of Science,* p. 3; see also pp. 21–31.

7. Ahlstrom, "Scottish Philosophy," pp. 257–72; John Vander Stelt, *Philosophy and Scripture: A Study in Old Princeton and Westminster Theology* (Marlton, N.J.: Mack Publishing, 1978); David K. Garth, "The Influence of Scottish Common Sense Philosophy on the Theology of James H. Thornwell and Robert L. Dabney," Ph.D. diss., Union Theological Seminary, Va., 1979; James E. Hamilton, "Nineteenth Century Holiness Theology: A Study of the Thought of Asa Mahan," *Wesleyan Theological Journal* 13 (Spring 1978): 51–64; E. Brooks Holifield, *The Gentlemen Theologians: American Theology in Southern Culture* (Durham, N.C.: Duke University Press, 1978), p. 206 and *passim;* George Marsden, *Fundamentalism and American Culture: The Shaping of Twentieth-Century Evangelicalism, 1870–1925* (New York: Oxford University Press, 1980), pp. 55–62.

8. Note, for example, the scientific or Baconian claims of the spiritualist

movement. R. Lawrence Moore, *In Search of White Crows: Spiritualism, Parapsychology, and American Culture* (New York: Oxford University Press, 1977), pp. 62–63.

9. Samuel Tyler, *Discourse of the Baconian Philosophy,* 2d ed. (New York, 1850), p. 15; and Benjamin M. Palmer, "Baconianism and the Bible," *Southern Presbyterian Review* 6 (1850): 250; both quoted by Bozeman, *Protestants in an Age of Science,* pp. 128, 130.

10. James S. Lamar, *The Organon of Scripture: Or, the Inductive Method of Biblical Interpretation* (Philadelphia: J. B. Lippincott, 1859), p. 176.

11. Ibid., pp. 26, 32.

12. See Charles Franklin Kilgore, *The James O'Kelly Schism in the Methodist Episcopal Church* (Mexico City: Casa Unida de publications, 1963); on Smith, see William G. McLoughlin, *New England Dissent, 1630–1883: The Baptists and the Separation of Church and State,* 2 vols. (Cambridge: Harvard University Press, 1971), 2:745–49; and Thomas H. Olbricht, "Christian Connection and Unitarian Relations," *Restoration Quarterly* 9 (September 1966): 160–86; on Stone, see William G. West, *Barton Warren Stone: Early American Advocate of Christian Unity* (Nashville: Disciples of Christ Historical Society, 1954); on the Campbells, see Robert Richardson, *Memoirs of Alexander Campbell,* 2 vols. (Cincinnati: Standard Publishing, 1913); and Alexander Campbell, *Memoirs of Elder Thomas Campbell* (Cincinnati, 1861). For primary accounts of the movements see Charles Alexander Young, *Historical Documents Advocating Christian Unity* (Chicago: Christian Century, 1904); Barton W. Stone, *An Apology for Renouncing the Jurisdiction of the Synod of Kentucky* (Lexington, Ky., 1804); Robert Marshall and James Thompson, *A Brief Historical Account of Sundry Things in the Doctrine and State of the Christian, or, as It is Commonly Called, the Newlight Church* (Cincinnati, 1811); Elias Smith, *The Life, Conversion, Preaching, Travels and Sufferings of Elias Smith* (Portsmouth, N.H., 1816); and James O'Kelly, *The Author's Apology for Protesting against the Methodist Episcopal Government* (Richmond, 1798).

13. For primary accounts of this phenomenon, see John W. Nevin, "Antichrist and the Sect System" (1848), in James Hastings Nichols, ed., *The Mercersburg Theology* (New York: Oxford University Press, 1966), pp. 93–119; and Charles Beecher, *The Bible a Sufficient Creed* (Boston, 1850). For recent studies on the democratization of religion in this period, see Nathan O. Hatch, "*Sola Scriptura* and *Novus Ordo Seclorum,*" in Mark A. Noll and Nathan O. Hatch, eds., *The Bible in America: Essays in Cultural History* (New York: Oxford University Press, 1982), pp. 59–78; idem, "The Christian Movement and the Demand for a Theology of the People," *Journal of American History* 67 (1980): 545–66; and Ronald E. Osborn, *Experiment in Liberty: The Ideal of Freedom in the Experience of the Disciples of Christ* (St. Louis: Bethany Press, 1978).

14. Alexander Campbell, *Christian Baptist* 3 (January 2, 1826): 209; Barton Stone et al., "Last Will and Testament," in *Historical Documents Advocating Christian Union* (Chicago: Christian Century, 1904), p. 22. See chap. 5, pp. 104–8.

15. Alexander Campbell, "An Oration in Honor of the Fourth of July, 1830," in *Popular Lectures and Addresses* (Philadelphia, 1863), p. 374; Thomas Campbell, "Declaration and Address," pp. 115, 75–76.

16. Alexander Campbell, *Christian Baptist* 3 (April 3, 1826): 229. See also his long series of articles entitled "A Restoration of the Ancient Order of Things," beginning in the *Christian Baptist* 2 (February 7, 1825).

17. See Robert B. Come, "The Influence of Princeton on Higher Education in the South before 1825," *William and Mary Quarterly,* 2d series, 2 (October 1945): 362–94.

18. Lester G. McAllister and William E. Tucker, *Journey in Faith: A History of the Christian Church (Disciples of Christ)* (St. Louis: Bethany Press, 1975), pp. 154–55. For other general accounts of the movement, see Winfred E. Garrison and Alfred T. DeGroot, *The Disciples of Christ* (St. Louis: Christian Board of Publication, 1948); James DeForest Murch, *Christians Only* (Cincinnati: Standard Publishing, 1962); and David E. Harrell, *Quest for a Christian America: The Disciples of Christ and American Society to 1866* (Nashville: Disciples of Christ Historical Society, 1966).

19. Winfred E. Garrison, in *Alexander Campbell's Theology: Its Sources and Historical Setting* (St. Louis: Christian Publishing, 1900), placed primary emphasis on Locke. F. D. Kershner, in *The Christian Union Overture: An Interpretation of the "Declaration and Address" of Thomas Campbell* (St. Louis: Bethany Press, 1923), pp. 155–57, argued that Campbell derived his psychology from Locke and his metaphysics from the Scottish philosophers. James Ellerbrook concluded, in "The Influence of Thomas Reid on the Thought-Life of Alexander Campbell," B.D. thesis, Christian Theological Seminary, 1947, that "the primary influence on Campbell was Thomas Reid and the common sense school from which he took his epistemology" (p. 32). Pointing to the influence of both Locke and Reid, Robert F. West, in *Alexander Campbell and Natural Religion* (New Haven: Yale University Press, 1948), pp. 220–21, 225, saw Campbell's thought as a complex and eclectic synthesis drawing from many sources.

20. Merle Curti, "The Great Mr. Locke: America's Philosopher, 1783–1861," *Huntington Library Bulletin* (1937): 108, 110–13, 117. See also Bozeman, *Protestants in an Age of Science,* pp. 23–25.

21. *Alexander Campbell at Glasgow University, 1808–1809,* transcribed with an introduction by Lester G. McAllister (Nashville: Disciples of Christ Historical Society, 1971), p. 4. Campbell's library at Bethany contained a copy of Jardine's *Synopsis of Lectures on Logic and Belles Lettres Read in the University of Glasgow* (Glasgow: University Press, 1804), which he had signed and dated December 10, 1808. According to Jardine, the chief accomplishment of Bacon's work was a "simple return to principles of unsophisticated reason" which would rescue people from "the dominion of art, and . . . restore them to the clear light, and unfettered liberty, of nature." *Outlines of Philosophical Education Illustrated by the Method of Teaching the Logic Class in the University of Glasgow,* 2d ed. (Glasgow: University Press, 1825), p. 152. See also Richardson, *Memoirs of Alexander Campbell,* chaps. 9–10; and Carisse Mickey Berryhill, "Sense, Ex-

pression, and Purpose: Alexander Campbell's Natural Philosophy of Rhetoric,"
Ph.D. diss., Florida State University, 1982, esp. pp. 54–86.

22. Alexander Campbell and Robert Owen, *Debate on the Evidences of Christianity: Containing an Examination of the "Social System" and of All Systems of Scepticism of Ancient and Modern Times* (Bethany. Va., 1829), 2:248–49, 4–6; cf. also 2:13–24. In the debate, Campbell also cited Reid's *Essay on the Human Mind* (2:48).

23. Alexander Campbell, *Millennial Harbinger* 1 (1830): 9; idem, *The Christian System, in Reference to the Union of Christians, and a Restoration of Primitive Christianity, as Plead in the Current Reformation* (Bethany, Va., 1839), p. 6. See also idem, *Millennial Harbinger* 5 (1835): 21–23.

24. Alexander Campbell, "Principles of Interpretation," in *A Connected View of the Principles and Rules by Which the Living Oracles May be Intelligently and Certainly Interpreted* (Bethany, Va., 1835), pp. 13–99.

25. Walter Scott, *The Gospel Restored. A Discourse of the True Gospel of Jesus Christ, in which the Facts, Principles, Duties, and Privileges of Christianity are Arranged, Defined, and Discussed, and the Gospel in its Various Parts Shewn to be Adapted to the Nature and Necessities of Man in his Present Condition* (Cincinnati: O. H. Donough, 1836), pp. v–vi; see also pp. 54–67. On Scott, see Dwight Stevenson, *Walter Scott: Voice of the Golden Oracle* (St. Louis: Christian Board of Publications, 1946); and William A. Gerrard, "Walter Scott: Frontier Disciples Evangelist," Ph.D. diss., Emory University, 1982. See also chap. 5, pp. 123–24.

26. Dwight Stevenson, *The Bacon College Story, 1836–1865* (Lexington, Ky.: College of the Bible, 1962), p. 10; Walter Scott, "The State System," *Christian* 1 (February –March 1837): 25–72.

27. James R. Wilburn, *The Hazard of the Die: Tolbert Fanning and the Restoration Movement* (Austin, Tex.: Sweet Publishing, 1969), pp. 29–35, 62–101, 176; Tolbert Fanning, "Spiritual Light (No. 10)," *Religious Historian* 1 (October 1872): 289–95; idem, "Metaphysical Discussions," *Gospel Advocate* 2 (November 1856): 326–29.

28. See Richardson's series of articles "Faith versus Philosophy," *Millennial Harbinger* (beginning March 1857); Robert Milligan, *Reason and Revelation* (Cincinnati: R. W. Carroll, 1868), p. 290; J. W. McGarvey, *Sacred Didactics* (reprint, Murfreesboro, Tenn.: DeHoff Publications, 1954), pp. 51–53.

29. For biographical information on Lamar, see the following: J. S. Lamar, *Recollections of Pioneer Days in Georgia* (n.p., 1906); W. T. Moore, ed., *The Living Pulpit of the Christian Church* (Cincinnati: R. W. Carroll, 1868), pp. 401–10; and J. Edward Moseley, *Disciples of Christ in Georgia* (St. Louis: Bethany Press, 1954), pp. 171–75 and *passim*.

30. Alexander Campbell, *Millennial Harbinger,* 5th series, 3 (February 1860): 100–101; W. K. Pendleton, "Biblical Interpretation," *Millennial Harbinger,* 5th series, 3 (February 1860): 84–85; Tolbert Fanning, "A New Book on 'Interpretation,'" *Gospel Advocate* 6 (1860): 30; Benjamin Franklin, *American Christian Review* 2 (December 20, 1859): 202; and A. E. Myers, " 'The Organon of

Scripture,' " nos. I–V, *American Christian Review* 3 (March 27–May 1, 1860): 49, 61, 65, 69.

31. Fanning, "New Book," p. 30. For Fanning's contention that "all the sacred records contradict the supposition that an interpreter is needed," see his *True Method of Searching the Scriptures* (reprint, Nashville: McQuiddy Printing, 1911), pp. 18–21.

32. Lamar, *Organon of Scripture,* pp. v, 140.

33. Ibid., pp. iii, 17. In his lengthy review of the *Organon,* A. E. Myer, one of Lamar's teachers at Bethany College, noted that, while Lamar was the first to systematize the inductive method and reduce it to rules, the method had been used "with the living voice and through the press for near half a century by our brethren." *American Christian Review* 3 (April 24, 1860): 65.

34. For examples of earlier works that belie Lamar's claim to originality, see James W. Alexander, "On the Use and Abuse of Systematic Theology," *Biblical Repertory and Princeton Review* 4 (1832): 171–90; Benjamin B. Smith, "Theology a Strictly Inductive Science," *Literary and Theological Review* 2 (1835): 89–95; Laurens P. Hickok, "Christian Theology as a Science," *American Biblical Repository,* 3d series, 1 (1845): 457–87; and Palmer, "Baconianism and the Bible," pp. 226–53. For other examples, see Bozeman, *Protestants in an Age of Science,* pp. 144–51 and *passim.*

35. Lamar, *Organon of Scripture,* pp. 18–33, 39–43.

36. Ibid., pp. 48, 56, 81.

37. Ibid., pp. 116, 121, 126.

38. Ibid., pp. 130–31.

39. Ibid., pp. 128–73.

40. Ibid., pp. 132, 134, 138–41, 148–50; idem, "The Christian Religion: I. The Elimination," *Christian Standard* 8 (June 21, 1873): 196.

41. Lamar, *Organon of Scripture,* pp. 174–75.

42. Ibid., pp. 187, 188, 189, 190–91, 188.

43. Ibid., pp. 191–92, 193.

44. Ibid., p. 181.

45. Ibid., pp. 240–63.

46. Ibid., pp. 196, 197, 194.

47. Ibid., pp. 213, 235. Despite his interpretive rule, Lamar on occasion could historicize and allegorize this "highly-colored imagery" in amazing ways. In a sermon, for example, he interpreted the seven parables of Matthew 13 as portraying the "various phases and fortunes" of the church throughout history. *Christian Standard* 11 (February 5, 1876): 41.

48. Lamar, *Organon of Scripture,* pp. 239, 245, 254–55, 248, 256–57, 239. See also idem, "Primary Concepts of Religion (III)," *Christian Standard* 9 (January 24, 1874): 84–85.

49. Daniels, *American Science,* pp. 118–37. Among the vast body of materials relating to the evangelical crisis after 1860, see the following: Marsden, *Fundamentalism and American Culture,* pp. 11–39; Paul A. Carter, *The Spiritual Crisis of the Gilded Age* (De Kalb: Northern Illinois University Press, 1971); Grant Wacker, "The Demise of Biblical Civilization," in Noll and Hatch, *Bible in Amer-*

ica, pp. 121–38; and James R. Moore, *The Post-Darwinian Controversies: A Study of the Protestant Struggle to Come to Terms with Darwin in Great Britain and America, 1870–1900* (Cambridge: Cambridge University Press, 1979).

50. See David E. Harrell, *The Social Sources of Division in the Disciples of Christ, 1865–1900* (Atlanta: Publishing Systems, 1973), esp. pp. 1–49; idem, "The Sectional Origins of the Churches of Christ," *Journal of Southern History* 30 (August 1964): 261–77; and idem, "From Consent to Dissent: The Emergence of the Churches of Christ in America," *Restoration Quarterly* 19 (1976): 98–111. See also Richard T. Hughes, "The Role of Theology in the Nineteenth-Century Division of the Disciples of Christ," in Edwin S. Gaustad, ed., *American Religion: 1974,* (Missoula, Mont.: Scholar's Press, 1974), pp. 56–78.

51. David Lipscomb, *Salvation from Sin,* ed. J. W. Shepherd (Nashville: McQuiddy Printing, 1913), pp. 235–62, 331–46; J. N. Armstrong, "Brother Foster's Article," *The Way* 3 (October 24, 1901): 239.

52. J. T. Poe, "Christian Liberality, No. 3," *Gospel Advocate* 17 (May 20, 1875): 498.

53. J. H. Garrison, ed., *The Old Faith Restated* (St. Louis: Christian Publishing, 1891), pp. 329–52; J. S. Lamar, "The Veiled Heart," *Christian Standard* 33 (March 26, 1898): 385–86.

54. For representative examples of Disciple efforts to refute evolution and higher criticism, see Clark Braden, *The Problem of Problems and Its Various Solutions: or, Atheism, Darwinism, and Theism* (Cincinnati: Chase and Hall, 1877); and George Plattenburg, "Materialistic Evolution," in *The Missouri Christian Lectures Selected from the Courses of 1886, 1887, and 1888* (Cincinnati: Standard Publishing, 1888), pp. 150–210. On the debate over higher criticism in the late nineteenth century, see Anthony L. Ash, "Attitudes toward Higher Criticism of the Old Testament in the Restoration Movement," Ph.D. diss., University of Southern California, 1966.

55. James S. Lamar, "Christian Union," *Christian Standard* 7 (May 18, 1872): 156, 172; idem, "The Christian Religion: II. The Interpretation," *Christian Standard* 8 (July 5, 1873): 220. Examples of how Lamar worked out these themes in his preaching during this period can be seen in his notebook entitled "Sketches of Occasional Sermons," Southern Historical Collection, University of North Carolina, Chapel Hill. Especially illuminating is a sermon of 1878 entitled "The Old Paths," pp. 110–113.

56. James S. Lamar, "How to Preach First Principles," *Christian Standard* 33 (January 1, 1898): 3; idem, "First Principles: XIII. The Place of Baptism," *Christian Standard* 26 (April 18, 1891): 323–24. Cf. also idem, "Settling in Jerusalem," *Christian Standard* 26 (January 10, 1891): 22; idem, "Going on to Perfection: XIV. Drawing Near," *Christian Standard* 26 (August 15, 1891): 681–82; idem, "Is the Sermon on the Mount a Creed?" *Christian Standard* 33 (February 26, 1898): 259; idem, "Veiled Heart," pp. 385–86.

57. James S. Lamar, "What Most Interests Me Now: II. The Passage of the Eternal into the Temporal," *Christian-Evangelist,* 20 (January 31, 1901): 137.

58. James S. Lamar, "What Most Interests Me Now: III. Light from the New Creation," *Christian-Evangelist,* 20 (February 14, 1901): 202; idem, "V. The Mean-

ing of Coal," *Christian- Evangelist,* 20 (March 14, 1901): 329; idem, "VIII. The Serpent in the Garden," *Christian-Evangelist* (April 25, 1901): 525. Lamar's views were shaped in part by the Presbyterian geologist Joseph Le Conte, whose evolutionary views strongly influenced American clergymen. See Lamar, "Religion and Science," *Christian Standard* 9 (March 28, 1874): 101. The dominant view that emerged among moderate and conservative Disciples was that Le Conte's teaching represented "unvarnished materialism." See B. J. Radford, "Le Conte and Materialism," *Christian Standard* 23 (March 31, 1888): 201. On Le Conte see Moore, *Post-Darwinian Controversies,* pp. 224–25; and Lester D. Stephens, "Joseph Le Conte's Evolutional Idealism: A Lamarckian View of Cultural History," *Journal of the History of Ideas* 39 (1978): 465–80.

59. "Letter from Bro. Lamar," *Christian Standard* 34 (December 23, 1899): 1648; idem, "The Old Man Himself," *Christian Standard* 38 (March 28, 1903): 433–34.

60. David R. Dungan, *Hermeneutics: A Text Book* (Cincinnati: Standard Publishing, 1888), p. 101.

61. See James B. North, "The Fundamentalist Controversy among the Disciples of Christ, 1890–1930," Ph.D. diss., University of Illinois, 1973.

Chapter 8. From Primitive Church to Protestant Nation

1. See Robert Frederick West, *Alexander Campbell and Natural Religion* (New Haven: Yale University Press, 1948), pp. 166ff.; Alexander Campbell, "Address on the Amelioration of the Social State," in *Popular Lectures and Addresses* (St. Louis: John Burns, 1861), p. 69; idem, "Prospectus," *Millennial Harbinger* 1 (January 1830): 1–2.

2. Cf. J. F. Maclear, "The Republic and the Millennium," in Elwyn A. Smith, ed., *The Religion of the Republic* (Philadelphia: Fortress Press, 1971), pp. 183–216; Lefferts A. Loetscher, "The Problem of Christian Unity in Early Nineteenth-Century America," *Church History* 32 (March 1963); Lyman Beecher, "The Memory of Our Fathers," *Works* (Boston: John P. Jewett, 1852–53), 1:176.

3. Alexander Campbell, "A Restoration of the Ancient Order of Things. No. 1.," *Christian Baptist* 2 (February 7, 1825): 136; Alexander Campbell and Robert Owen, *The Evidences of Christianity: A Debate* (St. Louis: Christian Board of Publication, n.d.), p. 395.

4. Campbell and Owen, pp. 385, 351.

5. Campbell, "Prospectus," pp. 1–2; cf. idem, "Preface," *Millennial Harbinger* 4 (January 1833): 3–4. Idem, "Millennium—No. 1," *Millennial Harbinger* 1 (February 6, 1830): 53–58.

6. H. Richard Niebuhr rightly perceived the utilitarian nature of restorationism in Campbell's thought when he noted the Disciples movement "was somewhat more interested in the social principle of union than in the individual principle of salvation of souls." *The Social Sources of Denominationalism* (Cleveland: World Publishing Company, 1957), p. 180.

7. Campbell, "Millennium—No. 1," pp. 55–56.

8. Ibid., p. 58.

9. Campbell and Owen, *Evidences,* p. 372.

10. Alexander Campbell, "Millennium—No. II.," *Millennial Harbinger* 1 (April 5, 1830): 13.

11. Ibid.

12. Alexander Campbell, "An Oration in Honor of the Fourth of July" (1830), in *Popular Lectures and Addresses,* p. 373. A good discussion of Campbell's attitudes toward and relations with Enlightenment thought may be found in West, *Natural Religion,* pp. 45–122.

13. Campbell, "An Oration," pp. 374–75.

14. Campbell and Owen, *Evidences,* p. 63.

15. Ibid., pp. 51, 145–46.

16. Ibid., p. 122.

17. Alexander Campbell, *Familiar Lectures on the Pentateuch,* ed. W. T. Moore (Cincinnati: Bosworth, Chase and Hall, 1871), pp. 374ff., cited in West, *Natural Religion,* p. 200.

18. Campbell and Owen, *Evidences,* pp. 261, 262.

19. Ibid., pp. v, 14.

20. Ibid., pp. 99, viii, 370.

21. Campbell, "An Oration," p. 377.

22. Alexander Campbell, "Letters to England—No. X.," *Millennial Harbinger,* new series, 2 (October 1838): 474; and idem, "Incidents on a Tour to the South, No. I," *Millennial Harbinger,* new series, 3 (January 1839): 8. Cf. idem, "Revival in Georgetown, Kentucky," *Millennial Harbinger* 2 (April 1831): 179; and idem, "Address on War" (1848), in *Popular Lectures and Addresses,* pp. 342–66.

23. Campbell himself participated in the Virginia constitutional convention of 1829 as a delegate from Brooke County.

24. Cf. Mircea Eliade, *The Quest: History and Meaning in Religion* (Chicago: University of Chicago Press, 1969), pp. 88–101.

25. Ibid. Also Charles L. Sanford, *The Quest for Paradise: Europe and the American Moral Imagination* (Urbana: University of Illinois Press, 1961), pp. 74–93.

26. For the English Puritan background, see James C. Spalding, "Restitution as a Normative Factor for Puritan Dissent," *Journal of the American Academy of Religion* 44 (March 1976): 47–63; for the Scotch-Irish background to Campbell, see Lynn A. McMillan, *Restoration Roots* (Dallas: Gospel Teachers Publications, 1983).

27. See G. R. Cragg, *From Puritanism to the Age of Reason* (Cambridge: Cambridge University Press, 1966), pp. 13–36, 114–35.

28. Cf. Oliver Read Whitley, *Trumpet Call of Reformation* (St. Louis: Bethany Press, 1959), pp. 47–67, 79ff., 96ff. Whitley calls the *Christian Baptist* "a veritable gold mine for the discovery of the evidence of sectarian traits in the early history of a religious movement" (p. 53).

29. Campbell believed that the record of a certain act indicated clearly that the act had been commanded but that the command had not been recorded in scripture. "A Restoration of the Ancient Order of Things. No. VII," *Christian*

Baptist 3 (September 5, 1825): 29. Alexander's father, Thomas Campbell, accepted the validity of the "approved precedent" in the cornerstone of the movement. *The Declaration and Address* (1809; reprint, St. Louis: Bethany Press, 1960), p. 26.

30. Thomas Campbell's argument appears in a sermon cited in Robert Richardson, *Memoirs of Alexander Campbell* (1897; reprint, Nashville, 1956), 1:235–37. On societies see Alexander Campbell, "The Christian Religion," *Christian Baptist* 1 (August 1823): 14–15; idem, "To Mr. Robert Cautious," *Christian Baptist* 1 (March 1, 1824): 157; idem, *Christian Baptist* 5 (May 3, 1824): 195; and idem, "Signs of the Times," *Christian Baptist* 5 (January 1828): 150. For a thorough discussion of Campbell's early opposition to societies, see Bill J. Humble, "The Missionary Society Controversy in the Restoration Movement (1823–1875)," Ph.D. diss., University of Iowa, 1964, pp. 34–42. On creeds see Alexander Campbell, "A Restoration of the Ancient Order of Things. No. II," *Christian Baptist* 2 (March 1825): 153. On fellowship with the unimmersed see idem, "The Christian Messenger," *Millennial Harbinger* 1 (October 1830): 474.

31. Alexander Campbell, "A Restoration of the Ancient Order of Things. No. XI," *Christian Baptist* 3 (March 6, 1826): 164. On one occasion, however, Campbell strongly implied that when a modern situation parallels a primitive situation that gave rise to a circumstantial or nonessential practice, that practice continues to be binding. See idem, "A Restoration of the Ancient Order of Things. No. VII," *Christian Baptist* 3 (September 5, 1825): 31.

32. Campbell, "Restoration of the Ancient Order of Things. No. VII," pp. 30–31; idem, "Reply," *Christian Baptist* 4 (July 2, 1827): 256.

33. J. H., "To the Editor of the Christian Baptist," included under Campbell, "Restoration of the Ancient Order of Things. No. XI," pp. 162–63, 165.

34. Campbell, "Restoration of the Ancient Order of Things. No. VII," p. 30.

35. A. S. Hayden, *Early History of the Disciples in the Western Reserve, Ohio* (Cincinnati: Chase and Hall, 1875), pp. 298–99.

36. Richardson, *Memoirs,* pp. 394–98. According to Campbell's biographer, the birth of his first child in 1812 forced him to the scriptures where he discovered to his own satisfaction that believers' immersion alone was biblical.

37. Barton W. Stone, *Christian Messenger* 4 (August 1830): 201.

38. Alexander Campbell and W. L. McCalla, *A Public Debate on Christian Baptism* (1842; reprint, Kansas City: Old Paths Book Club, 1948), pp. 100, 116.

39. Alexander Campbell, *Christian Baptist* 4 (April 2, 1827): 172.

40. Alexander Campbell, "To 'Paulinus.' Letter II," *Christian Baptist* 4 (April 2, 1827): 188–89.

41. Harold Lunger has observed that "from about 1831 to the middle of the following decade Campbell's conception of the church underwent a gradual transformation from that of the radical sect form to that of the characteristic American church form—the denomination." *The Political Ethics of Alexander Campbell* (St. Louis: Bethany Press, 1954), p. 115. Cf. Whitley, *Trumpet Call,* pp. 47–154.

42. Alexander Campbell, "Co-operation of Churches. No. IV," *Millennial Harbinger* 2 (October 1831): 436; idem, "Co-operation," *Millennial Harbinger* 6 (March 1835): 121.

43. Alexander Campbell, "Church Organization—No. III.," *Millennial Harbinger,* 3d series, 6 (May 1849): 270; idem, *Millennial Harbinger,* 3d series, 6 (December 1849): 694–95. For a thorough discussion of the evolution of Campbell's thought on the society question from the early 1830s to 1849, see Humble, "Missionary Society Controversy," pp. 48–128.

44. Alexander Campbell, "Any Christians among Protestant Parties," *Millennial Harbinger,* new series, 1 (September 1837): 411–14. See also Campbell's later clarifications in "Christians among the Sects," *Millennial Harbinger,* new series, 1 (November 1837):506–8; and idem, "Any Christian among the Sects?" *Millennial Harbinger,* new series, 1 (December 1837): 561–67.

45. Alexander Campbell, "To an Independent Baptist," *Christian Baptist* 3 (May 1, 1826): 204; and idem, "Any Christians among the Sects?" *Millennial Harbinger,* new series, 1 (December 1837): 564–566, and 561.

46. Alexander Campbell, "Address on Colleges" (1854), in *Popular Lectures and Addresses,* p. 297. Cf. Robert N. Bellah, "Civil Religion in America," *Daedalus* 96 (Winter 1967): 1–8. In an article with a different intent and thesis than the present study, Mont Whitson called attention to the element of "common religion" in Campbell's thought. See "Campbell's Post Protestantism and Civil Religion," *West Virginia History* 37 (January 1976): 118. See also Richard T. Hughes, "The Role of Theology in the Nineteenth-Century Division of the Disciples of Christ," in Edwin S. Gaustad, ed., *American Religion: 1974* (Missoula, Mont.: Scholars Press, 1974), pp. 63–64.

47. Sidney E. Mead, "The Theology of the Republic and the Orthodox Mind," *Journal of the American Academy of Religion* 44 (March 1976): 109.

48. Campbell, "Address on Colleges," p. 297.

49. Alexander Campbell, "On Common Schools" (1841), in *Popular Lectures and Addresses,* p. 259.

50. Ibid., pp. 259, 261; see also Alexander Campbell, "Address on the Anglo-Saxon Language: Its Origin, Character and Destiny" (1849), in *Popular Lectures and Addresses,* pp. 32–33; and idem, "The Destiny of Our Country" (1852), in *Popular Lectures and Addresses,* pp. 167–81.

51. Campbell, "Destiny of Our Country," pp. 174, 178; idem, "Address on Colleges," p. 297.

52. Alexander Campbell, "Sabbath Mail Report," *Christian Baptist* 7 (April 1830): 233–34; "Letter from Charles Cassedy, Esq.," *Millennial Harbinger* 4 (September 1833): 464–67. For early Disciples' attitudes toward the Sabbath, see David E. Harrell, Jr., *Quest for a Christian America* (Nashville: Disciples of Christ Historical Society, 1966), pp. 190–96.

53. Campbell, "Address on War," p. 350. Campbell here illustrates well Franklin H.Littell's thesis that "in crisis, the Protestants revert instinctively to use of state power to effect their ends." *From State Church to Pluralism* (New York: Macmillan, 1971), p. 80.

54. West, *Natural Religion,* pp. 209–10; Alexander Campbell, "Church Organization—No. V.," *Millennial Harbinger,* 4th series, 3 (September 1853): 488.

55. Campbell, "Address on Colleges," pp. 305–6.

56. Ibid., p. 299.

57. Campbell, "Address on Education" (1856), in *Popular Lectures and Addresses,* p. 244. Cf. idem, "On Common Schools," p. 258.

58. Campbell, "Address on Colleges," pp. 309–10, 305, 310. Cf. idem, "Address on Education," pp. 324–26. As early as 1830, Campbell had argued that the "perfection of education . . . is necessary to the millennial order of society." However, he seriously doubted "whether the present mode of training the human mind in common schools . . .was not almost antipodes to reason, and sailing against the wind and tide of human nature. It is worse than wrong end foremost. We begin in metaphysics, and end in physics." "Education—No. 2," *Millennial Harbinger* 1 (June 7, 1830): 252.

59. Cf. Sidney E. Mead, *The Lively Experiment* (New York: Harper and Row, 1963), pp. 66–71. Campbell identified this common faith as belief in the death, burial, resurrection, and ascension of Jesus ("Address on Colleges," p. 305).

60. Campbell, "Destiny of Our Country," p. 181.

61. The notion that the restoration of the primitive church would inaugurate the millennial age apparently continued to operate in Campbell's mind to varying degrees throughout his life. See Campbell, "The Millennial Character of the Harbinger," *Millennial Harbinger,* new series, 4 (December 1840): 561–62; idem, "The Coming of the Lord—No. I," *Millennial Harbinger,* new series, 5 (January 1841): 7; and idem, "Christology, Christocracy," *Millennial Harbinger,* 5th series, 4 (August 1861): 465. The persistence of this theme, when Campbell also was pinning his millennial hopes on the Republic, can be explained largely by Campbell's tendency in his later years to confuse the religion of the Republic with Christianity.

62. Campbell, "Address on the Anglo-Saxon Language," p. 44.

63. Campbell, "Destiny of Our Country," p. 170.

64. Ibid., p. 174.

65. Ibid., p. 179. In moving from the primitive church to Protestant America as foundation for the millennial age, Campbell but repeated a similar movement made by the New England clergy who also experienced the failure of a purely spiritual principle—in this case, the restoration of vital piety—some one hundred years before. When the conversions of the Great Awakening grew thin and the hoped-for millennium failed to appear, the millennial hopes of the clergy grew dim. But the colonial victory over French forces at Louisbourg in 1745 and the subsequent signing of the Peace of Paris in 1763 redeemed those hopes. By the time of the American Revolution, the New England clergy had focused their millennial aspirations far more on the ability of the colonies to rout the tyrannies of Britain than on any principle of pure and vital religion alone. As Nathan O. Hatch observes, the civil millennialism of the revolutionary period "advanced freedom as the cause of God and defined the primary enemy as the antiChrist of civil oppression." *The Sacred Cause of Liberty: Republican Thought and the Millennium in Revolutionary New England* (New Haven: Yale University Press, 1977), pp. 31–54, esp. 53. The differences between Campbell and his forebearers are obvious, but the basic shift from pure and vital Christianity to a form of civil religion prevailed in both instances. Other important works dealing with millennialism in eighteenth-century America are James West Davidson, *The Logic of*

Millennial Thought: Eighteenth Century New England (New Haven: Yale University Press, 1977); and Ruth H. Bloch, *Visionary Republic: Millennial Themes in American Thought, 1758–1800* (New York: Cambridge University Press, 1985).

66. Alexander Campbell, "Prophesy—No. I," *Millennial Harbinger,* 5th series, 3 (March 1860): 122–23; idem, "Christology, Christocracy," pp. 462–65; idem, *Millennial Harbinger* (1864): 3–4, cited in West, *Natural Religion,* p. 217. On the evolution of Campbell's millennial hopes, see West, pp. 163–222.

67. Ernest Tuveson, *Redeemer Nation: The Idea of America's Millennial Role* (Chicago: University of Chicago Press, 1968), p. 217.

Chapter 9. A Civic Theology for the South

1. See Theodore Dwight Bozeman, *Protestants in an Age of Science: The Baconian Ideal and Antebellum American Religious Thought* (Chapel Hill: University of North Carolina Press, 1977), pp. 23–31; and our previous discussion in chap. 7, pp. 154–56.

2. See chapter 1 for our earlier elaboration of how Christ's particularities and Nature's universalities were blended into an American primordium in the early nineteenth century.

3. Cited in H. Shelton Smith, Robert T. Handy, and Lefferts A. Loetscher, eds., *American Christianity: An Historical Interpretation with Representative Documents* (New York: Charles Scribner's Sons, 1963), 2:177. Cf. Donald Mathews, "We Who Own Slaves Honor God's Law," in *Religion in the Old South* (Chicago: University of Chicago Press, 1977), pp. 136–84.

While southerners typically sought to exclude from their region all arguments based on "Nature and Nature's God," some—like Thomas Dew—sought to redefine natural law and natural rights in the interest of slavery. See Carl Becker, *The Declaration of Independence: A Study in the History of Political Ideas* (1922; reprint, New York: Alfred Knopf, 1942), p. 247.

4. Clement Eaton, *The Freedom of Thought Struggle in the Old South* (New York: Harper and Row, 1964), p. 303; E. Brooks Holifield, *The Gentleman Theologians: American Theology in Southern Culture, 1795–1860* (Durham, N.C.: Duke University Press, 1978), p. 50.

5. See Holifield, *Gentleman Theologians,* pp. 110–54, for the importance of Common Sense Realism for the southern theologians.

6. Thomas R. Dew, *Southern Literary Messenger* 2 (November 1836): 768, cited in Eaton, *Freedom of Thought Struggle,* pp. 300–301, 316.

7. *The Eighth Census of the United States, 1860: Mortality and Miscellaneous Statistics* (Washington, D.C., 1866), pp. 500–501; and *The Monthly Journal of American Unitarian Association, January, 1860* (Boston, 1960), pp. 37–41; both cited in Eaton, *Freedom of Thought Struggle,* p. 316. Eaton notes that the three Unitarian societies were in Louisville, New Orleans, and Charleston, though the latter was without a pastor.

8. Two theses and one dissertation have been written on Benjamin Palmer: Wayne Carter Eubank, "Benjamin M. Palmer: A Southern Divine," M.A. thesis, Louisiana State University, 1943; John William Lancaster, "Presbyterian Preaching

in Time of Crisis: Benjamin M. Palmer," M.A. thesis, Austin Presbyterian Seminary, 1960; and Doralyn Joanne Hickey, "Benjamin Morgan Palmer: Churchman of the Old South," Ph.D. diss., Duke University, 1962. The best work providing a context for Palmer's civic theology is James W. Silver, *Confederate Morale and Church Propaganda* (New York: W. W. Norton, 1967). A more recent work on southern civic theology in the postwar period is Charles Reagan Wilson, *Baptized in Blood: The Religion of the Lost Cause, 1865–1920* (Athens: University of Georgia Press, 1980). See also Mark A. Noll "The Image of the United States as a Biblical Nation, 1776–1865," in Nathan O. Hatch and Mark A. Noll, eds., *The Bible in America: Essays in Cultural History* (New York: Oxford University Press, 1982), pp. 39–58.

9. Benjamin Palmer, "The South: Her Peril and Her Duty" (29 November 1860), in Thomas Cary Johnson, *The Life and Letters of Benjamin Morgan Palmer* (Richmond, Va.: Presbyterian Committee of Publication, 1906), pp. 207, 215. For an analysis of this sermon, see Wayne C. Eubank, "Benjamin Morgan Palmer's Thanksgiving Sermon, 1860," in J. Jeffery Auer, ed., *Antislavery and Disunion, 1858–1861: Studies in the Rhetoric of Compromise and Conflict* (New York: Harper and Row, 1963), pp. 291–309.

10. Ibid., p. 208.

11. Johnson, *Life and Letters of Benjamin Morgan Palmer*, p. 222.

12. Hickey, "Benjamin Morgan Palmer," p. 67; George Junkin, *Political Fallacies: An Examination of the False Assumptions, and Refutation of the Sophistical Reasonings, Which Have Brought on this Civil War* (New York: C. Scribner, 1863), p. 189, cited in Hickey, "Benjamin Morgan Palmer," p. 191. Cf. also Eubank, "Palmer's Thanksgiving Sermon," pp. 305–9.

13. Benjamin Palmer, "National Responsibility before God" (New Orleans: Price-Current Steam Book and Job Printing Office, 1861), pp. 11–13, a discourse delivered on the Day of Fasting, Humiliation and Prayer, appointed by the president of the Confederate States of America, June 13, 1861.

14. Benjamin Palmer, "The South: Her Peril and Her Duty," in Johnson, *Life and Letters of Benjamin Morgan Palmer*, pp. 212–13.

15. Benjamin Palmer, "Influence of Religious Belief upon National Character" (Athens: Banner Office, 1845), p. 29, an oration delivered before the Demosthenian and Phi Kappa societies of the University of Georgia, August 7, 1845.

16. Benjamin Palmer, article no. 13, *South-Western Presbyterian* (November 11, 1869), p. 2, cited in Hickey, "Benjamin Morgan Palmer," p. 228.

17. Palmer articulated the link he saw between Protestantism, the Bible, and Baconianism in an 1852 address at Davidson College, published under the title "Baconianism and the Bible," in two separate sources: *Southern Presbyterian Review* (1852): 226–53, and a tract published in Columbia, South Carolina, 1852. For a discussion of Palmer's Baconianism and Common Sense Realism, see Bozeman, *Protestants in an Age of Science,* pp. 128–31.

18. Thomas Smyth, "The Sin and the Curse; or, the Union, The True Source of Disunion, and our Duty in the Present Crisis" (Charleston, S.C.: Steam Power Presses of Evans and Cogswell, 1860), p. 8, a discourse preached on the occasion

of the day of Humiliation and Prayer appointed by the governor of South Carolina, November 21, 1860.

19. Ibid., p. 13. Ironically, some northern preachers took almost precisely the same position regarding Puritanism and infidelity as did southern preachers, but merely reversed the proper regional loci of the two traditions. Horace Bushnell provides a case in point. Bushnell lamented the omission of God from the Constitution and claimed that the Declaration was "an atheistic bill." The root cause of the Civil War, he said, was the substitution of the sovereignty of the people for the sovereignty of God that, in turn, led to the state rights doctrine of the South. Bushnell clearly recognized the synthesis of Jehovah and the God of Nature or, as he put it, of "New England and Virginia," and he sought to separate the two with fully as much vigor as did Palmer or Thomas Smyth. Unlike the southerners, however, Bushnell contended that Jehovah rightly belonged in the North while Nature's God was sovereign over the South. See Sidney E. Mead, *The Old Religion in the Brave New World* (Berkeley: University of California Press, 1977), pp. 99–104.

20. Palmer, "National Responsibility before God," p. 13.

21. Ibid., pp. 5–6, 13. For the southern preachers' concept of the South as a chosen people, see Silver, *Confederate Morale and Church Propaganda*, pp. 25–41.

22. Benjamin Palmer, "Address Delivered at the Funeral of General Maxcy Gregg," December 20, 1862 (Columbia, S.C.: Southern Guardian Steam Power Press, 1863), p. 10.

23. Benjamin Palmer, "A Discourse before the General Assembly of South Carolina," December 10, 1863 (Columbia, S.C.: Charles P. Pelham, State Printer, 1864), p. 24, appointed by the legislature as a Day of Fasting, Humiliation, and Prayer.

24. Palmer, "National Responsibility before God," p. 5.

25. Samuel S. Hill, Jr., *The South and the North in American Religion* (Athens: University of Georgia Press, 1980), pp. 30–31.

26. Benjamin Palmer, "Our Historic Mission" (New Orleans: "True Witness" Office, 1859), p. 19, an address delivered before the Eunomian and Phi-Mu societies of La Grange Synodical College, July 7, 1858.

27. Benjamin Palmer, "The Rainbow round the Throne; or Judgment Tempered with Mercy" (Milledgeville, Ga.: Doughton, Nisbet, and Barnes, State Printers, 1863), p. 29, a discourse before the legislature of Georgia, delivered on the day of Fasting, Humiliation, and Prayer, appointed by the president of the Confederate States of America, March 27, 1863.

28. Palmer, "Discourse before the General Assembly of South Carolina," p. 22.

29. Benjamin Palmer, "Baconianism and the Bible" (Columbia, S.C.: A. S. Johnston, 1852), p. 28, an address delivered before the Eumenean and Philanthropic societies of Davidson College, August 11, 1852.

30. Palmer, "Rainbow round the Throne," p. 25.

31. George Foster Pierce, "Sermon before the General Assembly of Geor-

gia," March 27, 1863 (Milledgeville, Ga.: Doughton, Nisbet, and Barnes, State Printers, 1863), pp. 10–11, 13.

32. Palmer, "Influence of Religious Belief upon National Character," pp. 27–28.

33. Smyth, "Sin and the Curse," pp. 17–18.

34. On the change in "natural rights" ideology following the Revolution, see Kenneth S. Greenberg, "Revolutionary Ideology and the Proslavery Argument: The Abolition of Slavery in Ante-bellum South Carolina," *Journal of Southern History* 42 (1976): 365–84. If the "natural rights" tradition of the Declaration would not serve the cause of slavery, the "natural law" tradition of Roman Catholicism, adapted to the antebellum South, sometimes could. For example, Bishop John England of South Carolina, appealing to a host of Catholic thinkers, argued that while the institution of slavery resulted from sin and was introduced by "the law of nations," it nevertheless was "perfectly compatible with the natural law." Still, England admitted that he "would never aid in establishing it [slavery] where it did not exist." See England, "Letter II" (October 7, 1840), in *Letters of the Late Bishop England to the Honorable John Forsyth, on the Subject of Domestic Slavery* (1844; reprint, New York: Negro Universities Press, 1969), p. 23.

35. Wilson, *Baptized in Blood,* p. 12.

36. Thomas Virgil Peterson, *Ham and Japheth: The Mythic World of Whites in the Antebellum South* (Metuchen, N.J.: Scarecrow Press, 1978), p. 48.

37. Thomas Cobb, "An Inquiry into the Law of Negro Slavery in the United States of America" (1858; reprint, New York: Negro Universities Press, 1968), cited in Peterson, *Ham and Japheth,* pp. 51–52; Peterson, p. 53.

38. *African Servitude: When, Why, and by Whom Instituted, by Whom and How Long Shall It be Maintained?* (New York: Davies and Kent, 1860), p. 5, cited in Peterson, *Ham and Japheth,* p. 48.

39. Palmer, "National Responsibility before God," p. 8.

40. Palmer, "Discourse before the General Assembly of South Carolina," pp. 13, 21.

41. Palmer, "Rainbow Round the Throne," pp. 31–32. Philip S. Foner, ed., *The Complete Writings of Thomas Paine* (New York: Citadel Press, 1945), 1:273.

42. Palmer, "Rainbow round the Throne," p. 39.

43. Benjamin Palmer, "The Present Crisis and Its Issues" (Baltimore: John Murphy, 1872), pp. 18, 20, an address delivered before the literary societies of Washington and Lee University, June 27, 1872.

44. Ibid., pp. 20–21.

45. Wilson, *Baptized in Blood,* pp. 61, 68–69, 100. See also Gaines M. Foster, *Ghosts of the Confederacy: Defeat, the Lost Cause, and the Emergence of the New South, 1865 to 1913* (New York: Oxford University Press, 1987).

46. Palmer, "Our Historic Mission," pp. 18, 11.

47. Palmer, "Discourse before the General Assembly of South Carolina," pp. 18–19.

48. Ibid., p. 10; Palmer, "Rainbow round the Throne," p. 34.

49. Benjamin Palmer, "Exhortation to the Washington Artillery," *New Or-*

leans Daily Delta, May 29, 1861, reprinted in Johnson, *Life and Letters of Benjamin Morgan Palmer,* pp. 238–39.

50. Benjamin Palmer, "Address to Soldiers of the Legion and Gentlemen of the Army," *Columbia, S.C. Daily Southern Guardian,* June 10, 1864, p. 1.

51. Palmer, "National Responsibility before God," pp. 18, 17.

52. Ibid., p. 26.

53. Palmer, "Discourse before the General Assembly of South Carolina," p. 12; idem, "Address to Soldiers of the Legion and Gentlemen of the Army," p. 1.

54. Palmer, "Present Crisis and Its Issues," pp. 13–14.

55. Ibid., p. 17.

56. Benjamin Palmer, "The Oath of Allegiance to the United States, Discussed in Its Moral and Political Bearings" (Richmond, Va.: Macfarlane and Ferguson, 1863), pp. 26–27.

57. Benjamin Palmer, "The South: Her Peril and Her Duty," in Johnson, *Life and Letters of Benjamin Morgan Palmer,* p. 219.

Chapter 10. Nature, Innocence, and Illusion in American Life

1. Sidney E. Mead, *The Nation with the Soul of a Church* (New York: Harper and Row, 1975), p. 60.

2. Carl L. Becker, *The Heavenly City of the Eighteenth-Century Philosophers* (1932; reprint, New Haven: Yale University Press, 1964); and idem, *The Declaration of Independence: A Study in the History of Political Ideas* (New York: Vintage Books, 1922). A lively debate on both the significance and the shortcomings of Becker's work has persisted into recent years. See e.g., Cushing Strout, *The Pragmatic Revolt in American History: Carl Becker and Charles Beard* (New Haven: Yale University Press, 1958); Raymond O. Rockwood, ed., *Carl Becker's Heavenly City Revisited* (Ithaca, N.Y.: Cornell University Press, 1958); and Leonard Kreiger, "The Heavenly City of the Eighteenth-Century Historians," *Church History* 47 (September 1978): 279–97.

Little has been done to focus specifically on the primitivist dimension of Enlightenment thought. An important step in that direction is Winton U. Solberg, "Primitivism in the American Enlightenment," in Richard T. Hughes, ed., *The American Quest for the Primitive Church* (Urbana: University of Illinois Press, 1988).

3. Becker, *Heavenly City,* pp. 52–53.

4. Ibid., p. 66; Becker, *Declaration of Independence,* pp. 58–59.

5. Jean-Jacques Rousseau, *Eloise* (1810), 1: 4.

6. Becker, *Heavenly City,* p. 87; and idem, *Declaration of Independence,* p. 62.

7. Becker, *Heavenly City,* pp. 97–99.

8. Ibid., pp. 103–4. Thomas Jefferson, letter to Benjamin Waterhouse, June 26, 1822, in *Basic Writings of Thomas Jefferson,* ed. Philip S. Foner (1944; reprint, Garden City: Halcyon House, 1950), p. 775.

9. Ibid., p. 139. Cf. p. 118: "It was as if mankind, betrayed by barbarism and

religion, had been expelled from nature's Garden of Eden. . . . [But] to the future the Philosophers therefore look, as to a promised land, a new millennium."

10. Joseph Priestley, *An Essay on the First Principles of Government; and on the Nature of Political, Civil, and Religious Liberty* (London, 1771), pp. 4–5.

11. John Adams, *A Defense of the Constitutions of the Government of the United States of America,* abridged in *The Political Writings of John Adams: Representative Selections,* ed. George A. Peek (New York: Liberal Arts Press, 1954) p. 117. Thomas Paine, *Common Sense* in *The Complete Writings of Thomas Paine,* ed. Philip S. Foner (New York: Citadel Press, 1945), 1:45. Again, Paine declared that "the present age will hereafter merit to be called the Age of Reason, and the present generation will appear to the future as the Adam of a new world." *Rights of Man,* in Foner, 1:449.

12. Lyman Beecher, "The Memory of Our Fathers," a sermon delivered on December 22, 1827, reprinted in Winthrop S. Hudson, ed., *Nationalism and Religion in America* (New York: Harper and Row, 1970), pp. 104–5.

13. Becker, *Declaration of Independence,* pp. 237ff.

14. Lyman Beecher, *Republican Elements in the Old Testament: Lectures on Political Atheism and Kindred Subjects* (Boston, 1852), p. 189.

15. Sidney E. Mead, *The Lively Experiment: The Shaping of Christianity in America* (New York: Harper and Row, 1963), p. 53.

16. Cf. Robert T. Handy, *A Christian America: Protestant Hopes and Historical Realities,* rev. ed. (New York: Oxford University Press, 1983); and Mark A. Noll, "The Image of the United States as a Biblical Nation, 1776–1865," in Mark A. Noll and Nathan O. Hatch, eds., *The Bible in America: Essays in Cultural History* (Oxford: Oxford University Press, 1982), pp. 39–58. See also Jerry Falwell, *Listen, America!* (Garden City: Doubleday, 1980), esp. pp. 29–54, 243–52.

17. James Oliver Robertson, *American Myth, American Reality* (New York: Hill and Wang, 1980), pp. 37–39.

18. Cited in Emily S. Rosenberg, *Spreading the American Dream: American Economic and Cultural Expansion, 1890–1945* (New York: Hill and Wang, 1982), pp. 32–33.

19. Edmund C. Burnett, ed., *Letters of Members of the Continental Congress* (Washington, 1926; reprint, Gloucester, Mass.: Peter Smith, 1963), 3:476.

20. David Trimble, *The Debates and Proceedings in the Congress of the United States,* 16th Congress, 1st sess. (Washington, D.C.: Gales and Seaton, 1855), col. 1768.

21. H. V. Johnson, *The Congressional Globe,* 30th Congress, 1st sess. (Washington, D.C.: Blair and Rives, 1848), Appendix, p. 379.

22. George Rockingham Gilmer, *Journal of the House of Representatives of the State of Georgia* (1830), cited in Albert K. Weinberg, *Manifest Destiny: A Study of Nationalist Expansion in American History* (1935; reprint, Chicago: Quadrangle Books, 1963), p. 83. For a brief discussion of "Indian removal," see Martin E. Marty, *Righteous Empire: The Protestant Experience in America* (New York: Dial Press, 1970), pp. 5–13.

23. John Winthrop, *Conclusions for the Plantation in New England,* in *Old South Leaflets,* no. 50, pp. 5–7, cited in Weinberg, *Manifest Destiny,* pp. 74–75.

Winthrop argued further that "this savage people ruleth over many lands without title or property; for they enclose no ground, neither have they cattle to maintain it." *Winthrop Papers,* ed. Allyn B. Forbes (Boston: Massachusetts Historical Society, 1929–47), 2:120. John Cotton concurred and argued that a country could be void of inhabitants even where inhabitants reside if those inhabitants had failed to replenish the earth and subdue it. Thus, "in vacant soil, he that taketh possession of it, and bestoweth culture and husbandry upon it, his right it is. And the ground of this is from the Grand Charter given to *Adam* and his posterity in Paradise, *Gen.* 1. 28. *Multiply, and replenish the earth,* and subdue it." (John Cotton, "God's Promise to His Plantations," 1630, in *Old South Leaflets,* no. 53 [Boston, 1896], p. 6, cited in Charles M. Segal and David C. Stineback, *Puritans, Indians, and Manifest Destiny* [New York: G. P. Putnam's Sons, 1977], p. 53.) The Puritans' conviction that they represented a primordial order and that Indians represented a fallen, decayed order of things may even help explain why Puritans were so reluctant to engage in serious missions to the Indians. For an illuminating discussion of this Puritan failure, see Henry W. Bowden, *American Indians and Christian Missions: Studies in Cultural Conflict* (Chicago: University of Chicago Press, 1981), pp. 111–33.

24. In John F. Cade, "Western Opinion and the War of 1812," *Ohio Archaeological and Historical Society Publications* 33 (1924): 435–36, cited in Weinberg, *Manifest Destiny,* p. 79.

25. "Documents and Proceedings Relating to the Formation and Progress of a Board," *North American Review* 66 (January 1830): 77.

26. Horace Greeley, letter in *New York Tribune,* June 1859, in James Parton, *Life of Andrew Jackson* (New York: Mason Brothers, 1861), 1:401n.

27. Weinberg, *Manifest Destiny,* pp. 168 and 185. The theme of subduing the earth, however, did not play the role in the campaign against Mexico that it played in Indian removal or even in claims to the Oregon Territory. The reason seems obvious: Mexico was a settled region. Thus a Whig diplomat, Waddy Thompson, argued in South Carolina that Mexico "is not the country of a savage people whose lands are held in common, but a country in which grants have been made for three hundred and twenty-five years." Cited in Frederick Merk, *Manifest Destiny and Mission in American History* (New York: Vintage Books, 1963), p. 165.

28. John Quincy Adams, *Congressional Globe,* 29th Congress, 1st sess., (Washington, D.C.: Blair and Rives, 1846), p. 340.

29. John L. O'Sullivan in the *New York Morning News,* December 27, 1845, in Conrad Cherry, ed., *God's New Israel: Religious Interpretations of American Destiny* (Englewood Cliffs, N.J.: Prentice-Hall, 1971), pp. 128–29.

30. Andrew Carnegie, "Wealth," *North American Reveiw* 147 (June 1889): 655 and 664.

31. Richard Slotkin, *Regeneration through Violence: The Mythology of the American Frontier, 1600–1860* (Middletown, Conn.: Wesleyan University Press, 1973), p. 558; Michael Paul Rogin, *Ronald Reagan, the Movie, and Other Episodes in Political Demonology* (Berkeley: University of California Press, 1987), p. 186; and idem, *Fathers and Children: Andrew Jackson and the Subjugation of the*

American Indian (New York: Alfred A. Knopf, 1975), esp. pp. 3–15. See also Winthrop D. Jordan, *White over Black: American Attitudes toward the Negro, 1550–1812* (Chapel Hill: University of North Carolina Press, for the Institute of Early American History and Culture, 1968), pp. 90–91.

32. Robertson, *American Myth,* pp. 123–24.

33. Albert Beveridge, "Our Philippine Policy," in *The Meaning of the Times and Other Speeches* (reprint, New York: Books for Libraries Press, 1968), pp. 84–85.

34. Charles S. Olcott, *The Life of William McKinley* (Boston: Houghton Mifflin, 1916), 2:109–11.

35. Orville Platt, *Congressional Record,* 55th Congress, 3d sess., vol. 32, pt. 1 (Washington, D.C.: Government Printing Office, 1899), p. 502.

36. James Henderson Berry, *Congressional Record,* 55th Congress, 3d sess., vol. 32, pt. 2 (Washington, D.C.: Government Printing Office, 1899), p. 1299.

37. Albert Beveridge, "The Command of the Pacific," in *Meaning of the Times,* pp. 188 and 194–95.

38. Charles Arthur Conant, *The United States in the Orient: The Nature of the Economic Problem* (Boston: Houghton Mifflin, 1900), p. 2.

39. Platt and McKinley cited in Weinberg, *Manifest Destiny,* pp. 290, 294; Weinberg, p. 284.

40. Albert Beveridge, "For the Greater Republic, Not for Imperialism," an address given February 15, 1899, reprinted in Hudson, *Nationalism and Religion in America,* pp. 117–19.

41. Albert Beveridge, "Our Philippine Policy," in *Meaning of the Times,* p. 71. Beveridge's own rejection of the jurisdiction of history over America emerged in his "March of the Flag" speech in Indianapolis, September 1898: "It is a glorious history our God has bestowed upon His chosen people; . . . a history of prophets who saw the consequences of evils inherited from the past and of martyrs who died to save us from them; a history divinely logical, in the process of whose tremendous reasoning we find ourselves today." In J. R. Conlin and C. H. Peterson, eds., *An American Harvest: Readings in American History* (New York: Harcourt Brace Jovanovich, 1986), p. 88.

42. Berry, *Congressional Record,* 55th Congress, 3d sess., vol. 32, pt. 2, p. 1297. Mark Toulouse has underscored the irony by which American clergy, typified by Lyman Abbott, fully identified the universal notion of "the kingdom of God" with particular visions of democratic societies during the Spanish-American War and its aftermath. Like the Enlightenment philosophers, Abbott also built his case on the notion of natural man or, as he put it, "man as man, not royal man, nor aristocratic man, nor priestly man, nor Anglo-Saxon man," for "to man as man are given the keys of political, as of natural, dominion." See Mark Toulouse, "In Defense of an 'Imperialism of Liberty': Lyman Abbott's Use of the Kingdom of God at the Turn of the Century," paper presented at American Academy of Religion, Atlanta, Ga., November 24, 1986, esp. pp. 6 and 9. The irony here is most apparent: the notion of "man in general," intended by eighteenth-century philosophers for use in liberation, finally was employed by nineteenth-century Americans for the sake of domination.

43. Rosenberg, *Spreading the American Dream,* pp. 38, 48–49, and 230–31.

44. Ibid., p. 230.

45. Andrew Jackson to Major William B. Lewis, August 25, 1830, in *Correspondence of Andrew Jackson,* ed. John Spencer Bassett (Washington, D.C.: Carnegie Institution of Washington, 1926–35), 4:177.

46. Cited in Robertson, *American Myth,* p. 272.

47. Cited in Rosenberg, *Spreading the American Dream,* p. 17.

48. Robert N. Bellah, *The Broken Covenant: American Civil Religion in Time of Trial* (New York: Seabury, 1975), pp. 114–15.

49. Rosenberg, *Spreading the American Dream,* pp. 232–33.

50. William R. Hutchinson, *Errand to the World: American Protestant Thought and Foreign Missions* (Chicago: University of Chicago Press, 1987), pp. 91–124.

51. Woodrow Wilson, message to the American people, April 15, 1917, in Wilson, *Why We Are at War* (New York: Harper and Brothers, 1917), p. 71.

52. Woodrow Wilson, message to the Senate, January 22, 1917, in Wilson, *Why We Are at War,* p. 16.

53. Rosenberg in *Spreading the American Dream* discusses the illusions of Creel's Committee on Public Information (pp. 79–81) and the Wilson administration policy on communication, industry, and raw materials (pp. 74, 79ff., 86, and 89).

54. By 1946, Americans had invested $39.4 billion abroad. By 1950, that amount had grown to $54.4 billion. U.S. Bureau of the Census, *Historical Statistics of the United States, Colonial Times to 1970,* Bicentennial Edition, pt. 2 (Washington, D.C.: Government Printing Office, 1975), p. 869.

55. Richard M. Nixon, *Setting the Course: The First Year: Major Policy Statements by President Richard Nixon* (New York: Funk and Wagnalls, 1970), pp. 28–30. See also chapter 9, "Neither Humiliation nor Defeat," in Robert Jewett, *The Captain America Complex: The Dilemma of Zealous Nationalism* (Philadelphia: Westminster Press, 1973), pp. 215–42.

56. Bellah, *Broken Covenant,* p. 1.

57. Ronald Reagan, State of the Union address, January 25, 1984, in *Washington Post,* January 26, 1984, pp. A16–A17.

Epilogue

1. Allan Bloom, *The Closing of the American Mind: How Higher Education Has Failed Democracy and Impoverished the Souls of Today's Students* (New York: Simon and Schuster, 1987).

2. Ibid., p. 370.

3. Ibid., pp. 179 and 314.

4. Ibid., p. 312.

5. Ibid., pp. 55, 191, and 97.

6. Ibid., pp. 33, 192–93, and 99–100.

7. Of the blame for American ills that Bloom placed on Nietzsche, Jack Miles perceptively wrote that "nothing so helps a story as a villain, particularly when the

story is about corrupted youth, and even now, there is no villain quite like a German villain. . . . Bloom provides American readers with something more of us seem to want than one could have guessed, namely, a foreigner to blame for the spiritual impoverishment of American life." "Allan Bloom as Best Seller," *Los Angeles Times Book Review,* August 30, 1987, p. 15.

8. Bloom, *Closing,* pp. 143, 148, 40, 55–56, 148, and 308.

9. Ibid., pp. 379, 375, 374, and 344.

10. Ibid., p. 37. Martha Nussbaum chastised Bloom for transforming the Socratic tradition from the search for truth into the discovery and contemplation of truth. "Undemocratic Vistas," *New York Review of Books,* November 5, 1987, pp. 20–26.

11. Robert Bellah and his colleagues, in their *Habits of the Heart: Individualism and Commitment in American Life* (New York: Harper and Row, 1985), also address the problems of relativism and radical individualism in American life. These authors argue that there are intellectual traditions in American life that can provide the basis for coherent moral discourse in America life, especially the biblical and republican traditions. Unlike Bloom, however, they find these traditions rooted squarely in America's historic particularities and therefore avoid absolutizing either heritage.

12. Leo Strauss, Bloom's mentor at the University of Chicago, felt that many great thinkers often obscured their basic intentions in order to avoid persecution from the masses who would not understand their real meaning in any event. On the Straussian tradition, see Gordon Wood, "The Fundamentalists and the Constitution," *New York Review of Books,* 35 (February 18, 1988): 33–40. For an interpretation of *Closing* as an example of Straussian concealment and misdirection, see Robert Paul Wolff, "The Closing of the American Mind," *Academe* 73 (September–October 1987): 64–65.

13. Sidney E. Mead, "Reinterpretation in American Church History," in Jerald C. Brauer, ed., *Essays in Divinity: Reinterpretation in American Church History* (Chicago: University of Chicago Press, 1968), pp. 170 and 192.

14. The definitive statement of the methodology of the "Chicago school" is Shirley Jackson Case, "The Historical Study of Religion," *Journal of Religion* 29 (January 1949): 5–14, originally published in the first issue of that journal in January 1921. In addition, the "Chicago school" published a collection of essays indicative of their methods and in honor of Case, in John T. McNeill, Matthew Spinka, and Harold R. Willoughby, eds., *Environmental Factors in Christian History* (Chicago: University of Chicago Press, 1939).

15. Sidney E. Mead, *The Nation with the Soul of a Church* (New York: Harper and Row, 1975), p. 10.

16. For one aspect of the restorationist underpinnings in Mead's thought, see Richard T. Hughes, "Civil Religion, the Theology of the Republic, and the Free Church Tradition," *Journal of Church and State* 22 (Winter 1980): 84–86.

17. Sidney E. Mead, "The Nation with the Soul of a Church," *Church History* 36 (September 1967): 1–22, reprinted in Mead, *Nation,* pp. 48–77. All references to this essay are to the later edition.

18. Mead, *Nation,* p. 63. The quotation from Tillich is in *Christianity and the*

Encounter of the World Religions (New York: Columbia University Press, 1963), pp. 96–97.

19. Mead, *Nation,* pp. 63, 59, and 9–10.

20. Ibid., pp. 21–22 and 60–61.

21. Ibid., p. 75.

22. Also basing his insights on the perspectives of Sidney Mead, Franklin I. Gamwell finally concluded that the ultimate purpose of public debate in America is not to arrive at some final answer or set of answers, since all particular answers are finite and bound by time and place to historic particularities. The ultimate purpose of the debate, rather, is to further the debate itself. "Religion and the Public Purpose," *Journal of Religion* 62 (July 1982): 283.

23. Mead, *Nation,* p. 76.

24. Reinhold Niebuhr, *The Irony of American History* (New York: Charles Scribner's Sons, 1962), p. 79.

Index

•